Y0-BUP-199

Winners and Losers of EU Integration

Policy Issues for Central and Eastern Europe

HC
240.25
.E825
W56
2000
west

Helena Tang
Editor

THE WORLD BANK
WASHINGTON, D.C.

© 2000 The International Bank for Reconstruction
and Development/THE WORLD BANK
1818 H Street, N.W.
Washington, D.C. 20433

All rights reserved
Manufactured in the United States of America
First printing March 2000

The findings, interpretations, and conclusions expressed in this paper are entirely those of the author(s) and should not be attributed in any manner to the World Bank, to its affiliated organizations, or to members of its Board of Executive Directors or the countries they represent. The World Bank does not guarantee the accuracy of the data included in this publication and accepts no responsibility for any consequence of their use.

The material in this publication is copyrighted. The World Bank encourages dissemination of its work and will normally grant permission to reproduce portions of the work promptly.

Permission to *photocopy* items for internal or personal use, for the internal or personal use of specific clients, or for educational classroom use is granted by the World Bank, provided that the appropriate fee is paid directly to the Copyright Clearance Center, Inc., 222 Rosewood Drive, Danvers, MA 01923, USA; telephone 978-750-8400, fax 978-750-4470. Please contact the Copyright Clearance Center before photocopying items.

For permission to *reprint* individual articles or chapters, please fax a request with complete information to the Republication Department, Copyright Clearance Center, fax 978-750-4470.

All other queries on rights and licenses should be addressed to the Office of the Publisher, World Bank, at the address above or faxed to 202-522-2422.

ISBN 0-8213-4427-7

Library of Congress Cataloging-in-Publication Data has been applied for.

Contents

TABLES

Foreword

In the spring of 1999, the Bertelsmann Foundation and the World Bank entered into a partnership to develop a network linking political and economic research institutes in the 10 Central and Eastern European countries (CEECs) that have applied for membership to the European Union (EU). The 10 countries are Bulgaria, the Czech Republic, Estonia, Hungary, Latvia, Lithuania, Poland, Romania, the Slovak Republic, and Slovenia. The objective of the network is to foster a cross-border dialogue on key political, economic, and social issues related to EU membership involving also governments, nongovernmental organizations, parliaments, the media, and other civil society organizations.

The network was formally launched in November 1999 at a conference held in Guetersloh, Germany, and hosted by the Bertelsmann Foundation. Representatives of 13 research institutes and nongovernmental organizations from the 10 CEECs attended the conference. Other attendees included researchers from EU member countries, staff from the European Bank for Reconstruction and Development, and representatives from the Bertelsmann Foundation and the World Bank.

Researchers from the CEECs and from EU member countries presented papers and exchanged views on some of the main policy issues for an enlarged EU. This publication includes the papers presented at the conference, as well as background country papers.

We would like to express our thanks to the teams in the Bertelsmann Foundation and the World Bank who conceptualized the project, organized the first conference, and launched the network. Specifically, we would like to acknowledge Dirk Rumberg, Cornelius Ochmann, Gabriele Schroers, Hafez Ghanem, Franz Kaps, and Helena Tang. We would like to especially acknowledge Helena Tang for managing the preparation of the papers and editing this volume, as well as the authors who provided us with their valuable perspectives on the different aspects of EU enlargement. We hope that the papers presented here will contribute to a wider public debate on the key issues pertaining to the accession of the 10 CEECs to the EU.

Werner Weidenfeld
Member of the Board,
  Bertelsmann Foundation
Director, Center for Applied
  Policy Research
Germany

Johannes Linn
Vice President
Europe and Central Asia Region
The World Bank

Networking toward EU Integration

The "EU Integration" network was launched by the Bertelsmann Foundation and the World Bank to facilitate the exchange of experiences between the 10 Central and Eastern European Countries (CEECs) that are candidates for EU accession, and the development of best-practice approaches as they address the common set of challenges related to accession. To date, 10 research institutes in the CEECs have joined the network. It is hoped that the network will expand over time with current network members recruiting new members from their own countries.

The network will hold three to four workshops a year, with each workshop focusing on a specific topic of common interest to all the CEECs. Network members will host these workshops, with the support of the Bertelsmann Foundation and the World Bank, and regional and international experts will be invited to share their experiences at these workshops. In addition to workshops, there will also be an annual meeting of network members to review accomplishments in the previous year and to discuss the work program for the following year.

An electronic network (http://www.euintegration.net) was launched on the Internet in January 2000 to support this network. A key feature of the electronic network is the "Discussion Forums," which allow the public at large to participate in discussions on a range of EU accession issues. Publications of network members on EU accession issues are also posted on the Web site, including the papers in this volume.

Contributors

Martin Brusis
Research Fellow, Bertelsmann Group for Policy Research, Center for Applied Policy Research, Ludwig-Maximilians-University, Munich, Germany

Center for the Study of Democracy
Sofia, Bulgaria

Jorge Braga de Macedo
Professor, Faculty of Economics, Nova University of Lisbon, Lisbon, Portugal

Kalman Dezséri
Senior Research Fellow, Institute for World Economics of the Hungarian Academy of Science, Budapest, Hungary

Economic Policy Institute
Sofia, Bulgaria

Jan Fidrmuc
Senior Fellow, Center for European Integration Studies (ZEI), University of Bonn, Bonn, Germany;
Research Affiliate, Center for Economic Policy Research, London, UK.

Jarko Fidrmuc
Economist, Foreign Research Department, Oesterreichische Nationalbank, Austria

András Inotai
General Director, Institute of World Economics, Budapest, Hungary

Maria Karasińska-Fendler
European Institute, Lodz, Poland

Vladimir Lavrač
Senior Researcher, Institute for Economic Research, Ljubljana, Slovenia

Atis Lejinš
Director, Latvian Institute of International Affairs, Riga, Latvia

Boris Majcen
Senior Researcher, Institute for Economic Research, Ljubljana, Slovenia

Sandor Meisel
Senior Research Fellow, Institute for World Economics of the Hungarian Academy of Science, Budapest, Hungary

Petr Pavlík
Research Fellow, Institute of International Relations, Prague, Czech Republic

Margit Rácz
Research Director, Institute for World Economics of the Hungarian Academy of Science, Budapest, Hungary

Elżbieta Skotnicka-Illasiewicz
European Institute, Lodz, Poland

Kazimierz Sobotka
European Institute, Lodz, Poland

Peter Stanovnik
Director, Institute for Economic Research, Ljubljana, Slovenia

Guoda Steponavičienė
Policy Analyst, Lithuanian Free Market Institute, Vilnius, Lithuania

Janusz Świerkocki
Professor, Department of International Trade and Finance, University of Lodz; Head of the Research Unit, European Institute, Lodz, Poland

Helena Tang
Senior Country Economist, The World Bank, Washington, D.C.

Ramūnas Vilpišauskas
Policy Analyst, Lithuanian Free Market Institute, Vilnius, Lithuania

CHAPTER 1

Overview

Helena Tang

Introduction

In the 10 years since the start of transition, the countries in Central and Eastern Europe have undergone dramatic changes in their political and economic systems, breaking with decades of communist rule and central planning. Reflecting their significant progress in building democracy and market economies, 10 Central and Eastern European countries (CEECs) have been invited to initiate negotiations to join the European Union (EU). The 10 countries are Bulgaria, the Czech Republic, Estonia, Hungary, Latvia, Lithuania, Poland, Romania, the Slovak Republic, and Slovenia.

There is widespread consensus among the authors of this volume that the benefits of joining the EU will outweigh the costs, especially in the long run. At the same time, pressures may intensify for certain economic, social, and political groups. This volume seeks to identify such groups so that measures can be designed to ease the accession process. More generally, accession will require policy adjustments on the parts of both the CEECs and the EU. The chapters on "Winners and Losers of EU Integration" focus on the challenges facing the accession countries. The chapter on "Internal Problems in the EU That Might Obstruct an Enlargement toward the East" focuses on the challenges facing the EU as it integrates the CEECs.

Among the issues addressed in the "Winners and Losers of EU Integration" chapters are the likely consequences of EU integration for specific economic, social, and political groups, including identification of the potential beneficiaries of accession and the groups at risk. The chapters highlight key issues of concern related to EU integration for policymakers and for the public, and should provoke further thinking, discussion, and analysis of these issues. Addressing these issues is important both for membership negotiations and for policymaking, including the formulation of measures for alleviating the costs for losers and increasing the number of winners.

A key message for the accession countries is the need for a strategy for disseminating information on the pros and cons of accession. This will provide a foundation for further analysis and for the much-needed public debate on accession that have so far been missing in most of these countries. This strategy is all the more important in the current environment, where public support for accession has been declining in many CEECs. In many instances, this decline in public support reflects a more realistic assessment among the population of what integration entails, correcting the overoptimism in the past.

The volume concludes with a study of the lessons for the CEEC candidates from Portugal's accession experience. This experience is relevant for three reasons. Portugal, like the CEECs, saw integration with the EU as the appropriate next step following the emergence of a democratic political system. Second, Portugal joined the EU more recently than many EU members, so its experience may be more relevant for the CEEC candidates. Third, Portugal joined the EU when its level of economic development was relatively comparable to that existing in many of the CEECs today.

The rest of this chapter highlights the main issues raised by the authors of the chapters in the volume.

Winners and Losers of EU Integration: Issues and Lessons

EU accession raises economic, social, and political issues. These are reviewed below.

Economic Dimension

Having a "functioning market economy" is a prerequisite for joining the EU. It is also a key objective of transition from central planning. Therefore, for many CEECs, the process of integrating with the EU overlaps with, and/or is a continuation of, the transition process. For some CEECs that are in a less advanced stage of transition, such as Bulgaria and Romania, the goal of integrating with the EU has the added benefit of boosting domestic political and public support for consolidating and continuing economic reforms.

The move toward greater competition with EU countries has much in common with the process of economic globalization that is also affecting the CEECs. Therefore, the challenges associated with accession identified by the authors in this volume overlap with those relating to transition and globalization. Some authors attempt to disentangle the effects of transition, accession, and globalization in their chapters, although this is not always possible. Therefore, this volume can also be viewed as offering broader lessons for policymakers in the CEECs as they confront all three issues.

Accession to the EU will bring both economic benefits and costs to the CEECs. Some of the main benefits are even greater liberalization of trade, which should improve competitiveness and boost exports; greater foreign investment inflows that could provide needed capital, technology, and skills; and access to EU funds, which could help upgrade infrastructure and boost regional development. All these benefits, in turn, should boost growth, raise living standards, and reduce regional disparities. EU accession will also bring higher environmental standards. At the same time, CEECs will face adjustment costs (unemployment benefits, worker retraining, and so on) arising from dislocation of labor in those industries that cannot withstand competition in the EU Single Market, and compliance costs relating to environmental and other regulations.

In general, consumers will benefit from higher quality and better prices of goods and services (because of greater competition and higher product standards) and cleaner environment (although they may have to bear some of the costs relating to the latter). Competitive producers will win while non-competitive ones will lose, generally implying a further expansion of the private sector at the expense of public production. There will be considerable pressure to streamline public administration, except for those parts that deal with EU-related work.

A systematic analysis of the issues of "winners and losers" has been undertaken by several authors in this volume who focus on the effects of the "four freedoms" (free movement of goods, services, capital, and labor), the Common Agricultural Policy (CAP), EU financial assistance, and Economic and Monetary Union, all of which are key elements for EU accession. Each element is discussed in turn below.

FREE MOVEMENT OF GOODS

With the entering into force of the Europe Agreements (EAs)[1] between the EU and the CEECs, the liberalization of barriers to trade in goods and services with the EU has already happened to a large extent in most of the 10 CEECs. Winners and losers from this process are already apparent in many of the countries. Not surprisingly, the reduction of trade barriers with the EU has benefited exporters and consumers at the expense of domestic producers that could not withstand external competition. To a large extent, the latter have either disappeared or been successfully restructured. In Bulgaria and Romania, the adjustment to greater competition was made more difficult by unsound domestic economic policies.

For many CEECs, the enterprises that most successfully weathered transition are also expected to benefit further from accession, as antidumping and other protection instruments that the EU can use currently are phased out. Some authors refer to these enterprises as "double winners." There is a large scope for such winners in small, open economies such as the Baltic states. Inotai is also positive about the prospects for the CE5 countries (the Czech Republic, Hungary, Poland, the Slovak Republic, and Slovenia), where he does not foresee the need for significant further restructuring after EU integration. Pavlik, however, sees risks for some parts of the Czech industry that have lagged in industrial restructuring compared with some other CE5s such as Hungary.

The situation is expected to be worse for Bulgaria and Romania, as their progress in industrial restructuring has been much slower in comparison with the other CEECs. This means that their remaining restructuring agenda is large, and will coincide with the process of EU integration. According to the Economic Policy Institute (EPI) and the Center for the Study of Democracy (CSD), the slower transition in Bulgaria and Romania means that the cost of accession may actually be higher, as industries will be exposed to further competition in the EU internal market before they are ready for it.

However, as Portugal's accession experience suggests, it is important that the needed industrial restructuring be undertaken. De Macedo notes that although Portugal's integration into the EU can be rightly seen as a success, there were several missed opportunities because of resistance on the part of potential losers from integration. In particular, Portugal missed the opportunity to carry structural reforms to completion, especially those pertaining to the discretionary regulation of private enterprises.

Integration with the EU will also entail adoption of the EU's Common External Tariff (CET). This will have varying effects on the CEECs. For Estonia, which currently has no external tariffs, adoption of the CET will benefit producers but hurt consumers. The effect on the other CEECs will vary according to product groups. In Hungary, for example, those exporters in duty-free zones that are now using duty-free imported inputs may lose, since there will be tariffs on these inputs under the CET.

A special situation arises for the Czech and Slovak Republics because of the customs union between the two countries. Both the Czechs and the Slovaks believe that the customs union has been important for sustaining trade between the two countries. Fidrmuc and Fidrmuc estimate that there will be a large decline in Slovak exports to the Czech Republic if the latter joins the EU first, and if the customs union between them is dissolved at that time.

FREE MOVEMENT OF SERVICES

As with the free movement of goods, consumers will win as competition will lead to higher quality and lower prices of services. Services that are already operating at a higher standard will win. These will include those that have already been privatized or are dominated by foreign presence. According to Inotai, such services would include telecommunications in most of the CE5s after the abolition of monopoly rights; and banking and insurance in Hungary, partly in Poland, and after consolidation in the Czech Republic. The transport sector is expected to benefit from accession in the longer term because of lower wages and geographic advantages. According to a Polish survey (probably applicable to the other CE5 countries), construction, highly specialized services in the renovation of monuments, and the exporting of cultural services are expected to be winners. Tourism, retail trade, and repair, all obvious winners of transition, will win if they can withstand the competition upon integration. State-owned monopolies (energy, public utilities, finance and insurance, railway, and aircraft) will be big losers.

FREE MOVEMENT OF CAPITAL

Foreign direct investment (FDI) has, by and large, played an important role in the creation of winners since transition. Hungary is notable as the largest recipient of FDI among the CEECs.[2] Dezséri and others attribute the improvements in international competitiveness in Hungary to FDI, which has resulted in faster increases in productivity than wages. According to Stanovnik and others, FDI has also played a positive role in industrial restructuring in Slovenia. Conversely, in Bulgaria and Romania where domestic economic reforms have lagged, so has FDI, which EPI and CSD see as contributing to the poor growth performance in these two countries.

On the whole, EU accession will make the CEECs more attractive for FDI. Both FDI itself as well as those sectors receiving FDI are winners. However, there may be some exceptions, such as in Poland where FDI has entered into protected markets (automobiles, trucks, food, and beverages) that will face greater competition after EU accession.

FREE MOVEMENT OF LABOR

This is likely to be a sensitive area of negotiation because of widespread fears in the EU concerning possible effects of migration into the richer EU countries from the poorer candidates. From the CEECs' point of view, the more liberalized the EU labor markets are, the more winners there will be.

EU fears of large-scale migration may not be warranted. Inotai suggests that demographic trends speak against large-scale emigration of labor. Analysis by Fidrmuc and Fidrmuc suggests that notwithstanding growing regional differences in unemployment rates and earnings, Slovaks are relatively not very mobile internally, and are likely to be even less mobile across national boundaries, given the linguistic and cultural differences and the lack of social networks for migrants abroad.

AGRICULTURE

Agriculture, like industry, has been a big loser of transition. Whether agriculture will continue to lose will depend on national strategies for agricultural restructuring, and on EU financial support and EU agricultural policies, specifically the Common Agricultural Policy, which is itself a moving target. The impact of the EU's CAP is expected to vary with the different CEECs. In the case of the Baltics, Vilpišauskas and Steponavičiene expect that farmers, mostly larger ones, will be winners of EU integration because of the higher level of financial support they would receive, while smaller farmers may lose because of greater competition.[3] For the CE5s, Inotai expects that some producers will win while consumers will lose because of higher agricultural prices after accession. Pavlík expects that the agricultural sector in the Czech Republic may win because of subsidies from EU funds. To the extent that some farmers lose out, agricultural lobbies within the CEECs may strengthen their opposition to EU integration.

EU FINANCIAL ASSISTANCE

All the candidate countries are beneficiaries of EU financial assistance, which currently includes various preaccession funds and will include structural funds after accession. These funds, if managed well, could contribute significantly to regional development as well as to the overall economic development of the candidate states.

The need for matching funds for the preaccession funds could complicate the "winners and losers" picture. Lejinš points out that SAPARD[4] requires matching funds from private capital, which means that the strongest economic sectors will receive the most funds.

Some authors highlight the policy challenge concerning the use of structural funds, which is the EU policy instrument for addressing regional disparities. These funds are designed to promote the development of less prosperous regions in member countries. However, some authors see merit in targeting the funds on the more prosperous regions in the CEECs, which have the best growth prospects, with other regions then benefiting through spill-over effects and internal labor migration.

ECONOMIC AND MONETARY UNION

Accession to the EU automatically implies ultimately joining the Economic and Monetary Union (EMU), which requires that countries meet the Maastricht convergence criteria on inflation, government deficit, public debt, long-term interest rates, and exchange rate stability. This will require sound macroeconomic management which, by itself, is important for successful integration. According to de Macedo, the Portuguese experience suggests that sound macroeconomic management coupled with well-functioning capital and labor markets, promotes financial stability. This, together with political stability, delivers the growth that is necessary for sustaining social cohesion during the accession process.

After joining the EMU, the loss of the exchange rate as an instrument of adjustment will further emphasize the importance of flexible labor markets. This will be particularly important for the CEECs where some sectors are expected to undergo rapid productivity increases. It is important that the resultant real wage increases in these sectors not spill over to other sectors, undermining their competitiveness.

PROPOSALS TO IMPROVE THE WINNER-LOSER BALANCE

Some authors propose acceleration of domestic economic reforms to improve the competitiveness of domestic industry and agriculture before exposure to further EU competition that will come with accession. This would help create more winners and reduce the number of losers.

Several authors propose enhancing labor mobility and education. Measures that would help enhance labor mobility include improved access to housing and better infrastructure. Education designed to address the needs of a market economy would help raise the skill levels, and enhance the flexibility and mobility of the labor force.

Free movement of labor is one of the more obvious benefits of integration. Several authors are concerned that delayed implementation in this area (through derogations) would have clear adverse effects on welfare in the accession countries. Vilpišauskas and Steponavičiene suggest that an active and innovative negotiation policy on the part of the accession countries would be needed to ensure free movement of labor upon accession.

Some authors suggest better use of preaccession funds. Lejinš suggests that information to the public about the potential of preaccession funds to raise living standards and convert some losers into winners will also help gain support for EU accession among the public in all three Baltic states. EPI and CSD propose that Bulgaria and Romania could improve the use of preaccession aid by training public administrators to better use EU transfers, by ensuring consistency between the activities being funded, and by ensuring that projects being funded are consistent with macroeconomic and overall development goals.

Accession countries and the EU need to balance the need for a deliberate approach toward accession against the risk that an overly prolonged accession period could lead to accession fatigue and also reduce the attractiveness of the CEECs to foreign investors. Several authors are concerned that delays in accession could lead to disappointment among business circles and the society at large, resulting in domestic political and economic problems. They are also concerned about the foregone gains in investments and growth, should accession be delayed. Furthermore, lower levels of investment and growth could spur emigration to the EU, which, with the exception of Poland, is limited today.

Social Dimension

EU integration will have different effects on social groups. It is likely that, unless corrective measures are taken, those social groups that have been excluded from the benefits of transition and globalization will also be excluded from the benefits of integration.

VULNERABLE GROUPS
Minorities in countries tend to be among the socially excluded groups,[5] for example, Russians in Latvia, and the Roma populations in Poland, the Czech and Slovak
Republics, Hungary, Bulgaria, and Romania. In the case of Bulgaria and Romania,
the prolonged economic slowdown has considerably worsened the position. Unless
corrective measures are taken, these vulnerable groups could continue to be losers
under integration. However, Lejinš points out that EU accession should upgrade the
social safety net. In addition, accession would provide stronger legal protection to
vulnerable groups.

AGE
Elderly (retired) people without liquid or convertible assets are expected to be the
losers throughout the CEECs. The picture for winners, however, is not as clear-
cut. In the Baltics, people in early middle age (ages 31–45) have lost out the least
during transition and are expected to gain from integration. This group has the
advantages of maturity and flexibility. Those under 30 are expected to face greater
risks in the Baltics. The situation appears somewhat different in Poland, however,
where Karasińska-Fendler and others have found that people over age 35 have
been openly discriminated against and where employers prefer to hire younger
people who have less experience and are ready to work longer than the legal working hours.

EDUCATIONAL BACKGROUND
Several authors indicate that those with university degrees are expected to benefit
the most from integration. In particular, the winners will be those with university
degrees in areas such as international law, economics, engineering, and banking
and finance. Foreign-language speakers will also win.

POVERTY AND INEQUALITY
Transition has brought with it rising inequality and poverty in the CEECs. In
Bulgaria and Romania, long-term unemployment and living below the poverty line
have led to de-skilling and human degradation. The group of long-term unemployed persons would be the most difficult to turn from losers to winners. The
Romanies are usually among the poorest in many of the CEEC countries. De
Macedo, drawing on the experience of Portugal, highlights the importance of dealing with poverty and inequality. In his view, the social dimension is the most fundamental long-term objective with respect to EU integration.

PUBLIC ADMINISTRATION
The public administration officials who are dealing directly with EU integration
tasks will be the winners. They will gain expert knowledge and receive special
training. Those parts of the public administration that will receive funds from the

EU for institutional restructuring will also benefit. Another group of winners is the decentralized entities at the regional level, both in terms of development resources from the EU and in terms of greater autonomy from the center. On the other hand, public administration reforms that will have to be undertaken to meet EU requirements will need to entail substantial downsizing, which will not be welcomed by the civil servants who will be the losers in this process. This group of losers could generate substantial opposition to EU integration.

The public in general will benefit from reforms of the public administration. These reforms should enhance transparency and financial control of government ministries and bodies. Lejinš points out that this is an area in which there is great potential for public support in the Baltics for the EU, since the society in all three Baltic states has become skeptical of the government's ability to resolve corruption and organized crime issues.

De Macedo underscores the importance of public administration reform, the absence of which was one of Portugal's missed opportunities in its integration into the EU. The public administration in Portugal has not been able to reform itself in areas such as justice, home affairs, social welfare, and education. De Macedo argues that the suspicion of widespread corruption in Portugal together with rising inequality, have become key social concerns and are threatening to erode the legitimacy of integration.

CIVIL SOCIETY

Civil society is developed to varying degrees in the CEECs. Karasińska-Fendler and others point out that civil society is quite well developed in Poland, where trade unions, lobbies, and nongovernmental organizations (NGOs) are key players in the political system. These groups are active in the decisionmaking process in the country, and could be considered winners of both transition and integration. NGOs seem to be similarly developed in Bulgaria and Romania, where the process of integration has given further impetus to NGOs that since the early 1990s have helped raise public awareness of citizens' rights in a democratic and free market system. However, Dezséri and others point out that civic organization in Hungary is emerging slowly. The role of NGOs has also been strictly circumscribed in the Czech Republic. Pavlík expresses the hope that the process of integration may help to rectify the situation of an underdeveloped civil society in the Czech Republic. In Slovenia, Stanovnik and others expect that political parties and pressure groups within civil society with predominantly nationalistic or local political programs will be the main losers of integration.

EU integration will change the dynamics of lobbying. In the Baltics, Vilpišauskas and Steponavičiene expect that there will be a shift in the balance of power between national lobbies in favor of consumers and exporters. A new group of winners could arise from groups lobbying for common external protection (such as farmers) after EU integration, although the results of their lobbying at the EU level are likely to be more modest than at the national level. Inotai suggests that influential pressure groups could also affect the position of winners and losers, and the redistribution of benefits and losses resulting from lobbying activities may lead to a suboptimal allocation of resources.

PROPOSALS TO IMPROVE THE WINNER-LOSER BALANCE

Social problems need to be addressed to avert declines in public support for accession. EPI and CSD are particularly concerned about the situation in Bulgaria and Romania, where rising social exclusion and social distress have accompanied transition. They propose education as an important measure for addressing the socioeconomic exclusion of the Roma group in Bulgaria and Romania, to help them gain employment and integrate socially. In addition, they also propose measures such as employment in infrastructure projects, public services, environmental programs, and so on, to improve the living standards of the socially disadvantaged groups and ethnic minorities.

Political Dimension

Many authors in this volume cite stabilization of democracy and democratic institutions as a main political benefit of joining the EU. More broadly, this also includes the safeguarding of human rights and the stabilization of the rule of law. For Bulgaria and Romania in particular, the political benefits of accession have been cited by EPI and CSD as key, reflecting the slower progress in achieving democratic stability in these two countries. Accession is also viewed by the authors as especially important in the aftermath of the Kosovo war for restoring political stability and continuing democratization.

Another main political benefit of accession cited by many of the CEEC authors is enhanced external and internal security. Inotai suggests that the benefit of enhanced external security is particularly important for those countries that are not yet NATO members.[6] Lejinš points out that integration with the EU has the added political benefit for the Baltic states with respect to the "Russian" problem, as they will no longer be viewed as "former republics of the Soviet Union," just as today Finland and Poland are no longer viewed as "former provinces of the Tsarist empire."

Internal security, which has deteriorated substantially since transition in many of the CEECs, is expected to improve with EU integration, as it will be a condition for membership given the importance the EU attaches to it. Pavlík suggests that compliance with the EU's *acqui* should help address some of the internal security problems, such as high crime rates, that have arisen in part because of inadequate institutions, loopholes in legislation, and weak law enforcement. He further suggests, by adopting the third pillar of the EU[7] (Justice and Home Affairs), CEECs should be able to improve their internal security through closer coordination with EU member countries.

There may be some losers arising from the adoption of the Schengen rules (which govern border regimes with non-EU countries). Inotai suggests that this is not a problem for the Czech Republic, and only a minor one for the Slovak Republic and Slovenia. However, it is a real challenge for Poland and maybe even more so for Hungary. There are large minority populations of Poles and Hungarians residing in neighboring countries that will not be candidates for EU accession for a long time. Adoption of Schengen rules could greatly reduce the flow of goods, capital, and labor between Poland and Hungary on the one hand and their neighboring countries on the other. This could mean the loss of economic benefits for Poland and Hungary, which currently benefit from economic relations with these minority groups abroad. Worse, it could generate anti-EU sentiments in these two countries among groups claiming that Poland and Hungary are selling out the interests of the ethnic Poles and Hungarians in those neighboring countries.

Public Education and Public Involvement

Broad social participation is important in shaping integration policies. This would help limit losses and ensure that benefits of integration are distributed as widely as possible. To this end, Inotai proposes setting up a continuous consultation mechanism between the government and different economic and social groups in the CEECs. This kind of consultation would also help generate greater public support for the integration process.

In order that the public could participate fully in these consultations, they need to be informed about the costs and benefits of integration, including those that have already materialized and those that are expected to materialize. This will help defeat illusions about integration and identify costs, which is the first step toward the formulation of measures to reduce these costs. While the public is becoming increasingly realistic in its assessment of the costs and benefits of EU integration in many of the CEECs, public opinion still suffers from misinformation or inadequate information. In this regard, the media and other organizations that are able to shape, educate, and orient public opinion have an important role to play.

EU Policy Challenges from CEEC Accession

In addition to the challenges facing the CEECs, Brusis (chapter 11) identifies six major policy issues confronting the EU in relation to an eastern enlargement. The first one relates to the inadequacy of the EU policy instrument—the structural funds—in dealing with expected increases in economic and social disparities within the EU after CEEC accession. Specifically, the structural funds favor current members over new members, and advanced candidate countries over those further from accession.

Second, several authors are concerned about the widening of domestic regional disparities that is expected to accompany the increase in competition following EU accession. Again, Brusis does not expect the structural funds to be able to address these increasing disparities, as past experience has shown that they have not been able to significantly alter the interregional disparities within the EU. Regional disparities could be a source of social crises in regions undergoing economic decline, thereby undermining political support for accession.

Third, agriculture is cited by many authors of this volume as a major problematic area for CEEC accession. Introduction of the EU's Common Agricultural Policy would raise agricultural prices for some accession countries. This could have an adverse effect on the poorer parts of the population in these countries. Brusis suggests that the EU will either have to allow different prices for agricultural products within the EU that would entail border controls and tariffs, or seek reforms of the CAP.

Fourth, eastern enlargement of the EU could exacerbate security problems relating to illegal immigration and transborder crime. The source of these problems may not be the accession countries themselves but those countries neighboring the accession countries to the east and southeast. The EU's requirement for members to introduce the so-called Schengen border regime vis-à-vis neighboring countries would conflict with the CEEC's commitment to ensure visa-free and open borders with their eastern neighbors. These internal security issues have been used by aspiring politicians in some EU member countries to weaken public support for eastern enlargement.

Fifth, adapting EU institutions to CEEC accession is also likely to be a considerable challenge. Experiences with previous reforms of EU institutions indicate that only incremental adaptations of existing arrangements are viable. Indeed, there is a risk that accession of a first group of candidate countries may further add to political inertia, with a wider and more fragmented EU finding it difficult to continue the enlargement process.

Sixth, the EU faces the challenge of managing an accession process in which the time lag between the first and last entrants may be significant. Because of the effects of the war in Yugoslavia, Romania and Bulgaria may lag further behind the advanced accession countries. This could negatively affect the pace of reforms in these two countries, further widen the gap between them and the more advanced accession countries, and weaken their prospects for an early accession.

To summarize, some of the constraints mentioned above may impede the enlargement process, while others may favor some accession countries over others. It would be useful if these constraints could be addressed, both to facilitate enlargement and to ensure that it is an inclusive process for all European countries as envisioned by the Copenhagen European Council.

Notes

1. The Europe Agreements (EAs), also known as Association Agreements (AAs), were signed in the first half of the 1990s between the 10 CEECs and the EU, and entered into force in the CEECs in the second half of the 1990s. The EAs cover political dialogue and economic cooperation in many areas, including provisions for trade liberalization.

2. According to Dezséri and others, on a per capita basis, FDI inflows in Hungary are exceeded only by FDI inflows into Singapore.

3. Their study assumes that the CAP will be implemented in its current form.

4. SAPARD is the Community Support for Pre-Accession Measures for Agriculture and Rural Development in the applicant countries.

5. See "The Baltic States: The Political and Social Dimensions" in this publication for a definition of social exclusion.

6. Three of the 10 CEECs are currently NATO members—the Czech Republic, Hungary, and Poland.

7. More precisely, this is the third pillar of the Treaty of Amsterdam (May 1, 1999), which encompasses all EU treaties including the latest modifications and additions.

Part I

Winners and Losers of EU Integration in Central and Eastern Europe: Cross-Country Reports

CHAPTER 2

The Czech Republic, Hungary, Poland, the Slovak Republic, and Slovenia*

András Inotai

Introduction

The process of accession preparation by the Central European candidate countries has entered a qualitatively new stage. First, political, economic, and social transformation has reached a critical level where, in most countries, hitherto untouched and politically delicate areas of changes must now be addressed and the conditions for sustainable economic development have to be created. Second, negotiations on accession with the EU are approaching the "hard core" areas, including agriculture, environment, and transportation. Third, the more negotiations on and preparation for accession advance and address important technical details, the more country-by-country differences of the "absorption and adjustment capacity" to EU requirements come to the limelight. The latest country reports prepared by the Commission are just one proof of this process.

Other relevant developments are intensified discussions on key issues of the accession process and attempts to identify potential gains and losses in the candidate countries. Finally, the increasing politics of the enlargement and accession process, mainly in some of the present member states (EU-15) but—to a lesser extent—also in the candidate countries, has to be considered.

In this context, a substantive survey of gains and losses and winners and losers is necessary and extremely timely. This paper is based on five country studies (Czech Republic, Hungary, Poland, Slovak Republic, and Slovenia).[1] It represents the initial stage of research and does not intend to present an in-depth and quantitative analysis of actual or potential gains and losses in different stages of the accession process.

It is not just a summary of the main findings of the individual country papers. Rather, it tries to identify some of the priority topics both for policymakers and for further research. The approach is interdisciplinary. It includes not only the economic effects but also the political and social consequences of preparing for membership in the European Union, because it is widely recognized that the process of accession and enlargement is expected to make deep changes in all areas of life.

Methodological Remarks

In the past several years, the five Central European candidate countries (CE5s) have been undergoing a unique change in a historically unprecedented short time. They have been affected by three overlapping and, in many cases, intertwining developments: socioeconomic transformation, catching up and adjusting to the EU, and the challenges of globalization.

As a result, in most cases, it is extremely difficult or impossible to separate the gains and losses of EU integration from the other components of the process. Most of the benefits and costs of preparing for membership in the EU can be attributed to those of transformation or globalization. They would have appeared, even if accession to the EU were not a priority task.

It is also difficult to differentiate between the gains and losses arising from the various stages of relations with the EU. The effects of the Association Agreements (concluded between 1991 and 1996), those of the preaccession period and those expected after reaching full membership, influence each other and partly overlap each other.

Most policy measures have a twofold effect. By redistributing costs and benefits across the national economy and the society, they create both winners and losers. Consumers generally gain by liberalization, while previously protected sectors lose. In turn, subsidies provide gains for some activities at the expense of others. Most residents will be affected as consumers, employers, or employees.

Cost-benefit analyses can have a static or a dynamic approach. Because the accession process covers a long period when the magnitude and distribution of gains and losses constantly change, it requires a dynamic approach to the analysis.

Measuring direct effects of the accession process may be relatively easy, but it is much more difficult to identify indirect consequences, which often may be more relevant because of substantive multiplier effects of the adjustment that nations must make to prepare sufficiently for membership in the European Union.

These multiplier effects include economic multiplier effects of economic adjustments, such as the longer term budgetary consequences of redistributing resources in favor of integration. They also include cross-sectoral multiplier effects, for example, when the economic adjustment process leads to non-economic multiplier effects, such as on the political, legal, social, psychological, and institutional spheres. An example of this is institutional and social flexibility or inflexibility from over-hasty adjustment.

The benefits and losses for the economy generally will differ from those arising from developments affecting individuals or employers. There is widespread consensus that integrating the CE5s into the EU has obviously positive effects on the macroeconomic level, related to growth, investment, competitiveness, living standards, environment, infrastructure and, probably with some delay, regional development. It is, however, difficult to convince losers of the overall benefit of the process by demonstrating to them what the macroeconomic gains are. Understandably, they are primarily, if not exclusively, interested in the adverse changes of their own situation. Thus, an in-depth microeconomic-level analysis in all critical areas must precede the determination of a general balance of costs and benefits.

Some of the benefits and losses cannot be quantified at all. More importantly, they may be more important for future development than the more immediate results that can be measured by statistics. These include security (both political and economic), changes in behavior and mentality of the society, business confidence, geographic location, and institution building, all of which generate and redistribute costs and benefits.

To identify winners and losers, parallel research on three levels is required: across the main sectors of the economy, between different regions, and over time. Changes over time are of crucial importance because first, costs and benefits are distributed over time unevenly. The CE5s have to bear substantial adjustment costs to qualify for membership, while an essential part of the benefits (including access to larger amounts of structural funds, free flow of labor, or, in some cases, free trade in agriculture) will materialize only after membership. Some interest groups in the EU-15, however, may consider that, because the CE5s already have undertaken comprehensive liberalization and they now have free trade in industrial products, they already have reaped most of the benefits. The next period of enlargement will impose additional costs, including competition in such still-closed areas as labor or agriculture and a higher contribution to the EU budget.

Second, short-term winners may turn out to be long-term losers, and vice versa. Different stages of the accession process, including the post-accession period, are likely to produce new winners and losers. Because the whole process of integration is fundamentally dynamic, it constantly develops a situation in which benefits and losses are created and distributed unevenly.

Winners and losers will be produced not only by accession or enlargement but also by non-enlargement or a delay in accession. These scenarios will negatively affect growth, investment, consumer demand, purchasing power, trade balance, migration potential, and sociopolitical developments.

Finally, both the size and the redistribution of benefits and costs are policy-dependent. Appropriate policies can increase the benefits and decrease the costs and, not less importantly, create a distribution pattern that not only creates more winners and reduces the number of losers but is able to manage and keep under control evident interest conflicts between winners and losers.

The Process of Transformation and Accession

Recent developments in the CE5s show that the speed and scope of the transformation process are strongly correlated with successful preparation for accession. The more advanced a country is in liberalization, efficient privatization, restructuring and international competitiveness, the better it is prepared to face challenges of adjusting to conditions for membership in the EU. In the areas or countries with the best transformation record, the winners and losers of the transformation process already have appeared.

Unlike in earlier accessions of less developed member countries, winners and losers from trade liberalization could be identified well before membership. Winners of liberalized trade as a result of the Association Agreements likely also will remain winners of the accession process. Those interests who already lost out because of the Association Agreements generally have disappeared or have been successfully restructured. Therefore, further big shifts are not expected.

Only in a few important cases, the sequencing of transformation may differ from the sequencing of preparing for membership in the EU. The CE5s need to continue to gain competitiveness to sustain high growth and further consolidate the transformation process. This priority may conflict with the too-hasty adoption of some elements of the *acquis communautaire*, mainly environmental and social standards. An overly hasty adjustment to the Maastricht criteria and surrendering of the flexibility of the exchange rate policy also may be detrimental to the transformation process in its decisive stage of consolidation. Adjustment to the CAP is another issue to consider. Most of these "asymmetries in sequencing" are expected to be abolished or prevented from generating harmful consequences through negotiations on temporary derogations.

In some countries, certain tasks of the transformation process have been delayed. First, in Slovenia, for example, apparently good starting conditions and a high priority given to social peace have diverted attention from making some fundamental reforms. "First-comer's advantage" was considered to remain unchanged over time and would save the transforming country from painful restructuring and politically not less delicate opening of the economy. Second, good macroeconomic indicators have allowed the Czech Republic to postpone some important reforms (such as in the fiscal area and the banking sector). Third, in some countries, the transformation process emphasized the opening of the trade sector, while certain sectors (banking and finance, infrastructure, and others) remained protected.

The delay in certain aspects of transformation gives rise to two negative consequences. First, it is difficult to obtain a true picture of the winners and losers of real (genuine and in-depth) transformation. Second, these remaining tasks of transformation likely will go with accession, which makes it difficult to distinguish between winners and losers of the two processes.

The CE5 countries differ substantially concerning the key transformation reforms to be taken at a time that overlaps with the decisive period of preparing for EU membership. The Czech Republic and the Slovak Republic still need to liberalize prices in such basic services as energy and housing, which evidently will create new winners and losers. In turn, Slovenia has to address the liberalization of financial services and, with the Czech Republic, maybe needs a major banking system consolidation. The negative budgetary and social consequences of rapidly growing unemployment are just coming to the agenda in the Czech Republic.

The CE5s also face some new and common challenges ahead. They derive partly from meeting the remaining stipulations of the Association Agreement (the last but painful part of trade liberalization, the Single Market-related dispositions). They also stem partly from the necessary further consolidation of various economic sectors, arising from both the achieved levels of capital accumulation, enterprise-building, and competitiveness and from the need to create a competitive economy before accession. As a result, the winner-loser pattern still may change in the next few years, even in those countries, such as Hungary or Poland, that have not experienced delays or missteps in the transformation process.

In sum, the effect of transformation and preparation for accession produces different conditions to identify winners and losers across the CE5. The more the two processes have been separated in time or, in other words, the quicker and deeper the transformation process was, the easier it is to separate winners and losers of the two processes.

Such a development has three important implications for the next few years. First, it is possible to ameliorate the negative consequences of transformation. Second, as clear winners and losers already have appeared in an increasingly competitive environment, potential "double winners" and "double losers" can be identified. Third, as some of the losers of the transformation process already have disappeared or have started a new activity, in which they may become a winner, the economic, social, and political burden caused by the potential losers of accession may be less heavy.

The Political Landscape

All CE5 countries benefit from accession to the EU, in terms of external security and of stabilizing democracy and democratic institutions. It is particularly relevant for the Slovak Republic and for Slovenia, which have not become members of North Atlantic Treaty Organization (NATO). Because the Slovak Republic also has not yet begun accession negotiations, it attaches particular importance to the political framework. Slovak politicians emphasize that a slower accession process has extremely negative consequences on the Slovak Republic's security and the sustainability of its democratic development. Although the Czech Republic, Hungary, and Poland already are members of NATO, membership in the EU represents a different quality of security, that is, in economic and social terms.

In the context of internal security, all CE5s were losers of the transformation. Rapid liberalization—accompanied by the necessarily slower process of building a new legal and institutional system, and social and economic polarization—have left many losers. This situation has seriously reduced the internal security standards enjoyed under the former one-party system.

Open borders and the simultaneous process of globalization also have exacerbated the situation. Membership in the EU is expected to improve internal security substantially. The growing importance attached by the EU to this issue (see the rapid upgrading of the Justice and Home Affairs pillar in the priority list of the integration) gives not only hope for a new "security umbrella" covering the new members, but it will become a condition for membership.

In the process of accession, CE5 countries have to give up part of their sovereignty and accept the "supranational" competence of Brussels. At first glance, it may be a heavy loss for all countries that either regained their independence just a decade ago, or have started again to build a new nation-state. There are groups in some countries that are not in favor of accession. For instance, there are rather strong concerns about sovereignty in Slovenia (both in politics and economics). The position of the new Czech government, however, has changed and is much less anti-European in security and political issues.

While anti-EU groups can be found in all countries, they do not have meaningful political influence. The partial loss of sovereignty is considered to be clearly compensated by gains of belonging to a larger Europe. The conviction also is broadly shared that small countries are unlikely to defend and implement their interests in *Alleingang* (in individual efforts), let alone to get relevant protection from adverse external effects.

It is possible that in the next few years, as the accession process accelerates and deepens and delicate topics manifest themselves, public attitudes will become more differentiated or even polarized. Strong influence groups that will be hurt by adjustment to the EU may become supporters of independence and "national interests." Populist parties will undoubtedly make use of this opportunity and will charge governments of "selling out" not only the economic assets of the country but also its political sovereignty. Old-fashioned Polish trade unions, partly involved in politics, with influence based on large industrial sectors in bad need of restructuring, may speak up against integration. Special support to this group may be provided by the influential Catholic church. Both in Poland and in Hungary, and to a lesser extent in the other CE5 countries, agricultural lobbies, expected to be on the losers' side, may also strengthen their opposition and fuel populist political movements. Almost certainly, any delay of the enlargement process would increase the influence of such pressure groups.

While all countries will be net beneficiaries in political terms, some may have to suffer painful sacrifices resulting from adoption of the Schengen rules. This is not a problem for the Czech Republic, and is a minor issue only for the Slovak Republic and Slovenia. However, it is a real challenge for Poland, and maybe even more so, for Hungary.

First, large minorities of Hungarians and Poles reside in neighboring countries that will not become members of the EU either in the first wave of enlargement or in the (very) long term. Second, open borders have fostered business contacts, favored the move of national capital into neighboring (less developed) transforming economies, and provided those economies with sizable economic benefits (such as in the case of Poland).

Third, both Poland and Hungary consider themselves as strategic bridges between the West and the East of the continent. Schengen borders may offer higher security, but they may lead to a loss of economic benefits (part of which would disappear anyway), a substantial loss in playing the "bridge role," and, probably most importantly, serious security and political implications. These issues may be efficiently used (misused and abused) by anti-EU groups claiming that Hungary, to join the EU, "sacrifices" several millions of ethnic Hungarians in neighboring countries.

Trade, Services, Capital, Labor

Trade

Trade liberalization stipulated in the Association Agreements created short and long-term winners of the integration process. In the short term, it helped companies previously oriented toward Eastern European (mainly ex-Soviet) markets to withstand the effects of the collapse of the Council for Mutual Economic Assistance (CMEA) (Comecon) by reorienting trade flows toward the EU. Also, asymmetric abolition of tariffs[2] created short-term winners. However, those companies that were unable to use the rather short time for quick and fundamental restructuring disappeared.[3]

Those who were able to restructure, modernize, and enter into privatization deals with foreign companies can be considered today the long-term winners. This group is certainly complemented by fully foreign-owned FDI, both in the framework of privatization and as green-field activities. New branches established mainly by FDI in the past years are clear winners of the trade liberalization (car industry, computers, electronics, and subcontracting networks of multinational firms). In turn, losers, in most cases, did not attribute their loss to the EU. Either they fell immediately victim of the market collapse (both Eastern and domestic) or of the transformation process. They may have attributed their demise to trade liberalization but did not attach it just to the EU, since, in fact, trade liberalization was not limited to the area of the EU-15.

In the next years until accession, the present winner-loser pattern will be changed only slightly by the still necessary liberalization in the CE5s. The effect may be different, depending on the scope and area of liberalization (or which goods will be affected), and, not less importantly, as a result of the continuing restructuring of affected production. Trade in agriculture will not be liberalized before membership, and the position of winners and losers, in general, will be influenced more by a clear agricultural strategy preparing for accession (if available) than by changes in the trade regime.

The CET of the EU, to be accepted at the moment of membership, may generate some changes already predictable today. As the EU and the CEFTA countries account for about 75 percent to 85 percent of the total trade of the CE5 group, introduction of the CET will have an influence on 15 percent to 25 percent of total trade. Major effects can be calculated only for those products that have very different tariff rates, rates not expected to be gradually harmonized between now and the date of accession.

Still, the major change is not expected from lowering tariffs to EU levels but from the rather sensitive area of raising tariffs to (generally relatively low) EU levels. Potential losers may be those mainly manufacturing sectors (firms) that use cheap imported inputs for production both for exports and domestic use (such as those multinationals that are importing from the Far East and manufacturing in Hungary for Western European markets, and subcontracting in Polish textile, clothing, and footwear sectors, and so on).[4]

The introduction of the CET may have serious implications, however, on the Czech-Slovak trade, if the two countries will not join the EU at the same time and, what is rather likely, Brussels does not provide temporary exception for maintaining the Czech-Slovak customs union. According to Slovak estimates, the main losers would be agriculture and the food industry.

The internal market is only partially represented in the chapters of the Association Agreement. Nevertheless, major challenges have to be faced in the preaccession period. They include compatibility with the *acquis* in such fundamental fields as competition, state aid, EU-conform compensation, some consumer, health, and technical standards, and others. The adjustment needs will be less significant for exporters and much more relevant for producers for the domestic market, as the domestic market of the CE5 becomes part of the EU's Single Market. Temporary derogations may reduce the adjustment burden or distribute it over some years after membership.

Services

Much of the service sector has not been affected by the Association Agreements and until now has remained in the shadow of integration. It has been one of the evident winners of the transformation, practically in all countries because of the emergence of private business and the temporary protection still prevailing in selected segments of the service sector. Over the next few years, winners and losers will emerge in this sector as the CE5 countries gradually liberalize their service markets. The effects will depend on the current state of liberalization in the countries, which has been rather uneven. Hungary and, somewhat, Poland have led the region, but Slovenia still has relatively high protection.

The most evident winner in the service sector will be the residents, who will enjoy more competition, higher quality, and lower prices. As for subsectors, long-term winners will be those areas already privatized or mainly dominated by foreign firms (telecommunications in most countries after the abolition of monopoly, and banking and insurance in Hungary and partly in Poland and after consolidation and privatization in the Czech Republic).

Some subsectors asking for temporary derogations may also become winners, provided that a subsequent restructuring occurs. One example is transport, which will be a winner in the longer term because of lower wages, favorable geographic location, and to-be-purchased modern vehicles. All activities that will receive larger EU funds after membership also may be winners, if the financial support helps to increase competitiveness and not to develop and strengthen the subsidy mentality.

According to a Polish survey (probably also applicable to other CE5 countries), construction, highly specialized services in renovation of monuments, and exporting of cultural services also all will become winners. Tourism, retail trade, and repair, all obvious winners in the transformation, may remain winners only if they will be able to face harsher competition. In this regard, the buoyant service sector of the Czech Republic, but also that of Slovenia,[5] Poland, and Hungary have to be restructured, which will imply declining job opportunities, higher profitability, and a serious concentration of capital.

As a consequence of the liberalization of the service sector, state-owned monopolies will be the most important losers (energy, public utilities, the finance and insurance sectors, railways, and aircraft). If privatization, largely to foreigners with powerful private domestic capital, is not carried out before accession, the costs of accession will be higher. Privatized companies that have guaranteed monopoly or quasi-monopoly rights and will lose them may be short-term losers.

Some services can compensate for the loss of domestic markets through expansion in foreign markets. Others (such as energy), however, will not be able to expand because they are generally weak in international competition. Those firms with foreign ownership that have to give up monopoly rights will not face serious problems of financing the necessary restructuring. For example, some EU-located firms (for example, Deutsche Telecom) enjoy contractually determined monopoly rights several years longer in an associated country than in the just-liberalized EU market. In this way, even if to a limited extent, losses from liberalization in Western

Europe can be financed by sometimes extremely high monopoly profits earned in much poorer CE5 countries.

It is not yet clear the extent to which domestic or foreign firms in the CE5 will be able to conquer two of the most promising new markets in the service sector, physical infrastructure and the environment, which will be among the most dynamic sectors of the next decade. Companies preparing for these activities, including proposing projects to submit to the EU budget for cofinancing, will be big winners. In most cases, however, big EU companies will dominate these proposals. Therefore, subcontracting from the larger firms also may become a profitable business for many small and medium-size firms.

Capital

As part of the adjustment to the conditions of the internal market, free flow of capital also has to be guaranteed. In this area, CE5 countries are rather unevenly prepared. Hungary, with most of its banking and insurance privatized to foreigners, seems to be in the winner's position with modern financial services, software, computer technologies, and others, while other countries still have to privatize and restructure large parts of this sector.

A common ground for concern is the selling of agricultural land to foreigners, for which all countries want to ask for relatively long derogations. This request is understandable in emotional, psychological, and political terms. However, it can hardly be defended with economic arguments. The extremely low price of agricultural land is a consequence of mistaken agricultural policies in all CE5 countries. Without changing the present rules of the game, that is, without relaxing the prevailing restrictions to buy and sell land, prices will not go up, even in the period of derogation, and may even go down further.

Here, the owners of land are the victim of a demagogy based on outdated nationalism. In fact, they are absolute losers if the restrictions are kept. In the case of gradual liberalization of the land market, they may still lose their land (which, in many cases, they are increasingly unable to cultivate), but get a honest price for it and improve their living standard. The big beneficiary would be the competitive agriculture and food industries, and, indirectly, the whole economy. In addition, regional development and rural investments may improve the situation of the "relative losers." In sum, having the misinterpreted interests of a small fraction of the population (except Poland) blocking the progress of a whole sector and, as a consequence, creating increasing losses, has to end.

Labor

The most dramatic changes in the labor market of the CE5 countries already have taken place. For each of the CE5s at different times, unemployment had risen to two-digit levels and has started to stabilize or decline as economic recovery has started. Hungary and Poland seem to have the most favorable unemployment picture; the unemployment rates were around 10 percent for both countries in 1998. Unemployment in Slovenia remained constant between 1993 and 1998 at about 15 percent. It rose in the Czech Republic from 4 percent to 8 percent during that period. Unemployment in the Slovak Republic was already high at nearly 16 percent in 1998 but may rise even further, once meaningful restructuring starts.[6]

While the overall level of unemployment will probably not grow in the decisive years of preparing for membership, sectoral redistribution of job creation and job destruction may reach sizable magnitudes. In this context, labor market rigidities will be a factor in increasing losses and reducing potential benefits. Labor market rigidities arise from inappropriate skills; limited housing facilities where jobs would be available; small differences between salary and social welfare benefits (which discourage the jobless to look for work); widespread gray market activities; as well as psychological barriers. Examples of psychological barriers are unwillingness or inability to work resulting from long-term unemployment and reluctance to learn new skills. Moreover, having been accustomed to social benefits for a long period of time, some of the unemployed have developed a "subsidy mentality," in which they look much more for different kinds of subsidies than for a job in the formal economy. Such "subsidies" or "temporary incomes" can come from tax evasion, crime, bribery, corruption, blackmailing, and other practices.

Free trade with the EU has had a twofold effect on the labor market. It has created new job opportunities in competitive sectors, while at the same time it also has destroyed many jobs in other sectors. As measured by the trade deficit, more jobs have been eliminated than created by exports to the EU[7] in practically all CE5 countries.

The winner-loser pattern on the labor market, to a large extent, will depend on the EU's position on liberalizing, and if so, under what conditions would its labor market be liberalized after accession. With no liberalization, labor market rigidities also would be increased in the CE5 group, with a clearly adverse effect on welfare. The biggest losers of labor market restrictions would be Poland, followed by the Slovak Republic. Slovenia and Hungary are expected to be modest job exporters; the former because of its internal rigidities and diversified economy and the latter because of job creation by multinationals and their subcontracting activities.

Demographic trends speak against large-scale emigration of labor. It is much more feared that labor from neighboring countries, including those joining at the same time, may appear on the domestic markets. Within the group, Poland represents a special case, because of its growing reserves of labor and the need for a fundamental restructuring of the agricultural sector.[8] This restructuring easily could create many new losers from land concentration and rapidly vanishing employment opportunities (including self-supply farms). If accession and agricultural restructuring are not planned carefully, the unemployment rate could rise substantially.

Manufacturing and the Role of FDI

In the first years of transformation, industry was a major loser. Following a decade of forced restructuring and free access to EU markets, a transparent picture of winners and losers has been emerging in the manufacturing industry. The group of winners includes most export-oriented activities carried out either by foreign or large, successfully restructured domestic companies. Firms integrated into the subcontracting network of multinational corporations are also winners.

Activities primarily or exclusively based on the domestic market proved successful only if, in the face of increased external competition, they could diversify production and/or develop clear specialization patterns. This pattern reveals two basic features. First, comparative advantages did not focus, as predicted by many experts, just on material- and labor-intensive production but included a rapidly growing number of skill- and technology-intensive products. Second, in recent years, a growing differentiation in production and export patterns between the CE5 countries can be observed. While more than 60 percent of Hungary's exports to the EU consist of machinery, electronics, computers, and transport equipment, the share of such product groups amounts to 40 to 45 percent in the case of the Czech Republic and Slovenia and to about 25 percent in the case of Polish exports to the EU.

The production and export sales of office and data processing machines, TVs, and communication equipment have been growing rapidly in Poland. The competitive sectors in the Czech Republic include car manufacturing, the plastics and rubber industries, specialized products of the food and glass sectors and, in the medium term, restructured machine building.

Membership in the EU will abolish its present practice of introducing temporary restrictions on different sensitive products. Some products may be beneficiaries of integration (for example, steel and other material-intensive goods). In Hungary (where foreign capital developed an international location for production), computers, electronics, transport equipment, and specialized machinery are the big winners. Many of them did not exist a decade ago. In contrast, Slovenian winners are concentrated in labor- and material-intensive production of specialized products, in which Slovenia already was competitive 10 years ago. It is expected that some of these winners are short-term beneficiaries, and further restructuring still will exert a major effect on the industrial structure, probably with the exception of FDI-dominated Hungarian production.

The big losers were traditional industries with no or slow restructuring, including mining, iron and steel, heavy chemicals, heavy machinery, shipbuilding, and after a temporary boom of subcontracting, textiles, clothing, and leather industries. Large companies not linked to international networks also lost. In the future, the further opening of the domestic markets will create more losers who have been protected either by tariffs or state subsidies.

Liberalization of energy prices in the Czech Republic and the Slovak Republic will add to the losers. Most probably, many of the still existing but highly indebted enterprises in the Czech Republic, the Slovak Republic, and Slovenia will find it difficult to survive. A special problem arises for the Slovak Republic if the customs union with the Czech Republic has to be abandoned.

Special attention has to be devoted to the development of small- and medium-sized enterprises (SMEs). It was a general assumption that this sector may become the engine of growth and, at the same time, a key factor of political stability. In fact, while there has been a real boom of SMEs in the service sector of all countries and in industrial production in Poland, its role has remained limited in other countries. This is particularly the case for Hungary, where large foreign-owned firms represented the engine of growth.

In the future, a strong differentiation process will affect the SME sector, both due to increased external competition and to the financial possibilities and constraints deriving from the necessity of growth and specialization. The bottom-up process of emerging SMEs is likely to enter a period of differentiation resulting in the selection of long-term winners but also many losers who used to be winners in the first stage of transformation. This characterizes the Polish development.

The other pattern of developing SMEs in a top-down approach, by increased clustering activities of multinational firms, may result in a different outcome. Most SMEs integrated into the subcontracting network of transnational companies are likely to be winners of the integration. This situation characterizes the Hungarian approach.

Although FDI has been playing an important part in the development of all transforming countries, both the macroeconomic importance and, more importantly, its basic orientation, were different from country to country. The two contrasting points are, again, Poland and Hungary. In the case of Poland, FDI, until most recently, concentrated on the domestic market and on privatization-related activities.

In the case of Hungary, after a short wave of privatization business, FDI started to develop an international production center based on comparative advantages, including geographic location, skill, and, not less importantly, openness of non-manufacturing sectors to foreign investment (banking, insurance, energy, telecommunications, and most business-related services). As a result, FDI became probably the most important beneficiary of the integration process.

FDI has not only been the unambiguous winner but also a key factor in accelerating the enlargement process. Large unrestricted European markets, existing or anticipated dynamic growth in Central Europe and rapidly growing domestic demand in the region, already have led FDI to establish production capacities based not only on free trade but also on full membership in the short to medium term.

In this context, FDI has become probably the strongest pressure group in Brussels for quick enlargement. Not less important, however, is the effect of FDI on the legal (and institutional) absorption capacity of the host Central European countries. FDI (mainly coming from EU countries) has enforced standards and regulations in conformity with the *acquis communautaire*, and started a bottom-up process of legal adjustment.

Still, FDI will face some challenges in the next years of the preaccession period. First, its profitability, highly above average in the last years, will come down to normal levels. Second, some of them have to restructure due to the enforcement in the CE5 countries of strict EU rules on health, environment, social safety, and standards (for example, for the tobacco industry). Third, FDI enjoying monopoly rights on a still closed domestic market will be facing harsh competition. Fourth, FDI-dominated manufacturing based on cheap imports from non-EU countries will have to absorb the effects of the common external tariff (mainly U.S. and Japanese investors). Finally, activities in customs- and tax-free zones will be seriously cut back as a result of membership,[9] in accordance with the competition rules of the internal market. Because this policy instrument was one of the attractive elements of locating FDI in Central Europe (and mainly in Hungary), in some cases major restructuring may be necessary to keep some FDI activities on the winning side.

Agriculture

Aside from outdated manufacturing based on uncompetitive goods and a highly undemanding but vast Eastern market before 1989, agriculture has been the other big loser of the transformation process. Loss of markets, overly hasty liberalization, the collapse of domestic demand due to declining real incomes in the first years of the changes and, to a large extent, ideology-driven and absolutely mistaken agricultural policies can be listed as the major factors of an unprecedented crisis. Still, agriculture remains a protected sector in the Association Agreements, at least in comparison to industry and some services.

Whether agriculture will be a winner or a continuous loser of the integration process fundamentally depends on two interrelated factors. First, a clear preaccession strategy for agricultural restructuring is needed. Second, the agricultural policy of the EU toward the new members has to be clarified. Benefits and losses will develop whether the CE5s will get compensation payments (as the EU producers do) or at least major financial support to modernize production. Also, the definition of production quotas in regulated agricultural markets has to be known before an assessment of winners and losers can be given.

Adjustment to the EU will result in more liberalized trade, even if full liberalization may need several years. Producers of competitive exportable products will be the winners as will be the food importers. At the moment, Hungary is the only CE5 country with a surplus in agricultural trade with the EU. With more liberalized trade, both the Czech and Slovak Republics should expect rapidly growing exports, since their agricultural protection level is much lower than that in the EU. In turn, the existing high protection level and high prices in Slovenia may mean that there will be no substantial benefits from trade liberalization. Therefore, Slovenia expects to receive compensatory payments that would increase the benefits and decrease the losses of agricultural integration.[10]

Agriculture will be characterized by growing polarization between winners and losers. First, market-oriented producers are expected to win, while farmers working in small, uncompetitive land will be losers. This is a particularly serious problem in Poland, which has a large share of its population in agriculture and therefore a potential for a large number of losers unless it can manage the process of restructuring, both in economic and in social terms.

Some of the Hungarian farmers will be losers, although their numbers are expected to be much smaller. About 8 percent of the active population are in the agricultural sector (320,000), about half of whom are expected to leave the labor market in the next few years for reasons of age (a clear difference from the Polish situation with a young agricultural generation). Around 120,000 are expected to be the potential losers in agriculture in Hungary.

Second, winners and losers will be distributed according to different production areas. The position of the CE5 farmers in strongly regulated sectors of the common agricultural policy will depend on the production quotas assigned to them. In general terms, milk, beef, and sugar beets producers may belong to the winners, while poultry and pork production will prove less advantageous in Poland.[11] Beef, hops, fruit, and milk belong to the winning sectors in Slovenia, while sugar beet and eggs are the losers. The future of other products depends on the implementation of compensatory payments (cereals, oil seeds, sheep) or on actual price growth (vegetables, potatoes, pigs, and poultry).[12]

Third, the balance between benefits and losses depends also on the financial and technical capacity of farmers to quickly adjust to the strict health and safety standards applied by the EU. Fourth, the number of winners can increase if farmers can connect their traditional production activities with (or partly replace them by) priorities that can be financed from EU funds (rural development, reforestation, and ecological environment). Almost certainly, producers of ecological goods (natural food) will be long-term winners.

Fifth, agriculture and food industry may follow different lines, one being more a loser while the other more a winner of the integration process. As a result of modern technology and large investments by foreign (and partly domestic) companies, the food industry can be a major beneficiary of trade liberalization by using imported inputs to a larger extent and relying less on the domestic production.

Finally, agriculture is supposed to be the only sector in which, at least in the medium term, some of the producers will win and consumers will lose. Prices of basic food products are still much lower in the CE5s (with the partial exception of Slovenia) than in the EU. During the preaccession period, further price harmonization will occur and, in some cases, a one-step bigger price increase cannot be excluded at the moment of membership, provided the new countries will become part of the common agricultural policy (without which, participation in the internal market raises substantial and not only technical problems).

Most likely, consumers will absorb the price increases with less opposition than some producers (or groups of producers) on the loser's side. In fact, agriculture is not a major production activity (its contribution to the GDP in the CE5 countries varies between 2 percent and 6 percent), and with the exception of Poland, farmers do not represent more than 4 percent to 8 percent of the active population. Still, their interest groups are influential, well organized and, in more than a few cases, open and inclined to populist trends. Therefore, they may affect domestic (and regional) politics and shape the pattern of winners and losers to the favor of a small, militant fraction of the society and to the detriment of other sectors.

Regional Policies

The CE5s reveal essential differences in regional development because of geographic, historical, cultural, economic, and even mentality-related and religious reasons. These differences can be observed between countries, as well as between different regions within one country.

On one hand, the Czech Republic and Slovenia, the historically more developed parts of previously larger countries (or federations), represent a higher level of homogeneity than the other three countries. Even in these two countries, there are regions at higher or lower levels of economical development, mainly due to the industrialization pattern of the socialist period (in the Czech Republic) or to a specific division of labor among differently developed republics in the former Yugoslavia (Slovenia). Still, these differences are relatively small and, more importantly, the historical and cultural background of the population is rather uniform.

On the other hand, Poland and Hungary have historically different regions, with a clear West-East gap of living standard, production structure, and cultural values. This gap is much wider in Poland than in Hungary. During the federation period, the same was true for the former Czechoslovakia, between the Czech and the Slovak territories. The modernization pattern implemented until 1989 has tried to narrow the historical gap, and, to some extent was able to do so in macroeconomic, structural, and partly infrastructural terms (less in terms of social values, mentality, education, and other issues). Unfortunately, the collapse of the Eastern markets has affected the newly industrialized regions much more than the traditional areas. As a result, the gap between the historically more and less developed parts of the countries has started to widen again.[13]

In macroeconomic terms, all CE5 countries will be net beneficiaries of the EU once they become members. Except for a few of regions which, depending on the design of regional entities, may reach 75 percent of the average per capita GDP of the EU, the whole area will qualify for structural funds. The largest beneficiaries will be those activities eligible for financing from these funds. It will include physical infrastructure and practically all areas of investing into environment and, depending on the level of participation in the Common Agricultural Policy, also rural development.

One of the not yet emphasized effects with substantial multiplier effects may be institution building and the fostering of cooperative mentality and behavior in policies funded by EU money. As a direct effect, winners will be generated by unprecedented investment activities in which domestic and foreign firms will participate. Indirectly, the development of the physical infrastructure, and better access to untapped or underused production factors will favor all activities in the geographic neighborhood of EU-financed developments. Most probably, grass-roots SMEs will start to prosper in this environment.

The evolution of winners of the process depends on various factors. First, the sooner a country becomes a member and gets access to these funds, the quicker winners will appear. Second, the later efficient administrative, financial, and human absorption capacities are created by the new entrants, the smaller will be the gains. Third, and most importantly, the size of the benefits will crucially depend on the pattern of resource allocation. According to available experience, direct financing of least developed regions leads to suboptimal efficiency.[14]

Therefore, to use EU funds most efficiently, those areas must be identified in which the critical mass of multiplier effects can be achieved in the shortest time with the smallest amount of resources. In general, these regions are the more developed, but not necessarily the most developed, parts of a country, where the critical minimum of financial, administrative, technical, human, and other resources are available, or quickly can become available, in a convenient mix.

At the same time, these regions, in any case, will benefit from accession, as they already have benefited during transformation and the preaccession period. Consequently, the first years of membership may widen the income gap, with accumulated gains in the more developed parts of the country. Evidently, the less developed parts of the country also will benefit from external funds, although they will be the relative losers. More importantly, in psychological terms, they will consider themselves as absolute losers of the process.[15]

The priority for a communication policy is to explain why the more developed areas can use resources with higher efficiency and how this resource allocation is more helpful to less developed regions than a direct inflow of money. It also has to be made clear that underdevelopment is not just a category of financial resources.

The level of education and flexibility of the labor market play a critical role in the catching-up process. It is not only an economic dilemma but a major political challenge that, in some countries, namely Hungary and the Slovak Republic, the most depressed regions have a high share of unskilled population mainly belonging to the ethnic group of Romas. While in rapidly developing areas of the CE5 countries, demagogy, extremism, nationalism, and hostility to the EU certainly will disappear or at least lose their social support, areas lagging behind may become the magnet to such forces (again mainly in Hungary and the Slovak Republic but also in Poland).

All CE5 countries definitely are interested in shortening the catching-up process as much as they can and in using EU resources in the most efficient way. Here, two conflicting areas may emerge in relations between the CE5 and the EU. First, funds of the EU budget will be distributed according to EU rules, which do not necessarily coincide with the development priorities and philosophy of the candidate country. While the EU may provide more direct support to least developed areas, the CE5s could prefer the option to create multiplier effects in the shortest possible time. Second, EU policies directed to provide large amounts of money to less (least) developed regions can strengthen (and not necessarily weaken) the political influence of nationalistic and anti-EU groups[16] (see the Country Report on The Slovak Republic).

Effects on Cross-Border Development

Cross-border regions have generally become winners over the last decade of transformation. If they are located at the external borders of an EU country (for example German-Polish or Austrian-Hungarian border), the multiplier effects deriving from the EU have created absolute winners. If they were depressed areas, the opening up of the borders, free flow of persons, and growing exchange of goods and services have helped them to compensate for the even more adverse effects of the transformation. Certainly, they felt like losers in comparison to other parts of the country, but they were clear winners in comparison to their previous situation or without this alternative.

Winners emerged on both sides of the border. For historical reasons, the West-East gap is even more evident on the Polish-Ukrainian or the Hungarian-Romanian border than along the German-Polish or the Austrian-Hungarian borderline. The western parts of Ukraine or Romania also are historically more developed already than the eastern parts of these countries. As a result, growing cross-border activities also have created winners in those countries for which accession negotiations have not yet begun. It has to be underlined, however, that also due to underdevelopment, many of the cross-border business covered gray or even illegal areas of activities, including commuting of illegal labor. It is questionable to what extent the winners of such a transformation process could remain winners in a more transparent, better regulated or controlled, and competition-oriented situation.[17]

Cross-border activities may have a longer-term effect on the distribution of winners and losers in different regions of a given country. The geographic location of the CE5 countries gives rise to three cross-border development patterns. The first category includes the relatively most developed regions of the CE5s bordering the more developed (although in the neighboring countries less developed) regions in Austria, Germany, and Italy. Second, the depressed regions of the CE5s have common borders (between the Czech Republic and Poland, Eastern Slovakia and Northeastern Hungary, and the Hungarian-Slovenian border). Third, regions that are developed to different extents may have common borders, to some extent between Northwestern Hungary and Southern Slovakia.

Clearly, the biggest winners stem from the first group, strengthened by the location choices of FDI in the last years. Winners of the second group belong to the category of "damage limitation," meaning that the decline in these areas would have been even more pronounced if some kind of cross-border activity had not been developed. In the longer term, the third group, currently not very present at the CE5 borders, could be an interesting test case of spillover effects creating winners on both sides of the border.

The EU could do a lot to strengthen cross-border activities and increase the number of winners by upgrading and locating interregional programs to the border regions of applicant countries. More importantly, a comprehensive plan of regional infrastructural development could substantially enhance the growth potential of the whole area, with fundamental spillover effects to other candidate or not-yet-candidate countries of Eastern and Southeastern Europe.

Preparation for and membership in the EU may, however, produce a different outcome. The introduction of Schengen rules at the new borders of an enlarging Europe would create losers in various aspects. Cross-border trade, investment, and partly illegal labor flows could decline rapidly as a result of visa regulations. This already has been the case for the Polish-Ukrainian border. Similar effects can be expected once other CE5 countries have to introduce visas for citizens of neighboring countries not on a Schengen border.

A special and extremely illogical situation could emerge if the Czech-Slovak border would become, even temporarily, a Schengen border of the EU. Ethnic minorities living on the other side of the border may become the losers. Because the negative effects of such a situation would clearly spill over beyond the narrow border area, however, losses manifested in decreasing stability also could be felt in the whole territory of Central and Eastern Europe, including the Schengen countries.

Public Administration

The EU has a twofold and significant effect on public administration in the CE5 countries. In a direct way, it enforces a restructuring, according to EU patterns. In an indirect way, it influences the redistribution of positions, gains, and losses through budgetary implications.

In practically all the CE5 countries, the public administration is seriously overstaffed and oversized. With or without enlargement, there is a need to streamline or substantially cut employment. Because this process is likely to take place during the crucial years of preparing public administration to meet EU requirements, many civil servants may perceive it as a direct and negative effect of accession to the EU.

As a result, losers of this process may easily become opponents to membership. More importantly, because they regularly have a stronger effect on shaping public opinion than several other pressure groups, opposition may spread beyond the circle of effective losers.

Winners will include public institutions and servants regularly dealing with the EU, be it an official negotiating with the Commission, an expert elaborating EU-related papers, or a person training staff in European integration. In short, everybody involved in the "EU culture" can be considered a winner. Unambiguous winners are and will be even more directly linked to the management, distribution, and monitoring of EU resources.

Public administration benefiting from EU money used either for training or for institutional restructuring also is a clear winner. Because of the regional philosophy of the EU and the entitlement of regions to structural funds, decentralized entities on the regional level represent a further group of clear winners, both in terms of development resources and in terms of more sovereignty from the center.

To some extent, the central government also can become a winner, at least against some influential pressure groups whose power can only be resisted, controlled, and broken with the support of the EU (or the overriding interest in joining the integration). Finally, and in a nutshell, all actors in the economy are expected to be winners because they will benefit from more transparent structures, provided the adjustment to the *acquis communautaire* will enforce such a development.

Among the losers will be those areas of public administration not connected to EU-related activities. Others, mainly relative losers, will emerge from those with no access to substantial EU funds. To some extent, the central government institutions also may be losers, because some traditional central functions will have to be abandoned, either to Brussels, or be relegated to the more independent regional level within the country.

Small communities (self-governments) not qualifying to be special entities eligible for EU funding will have to become part of larger regions and give up (part of) their self-government status in order to have access to additional resources. Finally, and linked to the last group, anyone on any level of public administration not ready to think and act in an interdisciplinary framework and refusing to network and cooperate will lose.

In more general terms, it is not yet clear how adjustment to the EU bureaucracy will affect the future of the public administrations in the candidate countries of Central Europe. More pressure and a higher workload coming from the EU may result both in higher efficiency (in the case of successful adjustment) or in growing opposition (in the case of unsuccessful adjustment). In any case, the selection and differentiation process within the national public administrations will be accelerated.[18] Moreover, this process will be crucially influenced by the continuing or planned reforms of public administration within the EU itself. The EU not only can produce both a more effective, downsized, and flexible administration but also can contribute to a more flawed bureaucracy in the CE5 group.

Budgetary Issues and Fiscal Policy

The budgetary effects of the preaccession and the post-accession periods are expected to be positive. The budgets of member countries will have a larger maneuvering room, for additional revenues from the EU funds will be higher than additional expenditures, both directly paid to Brussels and made available for cofinancing.

Beyond this general picture, however, three major changes will be generated. First, all sectors enjoying a net inflow of EU money will be winners, even if some may win more than others (infrastructure, environment, perhaps agriculture, and, of course, areas allowed to make use of temporary derogations).

Second, sectors that will be net contributors to the budget of the EU will have a declining influence in shaping and distributing the national resources available for the budget [customs duties, and part of value-added tax (VAT)]. Authorities in charge of allocating funds for subsidizing different and mainly uncompetitive production and services, including state-owned companies, will have to get accustomed to less influence in the struggle for the "budget cake."

Third, cofinancing will seriously modify the distribution of budgetary resources across sectors. While the budgetary income from traditional sources (that is, excluding financing from EU funds) will not increase dramatically, cofinancing needs will probably do so. Therefore, more money will have to be channeled to this purpose in order to draw on EU funds and, as a result, enhance total income of the budget. There will be a clear dominance of those sectors that are entitled to get EU resources.

Membership in the EU will challenge traditional pillars of the fiscal policy. The distribution of taxes will change due to the transfer to Brussels of some tax incomes still under the competence of national tax collecting authorities (customs duties, part of VAT). Also, accession criteria may include some change in the national VAT system, if currently multi-level VAT systems have to be simplified (to two basic VAT groups) and/or present tax levels have to be changed (for example, the difference between the higher and the lower tax rates has to be narrowed). An additional but not yet predictable element of change may come from EU-level tax harmonization. At the moment, most EU countries oppose such a step. However, developments in the monetary union may put this topic on the agenda of economic policy harmonization in the coming years.

A particular but "noisy" problem can emerge if tax exemption and tax preferences granted by national tax policies to special activities will have to be abandoned (or reduced). In this context, in Hungary probably the most critical issue is the tax exemption not linked to any obligation to declare income and given to several hundred thousand small-scale farmers, since this measure is not only a particular form of income and social support but a highly politicized issue as well. Once a CE5 country is member of the EU and of the Common Agricultural Policy, resources from the community budget can only be made available if farmers register their production and income. It is an open question how a large portion of farmers will behave and what will be the EU's position.

Potential Effects on the Central European Free Trade Association (CEFTA)

CEFTA plays a useful role, complementary to that of the EU, in regional cooperation. Accession to the EU will exert several influences on the future of CEFTA. Not all of CEFTA's seven members, certainly, will join the EU at the same time (most probably, not even in two different groups). For analytical purposes, however, CEFTA countries will be divided into those that already have begun accession negotiations and those that have not.

CEFTA countries already in accession negotiations will have clear gains from membership. First, their economic policies will have to be harmonized as a result of national adjustments to EU standards. Second, the potential in subregional trade will be realized. According to the author's estimates, membership would result in more dynamic intraregional trade than trade with the present EU member countries. In consequence, the share of first-wave CEFTA countries in each other's total trade can increase by several percentage points (from the present level of 8 percent to about 11 to 12 percent).[19]

Third, additional investments by foreign and local companies making use of the large, liberalized, and predictable regional market will fuel trade, financial, and other contacts. Fourth, infrastructural developments cofinanced by EU resources may result in a much higher level of cooperation, provided that national development plans are coordinated on the regional level. Finally, and partly as a result of the above mentioned factors, the Central European CEFTA countries already negotiating accession can become the most dynamic growth pole of Europe during the next decades.

Despite this clearly positive-sum game scenario, at the sectoral level, gains and losses will be distributed unevenly. Agriculture may be the main winner if the CE5 countries join the Common Agricultural Policy and if all trade barriers, a major element of dispute at the moment, are lifted. Concerning the key economic actors, foreign capital in general and multinational companies in particular are expected to be the most obvious winners in the short term. Large and competitive domestic companies and small- and medium-sized firms will, however, follow quickly, particularly if the indicated effects on growth, improved infrastructure, better predictability, and more efficient public administration materialize.

Once accession happens for those countries that already have begun negotiations, CEFTA will be split and probably the most competitive countries of the regional group will leave it. At the same time (or even earlier than accession to the EU), CEFTA can include new members from Southern and Eastern Europe. Some trade diversion may follow from CEFTA countries outside the EU toward EU-member CEFTA countries. This effect will not be very relevant, however, because trade and other economic relations among the two CEFTA groups are rather modest (relations between the Czech Republic and the Slovak Republic the only exception). Countervailing forces will be produced both by the Association Agreements signed, or to be signed, with the EU and the serious efforts of the remaining CEFTA countries to join the EU.

To reduce the potentially negative effects that mainly will not affect the economics field but will arise from security and sociopsychological concerns, clear and coordinated actions among Brussels, the new entrants, and the other CEFTA countries have to be elaborated and implemented. Large regional environmental and infrastructural programs can be the key instrument. In addition, cross-border cooperation between EU members and other CEFTA countries have to be substantially upgraded. The extension of current interregional programs of the EU, tailored to the needs of the new border areas, seems to be an adequate policy instrument.

Social Features of Winners and Losers

One decade of political and socioeconomic transformation has produced profound changes in the social structure of all candidate countries. Growing income differences and differentiated prospects of a large part of the society have been an unavoidable development after several decades of "artificial equalization." There is a clear picture as to who have been the temporary or long-term winners and losers of this process. In most cases, this pattern coincides with and is strengthened by the pattern derived from increasing globalization and sharper international competition. Integration into EU structures produces similar results with some specific elements. As a result, double (or triple) winners are emerging on the one side, while the danger of creating double (or triple) losers on the other side is growing, as well.

All country studies have confirmed that winners of the integration are or are expected to be the following groups:

- The younger generation, fully enjoying the benefits of integration and only partially sharing the costs of adjustment in the preaccession period;

- Dynamic people with entrepreneurial mentality, flexibility, mobility, and cooperative behavior;

- More highly educated persons involved in EU-related issues (mainly international law, economics, engineering, high-quality services, banking and finance, and so on);

- People speaking major foreign languages;

- Part of the public administration dealing with EU;

- Dynamic regions able to absorb resources efficiently, and generally people living in these areas;

- Urban population, particularly in comparison with depressed rural areas (which may catch up in the medium to long term);

- All consumers benefiting from competition affecting prices (except food prices), quality of products, and services;

- Peoples from cultures of small countries with languages that are not widely spoken (see the Irish or the Finnish cases);

- All groups that consider membership in the EU as a better forum to articulate and implement their interests than in the traditional national framework (from makers of foreign business policies to a large number of nongovernmental organizations (NGOs) able to be involved in international cooperation);

- All national minorities establishing a bridge to the mother countries not yet members of the EU, unless they will be artificially separated from them (for example, the Slovak, Croatian, or Romanian minorities in Hungary);

- Finally, all political parties or movements that get a better chance to become part of the decisionmaking or the public opinion-shaping process, irrespective of whether they are supporting the integration of their country or opposing it (particularly in the preaccession period, anti-EU groups may substantially benefit in political terms, since not everybody will be enthusiastic about accession).

It is more difficult to identify the losers, because, in the case of successful and quick integration, most of them can be qualified as relative and not absolute losers.[20] Absolute losers will include:

- Unskilled, immobile, inflexible population with no knowledge of languages;

- Farmers giving up land ownership and employment without getting anything in compensation;

- Ethnic minorities unable to cope with the requirements of transformation, integration, and globalization (mainly the large Roma minorities in the Slovak Republic, Hungary and, to a smaller extent, in the Czech Republic).

Most of the losers will belong to the group of relative losers (losers in comparison to winners but not in comparison to their previous situation). Despite this "relativity," they may consider themselves unanimous losers and will, most probably, be able to develop stronger resistance than the absolute losers. This group contains:

- People with no entrepreneurial spirit but still benefiting from some gains of integration;

- Regions unable to absorb large amounts of EU funds;

- People living in depressed rural areas and depressed small urban settlements;

- Public administration not involved in EU-related issues;

- Higher educated people with non-convertible knowledge (humanities, outdated engineering combined with no knowledge of foreign languages or basic computer skills);

- Most elder (retired) people, without liquid or convertible assets;[21]

- Short-term winners of the transformation process who will not be able to face growing competition resulting both from preparation for the EU and from the next (and natural) stage of transformation expressed in the concentration of capital (for example, retail trade, small private service companies, part of overstaffed banking sector, not yet privatized utility firms, and so on);

- Losers of the process of increasing transparency and adjustment to strict(er) EU regulations (invisible cross-border trade, smuggling, employment of unregistered cheap labor, even some criminal activities, and so on);

- Social groups and movements discredited in the process of transformation and integration (depending on the general balance between gains and losses and the success of related government policies, some extremists, ultranationalistic groups or parts of the Polish church can be mentioned in this context).

Based on the above characteristics, a new social structure is in the making, in which the dividing line between winners and losers is not defined by pre-transformation and post-transformation elites. On the contrary, from this point of view, a rather heterogeneous structure has been evolving, whereby part of the former elite with some crucial features of winners (skills, networks, languages, mobility and flexibility, and so on) could often build up a relatively large to decisive position. Adjustment and accession to the EU will be the next test for this group, and, most probably, not all winners of the transformation will remain winners of integration. There is some sentiment within the countries that those pre-transformation elites that became winners under the transformation should be removed from their current positions, although in many cases these elites have managed to keep their winning positions by virtue of their competitiveness and flexibility. Such an artificial division of this emerging new group of winners could not only weaken the group of winners as a whole, but more importantly could substantially reduce the benefits from integration.

Policy Instruments to Influence the Winner-Loser Pattern

The success of integration can be measured by the quantitative and qualitative distribution of winners and losers of the process. This can be influenced by appropriate policies implemented in various areas. Thus, it is not only the market and the mostly unilateral adjustment to the EU that creates winners and losers, but also deliberate policies on different levels and in different fields of governance (such as the economy, education, labor, social sectors, legislation, and public opinion-shaping) in the candidate countries.

The transformation and the accession process are developing at the same time and their conditions and consequences are in many cases similar (if not identical). It is therefore important that steps taken for the two processes be coordinated during the critical period of preparing for membership in the EU. At the same time, however, a separation or differentiation is needed in all areas in which cumulative adverse effects can be expected. In particular, it is important that the already registered negative consequences of the transformation process do not stop or substantially delay preaccession adjustment policies.

All policies should aim at increasing the competitiveness of CE5 countries in the preaccession period in order that they become economically healthy members of the Union from the very beginning of membership. In the first place, a predictable economic and sociopolitical environment is required, in which the actors can assess and forecast their gains and avoid or mitigate losses. Investment-oriented economic policies, further liberalization, streamlining of the privatization process, and intensive cooperation with FDI belong to this set of policy instruments.

In countries more advanced in the transformation process, governments should support networking between foreign and domestic capital through the establishment of subcontracting systems involving a large number of traditional or newly created small- and medium-sized companies. Also, more intensive contacts among different levels of public administration (central government, regional entities, and local self-governance) are needed.

Instead of passive, receptive policies, CE5 countries have to develop an active and offensive approach that speeds up and, to some extent, anticipates adjustment to EU criteria. In the short run, domestic companies able to survive and ready to adjust to the new environment can be supported by market-conform (indirect) instruments. However, activities also have to be intensified in areas in which the results will not become manifest immediately. Here, measures to enhance labor mobility (including housing, better infrastructure, and so on) and education have to be given priority. In a nutshell, government policies should consist of two basic elements. First, they have to create exit strategies to moderate losses, prevent would-be losers from losing, or even convert potential losers into (potential) winners. Second and more importantly, consequent government strategies have to *create* medium- and long-term winners of membership. According to all estimates, skilled, mobile, flexible and foreign language-speaking people will belong to the winners.

Derogations have to be selected and designed very carefully. At first glance, derogation requests of the countries negotiating on accession can be considered a good proxy to identify losers, both in absolute and relative terms. The former would include those who would be unable to adjust to the EU rules without temporary derogation, while the latter would like to keep part of current gains for a period well over the date of accession. Nevertheless, one has to be aware that the definition of derogations exerts multiple influences on the winner-loser pattern.

First, it evidently redistributes gains and losses both across sectors and over time. More derogations requested by a candidate country can easily be accompanied by more derogations by the EU, which may reduce the gains in selected areas in exchange for getting new or keeping old benefits in others. Also, more derogations are likely to prolong the negotiation process and deprive CE5 economies of quicker access to larger EU funds and of the dynamic gains deriving from full membership. Second, a long list of derogations, of which many items will have to be withdrawn during the process of negotiation on accession, may increase anti-EU attitudes, since nationalistic and populist political groupings would interpret such a step as the "selling-out" of the country to foreign interests in general, and to "EU dictate," in particular.

Third, many derogations may strengthen passive behavior of the affected actors and, in extreme cases, lead to "subsidy mentality," a well-known feature both inherited from socialist times and based on experience with a relevant part of EU funds directed to less developed member countries in the last decade(s).[22]

Fourth, derogations may be extremely counterproductive, once it turns out during the negotiation process that they will not be accepted by the EU. Since such a development may be the outcome of "package negotiation" in the last stage of the preaccession period, there will be no more time to efficiently prepare the affected sectors/firms to face competition. Therefore, some sectors or firms that could become potential winners as a result of consequent adjustment supported also by government policy means will most likely become real losers.

Benefits can be increased and losses reduced by adequately preparing institutions for absorbing and efficiently allocating future EU funds. The basic question here is whether these resources will mainly support activities for social reasons but without multiplier effects or become the instruments of an active, income-generating process. Due to the basic objectives of these funds and the widespread experience with its allocation, and the prevailing fundamental social problems in most CE5 countries, it is probable that at least part of the resources will be used for social objectives to contain "negative multiplier effects" rather than for the financing of activities with clear positive multiplier effects. The chances are all the higher because the delayed but unavoidable restructuring of the big social welfare systems (pension, health, and education) will have to be carried out just in the critical pre- and post-accession period.

Distribution of gains and losses is significantly influenced by the extent to which different political, economic, and social actors of a given country are included in the integration process. The closer this circle is, the higher is the danger that benefits will remain limited while losses will be higher. Under this scenario, potential benefits cannot be used, but all potential losses will materialize. At the same time, the integration process will have to face much greater opposition than if there were broad social participation in shaping the integration policies.

A permanent consultation and interest coordination among government, business, and trade unions is a necessary condition of successful preparation. A constant dialogue with interest groups and professional organizations helps abolish unjustified fears, identify the most important steps (either active or defensive), and reduce the danger of strong opposition immediately used (or abused) by populist politicians. This is the way to break up closed social structures and, at the same time, substantially reduce the danger of "ideologization" of the integration process. This is because the government cannot be sufficiently active in all areas, and a broad and efficient network has to be created in which nongovernmental organizations should play a leading role.

Public opinion in the CE5 countries is still in favor of accession. Obviously, the past years saw a shift from all too optimistic expectations often based on illusions, toward a more healthy, realistic, and balanced position. This can be attributed to the economic and social costs of the transformation which, to some extent, already have been connected with costs of preparing for membership in the EU. Also, as contacts with the EU become more intensive, temporary frictions in some areas (trade, agriculture, and competition policy) are necessarily emerging.

In addition, the advancement of negotiations toward more difficult chapters and into smaller but important details indicates further adjustment costs. As candidate countries advance toward membership, awareness is increasing among the population that everybody (or most citizens) may be affected personally. Finally, there is growing disappointment in some parts of the society, mainly those who may have come to the conclusion that they will, once again, be losers of the current process of integration. With the exception of Slovenia, where the share of supporters of integration remained on previous (in regional comparison not very high) levels, in all other CE5 countries public support has been decreasing. However, most of those abandoning this group did not become opponents but joined the group of indecisive, hesitant, and uncertain citizens. The radicalization (polarization) of public opinion is still rather limited.

In the present crucial period, the media and those organizations that are able to shape, educate, and orient the public opinion have an important role to play. The fundamental challenge is narrowing the difference between the expectations of the public and the actual outcome of policy measures with respect to the time frame and the distribution of costs and benefits of these measures. Balanced and open communication policies are needed for open discussions of real and potential benefits and costs. It is not enough, however, to defeat illusions and identify costs. In the first instance, there needs to be a realistic presentation of the tangible benefits of integration, both those that already have materialized and those still to be realized.

In the second instance, open discussions about real and potential costs have to be complemented by finding ways and means to avoid or to dampen them and by designing alternatives. In addition, attention has to be drawn to the responsibility of everybody in his/her role as citizen, employer, employee, consumer, member of a small community, and so on regarding the adjustment process.[23] One of the biggest challenges to the media is the uneven pressure exerted by winners and losers. While winners generally register the gains without any need to be communicated to the larger public, losers (or would-be losers) are much louder.

Some of the potential losers are certainly of sporadic character, in geographic, professional, and other terms. Some others, however, already have been organized in influential pressure groups (agriculture, trade unions in uncompetitive sectors, and parts of the public administration). Still, they represent the minority of all societies, and their domination of public discussion on critical issues of integration should be avoided. Balancing and contrasting the arguments of winners and losers is a unique challenge to the mass communication and public relations campaigns.

Finally, the timing of accession has an effect on the distribution of benefits and costs. Currently, CE5 countries have to make huge and at times rather costly efforts to adapt themselves to EU rules that are necessary preconditions of membership. They hope that after membership, present costs will be (more than) compensated by benefits. Of course, further costs will emerge following accession, as derogations are temporary and when they expire the pressure to further adjust will return. In turn, and despite all difficulties and additional costs, each CE5 country is convinced that quick membership offers much more benefits than losses.

First, any delay may lead to foregone gains in growth, investment, structural change, and integration into international production and service networks. Second, efforts to join the EU quickly may remain unrewarded and cause increasing disappointment among the business circles and the society at large, which could lead to domestic political and economic problems. Third, slow growth, a low level of investments and decline of attractiveness for the international business community, accompanied by psychological problems, may easily enhance the migration potential which, excepting Poland, is limited today. Therefore, it is not early membership that threatens the EU countries' labor markets and social order but the opposite—the absence of high growth and favorable prospects expected from quick membership.

The costs and the duration of the preaccession period are not necessarily inversely correlated. It is simply not true that the longer the preparatory stage lasts and, accordingly, candidate countries become better prepared, the costs of preparation will continuously fall. Obviously, a poorly prepared country needs some time and has to assume huge costs to get prepared adequately. However, there is a point where any delay of accession would not reduce but increase costs. First, there would be social and political costs that can hardly be quantified but that could reach dangerous levels. Second, expected benefits cannot be enjoyed as long as the accession process is postponed. In such a scenario, a substantial part of potential winners will, in fact, become direct losers due to lower growth potential and missing additional external resources.

Concluding Remarks

All country reports emphasize that accession to the EU represents an obvious net gain for the economy as a whole. While gains are expected to be much larger than costs, not everybody will be a winner. Benefits and costs will spread unevenly. It is the task of the governments to reduce large inequalities by keeping the engine of growth alive in more developed areas.

The possibility to clearly identify winners and losers, and the size and distribution of gains and losses, both depend on the progress reached in the transformation process. The more the transformation process and its consequences can be separated in time from the process of accession and its consequences, the easier it is to determine winner and loser positions, the higher the gains will be, as well as the higher the chances are of preventing the emergence of a risky "double loser" group.

The size and distribution of gains and losses are policy-dependent. This holds for the CE5 countries and advocates quick adjustment to EU rules. At the same time, and equally importantly, the EU also has to consider that it has to develop adequate policies to increase the number of winners and decrease that of losers. In this context, joint policies (including actions in border regions to be affected by Schengen rules and regional infrastructural planning) and an appropriate timing of accession are of crucial importance. Appropriate timing of accession in this context means that once the candidate countries are prepared, accession should not be delayed because any postponement would only result in higher costs but not higher benefits. Delays in accession would also lead to social and political disappointment in the EU.

The identification of "double winners" and "double losers" is relatively easy. Much more attention is required, however, in the management of the "conversion process," which could result in either the losers of the transformation becoming winners of the integration, or the winners of the transformation becoming losers of the integration. In particular, the latter case needs extreme care. In this context, the following basic question has to be answered: Which gains recognized by the transformation process can be converted into "sustainable gains" during the preaccession and accession stage, and what kind of policies should be pursued? And, not less importantly, Which are those gains that will not be sustained by the integration?

Influential pressure groups, both in the CE5 countries and in the EU itself, are affecting the position of winners and losers. Redistribution of benefits and losses resulting from lobby activities may lead to a suboptimal allocation of resources. Consequently, there will be a gap between potential and real influence on national welfare creation.

After membership, each of the CE5 countries will be entitled to have access to the EU's structural fund. Whether these funds will be allocated according to the requirements of economic efficiency, or whether they will be allocated for social considerations, will have a significant effect on the future distribution of winners and losers. The interests of the CE5 countries and those reflected in the guidelines of the EU budget for 2000–2006, as well as domestic political considerations based on the influence of political lobbies and on the given state of social peace, may provide different answers from country to country.

Finally, it is obvious that smooth and correct cooperation among different institutions involved in the accession process, and a cooperative mentality and attitude of the society will help to create more winners and less losers.

Some Suggestions for Further Research

Both the country reports and this paper tried to summarize the views in the current literature on winners and losers. They also attempted to outline some basic developments for the next few years in the accession process. In the process of this work, a number of areas could be identified in which in-depth analyses will be required to deliver basic and well-founded messages to policy makers and public opinion shapers.

Some possible suggestions for further orientation of the project include:

- Identification and separation of transformation-driven and accession-driven effects on winners and losers;

- In-depth analysis of problematic areas, such as agriculture, the future of depressed regions, and the integration of Romas into a modern society;

- Shaping of policies to influence the distribution of benefits and losses, including national policies and cooperation with the EU;

- The influence of integration on social cohesion and income distribution;

- The most efficient allocation of funds for regional development, in an interdisciplinary approach;

- How to ensure that the short-term winners of transformation will not turn into a new group of losers of integration;

- Policies to convert real losers of the transformation and would-be losers of the integration process into potential winners;

- Finding new and promising ways of supporting cross-border cooperation between potential EU members and other neighboring European countries;

- Instruments to increase the social approval of integration;

- Role of the media and public opinion in capturing benefits, reducing costs, and redistributing winner-loser positions;

- Potential influences of NGOs and other institutions on the pattern of winners and losers in the preaccession period;

- Analysis of expected losses and to-be-foregone benefits on the basis of the available derogation requests as submitted by the CE5 countries to the negotiations in the chapters already opened;

- Analysis of a scenario of delayed enlargement on the winner-loser pattern (together with a similar survey on EU member countries);

- The influence of not enlarging the EU on the distribution of costs and benefits in the CE5 countries and in the EU (also a joint and interconnected research);

- The effects on the regional distribution of costs and benefits of national vs. cooperative strategies among CE5 candidates.

Notes

*   Czech Republic (by Petr Pavlík)
   Hungary (by Kálmán Dezséri and Sándor Meisel)
   Poland (by Maria Karasińska-Fendler, Elzbieta Skotnicka-Illasiewicz, Kazimiers
       Sobotka, and Janusz Swierkocki)
   Slovak Republic (by Jan Fidrmuc and Jarko Fidrmuc)
   Slovenia (by Peter Stanovnik, Boris Majcen, and Vladimir Lavrac)
   The author acknowledges the valuable information from all authors of the country
reports. The views expressed in this summary report, however, are the author's responsi-
bility.

1. See the respective five country papers in this volume.

2. Asymmetric abolition of tariffs refers to the abolition in the EU of its tariffs on manufactured goods before the CEECs abolish theirs. In fact, the EU already has abolished these
tariffs, although the CEECs do not have to do so until 2001.

3. The beneficial impact of the Association Agreements on trade relations was certainly
larger in small, foreign-trade-intensive countries that already had more developed contacts
to Western Europe before 1989. Calculations are only known in Poland, where, between
1992 and 1997, 11 to 12 percent of the increment in exports and 15 to 18 percent of the
increment in imports was attributed to the impact of the Association Agreement (Country
Report on Poland, p. 169.)

4. In contrast to other CE5 countries, Hungary's trade with the EU has been balanced in
the last two and a half years. At the same time, there is a large deficit in trade with developing countries, mainly represented by Far Eastern emerging economies.

5. As an example, in Slovenia, there are 25 banks plus 6 savings banks and 70 smaller savings cooperatives. The insurance sector includes 10 companies and 3 re-insurance institutions. Financial institutions dealing with securities on the capital market consist of 46
investment companies and 15 mutual funds, plus 42 stock exchange trading companies.
Obviously, this structure cannot be sustained, no matter whether and when the country joins
the EU (Country Report on Slovenia, p. 244.)

6. Unemployment rates for the CE5 are from Countries in Transition, 1999, *WIIW
Handbook of Statistics*, Vienna Institute for International Economic Studies, 1999.

7. According to Polish estimates, the trade deficit with the EU was responsible for
200,000–250,000 thousand unemployed between 1992 and 1996 (Country Report on
Poland, p. 175).

8. More than a quarter of the active Polish labor force is employed in agriculture. Moreover, this sector has also been a partial absorber of industrial and urban unemployment in the first years of transformation.

9. At the moment, there are about 130 such areas in Hungary. According to some estimates, not more than 10 to 15 may (temporarily) remain working after accession. This is a major derogation request of Hungary in the present stage of negotiations.

10. For detailed calculations based on different assumptions, see the Country Report on Slovenia.

11. See the Country Report on Poland, p. 177.

12. Results of Slovenian calculations summarized in the Country Report on Slovenia, p. 242–43.

13. Two important remarks have to be made in this context. First, the widening of the economic gap both among and within countries has been partly offset (or compensated for) by the different speeds of diverging economic development and by social welfare benefits that are only slowly declining. Thus, the gap between regions that are doing well economically and those that are lagging behind has been, in fact, smaller than reflected by GDP per capita statistics. Second, economic differences within the individual CE5 countries are still smaller than in some EU member countries.

14. In this respect, several decades of socialism and even the subsidization policies followed in the past decade provide convincing arguments.

15. It has to be added that many irresponsible politicians rooted in and supported by depressed regions, already have promised "honey and milk" in case membership in the EU materializes. It is one of the basic and most urgent tasks of politicians and media to dispel such illusions and unjustified expectations.

16. See Country Report on The Slovak Republic.

17. Still, the sustainability of social peace during the transformation process in general and in the structurally depressed areas in particular is evidently linked to the spread of this kind of activities.

18. This refers to selection of staff to be employed in the public administration for dealing with the EU. Already, in Hungary, those dealing with the EU have to pass special exams. Since specialized skills (including foreign languages) will be required for dealing

with the EU, this will lead to income differentiation (with EU-related benefits added to salaries) between EU-related and non-EU-related staff.

19. The only exception may be trade between the Czech Republic and the Slovak Republic, where trade diversion is likely to continue (particularly if the two countries do not join the EU at the same time).

20. It has not been taken into account whether absolute losers are losing more or less with or without integration.

21. It is not true that all pensioners are poor or became poorer as the nominal rise of pensions remained below the inflation rate in many countries in the past years. Inherited assets or capital accumulated in their active years not only enable them to compensate for the decline of purchasing power of their pension but, in several cases, enhance welfare.

22. Long derogation on the free flow of labor may have the same negative effect in highly developed EU member countries.

23. People have to be reminded of their frequently contradictory interests (as consumers, employees, or investors). Their situation will become even more complicated in the future, since they may protest against adjustment to the EU while they are employed in a foreign firm owned by or a national firm exporting to the EU. As financial markets will be completely opened, citizens in the CE5 protesting against the EU may have substantial savings in banks and funds owned by EU-located companies or even participate as shareholders in stock markets in Frankfurt, London, or Vienna.

CHAPTER 3

The Baltic States: The Economic Dimension

Ramūnas Vilpišauskas
Guoda Steponavičienė[1]

Introduction

Economic integration is the merging of economies by eliminating barriers to the free movement of goods, services, capital, and labor; conducting common policies; and pooling of decisionmaking authority. All of these policies together imply significant changes in the patterns of economic activities in the participating states. Integration changes the political and economic environment in which production and economic exchange takes place. It could entail redrawing the boundaries between the state and the market. It also produces concrete benefits and losses for economic groups in each country. Support for or opposition to further integration depends on expectations of the balance between the benefits and costs that different economic groups are likely to experience.

Integration of the Baltic States into the European Union, in parallel with the implementation of the rules and institutions of a market economy and democratic governance, have a significant effect on the political economy of these three countries. The analysis of the actual and potential economic, fiscal, or regulatory consequences of integration on acceding countries, their economy, and interest groups has important implications for public policy. Although the Baltic States are constrained by the EU norms they are committed to adopt, there is still enough room for policies aimed at reducing the number of losers and creating conditions for increasing the scope of winners. Moreover, understanding the likely effects of integration measures on national economies and their sectors is also necessary for membership negotiations and rational policymaking.

Several factors should be considered in determining the degree and distribution of benefits and costs in the Baltic States resulting from integration into the EU:

- The distribution of winners and losers resulting from EU integration might be different in each country depending on the general economic policies pursued since the beginning of the decade. These economic policies conducted by each Baltic country have been influenced by the ideological orientation of the government, domestic interest groups, external actors, and other factors.

  Although the goals of reforms have been the same, concrete economic policy decisions have differed in each state. For example, Estonia has been pursuing a much more liberal trade regime than Latvia and Lithuania, which means that the adoption of the EU external trade policy will result in increasing trade barriers for Estonia, while it will result in decreasing or no changes to the trade barriers in the other two countries.

- Analysis of winners and losers arising from EU integration is complicated by the fact that, in some cases, economic policies are in line with integration policies, for instance in the case of trade liberalization. In these instances, it would be difficult to distinguish the effects on the distribution of winners and losers of the transition to a market economy from the effects of integration. In cases where accession into the EU involves changes in economic regimes, such as regulation of the agricultural sector or regional policies, the analysis is more straightforward.

  Also, analysis of winners and losers depends on the counterfactual that is used. Is the correct counterfactual the non-integration scenario? Or is it the current policy stance, in which case the difficulty of analytical distinction between transition and integration remains? Or is it the ideal market economy characterized by liberalized prices and trade, competition, and private property?

  More generally, the question is to what extent meeting EU membership criteria is consistent with the objectives of transition and policies conducted in the candidate countries.[2] The approach taken in this study is to take the ideal market economy as the correct counterfactual. This is because the general requirement of having a functioning market economy is what the Baltic States are aiming at irrespective of integration into the EU.[3]

  Assuming the obligations of membership involves adoption of the Union's *acquis*. This policy involves two types of investments. First is setting up the institutional structure and administrative institutions to oversee and monitor the implementation of *acquis*, which requires budgetary spending.

These costs, the bulk of which are likely to be covered by taxpayers, will be short term, while likely benefits will appear in the long term. Second is the investment that has to be made by economic actors because of the adoption of EU regulations; enterprises will face compliance costs, part of which are likely to be shifted to consumers.

- The timing of the effects of integration-related measures might result in the concentration of costs in time and issue area. This concentration might occur because integration is a long-term process extending far beyond the formal act of accession, while its influence depends on the issue area and economic group.

  Integration of the Baltic States into the EU already has started with the liberalization of trade and removal of other barriers to economic exchange, and it will continue with the adoption of *acquis*. As some analysts have maintained, "The costs of converging to the EU are not evenly spread across the societies in transition countries and emerge at various stages of accession process."[4]

The Study

This study aims at addressing the general political economy issues arising from the integration of the Baltic States into the EU. It addresses these issues: (1) identification of the economic groups that might benefit and the groups that might lose from integration of the Baltic States into the EU; (2) the dynamics of gains and losses in time; and (3) the possible political consequences of the economic effects of integration, and measures that could be taken to reduce the negative effect of integration on economic groups.

The study does not attempt to estimate quantitatively the economic effects of integration on the Baltic economies and economic groups or to provide a balance of the macroeconomic costs and benefits of EU membership. Rather, it provides a structured qualitative analysis of integration effects and the emergence of the groups of winners and losers in the three countries. It focuses on the effects of removing barriers to economic exchange between the EU and the Baltic States and the implementation of common EU policies and a regulatory environment in the Baltic countries.

The main dimensions of analysis are the measures of economic integration in selected areas and the time dimension, which distinguishes between the short-term and long-term time frames of the effects of these measures on economic groups in the Baltic States and the timing of implementation (stages of integration). Both dimensions are detailed below.

The measures of economic integration included in the analysis are: the removal of barriers to trade in goods and services; the removal of barriers to the circulation of capital; the removal of barriers to movement of labor; regulatory measures in line with EU *acquis* in the area of the internal market; and common rules in selected sectors including agriculture, the EMU, and external trade policy.

The "four freedoms" are analyzed because they form the basis of the EU. The areas and sectors are selected for their economic and political significance to the Baltic States (agriculture, for example) and for the depth of their integration inside the EU (EMU, for example). The selection of certain areas and sectors limits the extent of the analysis. This limitation is inevitable for such a study, although the text touches upon other, more general aspects of political economy of integration.

The study assesses the likely effects of the above mentioned measures, based on theories of economic integration and international economic relations and on insights from the studies of regulation. As noted, integration-related measures need to be analytically differentiated from transition measures or other measures of integration into the world economy that are to be implemented, independent of integration, into the EU. Therefore, the analysis focuses on integration measures set in the bilateral agreements between the EU and the Baltic States and EU treaties and legal norms, unilateral documents, and opinions.

The study assumes that other factors, such as EU policies and World Trade Organization (WTO) policies, are constant. This assumption implies that the EU implemented its policies in their present form, although in some cases, such as the CAP, it is not likely to be the case. Another important assumption concerns the transposition and enforcement of integration-related measures.

The complexity of the EU *acquis* and the limited administrative capacities of the applicant countries provide opportunities for misinterpreting the *acquis* and creating winners and losers that would not have emerged otherwise. While analysis of such cases when "transmission noises" distort the original message might be interesting and illustrate decisionmaking in the Baltic States, the authors assumed here that principles of the *acquis* are introduced properly.

The study will look at the temporal dimension of positive and negative effects of integration. This is important for the following reasons:

- First, the temporal patterns of costs and benefits to the economic groups in these countries have implications for the economic policies in these countries. While most costs are likely to be short term, benefits might occur only in the long term.

- Second, the integration measures are distributed in time. Some—such as the liberalization of trade—have been implemented since the bilateral free trade agreements between the Baltic States and the EU were signed. Some have been implemented since the entry into force of the Association Agreements. Some have been introduced on the basis of the White Paper. Some will be introduced before the membership, and some might result in transition periods after the accession.

The different timing of the integration measures has political implications in terms of the effects of the membership itself, and in influencing the distribution of benefits and costs in time. Therefore, the implementation of integration measures will be discussed along several temporal stages: the start of economic relations with the EU and the signing of the first economic agreements, preaccession measures, and membership itself and likely transition periods.

This paper first presents a brief description of the dynamics of economic relations between the EU and the Baltic States since the beginning of this decade. It follows with a discussion on the emergence of possible winners and losers in selected areas as a result of integration policies. It also supports these analytical findings with results of opinion polls conducted in the Baltic States, business attitudes, and economic statistics. The identification of the likely consequences of integration on economic groups in the Baltic States and their likely reactions toward actual or anticipated integration effects will provide the basis for suggesting policy recommendations. The paper concludes with general remarks, policy recommendations, and presentation of directions for further research.

Institutionalization of Relations between the Baltic States and the EU

Economic relations between the Baltic States and the EU were initiated at the start of the 1990s. Soon after the EU recognized the three countries in September 1991, bilateral Trade and Cooperation agreements were signed. They came into force in 1993, providing for Most Favored Nation trade status and for no discrimination in trade relations. With these agreements, the EU's Generalized System of Preferences has been extended to the Baltic States (see appendix 1).

Economically more significant have been the Agreements on Trade and Trade Related Matters, which the Baltic States signed with the EU in July 1994 and which have been in force since January 1995. These Agreements provide for the establishment of a free trade area between the parties. Certain products, including agricultural goods, fisheries, and textiles, are excluded from the general provisions. The EU has committed itself to free trade in industrial products by signing the agreements. Estonia declined to apply for any transition period, while Latvia and Lithuania received four- and six-year transitional periods, respectively, during which they agreed to gradually liberalize trade with the EU.

The next stage in the integration process of the three Baltic States followed with the signing of the Association (Europe) Agreements in June 1995. These agreements upgraded the status of the Baltic States to match the other Central and Eastern European candidate countries by explicitly acknowledging their wish to become EU members, although the agreements took effect only in February 1998.

The Baltic States joined the implementation of the preaccession strategy, consisting of the Association Agreements, the White Paper on preparing the CEECs to join the internal market, and the PHARE program (the latter has been applied to the Baltic States since 1992). In the second half of 1995, the three states officially applied for EU membership. In 1997, after the Commission announced its opinions on individual candidates, the European Council decided to invite Estonia to start accession negotiations, while Latvia and Lithuania were relegated to the group of "pre-ins." Their status did not change in 1998, although the EU reinforced its financial and technical assistance, aimed at helping the candidate countries prepare for membership and assume their obligations.

In October 1999, the newly formed Commission invited Latvia and Lithuania with the remaining "pre-ins" to start accession negotiations and join the first group of countries. The Commission maintained, however, that these negotiations should follow a "differentiated" approach, fully accounting for each candidate's progress in meeting membership criteria. Assuming that the EU will undertake reforms necessary for enlargement by 2002, it will be up to each candidate country to decide on the speed of its integration.

Currently, the Baltic States are participating in a number of bilateral and unilateral arrangements facilitating their integration into the EU, including the implementation of Association Agreements, the White Paper provisions, accession partnerships, national programs of *acquis* approximation, screening, twinning, and others. These arrangements have a significant effect on national economic policymaking and institutional structures of the three countries. At the same time, economic relations between the Baltic States and the EU have developed relatively rapidly. The EU has become the most significant trading partner of the three and the main source of FDI in the Baltics (see appendix 2).

Identifying Winners and Losers in Selected Areas

This section analyzes the winners and losers for each of the "four freedoms," the CAP, and the EMU. The analysis is also presented in a series of tables in appendix 3. The groups identified differ, depending on the integration measure and include consumers, exporters, importers, local manufacturers, farmers, financial institutions, and others. They are selected on the basis of the likely effect of integration. The effect is based on potential costs or benefits for these groups, which include profit losses (for business), higher expenditures (for consumers), or power losses (for state institutions). For the sake of simplification, the effects are evaluated as positive, negative, neutral, or uncertain.

Free Movement of Goods

The liberalization of trade so far has been the most advanced area of integration between the EU and the Baltic States. Except for trade in "sensitive" products, free trade has been the main principle and objective of economic relations between the EU and the three countries since 1995. Free movement of goods implies a number of measures for mutual trade, such as the abolition of quantitative and qualitative import and export restrictions and the application of the same regime to domestic goods as to imported goods from other parts of the free trade area (a principle of non-discrimination).

Dismantling barriers to trade reduces protection to domestic producers and increases competition. The main losers are domestic producers competing with imported products, currently protected by nontariff barriers. The main winners are consumers, exporters, and producers using imported goods as intermediate products in their production processes and participating in intra-industry trade with the EU. As some researchers maintain, the share of the latter is rapidly increasing in the Baltic States.[5] Estonia has the largest share of intra-industry trade with the EU, which in 1996 was estimated to equal about 35 percent of its trade with the EU. The shares of Latvia and Lithuania were 19 percent and 17 percent, respectively.[6] If this tendency continues, the scope of winners among producers will be the largest in Estonia.

The scope of winners will also depend on the intensity of overall informal integration. The EU has been the main trading partner of the Baltic States for several years (see appendix 2). The economic crisis in Russia has resulted in further increases in the EU's share of Baltic exports. Estonia leads with exports to the EU and imports from it, accounting, respectively, for 70 percent and 74.3 percent of its foreign trade at the end of June 1999.[7]

Analysis of product groups shows that for Estonia, most of the intra-industry trade with the EU is in such goods as electronics, footwear, wood, clothing, and parts of lifting machinery. In the case of Latvia, most of the intra-industry trade with the EU is taking place in such products as electric transformers, inductors, leather, clothing, and accessories. Most of the intra-industry trade between Lithuania and the EU is conducted in footwear, woven cotton fabrics, and some fishery products.[8] Producers of these goods are likely to benefit from further integration. The selection of product groups should be treated with caution, however, as market structures are rapidly changing, in particular in transition economies.

The small size of the Baltic economies, the large share of foreign trade in their GDP, and the importance of outward processing in these countries provide grounds to believe that the scope of winners is relatively large in all three countries. Due to the collective action problem, such groups as consumers have less influence on policymaking while domestic producers are better organized and in the case of Latvia and Lithuania have been able to have trade barriers introduced. Latvian and

Lithuanian farmers—the largest lobby groups in the two countries—have managed to receive import protection from their respective governments, even when such protection contradicted international obligations of the countries.[9] Membership in the EU will provide such domestic producers with new targets for lobbying for common external protection, although the results of the lobbying on the EU level are likely to be more modest.

The effect of integration on domestic producers is likely to differ, depending on the destination of their production. Those exporting to the EU are likely to benefit from the free movement of goods, especially after the EU phases out anti-dumping and other protection instruments with which it currently can threaten Baltic producers.

In 1998, the main products exported by Estonian producers to the EU included machinery, mechanical appliances, and electric equipment; wood and articles of wood; textiles; and base metals and articles of base metals. The main Latvian exports to the EU included similar products: wood and articles of wood, textiles, mineral products, base metals, and machinery and mechanical equipment. The main Lithuanian exports to the EU included textiles, products of the chemical and related industries, machinery and mechanical equipment, wood and articles of wood, and base metals.[10] Re-exports from Russia constitute a large share of the exports indicated above. Producers of the above products are likely to benefit from EU integration.

The other aspect of the free movement of goods is the harmonization of basic standards and mutual recognition. Adoption of the *acquis* in this area is a pre-accession measure, according to the White Paper, and takes priority according to the individual needs of each candidate. Currently, the main priority for the Baltic States is to sign the Protocols on European Conformity Assessment, which will involve recognition by the EU of certifications on product standards, issued by the relevant institutions in these countries. The adoption of these principles is likely to involve large short-term costs related to the upgrading of product and process standards ("EU conformity costs"). Although it is likely to be beneficial in the long term, the costs of regulatory load might also prove to be long term. This situation can be the case, particularly for such process regulations as environmental or social norms.

Free movement of goods is one element of the single market. The other one is the common external tariff which is applied uniformly and is part of the EU external trade policy. The common external tariff most probably will be adopted only after the formal accession of a candidate country into the EU.

The balance between the winners and losers on this issue depends on whether an applicant state has been applying a more or a less liberal trade regime before acceding into the EU. Estonia, which has been applying a zero-tariff foreign trade regime, will have to raise its external protection. This policy implies benefits to domestic producers but costs to consumers. The changes in its external trade regime are likely to be introduced in 2000.

The likely effect of common external tariff on the Lithuanian and Latvian economies is less clear and probably will vary according to product groups because the average customs tariffs in these countries are close to the EU average or lower. In 1999, the average customs tariff reported by Lithuania was 2.5 percent, and the average customs tariff for non-agricultural goods applied by Latvia was 3.71 percent.[11] Producers of some goods, such as agricultural products, have been protected by higher import duties.

Adoption of autonomous and conventional measures that constitute part of EU external trade policy (including import tariffs and commercial protection instruments such as antidumping duties, in particular) is likely to have divergent effects on producers and consumers in the Baltic States. It is likely that the level of protection might increase if regulatory barriers applied in high-standard EU countries are extended.[12] The EU has been characterized by the WTO as "one of the most frequent users of anti-dumping procedures."[13]

Domestic producers in the Baltic States might benefit from certain protective measures applied at the EU level, at the expense of consumers. As some have noted, it was "a safe bet that without Community, the United Kingdom and Germany would not have footwear protection today, that UK agricultural protection would be lower, that Denmark would not have an arrangement on Japanese cars, etc."[14]

On the other hand, more complicated procedures of initiating protection at the EU level, as well as control of state subsidies and other forms of aid for local producers by the Commission, might reduce the power of domestic producer lobbies in Latvia and Lithuania. As some observers have suggested, EU membership entails a major shift in the balance of power between national lobbies, strengthening the power of such groups as consumers and exporters, whose interests are often neglected in political decisions on trade policy.[15]

Free Movement of Labor

Free movement of labor is likely to become one of the sensitive negotiation issues because of widespread fears in the EU member states concerning possible effects of migration into the richer EU countries from the poorer candidates. Although the Baltic States have a comparatively small population (about 8 million altogether), this general attitude might influence the terms of their accession and could result in transition periods.

The Europe Agreements signed between the EU and the Baltic States contain provisions prohibiting discrimination against legally employed nationals by the other parties to the agreements. Free access to the labor market in the territory of the Union involves recognition of education degrees and professional qualifications, the right to transfer social security payments, and freedom of establishment and service supply. The White Paper contains provisions on mutual recognition of education diplomas and qualifications in selected occupations, such as medical treatment or transport. The Baltic States are implementing these provisions during the current stage of integration; they are included into the national *acquis* approximation programs.

The free movement of labor benefits both employees and employers in the Baltic States. They are likely to benefit from most measures related to free access to the labor market that provide them with more choice when looking for a job or an employee. Some measures, such as adjustment of training and activity rules for certain professions, will require investments and might be costly in the short term. The possibility of brain-drain from the Baltic States exists, but its likely negative effects are not significant.

The free movement of labor, and of people in general, is one of the most visible results of integration. Visa-free regimes agreed recently by the Baltic States and members of the Schengen zone provide an example of winners that could include all residents of the candidate countries.

Free Movement of Services

The free movement of services closely relates to the movement of labor. It implies freedom to establish enterprises or subsidiaries in other members of the Union and to provide services under the conditions the host state sets for its nationals. The treaty of the EU has provisions specifically for transport and financial services, detailed in the White Paper.

In transport, mutual recognition of qualification certificates benefits both service providers and consumers. More controversial is the adoption of safety and environmental requirements for vehicles and operation, adjusting technical requirements, administrative procedures, and meeting other requirements for entry into market. These measures require initial investment, and domestic service providers are likely to bear the costs or they might shift them to consumers.

The likely magnitude of costs can be illustrated by calculations for Lithuania. The cumulative investments needed to align environmental *acquis* in the regulation of air pollution alone will amount to 2.283 billion ECU by year 2020. Even when this regulation is omitted, the cumulative costs of the approximation of the remaining environmental regulations are estimated at about 15.2 percent of 1996 GDP.[16] The national environmental institutions estimate that for Estonia, reaching compliance by 2010 would cost about 2.21 billion euro. For Latvia, the relevant public investments are estimated to reach 1.2 billion euro and the cost for the private sector is estimated to be from 305 million to 742 million euro to reach compliance by 2015.[17]

The winners in this issue are service exporters already operating on higher standards. The requirement to separate transport infrastructure and operation is likely to benefit consumers because it is expected to introduce more competition and abolish the distortions resulting from state aid provided to this sector.

In transport, governments must establish specialized agencies to oversee the implementation of directives. Specialized agencies in this and other areas are likely to be financed from the budget. Although, in some cases, the EU might contribute part of the funds, the consumers are likely indirectly to finance the creation of a regulatory institutional network. Business will bear the regulatory costs.

Integration into the EU also requires adopting concrete measures in financial services. The Baltic States have to implement EU norms governing banking, securities, and insurance services, aimed at reducing the risks related to providing these services. The supervisory institutions have been created irrespective of integration. Detailed requirements for market entry and operation of financial service providers are set in the EU norms and require the Baltic States to take specific measures. Meeting such requirements as information disclosure, minimal capital, and deposit insurance might involve costs for service providers, although consumers are likely to benefit. As noted above, however, the balance of costs and benefits depends on the interpretation of EU norms in the Baltic States. For instance, in Lithuania, the adoption of money laundering prevention measures and setting up the norm of payments for mandatory insurance illustrate that EU norms can be interpreted with a bias toward more restrictions, and that imposes extra costs on economic operators.

Free Movement of Capital

Free movement of capital implies abolishing barriers to payments and investment among the candidate states and the EU. Both business and consumers benefit from these measures. Although some might lose because of competition from foreign investors, domestic business attracting investments will benefit.

Common Agricultural Policy

The CAP is one of the few policies harmonized at the EC level since the establishment of the organization. About half of the EU budget is used for CAP purposes, and the *acquis* for agriculture covers about 40 percent of the total EU *acquis*. This area is characterized by a very strong lobby of farmers in some member states and resistance to reforms, despite high costs of the CAP to EU consumers, international disagreements with WTO partners, and potential budgetary costs of extending CAP to acceding countries.

Adoption of EU norms regulating the agricultural sector implies both compliance with veterinary and other standards related to the free movement of agricultural products inside the Union and extension of support measures to farmers in the Baltic States. The former group alone represents about 1,000 measures aimed at ensuring product quality, and setting labeling requirements and standards of farming processes.

These processes include raising cattle, growing plants, using fertilizers, delivering products to consumers, and others. About 160 measures are essential requirements. The implementation of these measures requires setting up administrative infrastructure, including veterinary agencies and other institutions of certification and inspection.

Investments in the necessary infrastructure and support for its functioning are financed from national budgets, with some assistance from the EU. Implementation of EU standards will raise opportunities to export to the EU, although most exporters are likely to adopt standards before the accession. Currently, only some agricultural producers have been certified to export to the Union.

Most of these producers are in Lithuania, where 12 establishments are authorized to export milk and diary products and one company is authorized to export processed game meat. The growing regulation of agricultural production and trade also provides opportunities for domestic producers to use the product standards as nontariff barriers. Such was the case with the trade disputes between the Baltic States in the end of 1998 and in 1999.[18]

Some estimates have been made on the effects on agriculture of joining CAP in the Baltic States. It has been calculated that if Lithuania had joined the EU in 1999, its payments to the EU budget (VAT and GDP based) would equal 407 million litas, while receipts from the CAP would reach about 459 million litas, those from structural funds would be about 3.8 billion litas, and those from the Cohesion funds would be about 760 million litas.[19] It is very unlikely, however, that the current CAP rules will extend to the new member states.

Projecting the political economy of joining the CAP assumes implementing reforms discussed in the Agenda 2000. Extending the CAP to the Baltic States is likely to have significant effects on farmers and consumers, particularly in Latvia and Lithuania, where about a fifth of the labor force is employed in the agricultural sector in each country. Farmers in all three states are likely to benefit from CAP measures, which include import barriers against third countries, export subsidies, structural funds, price support, and direct income payments. Agricultural policy is likely to change most in Estonia, where new measures of domestic support for agriculture already were introduced at the end of 1998.

The current balance of trade in agriculture and food for all three countries with the EU is negative, while it is highly positive with the CIS. To predict how the balance of trade picture will change under CAP is difficult, however, because current market distortions (domestic subsidies and import tariffs) make it difficult to determine in which agricultural product groups the Baltic economies are likely to have a comparative advantage. This situation also makes it difficult to predict which groups of agricultural producers likely would benefit and which likely would lose under CAP.

It seems that small farmers will lose from increased pressure of competition, while the large farmers might win. According to some estimates, milk and beef producers in Lithuania would win.[20] Suppliers of agricultural equipment are likely to benefit also. At the same time, consumers are the clear losers of the CAP measures. Although the Baltic States are likely to receive more funds than they will contribute to the EU budget, implementation of CAP will redistribute resources from consumers to farmers.

Some economic groups are likely to have a mixed record. Food producers using imported products from third countries are likely to lose from most CAP measures and the resulting increase in prices. Food producers will benefit from upgraded quality of agricultural raw products supplied inside the EU. Producer exporters are likely to benefit from export subsidies.

Economic and Monetary Union

In 1999, the third stage of the EMU began with the participation of 11 member states. Accession of the new countries raises the question of their membership in the EMU. The EMU criteria are not formally treated as membership criteria for the EU, and it is very likely that candidate countries will join the EMU after a certain transition period. This would allow new members to participate for a defined period of time in the exchange rate mechanism (ERM2).

Participation of the Baltic States in the EMU will be judged on the same convergence criteria that current EU members willing to join the EMU had to meet. Meeting convergence criteria will affect the Baltic economies. The countries will have to maintain low levels of inflation and restrict budget deficit and state borrowing. Currently, the Baltic States meet the fiscal criteria.

If this situation remains, meeting the convergence criteria will not involve major policy changes in these countries. It will, however, limit the possibilities of borrowing, which is high on the agenda in the Baltic States because of the economic slowdown and budgetary deficits resulting from the Russian economic crisis. The fiscal targets of the EMU also might limit spending on integration-related measures and public investments needed to cofinance resources provided by the EU (SAPARD and ISPA programs).

The effect on enterprises doing business in the euro zone will be mixed. On the positive side, joining the EMU would eliminate exchange rate uncertainty and reduce transactions costs for economic operators. The benefits will be higher as the informal economic integration that has already occurred between the Baltic States and the EU intensifies. The degree of economic integration is reflected in the intensity of trade and capital flows between the Baltic States and the euro zone and the degree of production factor mobility.[21]

While the economic links between the Baltic economies and the euro zone have been expanding rapidly (see appendix 2), labor mobility might remain low, especially if the EU applies transition periods. On the negative side, joining the EMU could result in losses for domestic producers from the regulation of wage setting and participation in the euro zone itself. The model of wage setting by a trilateral council, imported from the EU, might result in rising wages exceeding the growth of productivity, thereby damaging the competitiveness of producers. Lower productivity and per capita income in the Baltic States also caution against quickly joining the EMU.

Participation in the EMU implies loss of national monetary and exchange rate instruments. Governments will lose the autonomy to conduct independent monetary and exchange rate policies. This will not involve a major policy change in any of the three Baltic States because they already apply monetary policies based on fixed exchange rates. Estonia and Lithuania have currency board regimes in place, which constrain national monetary policy. The change is also limited because, during the current preparation for accession, the euro is playing a major role for the Baltic economies. Estonia's kroon is directly pegged to the euro, the value of the Latvian lats is determined by a basket of currencies with a heavy euro weighting foreseen in the next revision in 2000, and the Bank of Lithuania has announced in October 1999 plans to peg the litas to the euro in 2001.

The powers to conduct monetary policy will transfer to the European Central Bank (ECB). The likely effects of the ECB's policy on business and consumers will depend on its autonomy, accountability, and the transparency of its policy. The powers of national banks, especially in Estonia and Lithuania, are likely to increase when they join the ECB and use monetary instruments, such as repo tenders, purchases and sales of debt instruments, interventions in the foreign exchange markets with swaps, and the lending and deposit facilities for commercial banks.[22]

Finally, joining the EMU implies introduction of the new currency euro. The loss of national currencies might cause adaptation problems for consumers. In the short run they include psychological adaptation as well as costs of adjustment that might be shifted on to them by banks.[23] There will be benefits, however, for those traveling in the Euro zone. Adoption of the common currency might exert a downward pressure on prices of imported goods. In the short term, the adoption of the new currency and the resulting adjustment of the payments and the banking systems are likely to impose costs on commercial banks but in the long term they are likely to prove beneficial. The transition might prove to be smoother if subsidiaries of euro zone commercial banks have a significant presence in the Baltic economies.

Conclusions

The broad picture that emerges from the analysis of the political economy of integration can be characterized briefly as gains from increased opportunities versus the costs of compliance. The main winners are likely to be competitive enterprises able to exploit comparative advantages and having established economic links (trade, production chain, and investment) with the EU.[24] They will have increased market access as a result of the removal of nontariff barriers, which are distorting trade between the Baltic States and the EU despite the principle of free trade. Farmers, mostly large ones, are another category of winners because they are likely to receive higher levels of support, although, at the same time, they will experience more competition. The enterprises still receiving state support and those trading with third countries (Russia, for example) will lose. The former will lose economic rents, and the latter are likely to face higher transactions costs relative to those trading with the EU.

Compliance with the EU regulatory system involves high costs for the Baltic economies. The costs of compliance or of "attaining EU conformity" include the costs of changing the economic and legal system, of meeting EU norms and standards, and of setting up the institutional structure of regulation and administration to oversee the compliance with regulations governing economic activities.[25]

The economic and fiscal effect of investing in the compliance with the system imposes (at least in the short term) costs on economic operators and consumers. The need for continuous administrative institutions fulfilling obligations of EU membership will remain in the long run, and taxpayers will have to finance them. Introducing environmental or social regulations will impose costs on economic operations, while setting up institutional structures to oversee their implementation will have to be financed from the national budgets. The compliance with EU norms might impose further limits on the already strained Baltic national budgets.

Consumers in the Baltic countries likely will benefit from the increase in competition after joining the Single Market, although part of the regulatory costs will shift to consumers. Consumers also are likely losers from the introduction of the CAP. Those groups in the population who have links with the EU and who frequently commute to the Union are likely to benefit the most.

This effect applies to all three countries. The economic structures of the Baltic States are relatively similar, and the balance of costs and benefits is not likely to vary much. Some differences are grounded in the inherited industrial structure or economic policies implemented during transition reforms.

The inherited industry includes the Ignalina nuclear power plant in Lithuania, whose closing might impose high costs on the economy; and the inherited economic policy includes larger shares of agriculture in Latvia and Lithuania, a more liberal foreign trade policy in Estonia, or more powers to intervene into the monetary affairs by the Central Bank in Latvia. The governmental integration strategies, however, are likely to be the most significant factors in determining the balance of costs and benefits and their distribution in time.

Optimal integration strategies require systematic understanding of the accession effect on the country's economy in the context of transition. The analysis of the abolition of barriers to economic exchange and the regulatory effect of adopting EU norms in separate issues as well as the whole economy is a precondition for sound integration strategy.

First, it will reduce the chances of costly misinterpretations. The EU regulation norms were developed to address particular economic and social problems. Automatic adoption of EU norms in the Baltic States, without considering the objectives of the regulations and their adequacy for the Baltic economies, increases the chances of not achieving the objectives and of imposing costs on economic operators. Analysis of the regulatory effect is a priority for further research and has clear implications for improving policymaking in the Baltic States.[26]

Second, well-informed policymaking will reduce the costs of uncertainty for business, costs arising from this complex and changing regulatory environment.

Third, understanding the accession effect on economies and economic groups allows the government to develop a better information campaign and to avoid making promises that it later could not fulfill. The problem of expectations can be reduced by an analysis of the effect presented to the public. At the same time, a clear plan of actions by the government would reduce uncertainty in the markets and allow for longer-term business planning.

Fourth, the integration strategy should aim at increasing the range of winners and reducing the range of losers, considering possible future scenarios. Returning to the introductory assumptions, the most relevant basis for reference and for policy proposals seems to be an implemented market economy. The consumers are the policy target group representing the interests of the majority. Examples of such strategic policy decisions include:

- Reducing the economic rents of enterprises before the act of accession would create incentives for them to transform, which is necessary sooner or later. It also would eliminate the apparent connection between a decrease in state support and the EU membership. In a similar vein, the agricultural sectors should be reformed before accession to provide the right conditions for markets to function. CAP reforms in any case will take effect, and the governments of candidate countries should anticipate the change by creating necessary conditions before accession.

- The Baltic negotiators should aim to avoid transition periods for free movement of labor, because this is one of the most visible benefits of integration and is crucial to the smooth functioning of the EMU. The relationship of the Baltic States with the EU has large asymmetries in political power and economic dependency, which imply that the Baltic States have weaker bargaining power, but an active and innovative negotiation policy might increase the scope of winners.

- Priority should be given to adopting EU product standards while spreading process regulations over a longer period of time. The former require less investments, while their positive economic effect from removing non-tariff barriers to trade is higher.

- The economic gains and scope of winners will be larger with the higher intensity of trade and investment flows between the EU and the Baltic States at the time of enlargement. Functioning markets and informal, integrated, economic exchanges create conditions for expanding the scope of winners of EU membership.

The benefits of joining the EMU will be larger as the level of productivity and per capita incomes of the Baltic States approach those in the euro area. The last two points raise the politically sensitive issue of the speed of integration. On one hand, large disparities in the characteristics mentioned above would neccessitate longer preaccession periods. On the other hand, long periods before accession might result in integration fatigue and lower attraction of foreign investments. The decisions concerning the speed of integration and implementing *acquis* should be made only after considering both arguments.

Appendix 1

TABLE 3.A1 THE MAIN BILATERAL ECONOMIC AGREEMENTS BETWEEN THE BALTIC STATES AND THE EUROPEAN UNION

Agreement	Signed	In force	Main provisions
Trade and Cooperation Agreements	11.05.92	01.02.93 (for Latvia, Lithuania) 01.03.93 (for Estonia)	Most-Favored Nation status, non-discrimination; extension of EU generalized system of preferences; economic cooperation in some areas
Agreements on Trade and Trade-related Matters	18.07.94	01.01.95	Liberalization of trade based on GATT principles; free trade in industrial goods (CN 25-97); 4-year transition period of gradual liberalization given to Latvia, 6-year transition period of gradual liberalization given to Lithuania; standard protection clauses; joint committees to oversee the implementation of the agreements
Association (Europe) Agreements	12.06.95	01.02.98	Objectives of Estonia, Latvia, and Lithuania to become EU members acknowledged; the provisions of free trade agreement incorporated; political dialogue; economic cooperation on issues, such as competition policy (EU rules), movement of services, capital and labor, freedom of establishment, protection of intellectual property rights, consumer protection, approximation of laws; cooperation in other issues, such as industrial policy, science and technology, energy, environment, etc.; Association Council to supervise the implementation of the agreement and Association Committee

TABLE 3.A2 INSTRUMENTS OF BALTIC STATES' INTEGRATION INTO THE EUROPEAN UNION

Instrument	*Main features*
Preaccession strategy	
(1) Europe agreements	See table 3A.1.
(2) PHARE program	Technical assistance for transition and preaccession measures in applicant countries.
(3) White Paper on preparation of the associated CEECs for integration into the Internal Market of the Union	Identifies key measures in each sector of the Internal Market and suggests a sequence in which the approximation of legislation with EU *acquis* should be undertaken.
Accession partnerships	Define country-specific need to support the applicant country in its preparation for the membership. Measures are based on the needs identified in the Opinions and aim to meet accession (Copenhagen) criteria. Provide financial assistance needed for further implementation of priority measures.
National Programs for the Adoption of the *acquis*	Define actions needed to reach objectives set out in the Accession partnership. Structurally are based on the Opinions and Progress Reports.
Screening	Analytical examination of the *acquis*.
Twinning	Aims at reinforcing institutional and administrative capacity. Consists of technical assistance, training programs, exchange of experts, participation of applicant countries' officials in the EU programs.
Accession negotiations	Aim at agreement between the EU and a candidate country on terms of accession (essentially, number and length of transition periods). Currently are taking place between the EU and Estonia. It is expected that Latvia and Lithuania will start negotiations in Spring 2000.

Appendix 2

TABLE 3.A3 GROSS DOMESTIC PRODUCT BY ECONOMIC ACTIVITY IN 1998, %

	Estonia	*Latvia*	*Lithuania*
Agriculture, hunting and forestry	4.6	4.5	11.7
Fishing	0.4	0.2	0.0
Mining and quarrying	1.4	0.2	0.5
Manufacturing	14.2	20.2	20.5
Electricity, gas, and water supply	5.5	3.9	4.2
Construction	4.7	5.2	7.7
Trade	15.6	17.5	16.5
Hotels and restaurants	1.1	1.0	1.8
Transportation, storage and communications	14.2	14.2	9.6
Financial mediation	4.7	3.2	2.4
Real estate, renting, and other commercial activities	12.6	5.9	7.2
State governance, national defense, and mandatory social security	4.7	10.0	5.9
Education	5.6	6.6	5.5
Health and social care	4.0	3.4	3.6
Other communal, social, and personal services	6.7	4.0	3.0

Source: Statistical Office of Estonia, Latvian Statistical Office, Lithuanian Department of Statistics.

TABLE 3.A4 EMPLOYED PERSONS BY ECONOMIC ACTIVITY, 1998, MAY, %

	Estonia[a]	*Latvia*	*Lithuania*
Agriculture, hunting and forestry, and fishing	9.5	18.7	19.3
Manufacturing, mining, and quarrying	23.0	19.2	19.5
Electricity, gas, and water supply	2.7	2.4	3.1
Construction	7.5	5.6	6.9
Trade and different repair works	14.0	14.6	14.7
Transport and communications	9.3	7.9	6.7
Other services	34.1	31.7	29.8

a. 1998, 2nd quarter.
Source: Statistical Office of Estonia, Latvian Statistical Office, Lithuanian Department of Statistics.

TABLE 3.A5 SELECTED MACROECONOMIC INDICATORS, 1998

	Estonia	Latvia	Lithuania
GDP per capita in current prices, US$,	3591	2611	2887
GDP per capita in PPS, expressed as % of the EU-15 average	37	28	31
Gross foreign debt as a share of projected GDP, %	36.8	10.8	15.0
State budget deficit or surplus, as % of GDP	0.3	0.3	−1.2
State debt as % of GDP	55.0	9.9	22.4
Export of goods and services, as % of GDP	79.8	47.7	47.4
Direct foreign investment, millions US$ (cumulative)	1811	1488	1625
EU share in direct foreign investment, %	75.5	40.1	60
Current account deficit, %	8.6	11.1	12.1

Source: Statistical Office of Estonia, Latvian Statistical Office, Lithuanian Department of Statistics.

TABLE 3.A6 EXPORT STRUCTURE BY TRADE PARTNERS IN 1998, %

	Estonia	Latvia	Lithuania
EU	54.8	56.6	37.4
Commonwealth of Independent States (CIS)	20.9	19.0	36.2
Baltic countries	12.4	11.9	13.9
Other	11.6	12.5	12.5

Source: Statistical Office of Estonia, Latvian Statistical Office, Lithuanian Department of Statistics.

TABLE 3.A7 IMPORT STRUCTURE BY TRADE PARTNERS IN 1998, %

	Estonia	Latvia	Lithuania
EU	60.1	55.3	47.3
CIS	14.2	16.0	26.0
Baltic countries	6.1	12.9	3.3
Other	19.6	11.5	23.4

Source: Statistical Office of Estonia, Latvian Statistical Office, Lithuanian Department of Statistics.

FIGURE 3.A1 GDP GROWTH, PERCENTAGE

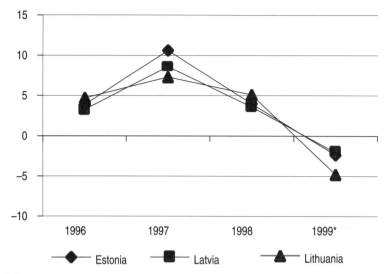

* August 1999
Source: Statistical Office of Estonia, Latvian Statistical Office, Lithuanian Department of Statistics

FIGURE 3.A2 INFLATION (DECEMBER–DECEMBER, PERCENTAGE)

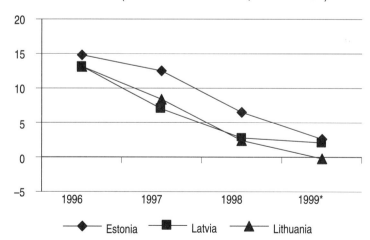

* August 1999
Source: Statistical Office of Estonia, Latvian Statistical Office, Lithuanian Department of Statistics

Appendix 3

The following tables present simplified classification of likely winners and losers in selected areas. The estimated effect is based on the principles and EU norms that the Baltic States have to adopt to be accepted into the Union. The documents used include bilateral free trade agreements, association agreements, the White Paper, the Treaty of the EU, and national programs of *acquis* approximation.

Evaluation: "+" — positive, "–" — negative, "0" — neutral, "?" — uncertain
S-term: short term (1 to 5 years), L-term: long term
Producers_Ex: producers unaffected by changes in the import regime
Producers_Im: producers that import capital and intermediary goods important for the production

TABLE 3.A8 LOSERS AND WINNERS: FREE MOVEMENT OF GOODS

| | Interest groups | | | | | | | |
| | Importers | | Producers_Ex | | Producers_Im | | Consumers | |
Measure	S-term	L-term	S-term	L-term	S-term	L-term	S-term	L-term
1. Abolishment of import duties and quotas	+	+	–	–	+	+	+	+
2. Abolishment of export duties and quotas	0	0	+	+	+	+	0	0
3. Harmonization of standards and rules	–	+	–	+	–	+	?	?
4. Mutual recognition of standards and rules	+	+	–	+	+	+	+	+
5. Nondiscriminatory regime	+	+	–	–	+	+	+	+
6. Abolishment of customs inside of Single Market	+	+	–	–	+	+	+	+
7. Common external tariff	?	?	?	?	?	?	?	?

Point 3. Positive: possibility of increased safety, negative: possibility of limited choice—existing products that will not meet higher required standards disappear from the market, the consumers with lower demands and low income will be disadvantaged.

Point 7 depends on the present tariff level. In the case of Estonia, it would mean increasing tariffs and benefits for producers-exporters and losses for other groups (consumers). In the case of Latvia and Lithuania it would differ depending on concrete product groups.

TABLE 3.A9 LOSERS AND WINNERS: FREE MOVEMENT OF LABOR

| | Interest groups | | | | | |
| | Employers | | Employees | | State | |
Measure	S-term	L-term	S-term	L-term	S-term	L-term
1. Free access to labor market	+	+	+	+	?	?
2. Recognition of periods for social security payments	+	+	+	+	–	–
3. Freely transferable social payments	+	+	+	+	–	–
4. Mutual recognition of high education diplomas and professional qualifications	+	+	+	+	+	+
5. Adjustment of training and activity rules for certain professions	–	+	–	+	–	+
6. Abolishment of customs	+	+	+	+	?	?

Point 1. Advantages related to incoming qualified labor force, disadvantages related to probable "brain drain."
Point 6. Advantage—expenditures saved from the budget for customs offices, disadvantage—possible illegal migration.

TABLE 3.A10. LOSERS AND WINNERS: FREE MOVEMENT OF SERVICES

| | Service providers | | Consumers (both individuals and corporate) | |
Measure	S-term	L-term	S-term	L-term
1. Nondiscriminatory conditions to provide services in respect to country of registration	?	?	+	+
Transport				
2. Mutual recognition of qualification certificates	+	+	+	+
3. Requirements for entry into market and operation	–	?	?	?
4. Safety and environmental requirements for vehicles and operation	–	–	?	?
5. Adjustment of payments for infrastructure	?	?	?	?
6. Separation of railroad companies and national states	?	?	+	+
7. Separation of transport infrastructure and operation	?	?	+	+
8. Establishment of control institutions (both economic and technical)	–	–	?	?
9. Adjustment of navigation systems	–	+	–	+
10. Adjustment of technical requirements and administrative procedures in civil aviation	–	+	?	?
Financial services				
11. Adjustment of requirements for establishment and operation for credit institutions	0	0	0	0
12. Adjustment of risk limitation measures for credit institutions	?	?	?	?
13. Mandatory deposit insurance	–	–	?	?
14. Requirements for publicly available information	–	–	+	+

(Table continues on next page.)

TABLE 3.A10 *(continued)*

Measure	Service providers		Consumers (both individuals and corporate)	
	S-term	*L-term*	*S-term*	*L-term*
15. Adjustment of rules of securities market and investment funds	?	+	+	+
16. Money laundering prevention measures	–	–	?	?
17. Common payment system	–	+	+	+

Effect of Point 1 for service providers will depend on their export level.
Transport. Points 3 and 4 are separate cases of harmonization of standards and rules
(see table 3.A8).
Point 5 will entirely depend on the new system, as for the moment there is no system of payments for infrastructure in the Baltic countries.
Points 6 and 7 for service providers. Advantage: for the private competitors of the state-owned monopoly, disadvantage: for the state-owned monopoly.
Points 8 and 10. Expected advantage: increased safety, disadvantage: costs for consumers (raised prices for service or budget spending).
Financial services. Point 12. Expected benefits—increased safety, disadvantage—business limitations to financial institutions and their clients.

TABLE 3.A11 LOSERS AND WINNERS: FREE MOVEMENT OF CAPITAL

Measure	Interest groups			
	Business		Consumers	
	S-term	*L-term*	*S-term*	*L-term*
1. Abolishment of barriers to payments and investment	+	+	+	+

TABLE 3.A12 LOSERS AND WINNERS: COMMON AGRICULTURAL POLICY

Measure	Interest groups									
	Farmers		Producers exporters		Producers importers		Suppliers of agricultural equipment		Consumers	
	S-term	L-term	S-term	L-term	S-term	L-term	S-term	L-term	S-term	L-term
1. Import duties from the third countries	+	+	–	–	–	–	+	+	–	–
2. Export subsidies	+	+	+	+	–	–	+	+	–	–
3. Structural funds	+	+	+	+	+	+	+	+	?	?

4. Price support	+	+	+	+	−	−	+	+	−	−
5. Direct income payments	+	+	+	+	−	−	+	+	−	−

Point 3 for consumers depends on their location. Those who work in supported area, buy products of supported company, or are in other way related to supported entity, benefit. The rest of population lose as their tax money is spent to support particular region.

TABLE 3.A13 LOSERS AND WINNERS: ECONOMIC AND MONETARY UNION

	Interest groups							
	Commercial banks		Consumers		Central bank		Government	
Measure	S-term	L-term	S-term	L-term	S-term	L-term	S-term	L-term
Convergence criteria								
1. Low inflation	0	0	+	+	+	+	−	−
2. Restricted budget deficit	0	0	+	+	+	+	−	−
3. Restricted state borrowing	−	−	+	+	+	+	−	−
Common currency								
4. Loss of national monetary and exchange rate instruments	?	?	+	+	−	−	−	−
4'. Introduction of EMU monetary and exchange rate instruments	−	−	−	−	+	+	0	0
5. Elimination of exchange rate uncertainty	?	?	+	+	0	0	+	+
6. Technical adjustment of banking systems	−	+	?	?	+	+	0	0
7. Introduction of a new currency instead the national one	−	+	−	+	0	0	−	−
8. Independent ECB and national central banks	?	?	0	0	+	+	−	−

Point 4 for commercial banks. Advantages derive from non-interventionist situation in money market. Disadvantages: loss of last lending source.

Point 5 is evaluated as a positive measure for consumers and business as a major share of the Baltic countries' foreign trade with EU countries. If foreign trade with non-EU partners dominates, the effect of this measure would be negative. For commercial banks, the effect could be twofold: positive, as uncertainty with EU currency is eliminated, and negative, as one source of income is closed.

Point 6. Advantages: improved services for clients, disadvantages: increased prices.

Point 8. Effect on commercial banks depends on the actual operation of central banks.

TABLE 3.A14 GENERAL TABLE: LOSERS AND WINNERS IN THE SELECTED AREAS

	Consumers		Importers		Producers_Ex		Producers_Im		Service providers		Farmers		Banks		Transport	
	S-term	L-term	S-term	L-term	S-term	L-term	S-term	L-term	S-term	L-term	S-term	L-term	S-term	L-term	S-term	L-term
1. Free movement of goods	+	+	+	+	-	?	+	+	+	+	-	-	+	+	+	+
2. Free movement of labor	+	+	+	+	+	+	+	+	+	+	+	+	+	+	+	+
3. Free movement of capital	+	+	+	+	+	+	+	+	+	+	+	+	+	+	+	+
4. Free movement of services (general)	+	+	+	+	+	+	+	+	?	?	+	+	+	+	+	+
5. Free movement of transport services	?	+	?	?	+	?	?	+	+	+	-	+	+	+	-	?
6. Free movement of financial services	?	+	?	?	+	+	+	+	+	+	?	+	-	-	+	+
7. CAP	-	0	?	?	?	?	0	?	0	?	?	+	0	?	0	?
8. EMU	?	-	?	?	?	+	+	+	+	+	?	+	-	?	+	+

Point 1 for consumers, point 4 for service providers, point 5 for transport companies, point 8 for consumers, importers, producers, farmers, and banks depends on the ability to exploit the opportunities of common market.

Point 5 for consumers, importers, and producer-importers, point 6 for consumers and farmers depends on the balance of actual costs and benefits of the current situation and the change after the implementation of integration measures.

Point 7 for importers, service, banks, and transport depends on concrete CAP measures and their implementation.

78

Notes

1. The authors are grateful to the World Bank, particularly Helena Tang, and the Bertelsmann Foundation for initiating the project and providing comments; to Dr. András Inotai and the Institute for World Economics for comments and the opportunity to discuss research issues in Budapest; to LFMI experts who provided helpful comments; and to Ikka Korhonen, Jorge Braga de Macedo, Klaudijus Maniokas, and Pekka Lindroos for their comments and suggestions.

2. One example of this issue and attempting to bridge the gap between the accession process and the general transition context is the study of Estonian integration into the EU produced by the World Bank. See The World Bank, Estonia. 1999. *Implementing the EU Accession Agenda.* Washington, D. C.: The World Bank.

3. The alignment of national regulations with EU *acquis* also might strengthen market reforms. As noted about transition countries in general, "harmonization of laws with the EU may be the most efficient way of stopping covert protectionism in the form of technological and procedural prescriptions and other forms of NTB [nontariff barriers]." Csaba, L. 1995. "The Political Economy of Trade Regimes in Central Europe." In Alan Winters, ed. *Foundations of an Open Economy.* London: CEPR.

4. Gacs, J., and M. Wyzan. 1999. "The Time Pattern of Costs and Benefits of EU Accession." In *Laxenburg: IIASA, Interim Report*, IR-99-015. May, ii.

5. Kaitila, V., and M. Widgren. 1998. European University Institute. RSC WP. "Revealed Comparative Advantage in Trade between the European Union and the Baltic Countries." Florence. December 22, draft.

6. Kaitila and Widgren, p. 12.

7. *Regular Reports from the Commission on Progress Towards Accession.* October 13, 1999.

8. Kaitila and Widgren, p. 13.

9. Vilpišauskas, R. 1999. "Regional Integration in Europe: Analyzing Intra-Baltic Economic Cooperation." EUI, Florence: Robert Schuman Centre. Working paper, draft.

10. Statistical Office of Estonia. 1998. *Estonia, Latvia, Lithuania. Foreign Trade.* Tallinn, 1999, 28–30.

11. *Regular Reports from the Commission on Progress Towards Accession.* October 13, 1999.

12. Moravcsik, A. 1998. *The Choice for Europe. Social Purpose and State Power from Messina to Maastricht.* Ithaca, N. Y.: Cornell University Press.

13. Cited in Pelkmans, J., and A. G. Carzaniga, 1996. *The Trade Policy Review of the European Union.* The World Economy. Global Trade Policy. Oxford.

14. Winters, A. 1994. "The European Community: A Case of Successful Integration?" In J. De Melo and A. Panagariya. *New Dimensions in Regional Integration.* London: CEPR.

15. Bofinger, P. 1995. "The Political Economy of the Eastern Enlargement of the EU." Discussion paper No. 1234. CEPR, London.

16. Ministry of Environmental Protection of the Republic of Lithuania. 1998. *Costs of Approximating Lithuanian Environmental Legislation with the European Union.* Final Report. p. 92.

17. *Regular Reports from the Commission on Progress Towards Accession.* October 13, 1999.

18. Vilpišauskas, R. 1999. "Regional Integration in Europe: Analyzing Intra-Baltic Economic Cooperation." Florence: EUI, Robert Schuman Centre. Working paper, draft.

19. "Strategy of Lithuania's Accession into the EU. The Alignment of Lithuanian Agricultural and Trade Policy with the EU Common Agricultural Policy," World Bank, March 22, 1999, p. 56.

20. Information provided by the Lithuanian Agricultural Institute.

21. On Baltic States' membership in EMU, see Korhonen, I. 1999. "Some Implications of EU Membership on Baltic Monetary and Exchange Rate Policies." Florence: EUI, RSC working paper. Draft, May.

22. Korhonen 1999, p. 26.

23. As noted about public attitudes in the EU, "[M]uch of the voting publics holds a strong attachment to its national currency for reasons having little to do with economics." Jones, E. "Playing with Money." In Moravcsik, A. ed. 1999. *Centralization or Fragmentation. Europe Facing the Challenges of Deepening, Diversity, and Democracy.* NY: Council on Foreign Relations. 70. Such sentiments might be even stronger in the Baltic States, which established their national currencies only recently.

24. This is also a view shared by business in the Baltic States. In November 1998, the survey of 52 Lithuanian enterprises from the largest 100 revealed that according to business, the main aim of the EU membership is access to its market, and the main winners will be exporters and consumers.

25. For a similar argument see Kiss, J. 1997. "The Political Economy of Hungary's Accession to the European Union." Budapest: Institute for World Economics. WP No. 77. March.

26. For examples of attempts to introduce the idea of regulatory effect analysis see OECD. 1997. "Assessing the Impacts of Proposed Laws and Regulations." Sigma Papers No. 13, Paris; also see *Proceedings of Taiex Seminar on Impact Analysis in the Hague*, June 4–6, 1997.

CHAPTER 4

The Baltic States: The Political and Social Dimensions[*]

Atis Lejinš
Latvian Institute of International Affairs

The Political Dimension

Theoretical Premises

With the EU's enlarging from 15 to 25 nations (and possibly 30, if we also include the Balkan States in the distant future), assumptions that all states that join the EU are winners in the end may not be so easily verifiable. At the very least, the process by which states will be able to assert their national interests in the EU may be more difficult. On the other hand, some have argued convincingly that the survival and even entrenchment of the state has gone hand-in-hand with increased centralization of the EU and that, despite the apparent paradox, the state and the international organization are capable of being mutually reinforcing.[1] These arguments suggest that a balance could be struck between the separate interests of each individual state and the need for common action.

Closer interdependence calls for increased cooperation both among states, as in the EU, and among regions (the United States-EU-Japan). Modern states now must arrange their economic systems in cooperation with other states, but this requirement is not a novelty of our age because "… sovereignty has always involved a compromise with the level of interdependence which prevailed at a particular time."[2]

The most salient demonstration of the need for common action, compared with other regions, is the present trade disputes between the United States and the EU over bananas, genetically modified food, and hormone-treated meat. Left on their own, the individual European states would be no match for the United States in these trade disputes. This comparison also holds true with managing relations with a chaotic Russia after the fall of the Soviet Union. Hence, the survival and entrenchment of each EU state is secured through the centralization of the EU.

Another manifestation of the confluence of the interests of separate states and the need for common action is the growing need for common political and military action, clearly demonstrated by the wars in Bosnia and Kosovo. Germany, the largest state in Europe, if left alone to deal with little Serbia, probably would have lost the war in Kosovo, barring a full-scale invasion and occupation.

This situation calls for more centralization of the EU that has led to the need to give credence to the second pillar of the Treaty of Amsterdam,[3] and to a common foreign and security policy (CFSP), that could translate into common military action by the EU. A common military action could help avert massive inflows of refugees from domestic conflicts in other countries in the region and would help individual member states unable to absorb many refugees. It remains to be seen, however, whether Dr. Javier Solana, NATO secretary general from 1995 to 1999, will be able to bring about such a policy. Only the defense ministers of the EU member states have not met within the regular EU meetings of ministers, but regular meetings of these ministers surely would arouse suspicion in the antifederalist circles of the EU.

The balance between the state and the union will become more complex and could lead some states to refrain from participating in common EU policy and actions, as demonstrated by the EMU example. Britain, Sweden, and Denmark have not adopted the euro. Until political scientists offer new theoretical postulates on the nature of the EU, however, one must accept those proposed before 1991, summed up as: "... as long as the Union rests upon a Treaty, and not a constitution, the member states have remained sovereign, and will remain so unless a fundamentally different order is introduced."[4]

Some Major Issues

Formulation of the Problem

We assume that no fundamentally different order will be introduced in the medium term, by 2006, or even in the long term, by 2010, though the next Intergovernmental Conference certainly will bring institutional changes that can radically affect the status of small states: that is, the possible loss of a commissioner. (Obviously, if this change should happen, it would be very hard to convince people in the CEE candidate states to vote for EU membership).

Some[5] have predicted that Estonia and Latvia will join the EU with Malta and the Czech Republic in 2004 or 2005, after Hungary and Poland (and Cyprus, pending a constitutional settlement). Lithuania, with Slovenia and the Slovak Republic, would join in 2005-2006, and Bulgaria and Rumania would join three or four years later. What happens in the distant future, by 2020, when the EU could have 30 states and possibly a "fundamentally different order," is beyond the time frame of this analysis.

The model for the Baltic States could be Ireland, a small country similar in size to the Baltics and with certain cultural and historical similarities. Ireland has successfully managed Community revenues and, within a few years, will be able to reach average EU living standards. It can be convincingly argued that "... the Union has been good for Ireland over the past quarter-century, in terms of increased prosperity, the enhancement of sovereignty, and growth in self-confidence."[6]

The Baltic States' becoming integral parts of the EU also will solve the "Russian problem," because whoever is in power in Moscow and whatever the future course of Russia, the Baltic States no longer should be considered "former republics of the Soviet Union" (a ghetto label), just as Finland and Poland no longer are viewed as "former provinces of the Tsarist empire."

The Timing of Accession

In the aftermath of the Kosovo war, political considerations moved the EU Commission, in its October 13 report to the EU Council, to state that full negotiations should begin with all "B" group states. Although the previous enlargement strategy, based on the two-group stadium model, now will be abolished, the principle that might enable the "slow-track" states to overtake those on the fast track by better adoption and implementation of the *acqui*, remains still in place in the new regatta system (first past the post). This means that there will be more competition all around, allowing the more successful of the late runners to catch up because the accession process now will be fully flexible with variable speeds. Under this scenario, only those chapters that can be realistically concluded in the short to medium term will be opened in the accession talks. Previously, the EU opened an equal number of the 31 *acqui* chapters for everyone in the "A" group.

Latvia and Lithuania were scheduled to finish their bilateral screening talks in November 1999 and were expected to begin negotiating the terms of admission at the end of the year. For Lithuania, only the Schengen (control of borders) *acqui* chapter in force since July remained to be screened. This chapter may cause problems in Lithuania because, like Poland, Lithuania has no visa requirements for Russians living in Kaliningrad. For Latvia, the government has announced that talks can begin on all 15 chapters opened with the "A" group states and that negotiations can be finished in two years, when Estonia also will conclude its negotiations. The statements issued by Lithuania on this issue are somewhat guarded.

The experience of both the EU and Latvia during the screening exercise will allow for a quick conclusion of the first 15 "easy" chapters, already finished by the "A" group. With regard to the more difficult chapters—for example, in the environmental protection sector—Latvia and Lithuania set the transition period at 2015, while Estonia puts it at 2018. The major hurdle between Lithuania and the Commission—that is, the closing of the Chernobyl-type power station—was removed when Lithuania finally agreed to a phased close-down, beginning with the first reactor in 2004.

Two issues with respect to the timing of EU integration are relevant for the analysis of winners and losers. The first is whether integration would take place before 2006, and the second is whether all three Baltic States will join at the same time. The year 2006 is crucial because the next Community budget term ends then, and the EU is certain to have admitted a number of new countries by then, all of which will be "cohesion states." Meanwhile, the Community budget has not been increased to accommodate enlargement but remains at 1.27 percent of EU GNP.

While there is no information on what the budget will look like after 2006, it is reasonable to assume that the "era marked by considerable generosity toward the poorer member states on the part of the richer members, particularly Germany," has come to an end.[7] Therefore, even if Ireland successfully manages its transition to a developed economy, as predicted by 2006, and loses its status as a "cohesion state," any state joining after 2006 may be a loser because less cohesion and structural money will be available, even if Spain or Portugal would follow Ireland. This possibility means those countries that join the EU first and are effective in husbanding transfers from the Community budget will be winners, while those joining later will be losers. Preaccession aid cannot match transfers in an era of increasing competition for diminishing funds. The fundamental advantage of states joining earlier, however, is opening up the EU market for their goods.

If the three Baltic States do not join at the same time, it raises the issue of whether the intervening time between each Baltic State's joining the EU could be significant enough to negatively affect: (1) the political, economic, and social development of the late joiners; (2) inter-Baltic integration, including the Baltic free trade agreement; and (3) the geopolitical security of the Baltics.

The Baltic cooperation model those countries have developed since they regained independence is the only successful example of cooperation in the whole post-Soviet era. In only a few years, Baltic cooperation has been able to achieve what the Nordics and Benelux countries failed until they joined the EU, mainly a free trade agreement including agricultural goods, despite the different trade subsidies of each country. Competition among Baltic businesses has provided excellent training and preparation for them to join the European market. Another aspect is the very close collaboration in military affairs, where some army, navy, and air surveillance units have been integrated and now serve in peacekeeping missions in the Balkans.[8]

The Geopolitical Security Situation

The geopolitical security of the Baltics must still be considered because of instability in Russia and the unpredictability of its behavior. Who will win the Russian
parliamentary and presidential elections in 2000 will be very important for Baltic
security. The Russian Foreign Policy and Defense Council, in its second report
(1999) on Russia and the Baltic States, says that how Russia manages to harmonize
its economic interests with the gradual integration of the Baltic States into the EU,
and if and how the Baltic States join NATO, in large measure will shape the future
of Russia. The report points out that Russia must invest heavily in the Baltics now
to have a foothold in the EU market.

On the other hand, in a letter to EC President Romano Prodi in August 1999,
Alexander Lifshitz, Russian President Boris Yeltsin's special envoy to the G7,
expressed 15 "points of concern" that, after enlargement, investments that would
have gone to Russia will end up in the Baltic States and Central Europe. Russia is
afraid that it will lose its export market, worth tens of billions of dollars a year, to
the CEE states. Russia thus may want to play a more active role in influencing EU
enlargement to the East than it has until now, after it invested so much energy in
stopping NATO enlargement.[9]

With the energetic lobbying of their Nordic neighbors, the Baltics overcame
the disadvantage they faced as "former republics of the Soviet Union" in joining
the EU (the European Agreements were signed in June 1995 and became effective
only in February 1998). The Nordic lobbying also helped to get a majority vote in
the EU for at least one Baltic State to join the fast-track accession negotiations at
the Luxembourg summit in 1997.

Although the Copenhagen criteria are of primary importance, the national
interests of present member states in promoting different candidate states in their
quest to join the Union cannot be denied. If the Slovak Republic did not have an
authoritarian regime, Estonia and Slovenia might not have landed on the fast track.
The original scenario for EU enlargement was that only the Visegrad states would
join NATO first and not all the Baltic or southeast states could be admitted. Estonia
and Slovenia were the compromise between contending parties in the EU as the
best northern and southern EU-aspiring states.

Power politics were even more evident in what the Commission said and what was
said at the December 1998 Vienna Council about EU enlargement. In its recommendations to the Council, the Commission singled out Latvia as the only candidate state in
the "B" group with which the so-called substantive accession negotiations "could begin
in 1999."[10] Subsequently, it became known that the Commission had thought that the
Council would set 1999 as the date when negotiations could begin, but that did not happen in Vienna. The EU's internal problems, especially reform of the CAP, subsequently partly resolved at the EU Berlin summit in March 1999, hindered the EU from
moving forward on enlargement in Vienna.

Preaccession Funding

In the accession process, the role played by preaccession funds also must be studied closely. These funds—first disbursed in 2000, in addition to the "new PHARE"—are known as IPSA (Instrument for Structural Policies pre-Accession, earmarked for transport, communications and the protection of the environment) and SAPARD (Community Support for Pre-Accession Measures for Agriculture and Rural Development) in the applicant countries of CEE in the preaccession period. They are similar to the structural funds and largely can determine the internal development of the candidate states, just as structural funds, when managed right, have done so in the economically delayed EU members by now. Even before their implementation, these funds already are helping the accession states.

For example, SAPARD will double the funds Latvia will invest in rural areas in 2000, and ISPA funding can be double that of SAPARD. Regional competition has intensified for these funds, including in the capital city of Riga, the richest region of all, and consequently has raised public awareness of EU integration issues enormously. This benefit cannot but enhance the "Link to the Citizen" component (designed to generate public support for EU integration) in future PHARE-supported programs. Latgale, in eastern Latvia, is the favorite contender, as the poorest region in Eastern Europe and according to Eurostat, the poorest region in Europe. Other regions, however, will be included, depending on their ability to design the best projects and establish the relevant institutional framework, such as regional development agencies that involve municipal government and the private sector.

The Internal Debate on EU Integration

As the preaccession funding translates more into visible real-life benefits, the minimal political debate in the Baltics against EU membership most probably will wither. The only question left to argue is how to join and the selection of priorities in the national integration plans, which are updated each year. The top echelons in the civil service of Latvia, for example, have not showed any resistance to EU enlargement for two years now. Possibly because the political elite is dead-set for EU membership, it simply may be too politically dangerous to oppose it.

An entrenched bureaucratic resistance to internal reform called for more transparency and financial control in the ministries and bodies under its supervision. These internal reforms, begun after the restoration of independence, now dovetail with the requirements of EU integration. This reform is another area with much potential for public support for the EU, because society in all three Baltic States has become skeptical of the government's ability to resolve major corruption and organized crime issues if the EU has the reputation as able to influence change for the better.

Regional Reform

Preaccession funding coincides with regional reform in Latvia and may play a decisive role in Latvia's decision to replace the 26 regions established during the Soviet occupation with either 9 regions plus Riga or 4 regions plus Riga. A powerful argument in the debate, unofficially from the EU, is that the four-plus-one formula would increase efficiency in acquiring and implementing the funds. The fewer regions correspond to the four historically determined cultural regions of Latvia and can only enhance the EU's popularity as the debate concludes and the unofficial EU position filters down to the public. Estonia also is reducing the number of regions, while Lithuania has set them at 10.

The Social Dimension

Winners and losers already have emerged since the restoration of independence in 1991. This phenomenon must be analyzed to investigate future trends as the Baltics integrate increasingly into the EU.

The Current Situation

In 1997, the GDP per capita (PPP US$) in the three Baltic states as a percentage of the EU average (see table 4.1 below) was 27 percent for Latvia, 30 percent for Lithuania, and 37 percent for Estonia. The average for EU candidate states was 40 percent.

The measurement of living standards depends, however, not only on monetary figures, but also on other indicators reflecting the quality of life. The UN introduced the Human Development Index (HDI) in 1990 for this purpose. The HDI is based on three indicators: the life expectancy index, the education index, and the

---

TABLE 4.1 GROSS DOMESTIC PRODUCT PER CAPITA USING PURCHASING POWER PARITY
(at current prices, in US dollars)

Country	Year 1995	Year 1996
Denmark	21,529	22,314
Estonia	4,138	4,431
Latvia	3,291	3,484
Lithuania	4,014	4,273
Finland	17,787	18,657

Source: 1998 Statistical Yearbook of Latvia, p. 319.
Purchasing power parity (PPP) is defined as the number of units of a country's currency required to buy the same amount of goods and services in the domestic market as one dollar would buy in the United States.

per capita income index. The index has ranked each UN member country, accordingly, in terms of human development.

These data (table 4.2, below) show that the three Baltic States have experienced a severe social trauma during transition, which has pushed them from the group of countries with a high HDI to the group with medium HDI levels. Latvia has experienced a social trauma more severe than that of Estonia and Lithuania. Latvia dropped to the 92nd position in 1998 from 48th in 1995 but moved up to 74th position in 1999.

Poverty is a serious problem. The gap between the rich and the poor is still growing. Social diseases are becoming more visible. Children are the most exposed group.

The elderly dependency ratio has increased in all Central and Eastern Europe countries, except Hungary and the Czech Republic. This ratio compares the percentage of the population that is 60 years and older to the percentage that is between 18 and 59 years of age. On average, the ratio in Central Europe is recorded to have increased to 23.4 in 1997 from 22.9 in 1990; in Eastern Europe, to 24.22 from 21.67; and in the Baltics, to 24.70 from 22.87. Latvia has the most unfavorable ratio of 25.50.

Public Opinion

In surveys by PHARE in 1997 (table 4.3) and by the Central and Eastern European Barometer (CEEB) in 1996 (table 4.4) about the potential losers and winners if Latvia joined the EU, the respondents stressed that they will benefit more as consumers (of goods, commercial and public services, in health and education) but none as producers. Especially worrisome is public opinion in Latvia on the future of Latvia's agriculture: Only 15 percent of farmers felt they would "benefit," while 63 percent felt they would lose. At the same time, nobody considered agriculture

TABLE 4.2   BALTIC STATES HDI VALUE AND HDI RANK, 1993–1999

		1993	1994	1995	1996	1997	1998	1999
Estonia								
	HDI Value	0.872	0.867	0.862	0.749	0.776	0.758	0.773
	HDI Rank	34	29	43	68	71	77	54
Latvia								
	HDI Value	0.868	0.865	0.857	0.820	0.711	0.704	0.744
	HDI Rank	35	30	48	55	92	92	74
Lithuania								
	HDI Value	0.881	0.868	0.769	0.719	0.762	0.750	0.761
	HDI Rank	29	28	71	81	76	79	62

Source: Latvia. Human Development Report 1998. Riga, 1998, p. 12. For each country, the first row of figures shows the HDI value and the second row the ranking of UN member states.

as not important at all. Until now, rural areas have lost more than urban centers, which affects their attitudes toward the EU.

The PHARE 1997 survey also shows that 21 percent of the respondents thought that low-income groups will benefit from EU integration, 27 percent thought that they will lose, and 18 percent thought that they will experience no changes, while 34 percent had no answer. The CEEB data show that 26 percent of respondents in Latvia in 1996 thought that low-income groups will be winners, 28 percent will be losers, and 22 percent would feel no effects.

Social Exclusion

We agree with András Inotai[11] that winners and losers not only are "created" by preparing for accession, but also emerge from the transformation and globalization processes. Those now excluded probably will remain excluded after EU accession. Those excluded will not be able to use the advantages of EU membership fully.

Social exclusion should be defined in terms of the failure of one or more of the following four systems:

- the democratic and legal system, which promotes civic integration;

- the labor market, which promotes economic integration;

TABLE 4.3 VIEWS OF RESPONDENTS ON WINNERS AND LOSERS (PHARE 1997)
(percentage of all respondents)

Do you think the following are likely to benefit or lose
out in Latvia as ties between Latvia and the
European Union increase?
What do you think will happen to:

	Benefit	Lose out	No impact	Don't know / No answer
Armed forces	55	2	6	37
Educational system	51	6	11	33
Private business	42	11	10	37
Health and social services	39	6	13	41
Consumers	39	8	11	41
Civil servants	20	10	25	45
Manual workers	22	22	19	37
People living on low incomes	21	27	18	34
State enterprise	19	26	9	46
Farmers	15	63	3	19

Source: Final Report on the project, "Survey on Public Access to EU Information." Talis Tisenkopfs un Aivars Tabuns. Riga, 1998, p. 60.

TABLE 4.4 VIEWS OF RESPONDENTS ON WINNERS AND LOSERS
(percentage of respondents)[1]

*Do you think the following are likely
to benefit or lose out in Latvia
(our country) as the European Union
increases?*

What do you think will happen to:	Benefit	Lose out	No impact
Educational system	56 (56)	10 (9)	13 (13)
Armed forces	52 (55)	6 (7)	13 (10)
Private business	50 (65)	15 (8)	13 (7)
Government civil servants	49 (40)	14 (15)	15 (19)
Health and social services	47 (53)	14 (12)	13 (12)
State enterprises	47 (40)	18 (28)	12 (9)
Manual workers	26 (37)	32 (26)	20 (14)
Low income groups	26 (33)	28 (24)	22 (18)
Farmers	24 (38)	45 (24)	11 (18)

1. Figures in parentheses are average data in candidate states.
Source: CEEB 7, 1996

- the welfare state system, promoting what may be called social integration; and

- the family and community system, which promotes interpersonal integration.

One's sense of belonging in society depends on all four systems. Table 4.5 (below) shows data on the extent of social exclusion in Estonia, Latvia, and Lithuania, according to the 1994 NORBALT survey.[12] According to the data, more than half of the Baltic population is at average risk of social exclusion, almost one-third is in the low-risk category, and one-fifth is in the high-risk group. The percentage of the total population for each country of those in the high-risk group was 15.1 percent in Estonia, 24.7 percent in Latvia, and 16.1 percent in Lithuania.

Latvia had been the most developed Soviet republic, but the Latvian indicators are higher because the GDP decreased more rapidly in 1992–1994, the population became more heterogeneous, and a larger share of the population was not citizens. The data suggest the share of native nationalities (16.5 percent) is much lower in the group of high-risk social exclusion than the share of Russians (22.50 percent) and others (21.0 percent) in the Baltic States.

Gender. Women are at higher risk of social exclusion than men because of the traditional role of women in society, hence their more frequent voluntary absences from work, and because most single parents are women. Women also are less politically active than men.

Age. People in early middle age (31–45) had the least risk of social exclusion. In a fast-changing society, the most active people in society are in this age group, which is mature, flexible, and adaptable. Those under 30 years of age face higher risks because their participation in society depends largely on their success in accessing the labor market. The highest risk of exclusion is among the oldest age group (older than age 60).

Education. People with university degrees have lost the least, and those with only a primary or basic education are the most vulnerable.

Inequality and Poverty. Stratification of the population according to material wealth continues. The Gini index in Latvia, according to data in a household budget survey for 1998, was 0.32, an increase from 0.30 in 1996 and 0.31 in 1997, and it reflects the rise in inequality. The majority of poor households are those with children and the unemployed.

TABLE 4.5 DISTRIBUTION OF RISK OF SOCIAL EXCLUSION BY GENDER, AGE, NATIONALITY, AND EDUCATION OF RESPONDENTS IN ESTONIA, LATVIA, AND LITHUANIA, ACCORDING TO THE NORBALT DATA
(percentages)

Risk of social exclusion	Low (0 – 6 welfare losses)	Average (7 – 9 welfare losses)	High (10–15 welfare losses)
Country			
Estonia	29.1	55.8	15.1
Latvia	23.6	51.6	24.7
Lithuania	30.1	53.8	16.1
Gender			
Male	36.5	50.7	12.8
Female	20.4	56.7	22.8
Age			
under 30	28.0	56.6	15.4
31–45	35.5	54.7	9.8
46–59	29.9	51.4	18.7
over 60	14.8	53.5	31.7
Education			
Primary	12.6	52.1	35.3
Basic	19.1	55.5	25.4
Secondary	28.7	57.4	13.9
Higher	48.5	43.0	8.5
Nationality			
Native	30.5	53.0	16.5
Russian	20.7	56.8	22.5
Other	24.7	54.3	21.0
Total (%)	27.6	54.0	18.4

Source: Estonian Human Development Report 1997, p. 16.

Explanatory Note: The more welfare losses for an individual, the more he or she experiences social exclusion.

Addressing Social Exclusion

The social dimension, the most human dimension, strongly depends on the economic and political dimensions. For average people, the opportunity to benefit from integration in the EU depends very much on the quality of internal decision-making and the degree of transparency.

Latvia's social welfare model is a mixture of features from other social democratic, conservative, and liberal models. A high degree of commodification (commercialization) of welfare services has been evident in recent years, and it has affected food prices, housing, health care, transport and communication, education, and other services. The value orientation in society, however, is still more egalitarian than liberal, opposite of the political elite.

The political elite has built a social policy model closely related to that of U.S. society but would prefer the European model, where social democratic features would dominate. Latvia has ratified the European Convention on the Protection of Human Rights and Fundamental Freedoms (1953) and its Protocol. In May 1997, Latvia signed the European Social Charter. Harmonization of legislation is proceeding, but officials always have cited the low level of economic standards as the main argument against adapting European standards of employee protection in current circumstances.

The EU basic documents (Treaty of Rome, new Amsterdam Treaty) underline the growing interdependence of the economic and social spheres. They are based on the understanding that the labor market is different from the market for goods and services. The European Employment Strategy calls for more investment in human resources. In all three Baltic States, the political elite needs to increase its understanding that social policy is an important factor of economic progress.

Social Security and Workers' Rights

The traditional concept of social security as defined in such international legal texts as the ILO Convention 102 on minimum standards for social security protection refers to a list of social risks or social contingencies. Estonian, Latvian, and Lithuanian officials wrote social legislation in accordance with this convention. Social insurance in Estonia, Latvia, and Lithuania has been restructured in accordance with the basic principles of social insurance in a market economy. Joining the EU would mean stricter controls for implementation.

Because joining the EU would upgrade the social safety net, from this viewpoint, all vulnerable groups should be considered winners. At least the legal positions of vulnerable groups should become stronger, and the protection of social rights for employees generally should improve.

Public Administration

The opportunity to use the advantages of Baltic membership in the EU closely connects with the development of an effective administration, the infrastructure, and the economy in general. For example, the benefits to gain from tourism depend largely on appropriate state policy for tourism.

The present integration process already places a burden on the bureaucracy, a very important actor in the Baltic States, but it also opens tremendous opportunities. About 46,000 public servants work in public administration in Latvia, and 17,500 of them are in the state civil service (fewer every year).

Estimating the number of public servants dealing directly with European integration tasks is difficult. Each of the 12 ministries has its own European Integration Unit, with 5-10 employees, and at least 100 are involved in the National Programme for Adoption of the *acqui communitaire*, in institution building and twinning projects. Those civil servants involved in these processes—that is, the EU integration tasks—gain expert knowledge and receive special training, including trips to the capital cities of the EU member states. This expertise raises the prestige of their positions, and they certainly are already winners.

The problem is how to convince the middle-level civil servants to stay in the ministries and how to multiply their knowledge and transfer it to the lower levels. Upon receiving expert training and knowledge, the middle-level civil servants often leave for the private sector.

One solution, presently attempted, would be providing social guarantees (such as educational courses designed to improve work skills) and raising the wages of the middle and lower levels of the civil servant corps. The high wages of the top bureaucracy are needed to retain them in the service of the state, but the gap between their wage levels and those below is too wide.

Until recently, Latvian top civil servants enjoyed extra pay based on "management contracts," which did not reveal to the public the sums involved. A new, transparent, and more equitable wage system, however, will create problems with the public, which will demand higher wages in return, as increased pay for school teachers and higher pensions.

A second solution could be to use top-level bureaucrat to train the lower levels, thereby also increasing the prestige of the trained. A strong civil service must implement legislation successfully, including the *acqui* the EU requires.

Preaccession Funds

The preaccession funds already mentioned in the political dimension can complicate the situation for winners and losers because of the need for matching funds. In the case of SAPARD, 50 percent of matching funds must come from private capital. This requirement raises the risk that the strongest economic grouping in the food-processing industry, for example, can get the largest share of the 12.3 percent, which will come from the state in order to attract the remaining 37.5 percent from the EU. This requirement is less of a problem with ISPA—which earmarks 75 percent of the funds from EU for improving transport, communications, and the environment—and with PHARE, which requires 10 percent to 25 percent of the state's own money for each project.

As mentioned above in the political dimension, the proper use of preaccession funds and especially informing the public about its potential to increase living standards and converting some losers into winners holds tremendous potential in gaining public support among all three Baltic States.

European Social Fund

A new EU fund, the European Social Fund (ESF), has appeared on the horizon. Financial support from this fund will be available only upon accession. Training seminars already have begun, however, because money from the social and economic cohesive component in the PHARE system can be released for projects designed to reduce long-term unemployment, especially for youth and minorities. Funding also has been earmarked for reducing regional disparities in unemployment and supporting small and medium businesses in hiring workers.

Conclusions

The Baltic States have managed the transition from communism to democracy and a market economy better and more quickly than many expected, particularly because they had the added disadvantage of occupation for almost 50 years by an extremely centralized world power. They have fulfilled the Copenhagen political and economic criteria (except Lithuania, which still does not quite have a functioning market economy, according to the 1999 EU Commission progress report). These countries still have much to do to improve their legal systems and crime prevention.

The social and economic upheaval, however, has inflicted heavy costs on society, as reflected in various sociological reports funded by the UN, the EU, and EU member states. The main challenge after stabilizing the political system in all three states is to ensure economic growth that will benefit most citizens and not just the small upper classes.

A specific feature of the Baltic integration into the EU is the Baltic cooperation model, the relatively high level of cooperation among the three states, which is similar to the Nordic and the Benelux cooperation models. The Baltic cooperation model, the only successful cooperation model in the whole former Soviet Union, plays an important role in the EU accession process because the Baltics have adopted common transit and customs procedures based on EU standards.

The Baltic free trade agreement, including agricultural goods, also has helped raise the competitiveness of Baltic goods. If the Baltic States do not join the EU at the same time, the cooperation model would help them overcome the negative effects of such an EU policy. For example, Norway decided not to join the EU after Sweden and Finland did in 1995 and today, Norway polices its border as an EU/Schengen border.

Notes

* The author acknowledges the contribution of F. Rajevska for the Social Dimension section of the chapter.

1. Paul Taylor, "The European Community and the State: Assumptions, Theories and Propositions." In Neil Nugent, ed., *The European Union* 1 (1996): 109. Dartmouth, Aldershot. Taylor and others have developed the theory of consociation, which qualifies aspects of such more traditional theories of integration as neofunctionalism, functionalism, and federalism. Consociation argues that integration in the 1980s and early 1990s has had a symbiotic character, as the state and the regional system are mutually supportive, each working with the other. In other words, practical adjustment to the need for more cooperation among states does not compromise the ideal of statehood or offer evidence of a step toward a federalist millennium. This view is also the theoretical basis of my analysis.

2. Taylor, p. 138.

3. The Amsterdam Treaty (May 1, 1999) encompasses all EU treaties, including the latest modifications and additions.

4. Taylor, p. 139.

5. The Economist, "Enlarging the EU: A New Pace?" pp. 32–33.

6. Institute of European Affairs. 1999. *Agenda 2000: Implications for Ireland.* Dublin, v.

7. *Agenda 2000*, ix.

8. For an analysis of Baltic cooperation, see Atis Lejinš, "The Quest for Baltic Unity: Chimera or Reality?" In Atis Lejinš and Zaneta Ozolina, eds. 1997. *Small States in a Turbulent Environment: The Baltic Perspective, Latvian Institute of International Affairs*, Riga.

9. *Uniting Europe.* 66 (13 Sept 1999): 3–4. Brussels. Of the "15 points of concern," 13 relate to economics and trade, and the other two concern political and security issues.

10. For an analysis of the Baltic States' accession process to the EU, see Atis Lejiņš, "Joining the EU and NATO: Baltic Security Prospects at the Turn of the 21st Century." In A. Lejiņš ed.. 1999. Joining the EU and NATO: Baltic Security Prospects at the Turn of the 21st Century, Helsinki, Aleksanteri Institute.

11. See Inotai, András, and A. Lejiņš eds. "Winners and Losers in EU Integration in the Czech Republic, Hungary, Poland, the Slovak Republic, and Slovenia" 1999. in this volume.

12. This is a social data project conducted continually between the Nordic and Baltic countries.

Bibliography for the Social Dimension

The Baltic Countries Revisited: Living Conditions and Comparative Challenges. 1997. The Norbalt (Nordic-Baltic) Living Conditions Project. Oslo, Fafo report 230, p. 79–104.

Demographic Statistics in the Baltic Countries. 1996. Tallinn, Riga, Vilnius.

Economic Development of Latvia. June 1999. Report. Riga.

European Commission. 1999. *Latvia Joint Assessment of Economic Policy Priorities of Latvia.* Riga.

Gosta Esping-Andersen. 1990. *The Three Worlds of Welfare Capitalism.* Polity Press.

Kutsar, Dagmar. *Multiple Welfare Losses and Risk of Social Exclusion in the Baltic States During Societal Transition.* Aadne Aasland, Knud Knudsen, Dagmer Kutsar and Ilze Trapenciere (eds.)

1998 Statistical Yearbook of Latvia.

Poverty Reduction in Estonia: Backgrounds and Guidelines. Tartu, 1999.

Rajevska, Feliciana. 1999. "Social Reform in Latvia: Achievements and Constraints." Paper, presented at TEMPUS project, JEP No 11389, Conference, April 24–28. *EU Enlargement: Present and Future*, Riga.

CHAPTER 5

Bulgaria and Romania

Economic Policy Institute, Sofia
Center for the Study of Democracy, Sofia

Introduction

During the past decade, Bulgaria and Romania have lagged behind the other Central European countries in restructuring and modernizing their economies. While major steps have been taken toward market-oriented reforms, both countries have experienced a slower and more controversial transformation process. In addition, they have been suffering from repeated problems of macroeconomic slowdown and internal and external disequilibria, including a high level of foreign indebtedness.

In their bid for accession to the EU, Bulgaria and Romania have to speed up reform measures to make up for their lower rates of economic growth and transformation to a market economy during the first half of the decade, and to catch up with the more advanced transition countries of Central and Eastern Europe already negotiating their entry into the EU.

During the second half of the 1990s, Bulgaria and Romania entered into a period of more profound and consistent reform measures in the areas of privatization, enterprise restructuring, building institutions, and administrative capacity. The reintegration into the world economy for both countries, experiencing the difficulties of servicing their external indebtedness, is proceeding with the more active support of international financial institutions. Nonetheless, Romania and Bulgaria still lag in their ability to cope with the competitive pressures and market forces within the EU.[1]

The profound changes under way in both countries, and the further changes still to be made, render more unstable the process of emerging winners and losers from the transformation and from integration to the EU. In analyzing the winners and losers to emerge from integration, it is important to delineate the factors arising from transition, from those emerging from accession, and the interdependence of these two trends. It is also important to take into account in this analysis the more controversial and painful transition of these two countries in comparison with other CEECs. Finally, it is important not to overemphasize the short-term costs and benefits and underemphasize the long-term costs and benefits associated with integration in these two countries.

The Political and Economic Background

Since the transition has started, Bulgaria and Romania have experienced the positive results of political democratization and of the reintegration of their countries into international economic and political relations. Nevertheless, overcoming the legacy of the authoritarian system was a rather inconsistent and slow process in both countries in the first half of the 1990s. As an overreaction to the earlier, rigid etatism and communist totalitarianism, transition in both countries followed a rather uneven path toward market-oriented development. The political commitment to reforms in both countries had depended to a great extent on various aspects of the emerging political structure. By the mid-1990s, the political situation in both countries could be characterized by the lack of a political force strongly committed and adequately skilled to carry out the reform policies.

In the second half of the decade, both countries experienced more radical political changes through the success of democratic coalitions, and they have undertaken more radical reforms for economic and social development. In both countries, these political outcomes have heralded an end to nearly six to seven years of procrastination under Socialist-dominated governments. The latter were not strongly committed to reforms and failed to achieve macroeconomic stabilization and growth. Structural reforms and the development of institutional and functional structures for a market economy were delayed.

The policies of the reformist governments in power in both countries show some similarities in their overcoming political uncertainty and social tension and the actual measures of transition and accession toward the EU.

First, the policy of accession to the EU has given an impetus to a kind of overoptimism of the political elite and the public for accelerating their integration into the EU. The high expectations of the population in both countries for speeding up reforms have provided an initial period of public confidence in the governments. This excessive optimism was not due to adequate awareness about the costs and benefits of integration into the EU. Rather, the tradition of etatism and *dirigisme* in these two countries has led the public to rely on centralized government decisions as a driving force for integration. Therefore, it has been political rhetoric rather than a true understanding of what integration entails—the establishment and the role of markets—that has led to the rather highly positive public expectations of accession to the EU in Bulgaria and Romania. As *Eurobarometer* surveys have shown in 1996–1998, Bulgarians and Romanians are the most fervent optimists among East Europeans for the chances of entry into the EU in the near future.[2]

Second, both countries have been unable to overcome economic slowdown and to initiate economic growth and sustainable economic development. There has been a recurrence of economic slowdown since mid-1998 in Romania and later in Bulgaria.

Third, the economic decline and worsening macroeconomic performance in both countries since the middle of 1998 and during the first half of 1999 have resulted in economic difficulties and a tendency to recourse to overcentralization and bureaucratization of government intervention in the economy. As one observer pointed out, the problems arise because " … the Romanian economy is still a very centralized and authoritarian economy. Reflexes are still inherited from the planned economy." (*Wall Street Journal*, March 28, 1998)[3] In Bulgaria, decisions at the highest level are the basis for policymaking in the central institutions.

The trend toward more centralization of the Bulgarian and Romanian economies may be considered a consequence of the economic slowdown, the slowdown in the privatization process, and remaining problems in the public sector with monopolies and corporate governance.

Fourth, the dominance of licensing (rather than registration) for economic activities in both countries is an impediment to economic development and a source of corruption. Corruption, a serious problem, is a bottleneck for economic development. Combating it requires building institutions, legislative measures, and social preconditions for respecting the rule of law.

Fifth, both among the political elites and in public opinion, the hardships of structural reforms have caused a growing sense of disillusionment as regards expectations of joining the EU. Official statements about the possibility of reconsidering the European integration priorities of the Bulgarian government, in the case of a delay of the start of negotiations with the EU, reflect this disillusionment.

Sixth, in both Bulgaria and Romania accession to the EU, above all, is a political goal. It involves the goal of achieving democratic stability and the goal of overcoming the post-World War II division of Europe and reintegrating into the world markets. Political leadership in Bulgaria has made the observation that any postponement of the accession process may have negative consequences, causing deceleration of the democratization process. (PHARE, November 1998)[4]

In recent years, the political elites of Bulgaria and Romania have openly voiced their disappointment with their exclusion from the group of countries that already have begun accession negotiations. The perception of a delay in starting entry negotiations with the EU has fostered fears that this delay would lead to further division among the countries of Europe. Any delay in the accession process for Bulgaria and Romania is considered harmful for their reintegration into the international economy and their market-oriented development.

The consequences of the Kosovo war have increased the fears of isolation of the Balkan region from the development of a stable European economic space. The Stability Pact for South Eastern Europe is expected to contribute to the reconstruction of the region, but there are concerns about the rate of foreign investment.

In the aftermath of the Kosovo war, EU accession becomes even more crucial for Bulgaria and Romania for restoring confidence in political stability and for continued democratization. Both countries have made more progress preparing for EU accession, compared with other Balkan transition countries.

Seventh, the political structures in both countries are reacting positively to integration with the EU. Governments in both countries are under strong pressure to speed up institution building, enhance administrative capacity, and adopt legislation harmonized with the *acquis communautaire* and the requirements of the EU Accession Partnerships.

The need to balance higher social expectations about EU accession with the reality of the cost of economic adjustment and of opening to the EU and the international economy has significant policy relevance in the medium term.

Political Criteria for EU Membership and Implications for Winners and Losers

Democracy in Bulgaria and Romania evolved in the 1990s under the increasing influence of international factors. EU accession policies and the implementation of the Copenhagen political criteria since 1993 have played an important role. The political objectives of accession have been well-received in Bulgaria and Romania and have constituted the main plank of their domestic and foreign policies since 1993. In spite of the political fluidity and instability, changes in governments, and political controversies, a national consensus has developed in both countries favoring EU membership. This political goal has been advocated well, though not quite implemented adequately enough, in these countries.

Since March 1998, Bulgaria and Romania have pursued preaccession strategies to meet the Copenhagen criteria. The accession process has provided both countries the grounds for building institutions that could not have been possible otherwise as a self-regulating process because of the insufficient demand of their underdeveloped markets. New institutions and regulations have emerged more as a result of policy measures developed in compliance with EU standards. In addition to introducing a new set of institutions, compliance with the Copenhagen criteria have also made it necessary to devolve power in both Bulgaria and Romania. As a result, the legacy of the former totalitarian state countries is being subject to increasing pressures to change in favor of the rule of law and in favor of institutional structures required for supporting a modern market economy. Officials in both nations also have started to regard institution building and enhancing of administrative capacities as an inherent part of the rule of law and a safeguard for human rights of their residents.

By working toward compliance with EU criteria for membership, Bulgaria and Romania are placing special emphasis on making the legislative, executive, and judicial branches of government more democratic and applying democratic values and principles in their societies. These two processes signify progress toward a higher level of democracy and increased abidance with the rule of law. More public awareness of individual rights is an essential part of this process.[5] Therefore, from the point of view of the functioning of the constitutional state and the creation of the institutional structure for a market economy, Bulgaria and Romania are in general on the winning side.

The efforts of Bulgaria and Romania to join the EU, by consolidating the legal and institutional frameworks of market economies and accelerating the implementation of market reforms, are particularly relevant for these nations, where the transformation process has proceeded more slowly for most of the past decade. The economic criteria for membership, although outlined broadly, imply fostering and sustaining market-oriented economic reforms that both countries still must accomplish more efficiently.

In case of delays in the actual negotiations, both countries may encounter reconsideration and opposition to the institutional development and adoption of the EU *acquis*. These reactions could promote public apprehension about the risks of ill-targeted priorities of the legal adjustment to EU standards. "The public opinion might come to perceive democratization and the establishment of the rule of the law as a response to external demands rather than as essential priorities of national development." (Sotirov and Todorov. 1998)[6] Under such conditions, political introversion and nationalistic trends may increase, and they could be detrimental to the democratization process. Therefore, delays in accession could make both countries losers.

Effects of Transformation and Accession on the Emergence of Winners and Losers

Transformation for Bulgaria and Romania has been slower than in the other CEECs. There have been delays in privatization and restructuring, which have resulted in low levels of foreign investments. The delays of these policies, together with the recurrence of macroeconomic instability and high external debt, all have been detrimental to the Bulgarian and Romanian economies. Unfavorable external developments, including the deflationary trends in the international markets for their main export products and regional instability, have exacerbated these internal economic problems. The Kosovo war has contributed significantly to the macroeconomic instability and the worsening of trade deficits in both countries, but especially Bulgaria. These internal and external problems have led to a deceleration in economic growth and a fall in industrial production.

The poor economic performance in both countries has led to many social groups and whole sectors of economies suffering from the transition. Many production activities, subsectors, enterprises, and social groups are sustaining losses while the two countries are gearing up to join the EU. With more liberal trade under the Europe Agreement, these declining industries and activities in Romania and Bulgaria have not been able to withstand the competitive pressure of EU industrial goods and have become double losers. The developments have been particularly unfavorable for the mining, chemical, and machine-building industries and for agricultural and some semiprocessed primary products.

Particularly disturbing is the situation of agriculture, which is not covered by the Europe Agreements. Lacking investments and entrepreneurship initiatives, the prospects for modernizing this sector soon are rather slim. The agricultural sectors in Bulgaria and Romanian likely will be unable to compete against the EU. The problems of the losers in the agricultural sector will worsen without supportive policies (better access to credit, clear legal regulation of ownership rights for agricultural land, and others) during the preparation for accession.

Compared with other Central and East European countries, Bulgaria and Romania will experience more interdependency and interaction between preparation for accession and continuing transformation. The key features of this interdependency include:

- The progress of adopting the EU *acquis* in the internal market is more rapid than domestic restructuring. This progress means that the economies of Bulgaria and Romania could be exposed to the competitive pressures of the internal market before they are ready for it.

- Given the slow progress in domestic restructuring thus far, Bulgaria and Romania are expected to tackle the remaining restructuring agenda while preparing to join the EU. This process likely will lead to high political and social tension and many "losers" expected with the still incomplete restructuring of the mining, chemical, and machine-building industries and public services and utilities. The preparation for accession will encounter the difficulties of dealing with the losers' situation in a vulnerable social and economic environment.

- Although the costs of transformation in Bulgaria and Romania have been low because of the slow progress, this delay in implementing reforms actually will result in higher costs of accession.

- Transition to a market economy in Bulgaria and Romania has been marked by the inefficiency of the legislative and executive branches and by not properly enforcing regulations and legislation. These factors, together with poor economic performance, have made Bulgaria and Romania unattractive to attract foreign investment.

- The "top-down" approach of transformation, performed under constantly changing privatization rules, has delayed privatization. At the same time, the countries have lacked the appropriate conditions for the spontaneous development of small and medium enterprises (a "bottom-up" type of economic development). Bulgaria and Romania will have to tackle these problems to become functioning economies. Thus, any potential winners in the future will have to emerge as a result of the "bottom-up" development.

- Both Bulgaria and Romania have had worse macroeconomic performance than those CEECs already negotiating EU membership. The unsuccessful implementation of adjustment policies resulted in political controversies and social unrest in Bulgaria in early 1997 and Romania in 1998. Both countries, however, have tried to address their macroeconomic situation. Bulgaria introduced a currency board in July 1997, which has helped it achieve macroeconomic stability in the past two years. Romania has worked on stabilization since 1998, with the objective of reducing inflation and overcoming the financial crisis. By the end of the 1990s, both countries have adopted more pragmatic approaches and better sequenced stabilization and adjustment policies.

- The crucial issue concerning the interdependence between the ongoing transformation and EU accession is the speed of transformation and accession. The winner-loser balance in the Bulgarian and Romanian economies may be much worse if accession is delayed. Acceleration in the preparation for accession will further keep on track the transformation process by the direct pressure of adjustment to the integration process. The possibilities of becoming an integral part of the internal market will create incentives for foreign investments into the Bulgarian and Romanian economies. It also may positively influence cooperation between Romania and Bulgaria, which will try to become partners rather than competitors.

Winners, Losers, EU Financial Support, and Macroeconomic Performance

The Effects of the Europe Agreements of Bulgaria and Romania

The implementation of the Europe Agreements of Bulgaria and Romania since 1995 has occurred during a period of unfavorable macroeconomic performance and structural problems in both countries. Therefore, an evaluation of the contribution of implementing the Europe Agreements to the worsening of the losers' problems must consider not only the nature and limitations of the association framework of the EU, but also the macroeconomic situation of the countries.

Association is not yet membership, and thus the focus on the winner-loser balance influenced by the association process so far should not blur the overall positive trend of fundamental changes in the relations of Bulgaria and Romania with the EU in the period concerned.

The limitations of the association are related to the approach adopted by the EU allowing for:

- Trade concessions and the creation of a free trade zone by the end of the transition period for all goods except agricultural products.

- EU protectionism in trade with sensitive products such as agricultural goods, wines, metal products, and others.

- Provisions for rules in the form of export quotas, safeguards, and rules of origin (in fact their arbitrary use may undermine the announced liberalization).

- Financial aid and assistance under the PHARE Programme, the main channel for the European Union's financial and technical cooperation with the countries of Central and Eastern Europe, and other EU instruments, though not included in the Europe Agreements Annexes and Protocols.

- Regional cooperation with neighboring countries in the framework of EU programs.

The many positive results of the association process include trade liberalization, trade creation, and financial assistance. Nevertheless, EU requirements remain contradictory when they call for trade liberalization and specialization according to comparative advantage while maintaining a managed protection of sensitive products. The major industrial exports of Bulgaria and Romania (apparel, steel, and metallurgical products) and particularly agricultural products still face substantial EU tariffs and nontariff barriers.

The situation is especially unfavorable for exports of agricultural goods to the EU, where protectionism bears more heavily on the weaker partners. Bulgaria and Romania pose no potential threat for EU with their agricultural products. Their agriculture has been hit severely by the transitional crisis and so far has not been able to expand supply to foreign markets, including the EU.

In general, the Europe Agreements of Bulgaria and Romania reveal the "soft-ness" of the EU support for trade liberalization with the Central and East European countries. The lack of "strong" support for better access by East European exports to the EU has prevented the relief of some of the economic problems the transitional countries have faced. The EU's two main motives for applying the Association Agreements—namely, trade liberalization only for most industrial goods and commitment to the internal market by unifying the EU countries' trade policies with the East European countries (Messerlin 1993)[7]—may explain the EU's "softness" of the Association Agreements.

Bulgaria and Romania have fully experienced the limitations of the Association Agreements, and these limitations have lowered the expectations somewhat for any easing of trade liberalization for newcomers to the EU markets. The effects of applying the Association Agreements relate to the disillusionment about the EU's managing trade liberalization toward the East European partners.

A positive consequence of this experience is that East European partners learn to understand better the EU's internal policies and the interests of socioeconomic groups and their lobbies, which they cannot ignore.

The costs for Eastern Europe of the Europe Agreements' restrictions against imports of agricultural goods in the EU have been much higher than expected. For Bulgaria and Romania, agriculture has been more supply-responsive during the period of reforms than industrial production, but it has not gained better access to the EU market.[8] The unpredictability of the EU import restrictions on agricultural goods often incurs losses, even for companies that have exported agricultural produce to the EU and have started developing their business. These losses are true particularly for dairy products, foodstuffs, live animals, and other goods. Thus, during the association period for agricultural production, both Bulgaria and Romania are losers or potential losers. These products have faced and still face substantial EU tariffs and nontariff barriers. Some reduction in EU protection in the future may apply to agricultural goods, wines, fish, and fish products.

The need to reduce the costs of restrictive EU trade policies toward agrarian exports from the CEECs will remain of crucial importance for the Eastern European nations during their efforts to gain access to the EU. Whether or not greater liberalization of the agricultural imports of the EU will occur in the future will depend on the reform of the CAP and the evaluated costs of the liberalization for the import-competing EU goods.[9]

Agrarian producers in both countries might benefit from preaccession restructuring aid for agriculture. At the same time, any further steps toward liberalization of trade in agricultural goods will make Bulgarian and Romanian producers face the competitive pressures of EU products in their domestic markets. It is difficult to foresee the possibilities of transforming Bulgarian and Romanian farmers from losers to winners in the preaccession period, although more changes in this direction may be expected.

EU Financial Assistance as a Factor in Determining Winners and Losers

EU financial assistance (through PHARE, various EU multicountry and horizontal programs, such as TAEIX, the SME program, the Large Scale Infrastructure Facility, crossborder and regional development and cooperation programs, ISPA[10] and SAPARD,[11] and others) is an important factor in creating winners in the association process. All forms of preaccession aid have contributed either to reducing disadvantages or to developing new potential. Though the overall aid disbursed to Bulgaria and Romania is much less than that to the more advanced transition countries (those that have begun accession negotiations), it significantly has provided them with possibilities of "learning by doing." The two countries have been somewhat slow to use the financial assistance efficiently, and thus their needs in the preaccession period will be much higher.

If accession is a real target for Bulgaria and Romania, then aid through the structural, cohesion funds and CAP may improve their position as beneficiaries. If they do not start accession negotiations in 2000, however, EU policies might disadvantage them as later entrants. The prospects for a catch-up development of Bulgaria and Romania could improve if EU policies for financial assistance would emphasize convergence.

Criticism of Bulgaria and Romania for not using EU assistance efficiently relates to their inadequate absorptive capacity. They have not applied aid efficiently because of inconsistent government policies, administrative limitations on access to information, and monopolistic structures. They also lack experience in complying with EU rules and procedures while they apply EU financial support. Finally, inefficient administration and political controversies also have blocked follow-up of implemented projects.

Both countries have improved their implementation of preaccession aid. They increasingly have applied financial assistance for investment priorities, rather than using it for technical assistance to support institutional building and policy development. This shift in priorities has contributed to structural reforms in Bulgaria and Romania, especially for industrial restructuring, privatization, SME development, trade and investment promotion, and research in science and technology.

Preaccession aid, although rather segmented, overall has helped Bulgaria and Romania so far, but the recipients could use the funds more efficiently and sustain the aid better if they coordinated funded activities better, by sector or related activities.

To turn losers into winners with preaccession aid, the EU should clarify the following criteria for the beneficiaries in Bulgaria and Romania:

• effectiveness of a given project over time;

• compliance with macroeconomic goals and developmental objectives;

- potential for enhancing labor productivity and improving the standard of living; and

- follow-up strategies for applying the EU transfers.

Government officials in both countries also need training to improve their institutions' capability (such as project design) to apply EU transfers better.

Bulgaria and Romania need to urgently improve their absorption of the EU's financial aid to focus on their problems of economic growth. The creation of winners in both countries during accession will rely very much on more efficient utilization of EU aid because of the capital shortage in their economies and insufficient foreign investments.

Bulgaria and Romania risk being left behind in terms of assistance policies geared to EU membership for the period 2000–2006. In case the EU decides to favor countries more prepared for membership, Bulgaria and Romania could find themselves in a losing position if significant amounts of transfers is conditional on the entry prospects of a country in the preaccession period, and the EU concedes long-term, transitional derogations from the *acquis communautaire* to only some of the countries with which it negotiates.

Macroeconomic Developments Impeding Catch-Up Strategies

The implementation of the Association Agreements confirms that the success of any country to meet the challenge of EU integration depends heavily on its own economic effort and performance. The unfavorable trends in their GDP growth from 1991 to 1998 accentuate the problems of the losers. Parallel with, and contributing to, the low or negative annual rates of economic growth in Bulgaria and Romania have been structural crises, new and inherited imbalances, wasted resources, distortions of the price mechanism, financial destabilization, and a high vulnerability to domestic and external shocks.

Compared with the already negotiating CEECs, as noted above, Bulgaria and Romania have not developed the appropriate and supportive economic environments for fostering higher rates of real growth.[12] In 1998, the GDP per capita for Bulgaria at purchasing power parity represented only 26 percent of the EU average, and the same indicator for Romania amounts to 23 percent to 24 percent of the EU average. (Poschl, J. 1999)[13]

Poor performance of its economy has resulted in chronic unemployment and an escalating need for social benefits in Romania. The official unemployment rate rose to 11.4 percent in May 1999 from 9 percent in October 1998.[14] Government spending related to unemployment is expected to rise to 1.5 percent of GDP in 1999, nearly twice the spending, 0.77 percent of GDP, related to unemployment in 1996.[15]

A third of the unemployed are young, and almost half of those who receive unemployment benefits should be considered long-term unemployed. Given that the volume of net investments in 1997 was only 52.8 percent of the level in 1989, a recovery of growth likely will not happen soon. For 1999 and 2000, Romania probably will remain in austerity with falling or stagnating GDP, which will only increase unemployment. With rising unemployment, more poor households need the support of social security. They are the greatest losers of transition.

Long-term unemployment and living below the poverty line leads to a loss or lack of necessary skills and human degradation. The United Nations Development Program (UNDP) studies on poverty in transition for Bulgaria and Romania have revealed a worsening of the problem and have discussed policy measures to improve the social assistance schemes. (ILO/UNDP 1998)[16]

The social fatigue from transition and the feeling of hopelessness among the long-term unemployed prevail in some industrially depressed regions where the closure of state enterprises has left people unprepared to provide their subsistence by a new occupation. This group of long-term unemployed—involved in prostitution, organized crime, and other criminal activities—would be the most difficult to turn from losers into winners. Attempts to reduce the losers of this type will depend on government policies to address long-term unemployment and social exclusion (see Policies for Social Cohesion).

The main issue in the preparation for EU accession will be how to guide the applicants through preaccession adjustment to reduce the number of losers in the transition and to assist the catch-up strategies of Romania and Bulgaria. The design of policy instruments to improve the situation for the losers needs to take into account the overall economic situations in the two countries (macroeconomic instability and the large, remaining agenda for structural reform). This design could consider the following proposals for supporting the catch-up policies for Bulgaria and Romania:

- linking EU transfers and financial support closely to the priorities of structural adjustment for accession;

- promoting private-sector growth through emphasis on investments in infrastructure and human capital (with the support of international institutions);

- certain derogations for cofinancing EU-funded programs, based on budget constraints in both countries;

- supporting social inclusion policies and reform of social services systems;

- increasing funds available for technical assistance and FDI support (for example, schemes provided by EU member countries for covering political risk) to facilitate the structural reform process;

- special support for the adoption of the EC's *acquis communautaire* and for derogations during the transitional periods of the accession; and

- stimulating crossborder and regional cooperation to create additional opportunities for investment and growth.

Structural Analysis of Winners and Losers and the Timing of Accession

The time pattern of the emergence of winners and losers in the accession to the EU will depend on the mode and speed of the accession process. Trends in the winner-loser positions arising from transformation may considerably influence the accession process. In particular, policymakers and politicians have a major concern for the increase in the number of losers. Public confidence in reforms is diminishing, given the lasting effects of the crisis for much of the middle- and low-income strata of the population in both countries. Low real wages in the public sector (for example, government administration, health services, education, and transport) also are having unfavorable consequences, especially in fostering corruption.

The short overview of the macroeconomic developments and transition paths of both countries reveals that, so far, the economy has sustained more losses, and the winners are still in a dynamic process of changes. General public opinion considers that the private sector generates winners. The shrinking domestic demand and unfavorable external factors, however, also make it difficult for normally functioning private businessess that are neither losers nor winners.

Concerning EU preaccession policies, winners are concentrated in the following sectors and professional groups:

- public administration and some public services that are beneficiaries of EU support for institutional building and training;

- state monopolies subsidized in the state budget or using restructuring funds from EU sources (electricity companies, railways, utilities, and water supply);

- oil and gas industries;

- infrastructure and its rehabilitation, renovation, and restructuring;

- market institutions, including stock exchanges and commodity exchanges;

- beneficiaries of EU regional cooperation funding at the municipality and regional levels;

- small and medium-size enterprises supported by different schemes; and

- university education, research, and development (only for the beneficiaries of EU funds; otherwise, state budget-funded entities are under strict budget constraints).

As for losers, several factors related to the transitional crisis make the process of emergence for them rather difficult to evaluate and influence. Any future analysis should distinguish these two types of losers:

- well-performing state-owned economic agents that are becoming losers because state budget or another institutional support is withdrawn; and

- loss-making state-owned enterprises, whose existence depends on state subsidies, or they otherwise are heavily indebted to the state budget.

Bulgaria already has eliminated direct and indirect subsidies in many sectors, except for energy and some natural monopolies. In Romania, direct subsidies still constitute a major policy instrument for several state-funded industries and activities. The main sectors where the loss of subsidies has made them losers are:

- industrial sectors, especially metallurgy, chemical industries, machine building, and shipbuilding;

- state monopolies, especially in the utilities sector;

- agriculture and forestry;

- fisheries;

- primary and secondary education and fundamental research;

- culture, arts, and the preservation of historical heritage;

- social policies, social inclusion policies; and

- health and social insurance systems.

Negative consequences for the losers will increase in the medium term with the opening of domestic markets. Further cuts in import duties and increased competition will put competitive pressures on several sectors and social groups, both winners and losers.

A special policy concern for Bulgaria and Romania will be to reduce the number of losers from the transition by consolidating the market economy, by introducing internal market regulations, and by restructuring and modernizing industries. Making these sectors and activities compatible with EU regulations also will benefit consumers. The loser sectors from the transition period, needing restructuring and modernization, include:

- the steel and iron industry in Bulgaria and Romania;

- the nonferrous metals sector, including mining, smelting, refining, and processing of metals (the downsizing and restructuring of this sector will be burdened with high costs, including for environmental protection);

- the mechanical and electrical engineering sector (includes car production in Romania);

- the chemical industries (exports for these industries have been declining because of delayed restructuring and loss of traditional markets; strategic foreign investors may make would-be winners of these enterprises in the medium term);

- the foodstuffs and food-processing industries (foodstuffs are predominantly in demand in the domestic market, though they have become more export oriented; the industrial structure in the processed food sector is impeding competition, and the increasing international pressures on the domestic market will cause high adjustment costs in this sector);

- the timber and furniture industries (these industries have an export potential, especially in Romania, but the need to suspend some subsidies may cause some problems and delays); and

- energy production (restructuring, privatization, and demonopolization remain valid issues both for Bulgaria and Romania).

The adoption and implementation of a realistic timetable and plan for the early decommissioning of four units of the Kozloduy nuclear power plant, as the Commission required in its 1999 Regular Report, is of both economic and political significance for Bulgaria. At present, the EC considers too distant the closure dates for these units that Bulgaria proposed (two units during 2004–2006 and the other two during 2010–2012) and not respecting the Accession Partnership priority. Public opinion strongly opposes conditioning the invitation to Bulgaria to negotiate accession on its progress in closing these units of its only nuclear power plant. Given the production and export loss that decommissioning these nuclear plant units will entail, it is important that Bulgaria devise a strategy to minimize the adjustment costs.

Creating winners in the preaccession period may not necessarily provide conditions to keep economic agents or social groups as winners after the accession. To keep these groups as winners after accession, there is a need for more investment-oriented use of EU funds. Priority should be given to funding the restructuring of the real sectors of the economy to increase their competitiveness.

In the medium term, the compliance with EU regulations in legislation, free movement of goods, capital and labor, consumer protection, environmental protection, social policies, health, and other issues will increase costs, and challenge both economic agents and the system of financing the adjustment.[17] Adopting EU regulations must consider that any cost "threshold" that is too high for businesses to implement EU regulations will tend to stimulate the shadow economy. Thus, the timing of accession is relevant to the success of applying the EU legislation and enforcing it in practice.

EU accession is a priority for Romania and Bulgaria in their overall strategy for reintegration with the world economy. Not including them in a clear timetable for EU membership may decrease the positive effects of their preparation for accession on their overall economic development.

Opening negotiations with the EU will help establish the mechanism and policy instruments to continue their preaccession adjustment. Their preparation for accession now must contribute to:

- adoption of policies to close the productivity and income gaps between them and the EU; and

- the concession of medium-term transitional derogations from the Community *acquis communautaire* to diminish the risks of creating more losers than winners during the accession.

Policies for Social Cohesion

Guaranteeing basic individual human rights becomes crucially significant to the reinforcement and irreversibility of the positive developments of the transformation toward political democratization and market economy. The protection of human rights and the democratic process of institutional building, based on the adoption of the EU *acquis*, have become important in the two countries as preconditions for long-term social and economic development. These efforts within the framework of accession to develop strategies and policies to protect human rights and minorities are important for addressing social cohesion issues in Romania and Bulgaria.

These strategies move the nations toward recognizing the needs of ethnic minorities and socially disadvantaged groups, which have much lower living standards, and politically incorporating them in the society. The Roma remain one of the most socially excluded groups, and the prolonged economic slowdown in Romania and Bulgaria has deteriorated their position considerably.

These groups may be losers of transition and become a risk group because of rising illiteracy, social diseases, and crime. In general, both Bulgaria and Romania have gained support from international organizations for acknowledging the existence of social exclusion problems.[18] The measures these two countries adopted to improve their social situation reflect the positive influences of the protection of basic human rights and freedoms. These approaches and mechanisms of social protection and inclusion, however, must improve further.

The problem with the Roma population in Bulgaria is rather socioeconomic in nature, not so much restoring curtailed basic human rights and freedoms. The Roma's unfavorable social and economic situation leads to their rising involvement in crimes, prostitution, and fraud. The social inclusion of this minority will be a challenge for the social and employment policies in the medium term.[19]

It is therefore important that policies addressing the issues of these groups not focus exclusively on "not losing the losers," that is, not just occasionally helping them to survive with social net programs. There is a strong need to take further steps to integrate these groups and minorities socially by providing conditions for increased employment. Even limited measures to involve them as employees or self-employed and educating their children may contribute substantially to their social cohesion.

No doubt Bulgaria and Romania will need much financial support to solve these social problems. Maintaining lower ratios of state budget deficits to GDP and the difficulties of raising budget revenues present a challenge to the state budgets in Romania and Bulgaria for adequately financing their policies. The success of social cohesion policies, therefore, will depend on securing funding for better designed and more effective initiatives. Limited government budget sources could cover only short-term measures. Support by the EU and other international financial institutions may be of primary significance to:

- fight poverty by creating employment and self-employment opportunities and improving access to the labor market;

- improve access to and raise the quality of social services, including education, health care, and social assistance; and

- reduce illiteracy by guaranteeing conditions for obligatory primary education and better access to secondary and high school training of the children from poor families, including ethnic minorities.

Conclusions and Some Considerations for Further Research

Conclusions

Preliminary evaluation of preaccession problems suggest that, from 2001 to 2006, both Bulgaria and Romania will reach the final stage of trade liberalization foreseen under the Europe Agreements. EU competitive pressures, especially in industrial goods, will approach their peak during this period, and the adjustment costs for the industrial sectors of Bulgaria and Romania will be the highest in the medium term as they approach membership.

The countries should make better use of preaccession aid by giving priority to those projects and actions that produce more winners. Regional development and crossborder cooperation between Bulgaria and Romania and with neighboring countries could also be an important instrument for creating winners and for opening new business and economic growth opportunities. Until now, similar economic problems in both countries did not encourage them to cooperate in any mutually beneficial activities, but rather created tensions, such as the construction of a second bridge over the Danube. EU accession might bring a new attitude and approaches to regional and crossborder policies.

The social aspects of the policies toward winners and losers seem to be gaining political importance because of the social depression, social exclusion, and social fatigue of the 10 years of transition. EU accession may become a worn political promise from the political elite if the creation of losers continues to deepen social differentiation and social distress. Thus, policies to reduce losers will help promote the creation of functioning market economies and EU accession.

Both countries need policies and programs to improve the living standards of the socially disadvantaged groups and ethnic minorities. For example, the governments should help support self-employment for these residents and their employment in infrastructure projects, public services, forestry preservation, agricultural-environmental programs, and environmental protection programs along the coasts of the Danube River and the Black Sea.

The timing of accession will be crucial for Bulgaria and Romania to win or lose economically in the EU. Both countries have a goal to meet the Copenhagen criteria but, in the preaccession period, they have growing needs of financial and investment support. The European Commission's Agenda 2000 anticipates that, beyond 2001, policies of financial support for new members and for the later entrants will tend to diverge somewhat. If this trend becomes actual policy, then new members will have an advantage with financial support, compared with those who join later. This difference will make the task of catching up more difficult for Bulgaria and Romania.

Suggestions for Future Research

Bulgaria and Romania have to take into account in their National Accession Strategies certain quantification of the benefits and losses at different stages of the preaccession process. Few studies in either country assess the cost-benefit (impact) analysis of EU accession as a basis for medium- and long-term policymaking. Studies should be carried out to evaluate the effects of alternative scenarios, such as a more gradual or radical liberalization of the domestic markets. The framework for calculating the benefits and costs of EU accession could consider several assumptions:

- consolidation of the market economy in the medium term;

- application of the EU financial aid and funding for adjustment purposes; and

- effects and costs of adopting the *acquis communautaire* at different stages of transition and accession.

Notes

1. "Bulgaria has continued to make progress in establishing a functioning market economy but further steps are needed and it is not yet in a position to cope with competitive pressure and market forces within the Union in the medium term." In *1999 Regular Report from the EC on Bulgaria's Progress Towards Accession*, October 13, 1999.

"Romania cannot be considered as a functioning market economy and it is not able to cope with competitive pressures and market forces within the Union in the medium term." In *1999 Regular Report from the EC on Romania's Progress Towards Accession*, October 13, 1999.

2. *Eurobarometer*, Gallup International, 1996–1999.

3. *Wall Street Journal.* 1998. Tismaneanu, Vladimir. "Romania: Running on Empty." In *Central European Economic Review*, as quoted in the *Wall Street Journal*, March 28, p. 20.

4. PHARE. November 1998. Convergence, Ministry of Foreign Affairs of Bulgaria, p. 3.

5. Since the beginning of the 1990s, many NGOs, especially in Bulgaria, have helped to raise public awareness of citizens' right to choose their own government and to live under a system of the rule of law. They also have helped people acknowledge that both political freedom and a free market are necessary for intellectual, economic, and political prosperity and

supported minority rights. NGOs also could contribute more, however, to assessing and implementing pilot projects fighting poverty, supporting self-employment schemes, and microcrediting.

6. Sotirov, V. and A. Todorov. 1998. "The Democratic Institutions, the Rule of Law, Human Rights and the Protection of Minorities." In *Bulgaria and the European Union: Towards an Institutional Infrastructure.* CSD, Sofia. www.csd.bg/publications/inst-infrastructure-eng/index2.html

7. See Messerlin. P.A. 1993. "The Association Agreements between the EC and Central Europe: Trade Liberalization vs. Constitutional Failure?" In *Acta Oeconomica* 45.

8. The agricultural sector provides 25.9 percent and 18.8 percent of GDP for Bulgaria and Romania, respectively.

9. Some estimates of the effects of the EU's eventually, unilaterally easing imports from the first four countries with Europe Agreements (Hungary, the Czech Republic, the Slovak Republic, and Poland) show that it would reduce outputs in the four EU sectors (agriculture, steel, textiles, and chemicals) by only 2 percent to 4 percent at most, and only in agriculture and apparel. See Aghion, Philippe and R. Burges. 1992. *Toward an European Continental Common Market.*

10. Instrument for Structural Policies Pre-Accession.

11. Community Support for Pre-Accession Measures for Agriculture and Rural Development in the applicant countries.

12. After 1995, following two to four years of recovery and positive growth, economic growth in Bulgaria and Romania declined again. After a short recovery in 1998 in Bulgaria, but not Romania, the increasing imbalances and unfavorable domestic and external factors weakened the economy further in 1999 in both countries.

13. Poschl, J. et al., February 1999. "Transition Countries in 1999: Widespread Economic Slowdown with Escalating Structural Problems," *WIIW* 253.

14. *1999 Regular Report from the Commission on Romania's Progress Towards Accession,* 52.

15. Authors' calculations, based on IMF documents.

16. *Poverty in Transition.* ILO/UNDP. Republic of Bulgaria. 1998. *Poverty in Transition.* ILO/UNDP, Romania.

17. At the same time, of course, adopting these regulations will confer benefits to the consumers through high-quality products and will contribute to better consumer protection, better environment, and a higher level of safety.

18. *Bulgaria and Romania Poverty Assessment Studies of the World Bank*, 1996. *Poverty in Transition, Republic of Bulgaria*, ILO/ UNDP, 1998. *Poverty in Transition, Romania*, ILO/UNDP, 1998.

19. According to the latest population census (1992), the Roma population in Bulgaria was 313,396, or 3.7 percent of the total population. In Romania, the official count of the Roma population was 400,000. The EU Commission, in its 1997 Opinion, estimated this population at 1.1 million to 1.5 million for Romania, and its 1999 Report for Romania asserted no need to adjust this estimate.

PART II

Winners and Losers of EU Integration in Central and Eastern Europe: Country Reports

CHAPTER 6

The Czech Republic

Petr Pavlík

Background

Three macroprocesses are under way simultaneously in most countries of Central and Eastern Europe. The Czech Republic (CR) is no exception in this respect. One is a multilevel and multidimensional transformation process. Another is the process of integration into the European Union. Both these processes are occurring in the context of the process of globalization. All three macroprocesses are strongly interrelated and, indeed, it is sometimes difficult or even impossible to distinguish and separate clearly the transformation, integration, and global influences on the economies and societies of the transition countries.

Czechoslovakia, East Germany, and Romania were among the most hard-line communist regimes in Central and Eastern Europe. Even more so after the Soviet invasion of 1968, Czechoslovakia was one of the most loyal members of the Warsaw Pact and of Comecon. Before 1989, Czechoslovakia had only three political parties, with the Communist Party playing the lead role, as the Constitution provided.

The Czechoslovak economy had remained a typical Soviet-model, centrally planned economy, practically unreformed all the way until the changes of November 1989. Unlike Poland and Hungary, Czechoslovakia started its transformation process from a position of virtually complete state ownership of the economy. Only 1.2 percent of the labor force, 2 percent of all registered assets, and a negligible fraction of the nation's GDP belonged to the private sector in 1989. This low share did not change much in 1990, when official statistics still attributed only 4 percent of GDP to the private sector.

In sociological terms, the society of communist Czechoslovakia, with East Germany, was one of the most equalized in the Soviet bloc, especially in income differentiation. For example, the differences were negligible between salaries of university-educated employees such as teachers and physicians on the one hand and wages of unskilled workers on the other.

The so-called "Velvet Revolution" of November 1989 brought radical changes in Czechoslovakia, which have affected practically all spheres of human activity. The political system changed from a totalitarian regime into a pluralist, parliamentary democracy. The leading role of the Communist Party was abolished in December 1989, followed by the adoption of a law on political parties in January 1990. The first free elections after five decades of totalitarian regimes occurred in February.

At the beginning of the changes, the political movement the Civic Forum played an important role, which encompassed various political trends that had united together to oppose the preceding communist regime. The Civic Forum won the first free elections but later split into several political parties. The political spectrum gradually started to resemble the standard spectrum that exists in most developed countries. Thus, after the break-up of the federation at the end of 1992, the CR inherited a relatively stable structure of political parties. All major political streams are represented in the Czech political spectrum at present.

Despite all of its imperfections, the CR is a sovereign and democratic state governed by law, based on respect for the rights and freedom of the citizen. The Charter of Fundamental Rights and Freedoms forms a part of the constitutional order of the CR. The legislative power is vested in the Parliament, which consists of two chambers: the Chamber of Deputies, elected for four-year terms, and the Senate, elected for a term of six years. The executive power is vested in the president of the republic and in the government of the CR. The judicial power rests in independent courts, which consist of the Constitutional Court and a system of common courts.

Major steps taken so far to transform the economy—such as liberalization of prices and foreign trade, privatization, introduction of currency convertibility, tax reform, and establishment of standard market institutions—together have formed a relatively consistent program of economic reform. Since 1990, the Czech Republic already has accomplished all the basic systemic changes, but it has finished none of the transformation steps completely. In a simplified way, the radical economic reform is more or less over, but the complex transformation process will continue for many years.

In its foreign policy, Czechoslovakia had to redefine its orientation because it switched practically overnight from the Soviet bloc to independent republic.

Immediately after November 1989, the new democratically elected representatives attempted to establish contacts with all significant international organizations and institutions.

An important goal of foreign policy has become the integration of Czechoslovakia, and later the CR, into all relevant Euro-Atlantic political and social structures. Already in December 1990, official talks on an association agreement with Czechoslovakia, signed one year later, started in Brussels. Because of the disintegration of the country, its leaders had to sign new Association Agreements with both parts of the former federation.

Since the break-up of the federation, the Czech Republic has actively sought entry into the EU and NATO. On March 12, 1999, the CR, with Hungary and Poland, acquired full NATO membership. In October 1993, the CR and the EU signed an Association Agreement, and the CR submitted a formal application for membership in the EU in January 1996. The Czech government expects the country to be ready by January 2003 for EU accession, now the top priority of Czech foreign policy.

Winners and Losers since Transformation

This section briefly outlines the winners and losers of the process, beginning with transformation and followed by EU accession, until the present. Whenever possible, this section will attempt to separate the effects of integration from the influences of transformation.

External and Internal Security and Stability

After the artificially stable, bipolar world came to an end, the countries of Eastern and Central Europe found themselves in a security vacuum. At the beginning of transformation, the prospects of NATO membership were very hazy and, at best, seemed very far away. In this respect, starting the process of integration into the EU has increased the level of external security of these countries considerably.

Because the Czech Republic expects to enter the EU soon, potential foreign investors see it as a much safer country. On this issue, the whole Czech society can be considered a winner. The CR's recent entry into NATO certainly has made the country's external security almost absolute.

Regarding internal security, since the fall of the communist regime, there has been a tremendous increase in reported crime activities in the CR. The opening of borders and the free movement of people have contributed much to the internationalization of the crime scene in the CR. Criminal activities originating in many other parts of the world have started to operate in the Czech Republic.

New types of crime, such as drug trafficking, money laundering, and racketeering, have come into the country. There has been a striking increase in car thefts and bank robberies recently, and prostitution, especially in Prague and in border regions close to Germany, has risen. According to Czech police statistics, the crime rate has increased almost fourfold since 1989.

At the same time, a wave of white-collar crime has emerged, mainly tax evasion, insider-trading on the capital market, and various kinds of financial frauds. Obviously, the level of internal security has dropped significantly in the CR, though the situation is not yet as bad as it is in some other countries of the region. The whole country is a clear loser in terms of internal security.

The internal security problem certainly did not develop from the integration process. On the contrary, the accession process likely will improve internal security in the future. Aggravating the high crime rate are the inadequacy of institutions, loopholes in legislation, and problems with law enforcement. The process of conforming Czech laws with the *acquis communautaire* may help to address this problem. The third pillar of the EU (Justice and Home Affairs) also should improve internal security through a better organized and close coordination with EU member countries.

In general terms, the accession process has contributed positively to the country's stability, a very different kind of stability, however, than in the previous communist regime. This stability links to freedom and respect for basic human rights, with much more dynamism in it. At the same time, elements of instability in the CR are linked mainly to the unfinished transformation.

An important source of internal instability is the Roma issue. The living conditions for the Czech Romanies are very poor, their education level is low, and unemployment among them is very high. All these factors contribute to the high rate of crimes they commit. Also exacerbating the Roma problem are activities of various extremist, right-wing groups, often directed against the Romanies.

Political Structure

Within the Czech political system, the large political parties, namely the Social Democratic Party and the Civic Democratic Party, especially are the winners of the transformation process, compared with other elements of civil society. (These two parties signed a so-called "opposition treaty" last year.)

Since the collapse of communism, several NGOs have appeared, dealing with such concerns as the environment, human rights, and ethnic minorities. Their combined membership, however, remains relatively small.

The precedent Klaus government tended to view its role negatively. It had been particularly keen to limiting its own influence on political decisionmaking by stressing the primacy of formal representation. That government also had obstructed its own activities by delaying the law on nonprofit organizations and by not making charitable donations tax-deductible. Thus, so far, the NGOs are losers in the transformation process.

Influential political lobbies in the CR are connected mainly with large enterprises, banks, and financial institutions, where the stake of the state is still significant. The role of civil society has been strongly underestimated in the CR, and it certainly has much to accomplish on this issue. The integration process, however, may contribute to the development of civil society in the CR.

After the early elections for Chamber of Deputies, on June 19–20, 1998, five political parties passed the 5 percent limit necessary for obtaining seats in the Chamber. The Republicans (SPR-RSC), who strongly oppose the CR's membership in both the EU and NATO, did not meet this limit.

Of the five parliamentary parties, only the Communists (KSCM) have substantial reservations about EU membership. The CSSD (Social Democratic Party), KDU-CSL (Christian Democratic Union-Czech People's Party), and US (Freedom Union) are all strongly pro-European.

The ODS (Civic Democratic Party) considers the CR's all-sided participation in the process of European integration an important goal and has explicitly mentioned it in its electoral program, but many of its top leaders, especially Václav Klaus, often have expressed Eurosceptic remarks. Above all, ODS does not want to dissolve the country in supranational structures or in a "Europe of regions," without a clearly defined statehood. Although the Social Democrats promised to accelerate the CR's preparations for entry into the EU during their campaign, since their election, the performance of their government on this issue has been rather disappointing.

Economic Actors

Tremendous changes have hit the economy of the Czech Republic. The biggest winner is the whole services sector. There has been a large increase in the range of financial service offered. The personal incomes in the services segment, by far, are also the highest, compared with all other parts of the economy.

Among the deepest losers are agriculture and large parts of the heavy industry, especially steelworks and mines. In general, most segments of the Czech industry tend to be losers in both the transformation and the integration process, largely because of the slow restructuring, low productivity of labor, and low competitiveness of most branches of the Czech industry and individual firms.

There is some hope, however, linked to the increase of foreign direct investment. Nevertheless, some parts of the Czech industry may not survive the shock connected with the country's entry into the EU. Otherwise, the situation of Czech agriculture may improve after accession because of subsidies from EU funds.

Concerning basic macroeconomic indicators (table 6.1, below), the development was very promising in the first years of transformation, despite the sharp but necessary economic decline in 1991. The past couple of years, however, have been very disappointing, mainly because of the economic recession caused by serious mistakes in economic policy and an inadequate legal framework for economic transformation.

The Czech GDP still has not attained its pretransformation level in real terms. In 1998, it was at 95.5 percent of its 1989 level, although real wages already reached its 1989 level in 1996. The Czech Republic often was praised for its fiscal discipline, reflected in a relatively low public debt and occasional state budget surpluses. Some of the internal debt, however, has remained hidden in extrabudgetary institutions, for example, Konsolidační Banka, where many bad debts from commercial banks have been transferred.

The CR has been rather successful in controlling inflation, such that the policy of the Czech central bank is considered too restrictive and, in fact, undermining economic growth. Unemployment, which many foreign observers consider curiously low during many years of transformation, has risen substantially.

Social Cohesion

Despite its right-wing stance, the policy of the Klaus government was very considerate from the social point of view. For a very long time, the unemployment rate was very low and, as a consequence, the level of social cohesion during the first stage of the transformation process was reasonably high. The unusually low unemployment rate, however, was in large part artificial because the government did everything to prevent bankruptcies of larger enterprises. Thus, there was much hidden unemployment.

This kind of policy, obviously, had a negative effect on the restructuring process. The restructuring of enterprises finally has accelerated, and the unemployment rate is rising quickly. As a result, social tension is increasing, but paradoxically under a Social Democratic government. Under the right-wing governments, trade unions played a relatively limited role during the first period of the transformation because the economic situation was relatively good. Thus, it was possible to maintain social peace without major problems. Since then, however, the worsening economic and social situation has led to radical rumblings in trade unions.

TABLE 6.1 BASIC MACROECONOMIC INDICATORS (PERCENTAGES)

Years	1990	1991	1992	1993	1994	1995	1996	1997	1998
Inflation rate[a]	10.0	57.9	10.9	20.8	10.2	9.1	8.8	8.5	10.7
Unemployment rate	0.7	4.1	2.6	3.5	3.2	3.1	3.5	5.2	7.5
GDP growth	−1.2	−11.5	−3.3	0.6	2.7	6.4	3.9	1.0	−2.7

a. The figures for 1990–1992 are for Czechoslovakia.
Source: Czech National Bank.

As for winners and losers, those who benefited most from the transformation took advantage of the privatization process, the capital concentration, and the lack of transparency of the financial markets. Although the situation of pensioners and young families with children remains rather difficult, in general, given the rather generous social security system, it is not the lower social groups who are considered the main losers of the transformation.

Undoubtedly, the middle class has been the main relative loser, although in absolute terms, many people in this group are still winners. In this context, the Czech middle class includes small entrepreneurs, teachers, medical doctors, scientists, artists, and other people, that is, very often people who are expected to form the main driving force of the "new Czech capitalism." The Czech Romanies, whose situation seems almost hopeless now, are also losers. Only if the CR is able to cope adequately with the problem of rising unemployment will social cohesion not deteriorate in the course of integration and after accession.

Public Opinion

Most public opinion surveys in the CR reflect, after the initial euphoria at the beginning of the transformation, an atmosphere of disillusionment now all over the country. This disappointment results from the deep economic crisis in the country and expectations of the population that were too high in the first years of the transformation.

Public support for EU accession has decreased somewhat recently, but quantifying this support depends very much on the particular methodology applied and the type of question it poses. According to the Stredisko Empirickych Vyzkumu (Center for Empirical Research), almost 64 percent of respondents favored the CR's entry into the EU in March 1999, compared with 72 percent in July 1998. This support has decreased among the members of all political parties but, significantly, the number of Czech citizens who oppose EU accession has not increased. Table 6.2 shows the development of the support of CR's entry into the EU done by the Institut pro Vyzkum Verejneho Mineni (Institute for Research of Public Opinion).

TABLE 6.2 SUPPORT OF THE CR'S ENTRY INTO THE EU (PERCENTAGES)

Answer	May '93	Mar '96	Nov '96	Jan '97	Sep '97	Feb '98
Yes	66	42	51	58	58	61
No	12	21	26	23	22	15
Does not know	22	37	23	19	20	24

Source: Institut pro Vyzkum Verejneho Mineni (Institute for Research of Public Opinion).

Factors Affecting the Evolution of Winners and Losers

Trade

The orientation of the Czechoslovak and later the Czech foreign trade has changed dramatically in the transformation period. The liberalization of foreign trade in 1991 more or less coincided with the loss of eastern markets after the abolition of Comecon. The Czechoslovak currency was devalued three times at the beginning of the transformation, and the undervalued crown helped the domestic exporters very much in finding new markets for their products.

Table 6.3 shows the radical change of the structure of Czech foreign trade. In 1989, half of the exports went to the Soviet Union and other socialist countries, but most exports now go to developed market economies. At the same time, imports from developed countries to the CR increased significantly. More than 60 percent of the Czech foreign trade turnover is now with the countries of the EU, with Germany the CR's biggest trading partner. The Czech consumer has been the greatest winner of this trade liberalization. The quality and choice of goods in the Czech shops have improved enormously.

On the other hand, many Czech firms that had no problems exporting to the soft markets in the Soviet bloc and to "friendly" developing countries, now have a difficult time with their competitiveness in much more demanding markets. Those who will not restructure and invest sufficiently in modernization and innovation certainly will be losers because they otherwise will not survive the changes. The integration process is pushing the Czech producers to increase their productivity, efficiency, and effectiveness. On a macro level and in the long term, the whole country should benefit. In the short term and the medium term, it still may cause many difficulties in the economy with serious social effects.

Services

During the communist era, the importance of the services sector was underestimated. With the impressive expansion of this sector in Czechoslovakia and the Czech Republic since 1989, its share of GDP is now slowly approaching 60 percent. The

---

TABLE 6.3 TERRITORIAL STRUCTURE OF CZECH EXPORTS (PERCENTAGES)

Year	Former USSR and other socialist countries	Developed market economies	Developing countries
1989	50.0	37.2	7.5
1997	29.5	65.2	4.9

Source: Ekonom.

higher quality and larger selection of all kinds of services have contributed significantly to improving the standard of living of the Czech population. At the same time, the shadow economy has expanded the most in the services sector.

Despite improvements, the quality of services offered in the CR still lags behind that in most developed countries, particularly but not only in the tourism sector. The inferior quality of tourist services often does not correspond to the world prices charged for them. The worst example is the taxi service in Prague, even mentioned in most tourist guidebooks as one of the most dishonest ones in the world. Another example is the different pricing for Czechs and foreigners in many restaurants and hotels. The integration process is exerting pressure both directly and indirectly on the improvement of the quality of the Czech service sector, which hardly will reach EU standards before the accession.

Capital Markets

Securities are traded not only on the Prague Stock Exchange, founded in July 1992, but also at the RM-system,[1] founded in connection with voucher privatization. The RM-system mainly is a service for small shareholders who can buy and sell their shares directly without brokers. The capital market in the CR is small, compared with the level of its economic development. It is particularly small in view of the CR's objective to become a full-fledged market economy.

The Czech capital market also lags behind the capital markets in Warsaw and Budapest, which have much higher credibility and better reputations and which also are much more interesting for primary issuers. The capital market in the CR does not sufficiently perform the price-formation function, without which it cannot satisfactorily perform an allocation function and compete with the banking system.

The development of the Czech capital market has resulted in winners and losers because of the lack of transparency and irregularities associated with it. The Czech capital market was established for voucher privatization and has a long way to go to become a standard market. The process of voucher privatization was relatively fair at the beginning because, initially, the same rules applied to everybody.

The idea was not to give everybody an equal share, but rather, that the whole process is like a lottery. Like any lottery, some would be lucky and some not so lucky, but the end result would have been fair. In the CR, however, a group of insiders with privileged information and personal contacts benefited at the expense of minority shareholders.

It happened this way: At the conclusion of the second wave of voucher privatization at the end of 1994, ownership of large enterprises clearly had become excessively dispersed and there was a need to concentrate capital. At the same time, there was also demand for the establishment of strong domestic capital groups that would could compete with foreign institutional investors.

Some groups had a vested interest in keeping the capital market as transparent as possible for as long as possible. These groups managed to influence the government to establish rules of the game that would suit them best and allow them to have privileged access to information. At the same time, the protection of minority shareholders was completely ignored.

Consequently, a few clever insiders took advantage of the situation and have become enormously rich very quickly with minimum effort, at the expense of others and without having created anything positive. From this point of view, the Czech way of capital concentration was extremely unfair to millions of small Czech shareholders, because only a relatively small number of people really benefited from it.

This group of insiders probably invested their gains abroad, as substantial capital outflows from the country. At the same time, most Czech enterprises privatized by vouchers remain seriously undercapitalized. Their performance generally has remained poor, and they cannot contribute sufficiently either to economic growth or to the state budget in the form of taxes. Still, the Czech capital market has not played an important role in the development of the Czech economy thus far.

The big wave of capital concentration in 1995–1996 is over, but it has not brought the desired macroeconomic effect. With a downturn in GDP growth, the worst thing about the process of capital concentration, the accompanying unethical and criminal activities, has done a lot of damage not only to the image of the Czech capital market but also to the reputation of the whole country. This process also has aroused feelings of injustice, unfairness, and disgust in the Czech population.

Before entering the EU, the CR needs to have standard financial markets regulated according to standards applied in developed market economies. The introduction of EU standards could bring more justice and fair play to these markets. With proper regulations, the Czech capital market could contribute to economic growth in the future.

Labor Market

Unlike most other countries in transition, during many years of the transformation, unemployment in the CR was very low and not an issue that needed to be addressed. On the contrary, the CR had a serious labor shortage in many enterprises and state institutions. Changing rapidly now, the unemployment rate is quickly approaching 9 percent and was expected to surpass 10 percent by the end of 1999.

The major obstacle to addressing the unemployment problem is the low mobility of the labor force, partly due to tradition (the reluctance to move) and partly to the shortage of apartments, especially where economic activities are expanding.

The skilled but relatively cheap Czech labor force is approximately one-fifth the cost of the EU average, though recently, it has been rapidly approaching the level of the EU's poorest countries. Nevertheless, total labor costs of one employee are only around 6,000 EUR (220,000 CZK) per year in the CR, compared with 11,000 EUR in Portugal and 19,000 EUR in Greece, according to recent data.[2]

The combination of skilled labor force and low labor costs should make the country very attractive for foreign capital, but in the CR, bad laws and sometimes bad experiences discourage many potential foreign investors. Moreover, labor productivity is still much lower than in developed market economies, due in part to underinvestment in human capital in the country.

Another issue is the labor coming to the CR from abroad, especially from Ukraine and the Balkan countries. While foreign labor often works where it is difficult to find Czech workers, many foreigners also work in the CR illegally.

Finally, accession will bring new work opportunities in the EU countries for many Czechs. At the same time, some people from EU countries also may find interesting jobs in the CR.

Institutions Linked to the Integration Process

The Ministry of Foreign Affairs, in charge of coordinating the negotiations with the EU, has two departments for this work: one for political relations with the EU and another to coordinate other relationships with the EU. A deputy minister, the main negotiator, is responsible for coordinating the negotiations with the EU. The Chamber of Deputies also recently established a Committee for European Integration, but not as part of the Ministry of Foreign Affairs.

As of January 1, 1995, the Czech Republic had established the following institutions for the country's accession into the EU:

- The Government Committee for European Integration (its chairman is the Vice-Premier for Foreign and Security Policy);

- The Working Committee for the Implementation of the European Agreement (now called Working Committee for European Integration); and

- Working Groups (about 35 of them more or less correspond to the 31 chapters of the *acquis communautaire*; they deal with taxes, the environment, research and development, and other issues).

Besides the Ministry of Foreign Affairs and other ministries, the main institutions involved in the distribution of PHARE funds are the Delegation of the European Commission in Prague and the Centre for Foreign Assistance. The Czech Invest Agency also plays a special role in foreign investment, and the Czech Trade Agency plays a similar role in foreign trade promotion. An important institution in human resources development is the National Training Fund.

Although the system of institutions linked to the integration process looks very sophisticated, it is not very flexible or efficient. The main cause of this unfavorable situation is the low efficiency of public administration in the CR, which needs radical reform.

The Czech Republic does not yet have regional public administration because administrative self-governing units have not yet been established at the regional level, though the Constitution explicitly mentions them. They may be introduced early in 2000, but probably not until 2001.

Liberalization of Prices and External Payments

In January 1991, the Czech government abolished the administrative method of pricing, and it abandoned the cost-based approach to price formation in favor of market determination of prices. Since then, price regulation can apply only exceptionally. Most prices already have been liberalized, and those not liberalized constitute only about 5 percent of GDP.

The effect of these still-regulated prices on the consumption patterns of households and the behavior of firms is considerable, however, because they mainly concern rents, energy, transport, and food. The distorted structure of these prices has negative effects on labor force mobility and on energy costs for Czech industrial production. They lead to energy waste, housing shortages, and a flourishing black market for housing.

For currency convertibility, all current account and most capital account transactions have been liberalized. Czech corporate entities and private individuals, however, still cannot have overseas bank accounts or invest in foreign securities, unless they get prior approval from the Czech authorities, and foreigners still cannot purchase real estate in the CR. Nonetheless, the achievement of nearly full convertibility of the currency, with the CR's entry into the Organisation for Economic Co-operation and Development (OECD) as the first post-communist nation on December 21, 1995, are perhaps the greatest successes of the Czech economic transformation.

Privatization

Private-sector contribution to GDP is approaching 80 percent but state institutions still own a significant proportion of the equity of the two major commercial banks (Česká Spořitelna and Komerční Banka). Because these banks hold major stakes in many investment funds, which, in turn, hold controlling stakes in many private companies, the state still controls many allegedly fully privatized, large enterprises. These interlocking relationships, often not transparent, have been major obstacles to a quicker restructuring of large Czech firms. Both large commercial banks, however, will be privatized soon.

The transformation of ownership rights in the CR during 1991–1996 took several forms: restitution, transfer of state property to municipalities, small- and large-scale privatization, and transformation of agricultural and other cooperatives. The year 1948 was fixed as the time boundary for returning the property to its original owners; restitution of properties involving large-scale businesses was practically ruled out.

The small-scale privatization process in which small units (for example, restaurants, shops, service facilities, and small hotels) were privatized exclusively through public auction formally closed in December 1993. Most assets have been privatized through large-scale privatization, using several standard methods (public tenders, direct sales) and free transfers.

Under free transfers, of decisive importance was the so-called voucher privatization, which took place in two waves. The first wave lasted from the opening of the pre-round in February 1992 until January 1993. The second wave took place only in the CR from October 1993 to December 1994. The Slovaks decided not to do the second wave of voucher privatization.

The privatization process is a major influence on the winners-losers issue. Its character in the CR also has negatively influenced the support of the Czech population for the transformation process. It has significantly increased the feeling of social injustice in the population. Many people think that whoever is rich has acquired wealth by some fraud. Although it is not true in most cases, the present state of law enforcement in the country contributes substantially to this feeling. The privatization process in the CR is expected to conclude in the first years of the next millennium.

Income Differentiation

Income differentials rose after 1989. According to sociological surveys, the differentials for individual incomes have risen much more than for households, because lower-income families get significant social benefits that increase their household incomes. The individual income differentials increased largely because of the movement of the highest incomes upward as the lowest income categories remained relatively stable.

In the first period of transformation, social policy was more generous toward pensioners than toward families with children and the latter replaced pensioners at the foot of the income hierarchy. The highest incomes by region are concentrated in Prague (tables 6.4 and 6.5) and by sector in banking and financial services. Income differentiation by branches of the economy is in table 6.6.

Regional Imbalances

Even when compared with other post-communist countries, the Czech Republic inherited an exceptional degree of social homogeneity in regional terms, with all

TABLE 6.4 GDP PER CAPITA OF CZECH REGIONS FOR 1998
(EU average = 100 percent)

Region	GDP per capita in % (PPP)	Percentage of population
Prague	123.7	11.7
Central Bohemia	50.5	10.7
South Bohemia	59.3	6.8
West Bohemia	64.6	8.3
North Bohemia	60.5	11.4
East Bohemia	56.6	12.0
South Moravia	59.1	19.9
North Moravia	61.9	19.1

Source: Czech Statistical Office.

TABLE 6.5 GDP PER CAPITA
(in thousands CZK)

Region	1994	1996
Prague	196.7	283.4
Central Bohemia	86.7	115.8
South Bohemia	101.6	136.1
West Bohemia	107.1	147.7
North Bohemia	96.8	138.3
East Bohemia	98.5	129.7
South Moravia	104.3	135.3
North Moravia	100.8	141.1
Czech Republic	111.1	152.4

Source: Czech Statistical Office.

TABLE 6.6 GROSS WAGES ACCORDING TO BRANCHES OF THE ECONOMY
(percentages of average wage)

Branch	1989	1993	1997
Industry	104.4	101.3	100.5
Construction	111.2	112.3	104.9
Agriculture	108.2	87.7	79.5
Transport and communications	106.4	97.5	105.8
Trade	83.8	88.6	98.1
Health care	90.1	95.0	90.0
Education	89.8	90.3	88.1
Banking and financial services	98.3	177.7	174.5
Administration and defense	101.3	117.8	110.2
Whole Economy	100.0	100.0	100.0

Source: Czech Statistical Office.

major regional inequalities eliminated. The communist regime reduced regional inequalities, however, at the expense of a markedly inefficient distribution of labor and financial resources. The transformation process has deepened regional differences, and they are likely to increase further in the coming years. After accession into the EU, regional differences likely will start decreasing because of various EU policies.

Structural Analysis of Winners and Losers

Significant economic restructuring remains to be done, notwithstanding the progress made thus far. On the positive side, many new firms set up in the service sector have absorbed part of the labor force that has left the agricultural, industrial, and construction sectors. At the same time, however, very little has been achieved in the restructuring of large state-owned industrial enterprises, which still employ a significant proportion of the Czech labor force.

The structure of the Czech economy already resembles that of developed market economies (table 6.7). Since 1996, the shares of agriculture and industry have decreased further, and the share of services has increased. Still, unfavorable developments have occurred within each of the three major sectors, as discussed below.

Agriculture

Czech agriculture has changed significantly since 1989. Gross agricultural output has decreased by 30 percent. In 1997, the share of agriculture in GDP was about 4 percent. The share of labor force employed in agriculture fell from 9.9 percent to 5.5 percent between 1989 and 1997.

Agricultural production has suffered losses since 1991, except in 1995, when it recorded a small profit. Among major factors contributing to losses in agricultural production are the development of prices of agricultural products not reflecting the growth in the prices of components into agriculture and a significant cut in subsidies for agricultural production.

TABLE 6.7 SECTORAL STRUCTURE OF NATIONAL ECONOMY, ACCORDING TO GDP IN CURRENT PRICES
(percentages)

Year	Agriculture	Industry	Services
1989	10.5	58.9	30.6
1996	5.0	40.6	54.4

Source: Ekonom.

Given the relatively small size of Czech agriculture, it will not be a major obstacle for the CR's accession into the EU, compared with other Central European countries, especially Poland. Although Czech agriculture can be considered a " double loser" in both transformation and integration (as a consequence of the competition of heavily subsidized imports from EU countries), its situation may improve during the integration process. It may even become a winner after the CR enters the EU, also depending on how the EU's Common Agricultural Policy will evolve in the future.

Manufacturing

Industries producing specialized, research and development, and skill-intensive goods (machinery, transport equipment, and, initially, garments and textiles) encountered more difficulties in replacing their vanishing Comecon markets with new exports to developed market economies than did industries exporting standard natural resource-intensive intermediary goods.

The steel industry suffered the most from the decline in domestic and eastern external demand. Increased exports to Western Europe could not compensate for this demand shock. Given its outdated technologies and the declining demand for steel in both the world and domestic markets, the prospects of this branch of the industry seem very gloomy.

The machine-building industry, including transport equipment, is a branch of long industrial tradition in the CR. Despite the decline in output, its general revival is quite possible. This branch can turn from a temporary loser to a winner at the end. Foreign direct investment, such as Volkswagen's investment into the Škoda car factory, can play a major role in this regard.

The prospects of the textile and clothing industry, another branch with long tradition, already are less bright. This branch also has to cope with outdated technologies and, at the same time, face strong competitors not only from Europe but also from East Asia.

The chemical and rubber industry suffered less than other branches from liberalization and transformation in Eastern Europe and was able to increase the share of output to western countries, for example, in fertilizers.

The food-processing and glass industries can concentrate on a small number of such top-quality products as beer and Bohemia crystal.

As happened, for example, in Spain, Greece, Ireland, and the eastern part of Germany, accession into the EU likely will cause many less-competitive enterprises to close down, mainly in traditional industries. The expansion of investors from the EU, however, may revive some enterprises that would not have survived otherwise, and new greenfield investment from EU countries may bring many new work opportunities, with new technologies and skills. At the same time, the integration process also is exerting much pressure on the Czech firms to speed up restructuring and modernization.

Other Sectors

Despite its initial expansion, the banking and financial services sector, the most dynamic segment of the services sector, has been hit severely by the present recession. At the same time, the roots of the recession appear largely in this sector. The problem lies mainly with the large volume of bad loans and the lack of transparency in the capital market.

The integration process is the major driving force in improving the shape of the banking and financial sector. It is not only a question of better legislation but also of better behavior patterns. Without it, its improvement would have been much slower. The accession into the EU will bring desirable competition in this sector, which should further improve the quality of services.

The tourism sector also has been a major winner, with a large increase in tourist-oriented businesses—hotels, restaurants, retail trade, transport (taxis), and other such businesses. Though the tourist sector has problems with quality and differential pricing (discussed above), the sector has undoubtedly been a winner.

The construction sector, one of the most sensitive to the overall economic performance of the country, experienced a sharp decline in output directly after the liberalization process began and domestic demand fell. Since then, its output has declined and recovered several times. This sector appears to be a temporary loser but may become a big winner after the Czech economy soon recovers.

Finally, the private sector, the main beneficiary since 1990, has absorbed much of the excess labor force in agriculture, industry, and construction.

Regional Analysis of Winners and Losers

Regional differences in economic efficiency have increased much faster than social differences between regions since 1989, partly because of the equalizing role of the social security system. Nevertheless, the social differences between the regions also have already started to deepen.

An important indicator of these differences is the GDP per capita in purchasing power parity in the different regions, related to the EU average shown in table 6.4. By far the richest region in the CR, Prague has a GDP per capita estimated to be 123.7 percent of the EU average, while the whole CR is at 66.6 percent, according to the latest estimates of the Czech Statistical Office for 1998.[3]

The Prague statistic derives from:

- a specific economic structure of the country's capital (a high concentration of banking and financial activities and trading with real estate),

- a large concentration of foreign and international companies,

- a large number of people from other regions working in Prague,

- a high level of wages in the city, and

- many foreign tourists coming to Prague each year.

The Prague region also has the lowest unemployment rate. The regions most affected by high unemployment are Northern Bohemia and Northern Moravia. These regions are the weakest losers, and Prague is the strongest winner.

TABLE 6.8 AVERAGE GROSS MONTHLY WAGE IN CZK, ACCORDING TO REGIONS

Region	1995	1998
Prague	10,520	14,449
Central Bohemia	8,042	11,603
South Bohemia	7,635	10,525
West Bohemia	7,957	10,811
North Bohemia	7,987	10,959
East Bohemia	7,376	10,240
South Moravia	7,613	10,497
North Moravia	8,034	11,121
Czech Republic	8,166	11,688

Source: Czech Statistical Office.

TABLE 6.9 UNEMPLOYMENT RATE AT THE END OF THE YEAR (PERCENTAGES), ACCORDING TO REGIONS

Region	1995	1998
Prague	0.29	2.31
Central Bohemia	2.57	6.06
South Bohemia	2.03	5.59
West Bohemia	2.16	6.36
North Bohemia	4.80	11.40
East Bohemia	2.30	6.30
South Moravia	2.88	7.73
North Moravia	4.84	11.0
Czech Republic	2.93	7.48

Source: Ministry of Labor and Social Affairs.

Cultural-Sociological Aspects of Winners and Losers

The importance of age (connected with experience) as a factor determining economic success and advancement on the social ladder has sharply diminished since 1989. At the same time, the role of education and skills has risen significantly, as table 6.10 indicates. University-level education has had much more effect for employees in banking and financial services, management, and justice than in health care, education, and scientific research.

The absolutely strongest winners are top managers in banking and financial services, especially in companies with foreign capital. The climate for unskilled workers has deteriorated considerably, and their situation is likely to continue worsening in the coming years.

The contact network played an important role in getting a good post during the communist regime, and this role has not changed substantially, perhaps because personal contacts from the past have contributed increasingly to the economic success of a certain group of people.

As for the winners and losers, it is difficult to distinguish any cultural aspects specific to only the Czech Republic. The many common features, especially negative ones, for the whole region of Central and Eastern Europe include the role of corruption, old friendships, looking for ways to circumvent the law, attempts to get rich at the expense of others, and widespread dishonesty.

Policy Instruments to Influence the Distribution of Winners and Losers

National Policies

In the past, the Klaus right-wing governments refused to establish any explicit structural, industrial, regional, or other policies, though they implicitly implemented such policies, to an extent. On the other hand, the Social Democrats, who have

TABLE 6.10 GROSS WAGES, ACCORDING TO EDUCATION
(percentages of average wage)

Education	1988	1992	1996
Elementary	90.5	75.7	69.6
Special training	95.4	92.9	87.6
High school	101.4	103.7	106.9
University	134.0	144.0	164.7
Overall	100.0	100.0	100.0

Source: Microcensus 1989, 1992, and 1996.

just won the elections, are introducing ambitious policies on many issues and influencing everything from the top. The policies adopted in the future will depend very much on the compromise and consensus of the domestic political forces and on the pace of integration. After the country enters the Union, the role of various national policies probably will increase markedly.

The Potential Role of Preaccession Funds

Before the Czech Republic becomes a EU member, it can receive part of the approximately 7.5 billion euros assigned for all 11 applicant countries from the EU preaccession funds. The Czechs will have to fulfill several conditions to get the maximum amount: to prepare good projects, to find enough money in domestic budgets for cofinancing these projects, to control strictly the distribution of European and Czech money, and to create strong regions whose representatives will understand very well the complexities of the European regional policy.

For example, in the future region of Northwest Bohemia, the intention is to create 10,000 new working opportunities and to support 250 new entrepreneurs. The major problem is expected to be finding enough domestic financial resources for cofinancing the projects. The preaccession funds can especially help to improve infrastructure in the regions. By supporting small and medium enterprises in various sectors of the economy, they can stimulate economic growth and fight unemployment.

Membership and Access to Large EU Transfers

After the CR becomes a EU member, it can hope to acquire about 7 billion euros from the total sum of 40 billion euros assigned for new member countries. The CR and other candidate countries cannot count on such generous transfers from EU funds, as occurred with Spain, Portugal, Greece, and Ireland. Therefore, they will have to make the most of the relatively large but limited resources. The three main policies where CR resources should be directed include cleaning up the environment, modernization and development of infrastructure, and support of small and medium enterprises.

Management of Expectations

At the beginning of the transformation, the political elite, with the help of the news media, has aroused a lot of excessive, or even false, expectations in the Czech population. These expectations, reflected in the results of public opinion polls, concerned both the coming economic boom and the CR's early accession into the EU before 2000. The national euphoria was probably at its peak in 1995 when economic growth was 6.4 percent and unemployment was very low. With the start of the economic crisis in 1997 and the recession persisting since then, however, a wave of "bad mood" has spread all over the country.

The "bad mood" relates primarily to the social consequences of the economic recession and unfulfilled expectations that were probably too high at the beginning of the transformation. It also relates to the feeling among Czechs that honesty and hard work do not necessarily lead to success and that those who cheat, evade taxes, and commit financial frauds will not be punished because there is no political will to do so. Many Czechs believe that this situation will improve after the country joins the EU, especially because of the rule of law. Therefore, despite the "bad mood" in the country, support for joining the EU remains high.

In reality, no economic miracle occurred in the early '90s in the CR as Premier Klaus wanted the whole nation to believe (many problems were hidden under the surface). Nor is the situation as hopeless as the Communists have recently stated (public support for the Communist Party has exceeded 20 percent, according to some public opinion polls). Besides the Communists, many other populists (for example, the extreme right-wing Republicans) have taken advantage of the economic difficulties and political instability and have tried to offer quick and easy solutions for complex problems.

A realistic picture of the benefits and costs and winners and losers of EU integration must be presented to the public, to help prevent false expectations. The NGOs, an important element of civil society, could play an important role in informing the public about various aspects of integration.

The European Movement already has made efforts in this direction. Most recently, the newly established "Impuls 99" has set up a working group called "Integration into the European structures and the international position of the Czech Republic," which will organize meetings and discussions to present a realistic view of the contemporary situation and to look for solutions.

Conclusions

The strongest economic winner has been the private service sector, and the losers have been agriculture and heavy industry sectors. The Prague region has been the strongest winner, and the weakest losers have been the North Bohemia and North Moravia regions.

In social terms, the strongest winners have been those who took advantage of large-scale privatization and the lack of transparency of the capital market because of inadequate legislation and law enforcement. Among the winners are many members of the former *regime nomenclatura* and former secret police agents. They form a relatively small group of people, however.

More generally, the biggest winners have been urban residents with university educations (especially economists and lawyers) in the younger and middle-age groups. The general situation for many people with university educations has not improved significantly, however, either in absolute or in relative terms, and especially, employees in the health, education, and research sectors.

Thus, the middle class, which also includes many small business workers and which has been the main driving force of the transformation, hardly can be considered a winner. Nevertheless, it has justified hope that as integration progresses, the relative position of the middle class may improve substantially. The big losers are workers with specific skills from the declining industries and unskilled workers.

The sooner accession happens, the sooner the CR could reap its benefits. It would help the CR to become an overall winner of accession. Therefore, should the country think it is ready for accession, and if the Commission agrees, then there is no good reason for delay.

One way to alleviate the costs of integration, which could be of crucial importance, would be strengthening the public administration with better equipment and improving its organization and by employing fewer, but more skilled people. As a result, the administration could become more effective, more efficient, and even cheaper for the longer term.

Priorities for Further Research

An in-depth analysis of the standard of living and a comparative study of Central and Eastern countries could be useful. The research, however, should not reduce standard of living to one synthetic indicator, such as real wage or GDP per capita. Besides, the GDP shows only the potential standard of living of some of the country's population.

The research should evaluate standard of living by a whole set of indicators, both quantitative and qualitative. The indicators should be interdisciplinary and can be economic (for example, personal income), social (for example, the level of education, life expectancy, and infant mortality) and ecological (for example, emissions of sulfur dioxide). From a broader viewpoint, part of the standard of living is the internal security of the country, which is very difficult to quantify.

Notes

1. RM stands for "Registracni Mista," which means registration places. The RM-system is another stock exchange competing with the Prague Stock Exchange.

2. From the daily *Hospodarske Noviny* (Economic News).

3. The data on GDP in various Czech regions and their comparability with EU average should be interpreted with caution, because officials in the CR have had little experience estimating GDP below the national level. For instance, a firm registered in Prague actually could produce its output somewhere else.

Bibliography

Kaldor, M. and I. Vejvoda, eds. 1999. *Democratization in Central and Eastern Europe.* London and New York: Pinter.

Machonin, P., M. Tuček, et al. 1996. "Česká společnost v transformaci." *Sociologické nakladatelství,* Praha.

Pavlík, P. 1998. "Is the Czech Economy Ready for EU Accession?" In *Journal of Social Sciences.* Družboslovne razprave, University of Ljubljana. 14 (26).

Pavlík, Z., ed. 1996. "Human Development Report—Czech Republic 1996." Charles University, UNDP Project, Prague.

Svejnar, J., ed. 1995. *The Czech Republic and Economic Transition in Eastern Europe.* London: Academic Press.

Šafaříková, V. et al. 1996. *Transformace české Společnosti, 1989–1995.* Brno: Nakladatelství Doplněk.

Večerník J., ed. 1998. *Zpráva o Vývoji české Společnosti.* Praha: Academia.

CHAPTER 7

Hungary

K. Dezséri
S. Meisel
M. Rácz

The Context: Fundamental Changes in Hungarian Society

Hungary's integration into the European Union occurs simultaneously with two other fundamental changes in Hungarian society: the building of a democratic constitutional state and the transition to a market economy. All three processes are interrelated and, most of the time, mutually reinforcing.

In the decade since the collapse of Communism, the most important accomplishment in security and stability is the establishment of a constitutional state with effective and respected democratic laws and institutional structures. During the past 10 years, the party structure transformed successfully, with the creation of the Conservative, the Social Democratic, and the Liberal political parties in compliance with European traditions, while maintaining political stability. The three parliamentary elections in the recent past helped consolidate the party structure and helped Hungary attain a political structure that is transparent, understandable, and acceptable to its European partners.

During this time, the constitutional state functioned unquestioned, and its legal and institutional frameworks have consolidated, a stabilizing element in the Hungarian political structure.

> " ... [C]ontrary to overbidding, abusing ideology and radical competition, there are some stabilizing elements also in the party structure:

firstly, the insistence on democratic legal framework; secondly, the presence of some moderate and potentially ruler parties which can provide regime stability; and thirdly, the opposition of moderate parties representing the political majority to the radical aspirations of populist forces." (Fricz 1997)[1]

The Hungarian party structure deviates significantly from the European development trends in one important aspect. In the Western European democracies, the historical parties emerged from the bottom up in the course of organic development processes. The same parties in Hungary organized from above and in a fast process, which resulted in an unstable social basis for them. Consequently, each political party in Hungary "...was completely unknown [to] the others, and if the characteristically dominating cultural and ideological gaps among the party elites are also taken into consideration, the result is obvious: enormous distrust in each other."[2]

On this basis, the practical functioning of democracy can prevail through much contradiction and many disturbances. Because of these disturbances, the citizens and public opinion often are very wary and dissatisfied with the functioning of the parliamentary parties. This picture becomes more complicated because the civic organization of the society is emerging more slowly. Only the civic organizations, however, could help practical democracy succeed in Hungary more effectively than it does now.

On the economic front, after 10 years, the government apparently has succeeded in implementing a market economy in Hungary. It includes, for example, the completion of the privatization process and the establishment of regulatory frameworks supporting the functioning of a market economy.

The Hungarian privatization practice radically diverted at one point from those of the other transition countries. This point is the high level of FDI per capita in Hungary. (This ratio was higher in Singapore only).[3] This feature also determines the framework for enforcing interests. Moreover, it has implications on the priorities of economic policy. This particular situation also implies that any Hungarian government in power must consider the process of globalization, even if it modifies the policy priorities announced in the party's election manifesto. The Hungarian population also had to adjust relatively fast to the fact that the government social security nets were not as complete as was required by the numerous social groups adversely affected by the privatization. Due to the size of the FDI in Hungary, productivity increased faster than wages during the last decade. Consequently, the international competitiveness of the Hungarian economy has permanently improved. The economic lobbies also have organized accordingly. Big enterprises and banks play a substantial role in the lobbying of economic policies.

Because of the transition to a market economy in Hungary, the share of the black market economy is high and regional differences within the country are substantial. During the past decade, government policy has not addressed these issues. Government action to shrink the black economy and to reduce regional differences must be more substantial during EU accession and as the institutional structure of a market economy develops.

During the democratic transformation, the printed and electronic media became gradually independent. Aside from being commercialized, they have also become more outspoken in challenging the policy of the government in power.

Foreign capital and the media represent two exogenous factors that the government in power could not ignore without substantial political losses. This situation helps to stabilize and to define the democratic political system. Of course, it cannot take place without any tension. The presence of foreign capital implies that the market remains open and the market participants have to continuously adjust to international norms. Meanwhile, although the FDI constraint may have increased regional disparities, it may also have substantially facilitated the accession to the EU for the winners.

Winners and Losers: Causes and Changes over Time

On the economic front, Hungary faces two major interrelated challenges in the 1990s. One is to accomplish during a relatively (at least from the historical point of view) short period of time the transition to market economy, to create and modernize market economy institutions necessary for its functioning. The other parallel task is to meet the criteria for European integration (motivated by the provisions of the Europe Agreement and by the legal harmonization) and create the necessary economic conditions for accession to the EU. These two major tasks sometimes are interrelated, but in certain cases, they require different timing, sequencing, and priorities of economic policy steps.

The most important stages for reaching the first objective were:

- A general liberalization launched at the end of the 1980s and covering an important part of the economy,

- A radical transformation of the structure of ownership, and

- The creation of conditions favorable for increased participation of foreign capital.

The most prominent means in recent years to reach the second major objective, namely European integration, were:

- Concluding the Europe Agreement to meet Hungary's aim to make it a real tool for preparing for accession; and

- Harmonizing legal and institutional frameworks with the priorities the EU expressed. On this issue, the Hungarian authorities more recently have begun the necessary process of more systematically articulating Hungarian interests during the accession negotiations to gain the most benefits for Hungary.

Both major tasks of reorientation and economic and social transformation obviously are extremely complex and quickly and radically can modify the position of economic and social actors. These two processes also can amplify both negative and positive consequences when they work in tandem.

This section analyzes the effects of past and future steps of integration on actual and potential modifications in economic and social positions. Where applicable, it also will discuss the parallel and sometimes reinforcing effects of the transition to a market economy.

THE EUROPE AGREEMENT

Among the stages leading to European integration in the first half of the 1990s, the Europe Agreement has had the most obvious economic effect, particularly through the provisions to establish free trade in industrial products. (The agreement will deal later with provisions governing agriculture and agricultural trade.)

Liberalization of (industrial) trade according to the Europe Agreement involved radical mutual—but asymmetrical in time—market opening. The free trade rules had an immediate and direct influence after the agreement took effect. The new provisions and conditions of trade relations also mainly induced and transmitted the indirect effects of the Europe Agreement, at least in the first few years of it. These indirect effects include the increased role and participation of foreign capital in the Hungarian economy, changes in the structure of production, labor market effects, and even changes in the public opinion and modifications of the social attitudes toward integration.

The unilateral opening of the member states' markets before the signing of the Europe Agreements (and already started with the implementation of the Generalized System of Preferences scheme) exerted a different influence on the economic actors. A short-term, mainly passive and one-time effect reflected the fact that after the shock of losing the traditional East-European markets, even certain old-fashioned companies could survive temporarily. During a limited time, even those economic actors profited from the liberalization. They later could not withstand the competition from the EU, however, particularly such traditional branches of manufacturing as the textile and chemical industries, and they became losers in the liberalization. The active, long-term effect of opening the market was the emergence of a narrow but potentially growing circle of companies, able to integrate into the EU's industrial market on an upgraded and more reliable level. These companies, in most cases based on international capital, became the obvious winners of the opening of western markets during the first years of the association. They had an important indirect and positive influence not only on the structure and quality of Hungarian industry but also on the geographical location of the competitive parts of the industry. Indeed, this influence is one of the important roots of the growing regional disparities.

Opening markets to Hungarian exports showed certain sectoral differences. For most sectors, the market opened immediately, but it delayed access for others. This arrangement generally did not lead to an absolute degradation of the position of the economic actors. Nevertheless, a few companies assessed it as a relative disadvantage (for example, steel producers and producers of chemical fibers).

The influence of the Europe Agreement's trade provisions on imports, to some extent, is different from that on exports. The increased competition of industrial products in the Hungarian market, as a consequence, swept out the uncompetitive firms in the first half of the decade. The Europe Agreement did not directly influence this shakeout, although the competitive firms oriented at the same time to the EU and to the internal market certainly played a role in it. In the first period of implementation of the Europe Agreement, when its provisions disproportionately favored Hungary, the growing competition in the domestic industrial market resulted mainly from the general liberalization that started at the end of the 1980s. This liberalization focused on the quantitative restrictions in the import regime, and resulted in a large shock. (Ádám 1992)[4] Theoretically, Hungarians could have expected a similar effect after 1995, when the government began phasing out duties on industrial products of EU origin. Nevertheless, no such shock occurred; the effect was much softer than the consequences of the general liberalization. The uncompetitive companies already had disappeared before the customs liberalization under the Europe Agreement, and the remaining firms grew stronger or established solid contacts and cooperation with dynamic and competitive economic actors (in many cases owned by foreign capital). Thus, they could avoid the loser or "double loser" position.

With the transition and the first steps for European integration successfully completed, the effects of future stages of integration may become easier to absorb. First, the existing competitive Hungarian industry can enjoy its relatively strong position, developed during the sometimes painful restructuring in the transition process. Indeed, in light of the successful transition, these industries are now in a far better position to face the consequences of EU accession. A winner's position in the transformation can lead to a similar position after accession. Second, although the process of deeper EU integration may result in new potential losers, their position will be independent of the transition process. The picture will be clearer and the situation easier to handle. Government policies will be able to focus on handling the consequences of the pure integration.

THE POTENTIAL EFFECT OF DEEPER INTEGRATION
First, membership in the EU will impose stricter discipline on respecting the rules of EU competition policy (for example, in the case of monopolies of commercial

character and state (tax) preferences accorded before the accession). By the date of accession, Hungary should examine its conformity with EU's competition rules and company-level agreements concluded before the accession and, if necessary, revise them to comply with EU's rules. This examination may lead to withdrawing certain state preferences and the worsening of the relatively favorable position of the companies that have benefited from such preferences or state concessions. The need for a legitimate, EU-conforming compensation also may arise.

Second, deeper integration into the EU's Single Market will require harmonizing standards and regulations with those of the EU. Obviously, potential exporters will have to make permanent efforts to meet the Single Market requirements. Potentially more important, however, will be the future effects on the positions and actors of the Hungarian domestic market. If a company oriented toward the domestic market after the accession will be unable to comply with Single Market regulations, it could become a loser in the integration or would have to ask for temporary regulation (for example, as did producers of mineral water and chocolate).

Third, many service companies will face substantially increased competition after accession. These companies, fully or partially owned by the state, function mainly in the transport sector (railway, roads, and water transport) and in the telecom sector.

The Europe Agreement did not substantially liberalize the service sector. Indeed, at the time of negotiating the Agreement, many service markets were more restricted in the EU than those for goods. Thus, the Agreement docs not explain the position of the economic actors in the services sector and changes in their positions.

Many service companies will have to face substantially increased competition only after the accession. Companies in a particular service sector will win or lose from integration, depending on their ability to obtain national or Community financial resources, because they base their operations in many cases on infrastructure. Their position, however, may depend instead on the conditions of the accession.

The question becomes whether to postpone liberalization temporarily as a result of the accession talks (for example, for transport services). Without temporary measures, many service companies can join the losers, mainly because of the shortcomings in infrastructure. The relatively large number of requests for derogations in services and in related disciplines indicates the gravity of this problem. Here liberalization and the necessary restructuring will parallel integration.

Fourth, deeper integration also will have a strong effect on the agricultural sector. The provisions of the Europe Agreement regulating agriculture reflected only an initial and low level of integration; they stipulate nothing else than a partial and limited liberalization of agricultural trade. The agreement created limited pressures for adjustment in Hungarian agriculture.

Contrary to the industrial sector, the transition in agriculture from association to membership is not automatic. Regulations of the agricultural sector through the Europe Agreement and policies expected after accession are completely different, with no direct link between association and membership.

In the short term, this arrangement may be an advantage because Hungarian agricultural policy essentially can maintain its autonomy. Nevertheless, in the long run, this situation also can have negative consequences, with only weak pressure for adjustment and little effort to prepare the sector for membership in the EU. In this "comfortable" situation, it would be a mistake not to have an internal vision and strategy of agricultural integration, considering all implications of adapting the provisions of the CAP that can influence potential positions of the economic actors in this sector. Such a strategy is particularly important because the effects of accession on agriculture will be subsector-, and even farm-specific. Who will gain and who will lose also will depend on the progress achieved during the preaccession period to prepare for membership in the EU and on the conditions of accession.

CEFTA

During the preaccession period, the efforts to create a parallel process of integration among the Central European countries themselves through CEFTA emerged as another source of change to economic welfare. The implementation of the Europe Agreement and preparation for EU accession have dominated this period, but the effects of CEFTA should not be overlooked.

These consequences first affected trade and trade-related fields (for example, changes in employment due to increased trade competition), but the results of the CEFTA are certainly complex. Free trade agreements between the Central European countries apparently have become an indispensable tool for re-establishing "normal" levels of trade. (Some of these agreements are more liberal than the Association Agreements—for example, a quicker market opening and more important agricultural concessions.)

Increased trade resulted in additional production, employment, and income and created new winners in those economic actors able to take advantage of liberalization. It also relatively eased the "loser" position of those able to capture markets in the CEFTA countries (for example, exporters of meat and cereals), instead of the EU markets. CEFTA gave an initial push for the export of Hungarian capital to the neighboring countries.

The other side of the coin is that, for some industries, increased competition from CEFTA imports led many producers to lose in the transition. Competition from CEFTA sometimes was even stronger than market pressure from the EU exporters, as was the case of the steel industry in Borsod County, in northern Hungary. Competition from Czech and Slovak steel products practically swept out of the market the products of the Hungarian steel industry in that region. This process, an anticipated cost of adjustment, certainly also had labor market and regional implications. This uncompetitive production very likely would have disappeared later because of the EU integration.

CAPITAL MARKETS

Both transformation and the process of integration have affected the development of capital markets in Hungary. The former played an important role in the creation of the institutional framework of the capital market. At the same time, the functioning of the capital market is influenced by the different steps and measures of integration (for example trade liberalization, level of harmonization, and obligations coming from OECD membership, which is also integration in a larger sense). Compared with the services, EU accession in this field probably will not lead to a potential differentiation of positions of winners and losers. One contentious issue in Hungary is the liberalization of agricultural land, for which there is strong opposition from all the political parties. For this reason, the government may find it necessary to request a temporary derogation on the right of foreign residents to buy agricultural land.

LABOR MARKETS AND EMPLOYMENT

Changes in winners and losers in the labor market also derive from both transition and integration. The consistent implementation of the market economy (for example, bankruptcy law and the limited scope of state aids) resulted in more losers. At the same time, labor market tensions worsened in the short term because of:

- increased foreign competition (including EU),

- a reorientation of trade relations toward the EU (which made obsolete the skills of the workers formerly employed in industries that catered to the CMEA[5] markets), and

- the collapse of the eastern markets.

Structural and regional changes in production also resulted from the reorientation of trade toward the EU. Structural changes benefited skilled labor, and modifications of the regional location of production benefited those who live in the dynamic regions of the country. The potential economic dynamism derived from integration theoretically can decrease the number of losers, but only if labor makes the necessary adjustment.

Employment growth, however, does not relate directly to economic growth. Accession and integration into the Single Market can increase the number of losers in uncompetitive industries and regions, but they also can partly compensate unskilled, stationary labor, even in other industries, regions, and professional groups.

INTEGRATION BETWEEN COUNTRIES AT DIFFERENT LEVELS OF DEVELOPMENT

Most generally, the cost of EU integration for Hungary concerns the extent to which adoption of EU legislation—the *acquis communautaire*—will affect its economy. The EU's rules were designed for rich social democracies with expensive social security systems (for example, the social charter and environment standards). They thus are unlikely to be appropriate for poorer countries. Every Central European country needs primarily market economy rules. There is certainly some merit to adopting such preset rules as the *acquis*, but the *acquis* often may be a suboptimal set of rules for nations in the midst of their take-off stage of economic growth. Quantifying such costs is important, but very difficult.

Increasing the Winner-Loser Ratio: Some Preliminary Ideas

Until accession, national policies will preserve only limited opportunity for autonomous actions and modifying winner-loser positions. After accession, such actions will be more strictly defined by the terms and concrete conditions of accession. The government, hence, should consider acting now to correct as much as is feasible any unfavorable trends in the winner-loser ratio.

The government has requested temporary measures for only a restricted set of sectors or actors and, by implication, would rely on a forced and anticipated adjustment. In the short run, this may be a costly approach because, as discussed earlier, little adjustment has occurred yet on several economic issues. The success of efforts to minimize the number of new loser positions depends now on the possibility and the ability to finance this forced adjustment and on the efficiency of lobbying. A danger in this process is that, although a successful lobbying group will reduce the number of losers in its own sector, limited financial resources will increase the number of losers in other, perhaps more important, sectors. The other solution, to ask for temporary measures after the accession, is not without risks and costs, at least in the longer run.

The government aims to reduce the scope of transitory measures, which seems reasonable, and assumes that, in already integrated economic sectors, the unavoidable selection of winners and losers is over, and the winners are able to face the challenge of full integration. At the same time, this approach will force those sectors opened only partially to integration to adjust and bear the cost of adjustment. This approach also will mean a new distribution of winners and losers.

The ability of a public administration to manage the integration process will be a critical factor in improving the chances of winning. One potential issue here is that the administration's centralized and monopolistic approach to managing EU relations has weakened and, in some cases, even has ceased to exist. This trend results mainly from the increasing importance of the sectoral administrations in the day-to-day implementation of the Europe Agreement, in the preparatory work for the accession negotiations and, more recently, in the negotiations themselves.

The strengthened role of the administrations outside the EU may serve as a sort of training to learn EU thinking and "language." From this viewpoint, the proliferation of EU "culture" in public administration is beneficial. Nevertheless, this situation also has potential dangers. If one ministry's ability to communicate is weaker than that of others, it can get into a relatively disadvantageous position in the process of integration, and not only the ministry itself but also those supervised by it.

A government also has few chances for success in EU relations, if only an isolated circle of its specialists can communicate with EU partners. Therefore, the proliferation of the EU "culture" is important, not only among ministries but also inside them. This "culture" can be an element of getting into a winner's position. After the accession, the existence or lack of such a culture may make an even bigger difference.

Professional and interest groups of a successfully integrated country should be able to articulate and represent their interests not only toward their national public administration but also at the EU level. For this reason, these organizations need training and must participate in the integration process, especially if they must improve their direct contacts with their partners because they may lack money or competent staff. An interest group and those it represents easily can become losers by not successfully influencing respective lobbies in the decision making of the EU institutions.

Management of Public Expectations with Respect to Winner-Loser Positions

The public needs full information on the effects of EU integration to determine winners or losers realistically. The new quality of the Hungarian-EU relations emerging in parallel with the change of the political system in the first years of this decade resulted in illusions. The lack of information, lack of well-founded evaluations of the effects of integration, and unfounded expectations concerning the speed of integration (cherished sometimes by the administration itself) were at the origin of these illusions.

The widespread general feeling of being a winner was detrimental not only because of its simplistic nature, but also because the first signs of contradictions to the optimistic picture led to disillusions. The general feeling of being a loser is as false as the opposite. Disseminating up-to-date information to the public and involving the public in a continual dialogue on a subject can dispel simplistic notions and facilitate the acceptance and evaluation of the realities of integration.

Regional Analysis of Winners and Losers and Their Influence on Regional Stability

Despite its small size among European nations, in both area and population, Hungary traditionally shows prominent regional differences. Compared with the size of the country, the capital of two million inhabitants, a historical legacy, seems outsized. The regional differences generally have emerged over long historical periods. Only in exceptional cases could Hungarians reduce these regional differences rapidly. Such historical regional differences exist between the western and eastern parts and between the northern and southern parts of Hungary.

These regional differences emerged from different religions and cultural roots. Political writers often refer to Hunnia and Pannonia when they mention the eastern and western parts of Hungary. Pannonia integrates with its western neighbors in Europe on cultural, religious, and economic issues. Hunnia has preserved its national features. The cultural traditions of the capital differ from those of both eastern and western Hungary because of the intermingling of German, Slavic, and Jewish traditions there.

During the past 10 years, Hungarians built a market economy based on private ownership and these deeply rooted regional differences. Quite obviously, Budapest and at least a substantial part of western Hungary adjusted to the transformation more smoothly than eastern Hungary. The concentration of the so-called "socialist big industry," mainly in eastern Hungary, influenced this process but, because of better infrastructure, companies not in eastern Hungary weathered the transformation more easily and more quickly.

That almost no labor has migrated between Hungary's regions for the past 10 years partly explains the differences in traditions between those regions. (The Single Market of the EU, however, cannot be considered flexible enough, in terms of labor mobility.) The rigidity in labor mobility obviously relates to the structure of professions. Privatization and foreign capital investment affected this structure during the past 10 years, resulting in very substantial changes in the structure of production and the applied technology in Hungary. Labor mobility clearly is a function of education.

Infrastructure and FDI also have been important explanatory factors of these growing regional differences. Some infrastructural conditions (for example, information technology) can change quickly, while some (such as transport) change more slowly. Eastern Hungary, especially its northern part, is in an unfavorable situation with its transport. Because foreign capital takes rational and optimal decisions for itself within its own or often multinational structures, the regional breakdown of FDI reflects these infrastructure differences. The shares of Budapest and northwest Hungary dominate in the regional structure of FDI. The unemployment rates also reflect this structure. Thus, the social traditions, infrastructure, FDI, and the level of employment are almost directly interlinked in the process of transformation and exacerbated regional differences during the 1990s.

The government in power has the task of assisting those regions to catch up that a transformation has left behind. The Hungarian parliament has endorsed law No. 1998/35, a plan of regional development. This plan considers the features of the EU regional development policy and the pattern of the cross-border cooperation (CBC) programs and aims to develop cross-border economic cooperation. The infrastructure development plans of the CBC programs can integrate these territories. Hungary's original development plan endeavors to ensure adequate financial resources of the less-developed regions, especially for infrastructure development and job creation.

In the ideal situation, cofinancing together with the state can reduce regional differences in local transport, infrastructure, and education. The local public administration has an important role in solving these problems. In Hungary, the relations between the local and central public administrations have not yet stabilized enough. How much this small country will centralize its financial resources remains to be seen.

The relations between Hungary and the EU have and will have a significant role in the development and realization of regional development concepts. PHARE assistance and, later when Hungary is an EU member state, the use of the structural funds in the EU budget can contribute significantly to the development of regional infrastructure. Infrastructure provides a location advantage. The more developed the infrastructure, the more attractive the region will be for foreign investment.

EU relations basically motivate the changes in regional structure because the financial resources coming from the common budget and PHARE program are available only to larger geographical units than counties in Hungary. To reduce regional differences arising from EU financial support, Hungary must reorganize the existing public administration structure, which has remained unchanged through the significant historical changes of the 20th century.

Since 1997, the government and the parliament have considered reforming the administrative structure of the Hungarian county an important task, but the reorganization has proceeded very gradually and substantial changes have not yet been introduced. A significant development is the emergence of various regional lobbies as regional centers develop. Substantial, long-lasting changes expected for the entire Hungarian public administration will affect regions and will create numerous losers and fewer direct winners.

How the need to mobilize EU resources, however, will automatically and substantially change the regional structure of public administration is difficult to predict. For example, according to certain EU budgetary objectives, Hungary can be considered a single region, and even within the EU, the issues of the policies and means to mitigate the increasing tension among different levels of regional development are not resolved.

This regional problem also raises many aspects of the issue of cross-border cooperation, even before Hungary's membership to the EU. A part of the local population has traditional commercial links to those who live on the other side of the borders. Thus, if Hungary joins the EU sooner than the neighboring Central European countries, these cross-border economic and institutional links will have particular importance not only for the employment of people living on both sides of the same borders but also for the continental politics of the EU.

An outstanding example of the CBC cooperation is the development of relations between Burgenland and northwest Hungary. A negative example of the potential importance of CBC cooperation would involve increasing criminality in economically less-developed border regions and their neighboring territories. Preventing this adverse development is an important task in the medium term. The Schengen Agreement itself cannot protect the borders, but the abolishment of economic borders and the integration of infrastructures on both sides of the border will do so. The level of economic development and public administration obviously cannot be separated from the issue of cross-border cooperation.

Regional differences in Hungary have increased enough that they can cause serious political tension in the medium run, unless significant and effective changes take place. Extreme radical political forces may influence the population of the underdeveloped regions. For the past 10 years, such situations have not emerged, but such a possibility cannot be ruled out.

Cultural-Sociological Aspects of Winners and Losers

Recent research in Hungary has reached several tentative conclusions regarding the cultural and sociological characteristics of winners and losers from EU accession. First, it suggests that mainly men but not women consider themselves to be winners of the integration. Second, developments of the past decade obviously suggest that young, mobile, and skilled people have better chances of being winners because they live primarily in the dynamic western regions of the country and in the capital.

Third, certain groups of the population feel that integration can damage their position. They base their opposition to accession on fears that membership in the EU would destroy the deeply rooted system of their sometimes informal but profitable social relations. These groups include agricultural lobbies, interest groups and trade unions in the transport services, and local interest groups seeking development financing. These groups know well how to articulate and defend their interests in today's Hungary, how to argue for and acquire different state aids. They have well-established contacts, they know the "language" and the way of thinking of the country's administration, and they know how to successfully argue for improving their position in the national redistribution.

After the accession, however, this "specific" knowledge will have less value because an increasing share of the redistribution and the funds will come from the EU level. This completely new situation will have new and, at first, unknown rules, a new system of contacts, and new partners in the decisionmaking positions. The process of acquiring the new "subsidy mentality" evidently would lead to a new distribution of power among these groups.

In the tasks of a communication strategy is a certain asymmetry between winners and losers. "Winners" usually cause fewer problems and difficulties. While they certainly may exercise important pressure on the government's actions in the process of integration, they may themselves play a role in positively influencing public opinion. Coping with absolute or relative losing positions, the most important task of the communication strategy, is more complicated.

Indeed, articulation of the interests of the "losers" is different. Social groups in loser or non-winner (relative loser) positions are weakly organized and heterogeneous, but they can form a tacit opposition against integration. (These groups include elderly people, unskilled and unemployed workers, and people who do not speak foreign languages). In these cases, communication work has to be concentrated on the circle of civic organizations. Another group of losers or relative losers are those who are organized along strong political, professional, or regional pressure groups and can exercise their influence on the high political level (for example, agricultural organizations). Here, establishing an interactive, problem-oriented, solid partnership (if necessary institutionalized partnership) can play a decisive role.

In the past few years, several research companies have increased the number of regular investigations of the sociological and cultural aspects in Hungary. In the later stages of this research, it would be useful to analyze the emerging new and changing old tendencies.

Overall Conclusions and Priorities of Further Research

The balance of costs and benefits of Hungary's accession to the EU cannot be predicted unambiguously. One may and should, however, try to quantify them. But, what might be more important is that these costs will not be distributed evenly within any society, including Hungary. There will be losers and beneficiaries among various social groups and individuals. In most cases, the position will be temporary, only because integration into the EU is a complex process and its long-term effects are important to consider. The unequal distribution of advantages and disadvantages in the society will appear first in employment and earnings. Quantifying these effects is not easy at all, but several of them can at least be identified, which may serve as some basis of interest formation and necessary policy creation.

Precise distinctions are difficult or almost impossible between costs arising from the process of transition to a market economy and the costs of necessary changes required by the accession to the EU. The two groups of tasks closely link to each other because the main current political aims are the implementation of a well-functioning market economy and the endeavor to integrate with the EU. A full membership in the EU can occur only when a nation already has implemented a market economy. Making distinctions between the two types of costs obviously has serious difficulties. Nevertheless, for practical reasons, this analysis must define a standard of costs of EU accession. One approach is to consider as costs of accession those costs and expenditures incurred either to fulfill the criteria required by EU documents or to achieve the worst or minimum levels performed by any EU member state.

This analysis would allocate the costs of accession to the EU in different ways. Thus, their effects, which can vary widely, can be observed according to economic sectors or geographical regions. Some economic sectors can be affected more than others and, likewise, geographical regions can respond to the same influences very differently.

The winner-loser positions in the economy will change from the first steps of integration until the date of accession, both absolutely and relatively. Hungary has no solid means to improve the situation of losers and to create new opportunities for them because its welfare functions have not been extended since the beginning of the decade. In fact, these welfare functions have declined.

In the economic sectors already opened to measures of integration, the main groups of winners and losers already have emerged. After they join the EU, these groups would not change radically. At the same time, some sectors—such as important parts of agriculture and infrastructure—have been partly or completely hidden from integration. So the challenges for these sectors are ahead, which these sectors will experience after accession. The emergence of losers will seem to be unavoidable. This situation could be made easier with anticipated adjustment or, in some cases, with temporary measures after the accession.

Among the countries that already have begun accession negotiations, Hungary is probably in the most sensitive situation because it would have the opportunity to join the EU before the accession of most of its neighboring countries. Complicating the situation, many underdeveloped Hungarian regions are on the borders with such neighbors.

The less dynamic Hungarian regions already had to face losses from the first steps of integration. They probably can ease their losses after the accession with additional resources from the EU's system of redistribution or with cross-border cooperation. (Such Hungarian regions as the southern part of Zala County would profit from this type of cooperation, as would the northern part of Nograd and Borsod Counties with the accession of the Slovak Republic.)

Delaying the accession process would increase its costs. An important and the larger part of the Hungarian economy is practically participating in the integration and already faces EU competition. Only some sectors are hidden from integration, but upgrading them and reducing the number of losers is much easier in the framework of the EU. Certainly, the process will be costly and problematic. For those industries that have not yet faced the direct pressure of adjustment, the costs of such modernization are only postponed.

In the process of integration, Hungary might not be able to avoid "double-losers," but accession probably can facilitate the solution of such situations and, on the macroeconomic level, provides better opportunities also to ease the situation of "single-losers."

Before the accession, Hungary will have a referendum, and it stresses the importance of informing the public on costs and benefits of the accession, both in the short term and the long run. An open-minded dialogue is a precondition of a successful accession.

Research on winners and losers of the EU integration should be open to and consider any new information from the developments of the integration. This paper discusses only possible aspects and roots of winner-loser positions and draws attention to some elements of integration that may influence these positions. Most of these points would merit deeper analysis.

Notes

1. Fricz, T. Some features of the Hungarian party structure and parliamentary democracy. Lecture on 7–8 May 1997 HAS, p. 4.

2. Fricz, T., p. 9.

3. In Hungary, economic transformation of the market linked to modernization. The accumulated net values of FDI between 1989 and 1996 were: US$13.260 in Hungary, U $7.120 in the Czech Republic, and US$5.398 in Poland.

4. Ádám, Török. 1992. "A társulási szerzõdés kereskedelempolitikai vonatkozásai (Trade Policy Implications of the Europe Agreement)." Working Paper, Budapest: Society for Unified Europe.

5. Council of Mutual Economic Assistance.

Appendix

TABLE 7A.1. REGIONAL DIFFERENCES IN HUNGARY (1996)

Regions	GDP per capita as % of national average (current prices)	Number of employed persons	Employment 1993–1996 (1993 = 100%)	Unemployment in %	Monthly net average wage as % of national average	Number of registered companies end of 1996	Number of companies with foreign interests end of 1996	Regional distribution of quoted capital in %
Central Hungary	147.5	807,181	82.1	7.6	117.6	424,783	14,560	62.5
Budapest	186.2	671,293	83.9	8.0	121.8	330,471	12,921	54.2
Pest County	73.5	135,888	82.4	6.9	96.8	94,312	1,639	8.3
Central Trans-Danubia	91.2	255,686	87.6	9.6	97.4	106,886	1,815	7.5
Fehér County	102	101,060	92.3	8.3	102.9	39,267	529	3.1
Komárom-Esztergom County	89.3	66,974	8.0	12.3	95.8	28,035	528	3.1
Veszprém County	80.2	87,652	86.2	8.8	92.4	39,584	758	1.3
West Trans-Danubia	104.6	259,861	88.5	6.6	93.7	96,113	2,955	8.9
Győr-Moson-Sopron County	110.1	110,424	89.7	6.3	96.5	39,865	1,274	4.9
Vas County	108.8	75,816	90.4	5.2	91.3	22,341	678	2.7
Zala County	93.2	73,621	85.1	8.5	92.1	15,022	1,003	1.3
South Trans-Danubia	79.5	214,021	82.6	8.6	91.1	107,890	1,943	3.3
Baranya County	77.1	86,110	78.6	7.2	92.5	41,960	994	2.1
Somogy County	74.9	70,365	85.3	9.1	89.2	42,849	679	0.8
Tolna County	89.6	57,546	83.7	10.3	92.9	23,081	270	0.3
North Hungary	68.6	271,683	85.1	14.2	89.8	83,884	787	8.5
Borsod-Abaúj-Zemplén County	70.4	164,075	86.1	14.7	90.2	47,291	352	6.1
Heves County	72.8	66,604	84.3	12.0	92.3	23,212	270	1.9
Neves County	56.8	41,004	82.2	14.6	84.1	13,381	165	0.5

North Great Plaine	70.2	299,334	85.8	12.0	87.3	106,224	4.5
Hajdú-Bihar County	77.8	114,118	85.5	12.3	89.7	40,421	2.9
Jász-Nagykun-Szolnok County	75.7	88,085	85.1	12.3	88.0	28,350	0.9
Szabolcs-Szatm.-Bereg County	59.1	97,131	86.8	11.4	83.8	37,453	0.7
South Great Plaine	81.1	280,476	83.2	7.7	89.4	123,236	4.8
Bács-Kiskun County	75.6	105,287	65.8	8.5	87.2	48,494	1.4
Békés County	75.9	79,908	83.2	8.7	88.6	30,257	0.9
Csongrád County	92.9	95,281	81.4	5.8	92.4	44,485	2.5

Source: Central Statisztikal Office Annual Report 1996.

CHAPTER 8

Poland

Maria Karasińska-Fendler
Elżbieta Skotnicka-Illasiewicz
Kazimierz Sobotka
Janusz Świerkocki

European Institute
Lodz, Poland

From Transformation to Integration

Poland's integration to the EU is a strategic goal, seen as an anchor of the transformation process that may consolidate the process of democratization and systemic reforms and accelerate its economic development.[1] It means that the integration process links directly to general, systemic transformation and the process of opening up Poland's economy to market rules, global challenges, and an international approach to decisionmaking. That revolutionary change, inaugurated with the fundamental and successful effort of the "Solidarity" movement in the destruction of the post-Yalta political order in Europe, led to the destruction of the Iron Curtain and to the progressive inclusion of Central Europe again into the geopolitical and economic map of Europe.

An enormous political mobilization developed from residents' frustration with the shortages in the economy and violations of human rights, all of which had become clear to them, thanks to improved communication channels. Several public opinion polls conducted in the first years of the systemic reforms confirmed the enthusiasm and satisfaction of the Polish population toward the transformation and integration process.

At first, the transformation, supported by residents' enthusiasm, did not need the reinforcements of globalization, liberalization of trade, and integration, because the public broadly accepted it. In reality, there are spillovers between the process-es of transformation and integration.

Transformation entails the adjustment of Poland's economy and social system to market and democracy. Integration entails adjustment to the specific rules of the European Union's market and legal system and participation in the policies of the EU, all of which may facilitate further transformation as Poland is included in the funding support of the EU and has to adopt legal acts and other measures. Slowing down the transformation brings into question Poland's membership. Delay in the integration process affects structural and systemic adjustments and, consequently, the success of the transformation process.

Poland's transformation from a planned economy, worn-out and poorly func-tioning, started in 1989. At that time, Poland was widely considered a pioneer in transformation, and its first noncommunist government commanded much interest in Western governments, business, and financial circles. In 1998, not long before the 10th anniversary of the collapse of the old system, Poland again was widely considered one of the most successful pioneers in economic transformation. Given the "green light" by the EU in 1998 on the eve of the start-up of accession negoti-ations, Poland seemed to be once more a front-running economy in the Eastern Enlargement of the EU.

Nevertheless, since the official start of negotiations, some doubts have crept in about how smooth Poland's EU accession will be. Despite economic performance, some observers, arguing largely but not exclusively on the basis of Polish domes-tic political developments, have cast doubt on the country's readiness for EU mem-bership. In the worst case, observers have suggested that Poland might not be included in the group of advanced candidate countries for accession.

This evolution results both from the internal Polish situation and from the internal institutional and policy-driven debates within the EU itself. This paper does not analyze internal EU developments, but it is worth emphasizing that any potential delays in the target dates of enlargement may play an important role in slowing the speed of necessary adjustment, increasing pessimism of the public, and may create a spillover effect of a slowdown of the transformation process as the transformation and integration processes become increasingly interrelated.

Regardless of the pace of transformation and integration, even an observer without the necessary analytical instruments can easily see these two interconnect-ed processes as having both positive and negative consequences. These repercus-sions are distributed unevenly in Poland among economic sectors, social groups, and regions. They eventually may negatively affect the success of Poland's inte-gration with the EU, even if they do not block the process. For analysts of the inte-gration process and for the national and international politicians, knowing the distribution of the effects of integration is quite important. So then, who are and will be the winners and losers of EU integration in the candidate countries?

Who Are Winners and Who Are Losers?

The question of winners and losers is a complex, many-sided problem. Undoubtedly the losers will be those who will lose their jobs, although if they then work in the shadow economy, they may not perceive themselves to be losers.

There are absolute and relative losers. The absolute losers are those whose financal situation would deteriorate, while the relative losers are those whose financial situation is worse when compared with that of other social groups. The latter group would perceive themselves as losers, although in absolute terms they may not be worse off. Political factors also influence a person's sense of being an absolute or a relative loser.

An analysis of winners and losers should examine the balance of benefits and costs from economic, social, and political viewpoints. The economic perspective tends to be more objective because it can be measured, while the social viewpoint includes individual perceptions of real processes, attitudes that various factors (such as the news media or politicians) can influence and, in particular, residents' own—not necessarily objective—views of their situations. This report considers these circumstances in an attempt to identify obvious and possible winners and losers in the integration and transformation processes.

Political Aspects

Politics and Politicians

The general political objectives of Poland's integration with the EU include consolidating the results of democratic and systemic transformation, accelerating economic development, strengthening political stabilization, and increasing the security of the country and of the region. From this perspective, EU membership that contributes to extended security, democracy, safeguarding human rights, and stability of rules of law is a win for all residents and the country as a whole.

Membership in the EU requires fulfillment of the Copenhagen criteria, apart from the whole package of legal adjustments. Within the political framework, the Copenhagen criteria are of crucial value to residents. Poland has adopted all of the necessary legislation and fulfilled those criteria, which means guarantees for protecting human rights within a fully democratic political system. In that respect, all residents are beneficiaries of the transformation and integration processes. Special winners are those persecuted for political reasons and minorities. Possible losers are people previously involved in executing nondemocratic rules (that is, the security service).

A political analysis of "winners and losers" of integration in the candidate countries might use an institutional approach, because institutions determine (Steinmo, Thelen, and Longstreth 1992, Weaver and Rockman 1993):

- the capacity of governments to legislate and implement policies,

- the strategies of political or economic actors by virtue of the opportunities and constraints they provide,

- the distribution of power among political or economic actors, and

- who the actors are and how the actors conceive their interests.

This approach does not mean that only institutions alone determine state capacities, actors' strategies, and so forth, but that institutions operate within—and must be understood in the context of—the broader social, economic, and political setting in which they are embedded.

During the 10 years of transformation and integration in Poland:

- The parameters of economic policy debate have changed quite fundamentally, accompanied by subtle and not-so-subtle institutional changes (privatization of state enterprises, decentralization of wage bargaining, increased autonomy of central banks, the growth of legislation in line with European Union regulations, and others);

- The democratization of political life has led to the involvement of more actors in the political arena and the diversification of programs and channels of their participation in the political life of the country;

- The substantial change of the legal system has created a new institutional environment;

- The democratic, market-oriented, and systemic transformation has differentiated how residents form opinions (as opposed to the pretransformation period);

- Unions, firms, parties, nongovernmental organizations, self-governments, and electoral systems have become institutions clearly involved in the integration process; and

- Residents' potential opportunities in the participation in the decisionmaking process have increased substantially.

Assuming that, within the institutional approach, the potential winners of the process gather or increase power to articulate their interests, and losers yield or decrease that power, it might be said that the involvement of residents and of numerous partners in the decisionmaking process puts all new actors of the process on the side of winners. In that perspective all self-government institutions, non-governmental organizations, trade unions, and so on, are winners because they were created and gathered capacity to participate in the decisionmaking process.

Political System

A bipolar system (Solidarity versus Communists) developed in 1989 in semi-free elections to Parliament. The Solidarity party's *"raison d'être"* originally was based on opposition to the Communist Party and had to define its positive program (especially after the period of substantial fragmentation and electoral failure of 1993). The Left Democratic Alliance (SLD)—the successor of the Communists—had to look for a new formula to keep its role in the new political configuration.

An important characteristic of the 10-year transformation and integration period in Poland is that governments are based on coalitions, with the president's interference made possible by the 1997 constitutional settlement. As a result, the bipolar system was replaced progressively with a more complex one, in which the key players were: the governing coalitions, strong parliamentary opposition, the president, and the pressure groups outside Parliament (such as relatively well-organized farmers, workers in heavy industry, public sector employees, emerging groups of private sector employers and, importantly, regional interest groups).

"Post-Solidarity," effectively headed by Marian Krzaklewski, is much less well-integrated and less cohesive than post-communism, and the centrifugal forces within the Solidarity Electoral Action, Social Movement (AWS, *Ruch Spoleczny*) look difficult to contain. Three major strands are commonly identified:

- The Solidarity trade union element is the strongest and, in 1999, it was in the throes of transforming itself into a proper political party.

- The so-called AWS, or Social Movement, led by Prime Minister Jerzy Buzek (although many observers believe that this arrangement leaves Solidarity leader, Marian Krzaklewski, in de facto control).

- The "liberal-conservative" wing around the National Conservative People's Party (SKL) and the "Christian nationalists" around the Christian-National Union (ZChN).

SKL and ZChN seem to be competing over much the same ground for those nationalist, Catholic, conservative, and traditionalist voters who represent an important stratum in Polish political life. Notably, just as AWS has its trade union wing, so does SLD (the Polish Trade Union Alliance, OPZZ) and, leaping over a chasm of values, both organizations represent similar material interests.

The post-communist SLD, which Leszek Miller leads, is a disciplined grouping with a significant bedrock of support on the left and a strong trade union base, and it definitely will be a durable feature of the political scene. Strikingly, but not unexpectedly, Polish politics was not fertile soil for any significant noncommunist left-wing political movement. The post-Solidarity left organized itself as the Labor Party (Unia Pracy), but its few MPs lost their seats in the 1997 general election as the party narrowly missed the 5 percent voter threshold for parliamentary representation.

The Freedom Union (UW), the post-Solidarity group with a distinct identity and strong attachments to an emergent social stratum (the new business elite and middle class) also seems to have a reasonably firmly established position, but its elite attachments make it more marginal in quantitative terms. It is also a party with distinct internal right-left currents, but so far any internal debate has been subdued.

The Polish Peasants' Party (PSL) found itself squeezed in the 1997 election by SLD from the left and AWS on the right, but it is easily capable of making a comeback, given the importance of Poland's rural interests. Political parties that succeeded the Solidarity movement differentiate their positions toward integration. Some of them, especially from the extreme conservative right, are strictly against integration (such as the Confederation for Independent Poland, KPN, or Republican League, LR).

They do not have many members in Parliament, but they happen to be very vocal with street actions, and they have an audience reflected in public opinion polls. A core of AWS is positive about integration, but with special care of the defense of national interests. The ZChN changed its position from extremely against integration to conditionally supporting it. The UW, the most pro-integration party of the Solidarity tradition, wants quick membership.

SLD became a pro-integration party after it was neutral (in fact, silent) about it. PSL, a successor to the former United Peasants' Party (ZSL), acting during communist rule, situates itself with losers in the Europe Agreement, although it accepts the potential of being a winner if Poland is included in the complete system of support offered by the CAP.

An important actor in Poland's political scene is the Church. Its position toward integration has evolved from being rather hesitant to supportive, especially since the bishops' visit to Brussels in 1997. The position of individual priests and bishops, however, notably happens to differ from the official position of the Conference of Bishops. As the number of practicing Catholics has decreased systematically since 1992, one may wonder whether the Church as an institution will not lose from these processes.

Individual representatives of the Church have interpreted this decline as a consequence of the materialism of current lifestyles, linked to opening up information channels and developing the markets, and all resulting from transformation and integration. They even express their positions as definitely against integration. A very vocal representative is Father Rydzyk, the priest whose Radio Mary (Radio Maryja) hundreds of thousands of people hear.

One of the most important characteristics of the present political system is the decentralization of power that has happened in two steps. First, at the beginning of transformation, the communities (*gminy*) gained the capacity for self-governance. Second, reform of the administrative system of the country transferred substantial competencies from the national government to self-governing voivodships (provinces) and *powiaty* (counties).[2]

Preparations for future EU membership largely stimulated this reform because it was necessary to create a structure compatible with that in EU member countries. The new institutions, given substantial powers at regional and local levels, evidently are winners of the integration process. Those voivodships that lost their status in the reform process that reduced their numbers to 16 from 49 appear in this context as losers.

Last but not least, another change within the political system is officially establishing the roles of several partners whose opinions the government, the Parliament, and regional and local authorities should consider. These partners—including the trade unions and other social partners, several lobbies, and nongovernmental organizations—became active in the decisionmaking process and as such, generally, are winners in the transformation and integration.

The trilateral commission, which must be consulted in all important matters for employers and employees, has not been involved much in the integration process. Observers expect, however, that it will intervene more with the developing dynamics of negotiations. Within that perspective, its future involvement may reveal more of its perception of being a winner or a loser.

Trade unions—more diversified than the bipolar system of the communist era (Solidarity versus the official trade union OPZZ) and more vocal in some issues, such as agriculture, medical doctors, and nurses—articulate their opinions on several matters without special concentration on integration problems. The exception is miners, who make the clear link between the necessary cuts in production and preparations for membership.

The Polish labor movement, as noted, is closely intertwined with the party political arena. Solidarity is still an active player, although its influence is much diminished since 1980 or the early 1990s. Its strongest bases are heavy industry, defense industry, and larger state enterprises (such as the Ursus tractor factory outside Warsaw). The post-communist OPZZ trade union federation is much larger in membership (4.5 million, compared with Solidarity's 1.5 million) and is well-represented in the same, generally state-owned, sectors.

Because of the intricate link between trade unions and political parties in Poland, Solidarity and OPZZ take turns leading disputes. The Solidarity unions were less restrained in pressing grievances against the SLD-PSL coalition and much more circumspect after the AWS-UW government came to power in 1997.

For OPZZ, the reverse held true. The exception to this trend came from the countryside, where even Rural Solidarity was swept up by anti-government protests in early 1999. The agricultural lobby led by Andrzej Lepper (an extremely vocal leader of that faction, which blocks roads and organizes manifestations in Warsaw) considers integration a danger and not as an opportunity, and apparently sides with potential losers and may have the ability to slow down, if not to break, the process of integration.

General trade union solidarity seems to be in the past. On the other side of the employment contract, the vigorous development of private business has spawned new employer organizations, but their influence, together with that of individual firms, older-style lobbies, and powerful entrepreneurial individuals, remains unclear and would be a worthwhile topic for further research.

Economic Sphere

Macroeconomic Perspective

The reforms in Poland in the 1990s aimed to create a highly productive open market economy, able to compete internationally. A market mechanism replaced the command decisionmaking mechanism, the privatization process started, and the government gradually created new market institutions and radically liberalized the Polish market. The rate of systemic transformation, vigorous and dynamic from 1990 to 1992, lost its momentum and has stabilized as reforms reached a critical mass. It was, however, the most decisive factor of change in the 1990s.

From the beginning, Poland's government considered participation in the world economic system an anchor for its domestic reforms. As a result, Poland soon became a member of WTO (1995) and the OECD (1996), but its decision to enter the European Union was the most far-reaching reform.

In 1990, the EU included Polish exporters in the Generalized System of Preferences, which helped to reorient sales from the Soviet Union to Western markets and helped many companies to stay afloat. The formal integration process began in 1992, when the so-called Interim Agreement on trade issues between Poland and the EU took effect. It anticipated ratifying the Europe Agreement, which became binding in 1994. The successful implementation of the Agreement gradually strengthened the integration factor in reforming the Polish economy.

Before a discussion of the winners and losers at the microeconomic level, this paper will consider the overall balance of reforms and the role of integration in the performance of the Polish economy in the 1990s. Assuming that economic growth is the best measure of the effects of economic policies, Poland's achievements are impressive. According to its assessments, the European Bank for Reconstruction and Development (EBRD) expected the GDP level in Poland to be 20 percent higher in 1999 than in 1989; only 3 out of the 25 CEE countries are expected to produce more last year than a decade earlier.[3] Poland also managed to curb the hyper-inflation of 1989 to less than 9 percent in 1999 and reduced the rate of registered unemployment to 11 percent.

The role of integration with the EU was undoubtedly positive, but of secondary significance in this success. It should not be surprising, however, because integration was limited mainly to industrial trade, and the role of trade in a large economy, such as Poland's, obviously is less important than in smaller countries.

Polish experts estimated that the 5.8 percent average yearly growth rate between 1992 and 1997 was only 0.5 to 0.6 percentage point higher because of the consequences of the Europe Agreement. Similarly, only 11 percent to 12 percent of the increase in exports and 15 percent to 18 percent of the increase in imports between 1992 and 1997 can be attributed to the integration factor.[4]

As integration becomes more advanced, its positive influence will be stronger. Since 1999, almost all industrial trade with the EU is free, Poland receives more financial assistance, and the gradual harmonization of the law is in progress. All researchers in Poland who have quantified economic effects of accession agree that, in the long run, the benefits will exceed the costs. This is a common conclusion, irrespective of which models (macroeconometric or computational general equilibrium [CGE] models) they use for analysis.

In an example of such quantitative analysis, W. Welfe, A. Welfe, and W. Florczak (1997) estimated that if Poland joins the EU after 2010, its GDP growth would be 2.3 percentage points lower than if it joins in 2001. In other words, in 2010, the Polish GDP per capita would reach $21,300 if accession is early and $19,100 if it is delayed till 2010. This difference results from the larger inflow of capital induced by Poland's accession (private funds and from EU transfers), which should increase the investment rate and lead to the overall expansion of production, particularly for exports, and to the growth of consumption.

Integration also should help slow down inflation. (The average rate may be lower by more than 2 percentage points till 2010). On the negative side, accession at first may create extra unemployment (estimated at 600,000 people in 2010) because of a faster increase in productivity and also may deepen the trade deficit at least until 2005.

Researchers also share the opinion that, immediately after accession, some distortions will emerge in the labor market and in external equilibrium and that the final result of integration will depend mainly on the present and future domestic policies in Poland and not on EU assistance itself. In this respect, keeping the budget deficit under control is considered particularly relevant.

Fiscal tightness seems necessary to avoid the situation of EU funds' and private funds' helping to support a consumption level instead of stimulating investments. Thus, from the purely economic point of view, the much-discussed problem of the amount of money flowing to Poland is as important as its ability to absorb the funds and to allocate them effectively.

Sectoral Performance

The expected overall benefits will not be distributed proportionally among the economic actors. To project what may happen to individual sectors after accession, one can refer to the recent experience as a baseline. The start of transformation shook the economy, which, however, picked up growth after two years of recession.

It was a strikingly good result, considering that it occurred in a country that was isolated from world markets, exported mainly for less-demanding customers in the CMEA or Comecon, and stagnated during the 1980s after imposition of martial law. Entering the Single Market, Poland already has an economy open to external competition. Therefore, it seems that, even in the worst scenario, the effects should not exceed the effects of transformation. What may it mean for the sectors of the Polish economy?

Table 8.1 illustrates what happened in Poland after 1991, when the economy grew in the new environment.[5] One can presume that the sectors that lost their importance are the losers in the transformation and those that increased their importance are the winners. It is evident from the figures that industry kept reducing its share, while trade, financial services, and hotels and restaurants kept increasing their shares. This trend is more or less consistent with the changes between 1989 and 1992 and with what one could expect, knowing that in market economies, production of services dominates production of goods.

TABLE 8.1 GDP STRUCTURE IN POLAND IN CURRENT PRICES, 1992–97
(in percentages)

Sector	1992	1993	1994	1995	1996	1997
Agriculture, hunting, and forestry	6.7	6.6	6.2	6.6	6.0	4.8
Fishing	0.1	0.0	0.1	0.0	0.0	0.0
Industry	34.0	32.9	32.2	28.9	27.1	25.8
Construction	7.8	6.5	5.7	5.2	5.3	7.0
Trade and repair	13.1	15.0	13.5	13.1	14.7	18.5
Hotels and restaurants	0.4	0.5	0.6	0.6	0.6	0.8
Transport, storage, and communication	6.2	6.1	6.0	6.0	5.4	5.7
Financial intermediation	0.5	0.6	1.0	1.2	1.0	1.2
Real estate and business activities	6.5	5.8	6.0	6.8	7.1	8.5
Public administration and defense	6.1	5.2	4.5	4.8	5.3	4.7
Education	3.8	3.2	3.5	3.6	3.6	3.6
Health and social services	4.2	3.9	3.5	3.8	3.6	3.6
Other services	6.5	5.8	6.1	6.1	6.2	3.1
Customs duties	4.1	4.5	4.0	13.3	14.1	12.7
VAT	—	3.4	7.1			

Source: Statistical Yearbooks of Poland. 1995 table 6 (683); 1996 table 6 (687); 1997 table 7 (697); 1998 table 9 (544).

Within the biggest loser, industry, not all divisions declined. Some, such as the manufacturing of office and data processing machines and of radio, TV, and communication equipment, experienced a real boom. Others grew, such as clothing and furniture industries, partly because of the outward processing orders the EU countries placed in the former Yugoslavia. In other words, they were temporary winners of integration opportunities. In the rest of the main sectors, the trends are not so obvious, although agriculture and transport seem to become less important and real estate services more important.

Table 8.1 also shows that the present sectoral structure of the Polish economy is not much different from the structures of West European economies when their GDP per capita was similar to the current level of GDP per capita in Poland (that is, 20 to 35 years ago). If Poland follows those patterns of development, it should expect similar intrasectoral changes.

Trade and Trade Policy

For trade in industrial goods, the consequences of integration will result from adopting the rules of commercial policy of the EU and the rules governing mutual trade of member countries within the single market. Generally speaking, Poland will cede the present autonomy in creating its trade policy, will have to adopt the Customs Code and its procedures, and will have to "seal" its border with non-member states for goods and people, according to EU standards. This situation will have mixed effects on the positions of winners and losers.

During the Uruguay Round, anticipating its future membership, Poland bound the majority of its tariff rates for industrial goods to a level not lower than in the EU. Therefore, the adoption of the CET may create some winners and losers because these rates, as a rule, exceed the rates in the EU. Not many more will win because about 90 percent of Polish imports already originate from various free trade areas.

Generally, the accession will lower tariff protection (on average, roughly from 6 percent to 3 percent). Consumers will gain (especially if the decrease in tariff rates passes on to them in lower domestic prices), but specific industries will face more adjustment pressure, particularly those competing with suppliers from outside EU, European Free Trade Association (EFTA), and CEFTA.

The largest such effects (because of 20 percent to 35 percent differences in tariff rates) may be expected for automobiles, trucks, tractors, hides, linen goods, and watches. Some rates, however, will rise slightly in Poland (for natural gas and bicycles) and benefit producers at the expense of consumers.

For some industries, another benefit stems from adopting the EU customs procedures. They may force Polish customs officers to apply existing tariff rates more strictly. This application may stop imports at artificially low prices, which was a practice to lessen the burden of existing rates and especially eliminate producers of consumer goods (clothing, textiles, and footwear).

In agricultural and food trade, the picture of potential winners and losers is far less clear because detailed bilateral preferential agreements with other countries determine the scope of protection, and the methods of protection are less transparent in these sectors. The agriculture and food industries enjoy the highest effective protection in Poland (Marczewski 1998).

Nominal tariff rates are generally higher in Poland than in the EU, and many powerful barriers still exist in mutual trade. Fast accession to the SM probably would lead to more losers in the agriculture and food industries than elsewhere. One would expect that the government, anticipating these dangers, should immediately start exposing both activities to more import competition. Unfortunately, since 1998, the policies have gone exactly in the opposite direction (Szot 1999).

The free flow of goods within the SM will endanger firms that previously did not export or compete with imports. Even those selling on their local markets will feel the pressure because they will have to comply with EU technical norms (product and process-related). For consumers in Poland, this requirement is very good news. For some industries, however, it may be quite a challenge. For instance, less than 5 percent of the milk factories in Poland now qualify to export to the EU. Thus, free access to the SM will create opportunities only for those that will manage to supply products according to EU norms.

Fulfilling this condition will require investments in modern equipment. Those companies that do not upgrade their technology will find themselves losing. Compliance with process-related technical norms, established mainly to protect the natural environment or to provide social protection to employees, would be particularly costly. The harmonization of Polish law on this issue will have to last longer if accession will not hamper the growth of the Polish economy. Otherwise, consumers living in a healthier environment and firms supplying equipment for environment protection may find themselves on the winners' side of integration.

To obtain a better idea of the potential static and dynamic effects on merchandise trade, Orłowski tried to quantify them for the first five years after accession with a CGE method (Orłowski 1997). In his calculations, he assumed that firms would bear the costs of adjusting to technical norms and of adjusting to increasing costs of labor and that they would take advantage of the additional demand generated by growing incomes. He found that Polish imports would grow faster than exports, worsening the trade balance with the EU and the rest of the world by $4.1 billion. This would require transfers of at least an equal amount of public and private capital from abroad.

Orłowski also found that many industries that were leaders in the Polish economy so far would become uncompetitive in the medium term. Among the potential losers in integration are manufacturers of office equipment, tobacco products, vehicles, textiles, leather goods, and metal products. More growth opportunities would occur in the manufacturing of furniture, clothing, wood, TV equipment, and electrical machinery. Some losers in integration possibly can stay afloat, however, by selling their products (such as automobiles and office equipment) on the growing domestic market

Services

The service sector plays a major role in GDP but constitutes only 25 percent of external merchandise trade in Poland. It means that joining the SM will expose more activities in this sector to foreign competition than in the industry sector. Some of them, such as telecommunications, railways, and pipeline transports, are highly monopolized. They also are politically sensitive and considered of strategic importance for the country. In Poland's external trade, transport, construction, insurance, and tourism are the most important so far.

The liberalization of services in the SM is less uniform and less advanced than for goods, so the potential effect of accession should be analyzed separately for specific activities. The group of winners in integration may include (Pietras and Jednolity 1997) road transport (many private companies can exploit Poland's geographical rent), construction (lower wages), highly specialized services in the renovation of monuments, tourism, computer programming, and exporting culture services.

Lowering barriers between Poland and the EU may result in a fast-growing service trade. Poland probably would import more financial, consulting, marketing, and auditing services, and service networks in the EU will connect better with networks in Poland. In some cases (such as telecommunications), this networking will stimulate mutual trade in more sophisticated services (programming, designing, and computer systems). In the financial sector, the active role of foreign investors (60 percent of the banking industry has foreign owners) will facilitate adjustments to EU law.

Some services, however, may worsen after integration. The national carrier Lot Airlines will face more competition, and Poland will have to invest extensively in infrastructure (airports and control and communication systems) to adapt to EU standards.

In tourism, the so-called "shopping" visits probably will end, because price differences between Poland and the EU will disappear. Subsequently, some regions of Poland (especially in the west) will lose an important part of their income. Only "true" tourists will visit Poland, demanding higher quality service in hotels and restaurants. Integration opportunities for construction services will depend mainly on the extent of free movement of Polish labor to the EU countries.

The same condition applies to business services, although some technical barriers (recognition of diplomas) will create additional problems for Polish lawyers, accountants, or nurses. Therefore, Poland should start to harmonize its education standards as soon as possible. Telecommunication services are much less developed and overregulated.

The entrance of foreign competitors will make life difficult for the national operator, TP S.A., but consumers and businesses may benefit from cheaper and better service. The service sector is very heterogeneous and complicated by nature. This sector may become a particularly big supplier of winners from integration. To facilitate its adjustments and reduce the number of losers, Poland should try to adopt as many EU legal standards as possible before accession.

Labor Market

The flow of labor between Poland and the EU is a very controversial issue in the negotiations. The EU, afraid of immigration of Polish workers, demands a transitory period before allowing full freedom of movement. As indicated above, this demand may increase temporarily the number of losers in the Polish service sector.

Some analysts (labor economists) consider this demand as a way for EU countries to export unemployment to Poland. For instance, the EU's trade surplus with Poland in 1992–1996 is estimated at 200,000 to 250,000 unemployed (Kwiatkowski 1997). Because the trade deficit is expected to deepen after accession, more people in Poland will lose their jobs. Thus, the overall balance of integration for the labor market is negative in Poland, at least in the medium run.

The labor market in Poland has three main characteristics, which may be decisive for winners and losers. First, Poland has growing reserves of labor because of the natural increase in population. This growth might become an asset after accession, provided that the quality of work improves. Notwithstanding some opinions, the labor in Poland is neither cheap nor well-educated. Low wages, with high labor taxes and low productivity, make the real cost for the employer comparable to the cost in some Western European countries.

Poland also has one of the highest percentages of functionally illiterate adults in Europe. These people are losers in the transformation, with little chance to become winners in integration. The poor quality of human capital is a heritage of the communist system.

The transformation has brought here some dramatic improvements. Between 1989 and 1999, the number of higher education students tripled. In 1999, there were 145 private higher education schools that were nonexistent in 1989. Many of the higher education schools are located in smaller towns without academic traditions. Various training courses (such as MBA programs) have become increasingly popular. The structure of studies has become more market-oriented (business management, economics, law, and finance). The education industry, supplying better human capital, increases not only the potential for economic growth in Poland but probably also the number of winners from integration.

The second characteristic relates to the spatial differences in the labor market and to the low mobility of labor. So far during transformation, some employers openly have discriminated against people over age 35, preferring young people with not too much professional experience but knowing foreign languages, ready to work longer than the legal working time, mobile, and flexible by occupation.

Demand for such people is concentrated first in foreign-owned companies, and most of these are located in a few big cities. Workers from other regions could supplement their local supply, but the high costs of changing a residence limit such migrations. Affordable housing, better roads, and faster trains could mitigate the difficulties of increasing the number of winners from integration among employees.

The third characteristic stems from the scale of unregistered unemployment, which probably matches the official rate. Any serious attempts to modernize agriculture and big state enterprises would increase the labor supply significantly. Considering the relative scarcity of capital in Poland, additional workplaces should be rather labor-intensive to ease the problem of unemployment.

The small business sector creates such places. In 1997, 61 percent of employees worked in small business, up from 59 percent in 1993 but less than the EU average (66 percent). Lowering barriers to development of this sector will help to change losers into winners in integration.

Capital Market

FDI has a strong effect on the relative positions of winners and losers during transformation and integration. Industries and regions attractive for foreign investors have good chances to gain. In spite of the economic reforms and implementation of the Europe Agreement, the flow of capital to Poland was insignificant until 1995.

The situation changed after the London Club arrangement. Since 1996, the inflows have gained momentum. According to the State Agency for Foreign Investments, the total of FDI accumulated until June 1999 amounts to $35 billion. This FDI is almost 30 percent of the net value of productive assets in Poland. The experience of formerly less-developed candidates to the EU shows that accession may significantly increase the availability of private funds, an important winner-creating factor.

In absolute terms, financial intermediation, food, drinks, tobacco products, transport equipment, trade, and repairs absorbed most of the FDI in Poland. Comparing the capital invested with the net productive assets of a given activity, however, the role of FDI is less pronounced in the food, drink, and tobacco industries. Branches with a smaller presence of foreign capital will have more difficulties with integration adjustments.

The long-term assessment of the winners' position also should consider that some foreign investors came because of heavy protection in the domestic market (automobiles, trucks, food, and drinks), and are not much export-oriented. Their real abilities to compete internationally will become clear after accession to the EU, or when their privileges end.

Definitely unattractive to foreign capital were quarrying and mining, agriculture, real estate, renting, business activities, power, gas, and water supply. These activities were losers from transformation, but not all of them are hopeless yet. At least water supply offers a high potential for foreign investors, but on the condition of privatization and deregulation. Integration with the EU will stimulate these policies.

The regional concentration of FDI is very distinct in Poland (also see figure 8.1). Half of the major foreign investors came to three (out of 16) voivodships (provinces): Mazowieckie (Warsaw), Silesian (Katowice) and Wielkopolskie (Poznan). The biggest winner is undoubtedly Mazowieckie, which attracted 25 percent of total FDI. Silesia owes its prominent position partly to the magnet of special economic zones offering tax exemptions for investors.

Their presence in a region dominated by potential losers, such as the coal and steel industries, is very helpful from the social point of view. Economic evaluation should consider, however, that the rest of the country simply paid for the attractiveness of Silesia. The voivodships (provinces) in eastern Poland aroused little interest among foreign investors during the transformation. This situation may continue after accession because this part of the country will be on a periphery of the EU.

Agriculture

The Polish agriculture sector employs 26 percent of all those employed in the national economy but produces only 5 percent of total GDP. The average low productivity of agriculture in Poland does not mean that it will cease to exist after entering the SM, but because of economic backwardness, this sector is probably most vulnerable to market adjustments.

At the same time, the evolution of the losers and winners process here is probably least clear. First, the goals of transformation and integration do not necessarily coincide in agriculture. Transformation aims to establish an open market economy, but the strongly regulated and protected EU market in agriculture hardly conforms to such a model. Consequently, food in the EU is expensive.

Therefore, many Polish experts suggest postponing the adoption of CAP solutions until after the accession because such a strategy would cost consumers and the state budget less (Piskorz and Plewa 1995). This suggestion is contrary to recommendations for other sectors, and it certainly goes against expectations of the agricultural lobby in Poland. In other words, the optimum integration policy for agriculture is inconsistent with the overall optimum for the economy.

Second, the shape of the CAP at the moment of Poland's accession and its evolution during the first period of membership is to some extent an unknown. It will depend on the results of negotiations with the WTO and on the reforms of the CAP. For example, from the losers-winners perspective it makes a difference whether the quota system for milk survives only until 2006 or longer.

The other important unknown is the outcome of accession negotiations, first of all the scope of compensatory payments for Polish farmers, and the size of production quotas allocated to them. If the quotas exceed the average production levels during the transformation, agriculture in Poland will develop and more farmers will become winners of integration.

Third, the social function of Polish agriculture is probably as important as the economic one. During the transformation, it accommodated many potentially unemployed people who worked there to produce for their own needs and not for the market. Farming is a main source of living for only one-third of the people working in agriculture. The integration with the EU will be a chance mainly for this minor group.

The majority, consisting of elderly or poorly educated owners of small plots, will have problems applying for EU grants, keeping books properly, and complying with veterinary or phytosanitary standards. The state should provide them with a safety net for purely social reasons for as long as necessary. This specific group neither participated in transformation nor would participate in integration.

In general terms, the winners from integration will be market-oriented farmers whose earnings will increase, because of higher agriculture prices in the EU than in Poland and because of a larger demand in the SM. The average price gap, significant in the beginning of transformation, has been diminishing. Only the production of milk, beef, and sugar beets will generate more easy profits, because production of poultry and pork probably will become less advantageous (Rowiński 1997).

The rising prices that will result from joining the CAP will hurt the consumers, who spend around 40 percent of their income on food. The expected wage increase in the Polish economy somewhat will alleviate this tendency. Long-term winners will be farmers who will respond to more competition from the EU with better quality and more variety of products. This improvement also will benefit consumers. Cheaper agriculture raw materials than in the EU may attract foreign investors to the food-processing industry, which would be advantageous both for farmers and consumers in Poland.

Backwardness and overpopulation of Polish agriculture may become its asset in some cases. The growing popularity of ecological food will create better opportunities for farmers who traditionally used less pesticides, applied manure rather than chemical fertilizers, and fed livestock with natural feeds. Ecological farming also will give work to more peasants than modern intensive methods. Exploitation of this advantage will depend on development of the economic and institutional environment for agriculture. Such activities could get support from the state and the EU. Poland may have comparative advantage in the production of labor-intensive crops, such as some fruits and vegetables. After Poland joins the EU, its exports no longer will be hampered by antidumping duties.

Regional Disparities

Because of historic heritage, the present territory of Poland can be divided into four main areas: three areas of "old territories" and one "new territory." The "new territory" (western and northern areas) was allocated to Poland after World War II as a compensation for the lost territory allocated to the Soviet Union. For many inhabitants, migration was compulsory.

These circumstances have determined the land use and ownership structure in agriculture, demographic, and sociological characteristics of the population, and infrastructure equipment. In this territory, about half of the agricultural land was given to state farms, and the individual farmers were given relatively large farms, so that the average size of a holding is much larger than in the rest of the country.

The other three parts of Poland are territories that belonged to Poland before World War II but before 1914 belonged, respectively, to Russia (the largest portion in central and eastern Poland), to Prussia/Germany (central-western part and central-northern part), and to Austria (southeastern part). The main characteristics of those four areas differ in density of population, size of farms, density of towns distribution, demographic figures, GDP per capita, level of education, and other factors. The transformation and integration processes seem to reinforce the disparities.

An important question that arises from this situation is whether such a differentiation may be compensated with cohesion and structural policies, or whether the transformation and integration will stimulate development in regions that already are "locomotives" of growth, such that the living conditions and standards in the remaining parts of the country will be even more worse off relatively.

The statistics seem to confirm that differences have become more pronounced. This trend could lead to the conclusion that historically well-equipped regions evidently will be winners of integration and poorly equipped regions will be losers in the process (see table 8.2). One element frequently quoted as a lever to growth is foreign investment, and the data confirm (see figure 8.1) the attractiveness of some regions (poles of growth), compared with the lack of investment in poor regions.

In that respect, knowing which solidarity and cohesion policies would apply to Poland once it becomes a EU member will be extremely important because these policies may contribute to improvements in infrastructure and economic growth of the poorest areas. If those policies are opened to Poland, the potential relative losers may become net winners of the process because the poorer regions could be the main recipients of cohesion and structural funds.

Some specific problems link to industrial concentration in particular regions (such as textiles in Lodz, coal mining in Silesia, and shipbuilding in Gdansk and Szczecin). For instance, the region of Lodz evidently would be a loser in integration, if its textile industry loses markets and closes factories, thus raising unemployment, but with no parallel support for retraining or creating small- and medium-sized enterprises. In the longer perspective, if Poland makes the necessary adjustments to market rules arising from integration, with special financial support for employees leaving the dominant sector (for example, the coal industry in Silesia), then a region may become a winner.

FIGURE 8.1 REGIONAL DISPERSION OF COMPANIES WITH FOREIGN CAPITAL IN
POLAND IN JUNE 1995

Source : Profile regionalne, PARR (Polish Agency for Regional Development), Warszawa 1997
(mimeo).

Another specific problem for eastern Poland arises from integration-driven
changes in the Polish legal system. The need for reinforced control at the eastern
border of Poland has led to a new visa regime, which has resulted in a substantial
decrease in economic activities (specifically linked to the intensive border trade
between Poland and its eastern neighbors). As that policy significantly affected
people from the poorer areas of Poland, it has been perceived as a special negative
effect, and residents of three eastern voivodships perceive themselves as evident
losers in the integration process.

Main Policy Issues

High sustainable economic growth is the most comprehensive measure of economic benefits from integration (Orłowski 1998). Another necessary condition is
to ensure a positive overall balance in the winners-and-losers account. High growth

TABLE 8.2 GDP PER CAPITA IN VOIVODSHIPS (PROVINCES), 1995–97

Voivodship (and main cities)	GDP for Poland =100		
	1995	1996	1997
Dolnośląskie (Wroclaw)	99	94	94
Kujawsko-Pomorskie (Bydgoszcz)	91	87	84
Lubelskie (Lublin)	73	73	73
Lubuskie (Zielona Gora)	91	86	86
Łódzkie (Lodz)	98	96	94
Małopolskie (Krakow)	90	89	90
Mazowieckie (Warszawa)	136	144	151
Opolskie (Opole)	89	87	86
Podkarpackie (Rzeszow)	77	76	75
Podlaskie (Bialystok)	76	74	72
Pomorskie (Gdansk)	103	102	100
Śląskie (Katowice)	118	118	115
Świętokrzyskie (Kielce)	73	71	69
Warmińsko-Mazurskie (Olsztyn)	77	75	77
Wielkopolskie (Poznan)	105	107	108
Zachodnio-Pomorskie (Szczecin)	98	98	97

Source: Profile regionalne, PARR (Polish Agency for Regional Development), Warszawa 1997 (processed).

would lead to either larger numbers of winners or more gains for winners. It also could generate more funds for compensating losers or help them become winners.

A resulting policy dilemma is that such growth-oriented policies as disciplining of the state budget would need reconciling with more spending for restructuring of the coal industry and for investment in infrastructure. These outlays may help to improve the balance of winners and losers, as the experience of transformation has shown that the market mechanism by itself has not been able to cope with social protection, and the private sector has been too weak financially to find solutions.

From this perspective, integration will positively influence domestic economic policy in Poland. Regarding economic growth, the adoption of the EU regulatory framework will be conducive to more economic freedom through better protection of property rights, more secure contracts, more business-friendly administrative procedures and regulation, fewer trade barriers, better law enforcement, lower inflation, more investment in human capital, and other results.

The government in Poland will have to observe the rules of common competition policy and public aid policy. These rules are not perfect, but they seem more transparent and more efficiency-oriented than such policies in Poland. Their adoption may stop the practice of perpetual support of state-owned enterprises and may subordinate such practice to the rules of cost-benefit analysis.

This adoption will free up resources for profit-generating activities, which will create more winners and stimulate economic growth. Integration will strengthen the position of authorities (legislators and regulators) responsible for economic policies in relation to various vested interests groups that so far have managed to exert pressure on the government about the use of social funds.

This, in turn, may help the government to earn more social support for unpopular decisions. As for redistribution, the adoption of the EU regulatory framework, based on the principle of economic and social cohesion, may facilitate adjustments in poor regions, increasing the number of winners from integration.

Not all EU solutions, however, are worth recommending. Some, such as the CAP measures, will have to be introduced after accession, irrespective of their negative effects on the whole economy, because they are a part of the *acquis*. As a member state, Poland will be able to help shape them. The others are not obligatory, such as the Social Charter, and may be negotiated. The sequencing and timing of implementation of ecological and social standards should be subordinated to long-term growth requirements.

Otherwise, Polish firms will have to close down on a massive scale. In such a case, better environmental or stricter work safety norms would be a Pyrrhic victory. Some other regulations do not have to be copied at all because they are in competencies of member states. For example, the average working time and the income and personal tax systems vary among the EU states. Poland may choose the measures in these issues to stimulate investments and restructure industries. For example, such measures as training and education would improve the mobility of labor and develop small businesses.

Policies to spread education and training will play an important role from the point of view of reducing the number of losers from integration. Aside from building human capital, discussed earlier, such policies also are important for weaning those who continue to think their welfare is the responsibility of the government and not their own.

According to this thinking, the government should guarantee minimum selling prices, buy the production, eliminate the competition of other suppliers, guarantee decent wages, or subsidize exports. By the same token, the "good" minister of finance should satisfy the needs, regardless of budgetary discipline. In other words, they are convinced the government bears the responsibility for their losing. Unless such socialist-like attitudes are eliminated, any policies to create winners will have very limited success.

Social and Public Opinion's Perspective

Since the beginning of transformation, the direction of change in the social, political, and economic life of Poland proposed by the democratic opposition before 1989 and realized after June 4, 1989, was decisively pro-Western. The changes were meant to lead toward a western European model socioeconomic and political system. Only gradually did the politicians start to understand formal integration with European structures as the objective itself.

The determination of such a long-term objective was based on the strong conviction that it was the only way that would secure the economic well-being and political security of Poland and its residents and protect Poland and the Polish society from falling again into Soviet and later the Russian sphere of influence. It also was accepted that carrying out this objective would imply costs and sacrifice. To abandon this challenge, however, would leave Poland in a marginal position in Europe in economic and political terms.

At the starting point (1989, the opening of Balcerowicz's reform), Poland had an "equality of chances," with no striking discrepancies between income levels and chances for success in both economic and social terms, and the enthusiasm shared by most people at the beginning of the process drove the society. At that time, few people thought about or experienced the gap between those successful and those who might be losers in the process.

The systemic changes have had a positive effect on the situation for young people, opening to them almost unlimited possibilities. The first years of transformation divided Polish society into two groups: the ones who can function in the new economic system thanks to age, education, and mental characteristics (for example, as a man with initiative) and those who will not adjust to the new situation. This division probably will deepen with the rules of market economy and competition in the labor market within the Single European Market. It will be the boundary between the winners and losers from European integration.

Gradually since 1990, Poland has developed a fast-growing gap between the groups at various income levels. The general support for integration, however, has not been perceived as linked with specific expectations of chances to open for individuals. At some stage, the "general" support for integration was very high (80 percent in 1996), although individual perception of success was not linked directly with integration (28 percent in 1996).

The public's perception of the consequences of the integration process has become increasingly more realistic. The currently observed decrease in public support for integration should be interpreted from the perspective of gradual elimination of illusions, that is, overoptimism in the past, rather than actual disappointment with integration as such. In May 1999, the percentage of citizens that in a potential referendum would vote for Poland's accession to the EU was only 55 percent, while in December 1998, it was 64 percent. The decrease in support for integration runs beside the growing conviction that Poland is not yet properly prepared for membership in economic terms. This opinion is not based, however, on adequate knowledge of the Polish economy. Other factors that could have contributed to this opinion are the approach of actual accession and the general deterioration of the social outlook on Poland's future. It is difficult to predict how public opinion will evolve in the near future and how far and to what level the support for integration will fall.

Support for integration positively correlates with the sociofinancial status of the interviewees. The higher the level of education and per-capita income in the family, the stronger the support for integration with the EU. The most ardent critics of Poland's membership in the EU are the farmers, 48 percent of whom are opponents, compared with 34 percent who are supporters. More often than in other social groups, the negative attitude toward integration exists among unqualified workers, although generally there are more integration supporters. The opinions about integration differ among:

- Various age groups ("yes" declared by 67 percent of those under 24 years of age, 38 percent among the population over 65). Younger people are apt to use the opportunities created by the new socioeconomic situation, but, for example, old-age pensioners are obvious losers because they lack adaptability, fear the unknown, and are used to the "comfort" of the socialist welfare state.

- Groups representing different political views: two-thirds of right-wing party supporters and only a little more than half of those representing left-wing positions would vote for integration, but the members and supporters of the Freedom Union (UW) are the most ardent proponents of integration. Among those most skeptical are the supporters of the Polish Peasants' Party (PSL).

The social groups mentioned above (farmers, old-age pensioners, and unqualified workers) are commonly perceived more often than other groups as the largest losers in the integration process. According to *Eurobarometer* (autumn 1997), the public perceives employees of the education system as the top beneficiaries of the integration process (60 percent), less so the workers of state-owned enterprises (38 percent). As for losers, the respondents mention most often farmers (43 percent), employees of state-owned enterprises (35 percent), unqualified workers (30 percent), and the groups with lowest incomes (28 percent).

The toughest problem seems to be among people with "acquired helplessness syndrome,"[6] sometimes called the communism orphans or those who are not adaptable. These people are usually from northwestern Poland, previously dominated by the state-owned farming industry. They include the former employees of these enterprises, a large group of unqualified workers, and all those who were able to function somehow under the communist system.

Since 1989, these groups have been collapsing systematically in social terms. They have quite pessimistic views on democracy and free markets because these benefits have not brought the promised equality of chances. These people also should be considered the greatest losers in the transformation process, but not in the integration process. The attitudes toward integration of this group may be either negative or positive, and further and deeper study should examine their situation.

In an opposite phenomenon, however, the members of the former political system's elites have become the beneficiaries and the chief winners in transformation.

They have been equipped since the beginning with better possibilities (economic conditions, financial situation of families, place of residence, and other benefits). These advantages have enabled them to take advantage of the new possibilities opened by the transformation process, again rendering insignificant the social groups that were the original proponents of the systemic changes. It is common thinking that these elites also are the foremost beneficiaries of transformation and integration.

All political parties that won seats in the Polish Parliament in the 1997 election declared in their programs the willingness to continue the processes leading to accession to the European Union. In the autumn of 1998, the general support for integration in the Parliament was broken for the first time with the creation of a tiny anti-integration parliamentary group "Our Circle" (Nasze Kolo).

Parallel to the creation of the parliamentary group opposing Poland's membership in the EU is the formation of about 30 organizations (registered as various associations) whose statutory objectives provide for actions aimed against Poland's membership in European structures. This breach of the "assent for integration," which so far has been one of the determinants of the proper direction of political development in Poland, probably to a large extent has induced the considerable decrease in public support for Poland's integration with the EU.

Debate on the integration question (integration—yes or no?) has turned into an ideological confrontation. This conflict, in turn, has deepened the division between the supporters and opponents and has added to the dangerous polarization of standpoints among politicians and, in consequence, the voters. All of these divisions have resulted in increased information chaos, a definitely negative factor for the integration processes.

The turning of the integration question into a political ideology by the political elites seems to be even dangerous, because the social consensus on integration is rather shallow. The views presented by political elites addressed to certain social groups may influence their already existing sense of being losers. This impression seems to be the case with the farmers and their party, which are persuading their electorate that the city wants to destroy the peasants with the help of the European Union and let Polish land fall into foreign hands.

Applying ideology and making the "integration question" instrumental in the political struggle is reflected partly in the fact that, depending on the political standing of the politicians (in power or in opposition), the perception of both their own political environment (winners or losers) and the views of the electorate change. The best example of this phenomenon is the increase in anti-integration arguments among the Polish Peasants' Party (PSL) after the lost elections and the increased presentation of the farmers as the main group of losers. Similarly, the intensification of "leftist" anti-integration tactics in the discourse of the Left Democratic Alliance (SLD)—not in power, either—very often stands in clear contradiction to the party's active support for integration into the EU.

In sum, the parallel integration and transformation processes produce a situation in which the losers in the transformation process also are apt to be the losers in the integration process. Whether these losers attribute their situation to integration depends on the news media, politicians, and the strategy for communicating the progress in integration because, as ordinary people, they may not have the proper knowledge to assess the real factors that make them losers. A strategy that accurately communicates to the public the actual benefits and costs of Poland's integration with the EU is important, now that accession negotiations are about to begin.

After the actual accession to the Union, with the opened possibilities of using regional policy grants, the situation of losers—both absolute and relative—may have a chance to improve. This possibility depends on certain conditions, including the framework in which the newcomers in the EU will take part in structural policy.

Further research might analyze the sources of various societal groups' sensing they lose in the integration process. This research should entail economic analysis, based on statistical data and sectoral analysis of production, trade, and services (identification of objective factors). It also might examine psychological factors determining the "losers" and the influence of media and political elites (subjective factors). The sociological part of this project should include opinion polls, interviews with politicians, and media studies.

A particularly interesting subject for further studies would be a comparative analysis of communication channels between the state authorities and the society with regard to integration issues. Given the dissonance between being a loser in absolute and relative terms and the phenomenon of "blame transfer"—that is, blaming the integration process for any misfortunes, which is popular among politicians—the news media and NGOs realized a need for adequate information and educational policies. The number of such organizations is still growing in Poland, and they seem to be the best proponents of integration, thanks to their nature (direct contacts with people). These organizations will be able to present most convincingly the objective gains and inconveniences resulting from the integration process.

Notes

1. That formulation of the main objectives of Poland's motivation for membership in the EU is in the *Pro Memoria* (April 11, 1994), and developed further in these documents: *National Integration Strategy* (Council of Ministers Document, 1997), and National Programme of the Preparation to the Membership (*Document of the Committee for European Integration*. April 29, 1998).

2. Each voivodship is divided into several powiaty (counties), which in turn consist of several communities (*gminy*).

3. *The Economist*, April 24, 1999.

4. Kawecka-Wyrzykowska, E., 1998, 274–86.

5. Strictly speaking, one should take 1989 as a starting point, but it is not possible, however, because of the lack of compatible data on GDP and its structure.

6. This is the attitude ascribed to those people who, after the collapse of communism, have not been able to make a living, because they are so used to having decisions and their livelihood taken care of by the state.

Bibliography

"Czy Polska ma doktrynę integracyjną?" *Ośrodek Myśli Politycznej.* Kraków 1998.

The Economist, April 24, 1999, 11.

Eurobarometer, autumn 1997.

Kawecka-Wyrzykowska, E., ed. 1998. "Ocena stopnia realizacji Układu Europejskiego Ustanawiającego stowarzyszenie między Rzeczpospolitą Polską a Wspólnotami Europejskimi i ich państwami członkowskimi IKiC HZ, Warszawa październik 1998. (processed)

Kawecka-Wyrzykowska, E. (b). 1999. *Polska w drodze do Unii Europejskiej.* Warszawa: PWE.

Kwiatkowski, E. 1997. Społeczne konsekwencje dostosowań i procesu integracyjnego. Przekształcenia rynku pracy i problemy bezrobocia. (processed)

Marczewski, K. 1998. "Efektywna protekcja celna w latach 1997–1998." In *Zagraniczna polityka gospodarcza Polski*, 1997–1998. Warszawa: IKiC HZ.

Orłowski W. M. 1997. "Uwarunkowania i skutki przystąpienia Polski do unii celnej UE." (processed)

Orłowski W. M. 1998. *The Road to Europe, Macroeconomics of Accession to the European Union.* European Institute in Lodz.

Pietras, J., and Rynek Jednolity. 1997. "Konsekwencje Dla Sektora Usług." (processed)

Piskorz, W., and J. Plewa. 1995. "Scenariusze integracji rolnictwa polskiego z UE, FAPA, SAEPR, październik."

Polska i Kościół w procesie integracji, KAI, Warszawa 1998.

Rowiński, J. 1997. "Problemy integracji gospodarki żywnościowej i regionów wiejskich." (processed)

Sfera, Społeczna and Polsce. 1998. *Przesłanki rozwoju.* Warszawa: RCSS, Czerwiec.

Steinmo, S., K. Thelen, and F. Longstreth, eds. 1992. *Structuring Politics: Historical Institutionalism, a Comparative Analysis.* New York: Cambridge University Press.

Szot, E. 1999. "Rynek chroniony przed importem." *Rzeczpospolita.* No. 216.

Weaver, R. Kent, and Bert A. Rockman, eds. 1993. *Do Institutions Matter?* Washington, DC: Brookings Institution.

Welfe W., A. Welfe, and W. Florczak. 1997. "Długookresowe prognozy gospodarki polskiej do 2010 roku." *Gospodarka Narodowa*, Nos. 11-12.

CHAPTER 9

The Slovak Republic*

Jan Fidrmuc[†]
Jarko Fidrmuc[††]

Abstract

The Slovak Republic has a special position in the process of the Eastern Enlargement of the European Union. This special position comes from its close economic relations with the Czech Republic. The economic impact of EU enlargement on the Slovak Republic will depend crucially on whether the Slovak Republic accedes to the EU simultaneously with the Czech Republic and whether the Czech-Slovak customs union will be sustained if the Slovak Republic joins the EU after the Czech Republic.

The potential gains and costs resulting from EU accession will distribute unevenly in the Slovak Republic. Some industries will face substantial adjustment costs resulting from the adoption of EU regulations, whereas others will benefit from increased trade liberalization. EU membership is unlikely to cause a major emigration from the Slovak Republic to the current EU members, although there may be some outflow of highly skilled and educated workers. Finally, EU membership can stabilize the political environment in the Slovak Republic and put the country firmly on the road to democracy and economic liberalization.

Introduction

The Slovak Republic has a special position in the process of the Eastern Enlargement of the European Union. On the one hand, the Slovak economy is oriented toward the European Union and to its Central European neighbors, which already have begun accession negotiations with the European Union. Moreover, the Slovak economy in many aspects is very similar to these Central European countries. This is reflected in the fact that the Slovak Republic expects to join the OECD in 2000, in the footsteps of the Czech Republic, Hungary, and Poland, and ahead of such other EU hopefuls as Slovenia, Estonia, and Cyprus.

On the other hand, the political development in the Slovak Republic has been rather negative since the country gained independence in 1993. Between 1994 and 1998, the policy of the Slovak government headed by Vladimír Meciar, resulted in increasing tensions within the country and several cases of possible violations of the constitution, human rights, and the rights of minorities. This period also widened the gap with the European Union, neighboring countries, and international organizations. The developments in 1999 showed that this gap would be more difficult to fill than expected.

Between 1994 and 1998, the surprisingly weak reaction of Slovak policy, voters, and various interest groups and firms to a multitude of signals confirming the exclusion of the Slovak Republic from the first wave of Eastern Enlargement of the European Union reflects the relative importance of short-term issues in the Slovak Republic. The dominant issue in Slovak domestic policy at that time was the privatization of state property.

The reaction of policymakers and the public at-large also has been weak because adjustment costs are expected to be large and unevenly distributed while benefits are uncertain. Processing industries (including iron and steel industry and less-processed machinery) are likely to face significant adjustment costs, while the potential gains—after the introduction of higher environmental standards and increased wages—are uncertain. These adjustment costs will be highly concentrated regionally, and they already have given rise to strong regional segmentation along political party lines.

Major Developments in the Slovak Republic with EU Accession

The Slovak Republic became an independent country after the break-up of the former Czechoslovak Federation on January 1, 1993. While the Czech Republic secured its position on the fast track to EU accession, the Slovak Republic initially was excluded from this track mainly because of the lack of democratic practices, flagrant violations of constitutional and basic human rights, open and covert abuse of minorities, and corruption in the privatization process. These concerns prevented the Slovak Republic's inclusion into the Western European and Atlantic structures, despite its relatively good economic developments. The Helsinki summit in December 1999 reversed the European Commission's earlier decision and invited the Slovak Republic to participate in accession negotiations.

The developments at Helsinki reflect the geopolitical concerns of EU members, but it is nevertheless true that the Slovak Republic has made important progress on some fronts and has improved its standing with the European Commission. The new Slovak government has undertaken some important changes aimed at improving the treatment of national minorities.

Nationalist views, however, have remained a common feature of Slovak politics. Their role even increased during the controversial presidential campaign in early 1999. Although an ethnic Hungarian party is participating in the current government coalition, the recently adopted Law on Minority Languages failed to gain the support of the Hungarian party, whose members saw it as insufficient.

The Slovak Republic also has attracted criticism for its treatment of the Romany minority. In particular, the Romanies have faced racially motivated attacks and both open and covert discrimination in the labor market. The problem culminated in the Romany exodus to the United Kingdom in 1998 and Finland in 1999. In 1998, the United Kingdom and Ireland reintroduced a visa requirement for Slovak citizens, with Finland, Norway, and Denmark following suit in 1999.

Furthermore, in 1999, the Slovak Republic made little progress on the economic front for beginning accession negotiations. Because of a high current account deficit, the Slovak Republic reintroduced an import surcharge in June 1999 as a part of a macroeconomic stabilization program. Nevertheless, this reform package often has been criticized as insufficient. Postponing the necessary reforms could lower the growth prospects of the Slovak economy in the short run and prolong the economic crisis.

While the Slovak Republic seems to be gathering pace in its progress toward EU accession, the Czech Republic recently has been increasingly criticized for lagging behind in adopting the *acquis*. Ironically, this may remove an important point of contention that could arise if the Czech Republic gains EU membership before the Slovak Republic.

Since the break-up of Czechoslovakia, the Czech and Slovak republics have sustained a customs union, allowing (nearly) unrestricted mobility of labor, and implemented a rather liberal border protection regime. The EU currently insists that the Czech Republic would have to abandon the customs union and free movement of labor with the Slovak Republic and intensify the border enforcement.

The loss of preferential trade relations clearly would have adverse economic implications for the Slovak Republic because the Czech Republic is the Slovak Republic's most important trading partner, accounting for 27 percent of total exports and 23 percent of total imports in 1997. Nonetheless, in light of the recent improvements in the Slovak Republic's progress toward EU membership and the lack of progress in the Czech Republic, it now seems increasingly likely that the two countries indeed will gain EU membership at the same time.

Major Economic Developments since 1989

Recent macroeconomic developments in the Slovak Republic were crucially affected by two major economic and political events: the start of economic reforms in 1990 and 1991 and the dissolution of Czechoslovakia in 1993.

Until the dissolution, the economies of the two republics, to a large extent, were subject to centralized economic policies, both before and after the collapse of communism and central planning in 1989. The reform program implemented in 1991 and 1992 also followed a centralized scenario, without much differentiation in policies implemented in the two republics, although the effects of the reforms were different. This extensive initial centralization of economic policies and a close interdependence of the Czech and Slovak economies were important factors underlying the macroeconomic developments in the two countries since the collapse of communism.

The economic relationship between the Czech Republic and the Slovak Republic before the disintegration of Czechoslovakia had two important features: a high degree of economic interdependence through Czech-Slovak trade and the dependence of the Slovak Republic on a transfer of resources from the Czech Republic.

The importance of this transfer could be seen in the evolution of the ratio of Slovak and Czech per capita national income, in particular per capita disposable national income (figure 9.1). Slovak disposable national income per capita exceeded its produced national income per capita in every year from 1950 to 1991.

Although this difference between produced and disposable national income also might result from Czech-Slovak trade or net borrowing by the Czechoslovak government, clearly the transfer from the Czech Republic to the Slovak Republic was substantial during the postwar period, especially until the late 1970s. The transfers probably increased again in the early 1990s, in response to the asymmetric effects of the reforms.

According to estimates Hajek et al. suggested, the net transfer amounted to 1.5 percent, 2.6 percent, and 4.4 percent of Slovak GDP in 1990, 1991, and 1992, respectively. OECD (1994) put the estimate for 1992 even higher, at 8 percent of Slovak GDP. Hence, the transfers were far from negligible, and their elimination after Czechoslovakia broke up in 1993 had important effects on macroeconomic developments in the Czech and Slovak republics.[1]

The economic reforms in former Czechoslovakia started in earnest in January 1991, more than a year after the collapse of the communist regime. The Czech Republic and the Slovak Republic implemented the same stabilization and liberalization policies before the break-up, but despite this centralized approach, the effects of the reforms largely were asymmetric. The transformation depression started in the Slovak Republic in 1990, one year earlier than in the Czech Republic, with a 2.5 percent fall in GDP. The major effect of the reforms in 1991 again was more profound in the Slovak Republic, with its GDP falling by 14.6 percent, com-

FIGURE 9.1 SLOVAK PER CAPITA NATIONAL INCOME (SOLID LINE) AND PER CAPITA
DISPOSABLE NATIONAL INCOME (DASHED LINE) AS A FRACTION OF THE CZECH
LEVELS, 1950–91

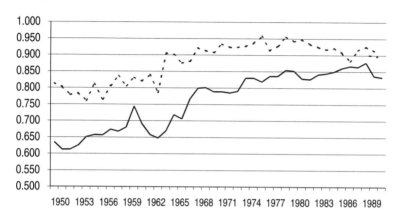

Sources: *Historical Statistical Yearbook of Czechoslovakia* (1985) and *Statistical Yearbook of Czechoslovakia* (various volumes), Federal Statistical Office of Czechoslovakia.

pared with 11.5 percent in the Czech Republic. The cumulative contraction of output was 10 percentage points larger in the Slovak Republic than in the Czech Republic and lasted one year longer.

Eventually, growth resumed in 1994, with the Slovak Republic growing faster than the Czech Republic. The renewal of growth started with export expansion and import contraction (introduction of trade barriers) that year.[2] The Slovak economy, like most small economies, strongly depends on foreign trade, with imports and exports each as a share of GDP ranging from 60 percent to 80 percent.

Later, from 1995 to 1997, the government tried to sustain high growth rates in excess of 6 percent by expansionary policies, in particular through large infrastructure investments financed by public debt.[3] This approach resulted in high fiscal and current account deficits in 1998 and 1999. The government accumulated sizable debts. As a result of this controversial policy, however, the Slovak Republic was among the first of the Eastern European countries, following Poland, to approach its pre-reform GDP level.

After sustaining impressive growth for several periods, the economy also turned out to need further reforms and austerity measures. Neither the voucher privatization favored before the break-up of Czechoslovakia nor the crony privatization after independence delivered effective ownership structures. Enterprise restructuring was delayed because owners and managers found it more profitable to divert assets to their own means.

The economic situation became grave in late 1998, following the election and change of government. GDP growth slowed down in 1998, and the economy was expected to stagnate in 1999. The unsound macroeconomic policies and structural reforms pursued earlier have led to lower short- and medium-run growth prospects of the Slovak economy, just when it is at the threshold of European integration.

The Special Position of the Slovak Republic in the Eastern Enlargement of the European Union

Slovak Trade with the Czech Republic

To mitigate the economic effects of Czechoslovakia's disintegration, the Czech Republic and the Slovak Republic retained a common currency and a common labor market and established a customs union. While the customs union and the free movement of labor were intended to remain in place indefinitely, they conceived their monetary union to be a temporary measure, initially to last for at least six months. However, the monetary union proved to be unsustainable, and the countries abandoned it on February 8, 1993. Thus, the Czech-Slovak Monetary Union ceased to exist less than six weeks after the break-up of Czechoslovakia.

The extent of bilateral trade between the Czech and Slovak republics always has been relatively high. Because the population of the Czech Republic is roughly twice that of the Slovak Republic, the Slovak Republic has been more dependent on the Czech Republic than vice versa. In 1991, the Czech Republic accounted for about half of Slovak exports and imports, while the Slovak Republic accounted for only about a third of Czech trade.[4] After the break-up, the share of Slovak trade with the Czech Republic fell to about 25 percent of total exports and imports in 1997. Czech trade with the Slovak Republic declined to 13 percent and even 8 percent of total exports and imports in 1997, respectively.

This relationship points to an extraordinary interdependence between the two countries before the split. The Slovak Republic was the Czech Republic's most important trading partner, and vice versa, until the split. Such a pattern of bilateral trade is rather atypical for two small open economies.

For example, Norway accounts for only 6 percent of Sweden's exports—although these two countries compare with the Czech Republic and the Slovak Republic in their similarities in culture, language, relative size, geographical proximity, openness, and liberalization of mutual trade. The Czech Republic's share in Slovak exports is similar to, for instance, Germany's share in Dutch exports (28 percent)—though the Czech Republic's population is only twice as large as that of the Slovak Republic, but the population ratio between Germany and the Netherlands is 5-to-1.

The intensity of trade relations between the Czech and Slovak republics has declined continuously since the break-up of Czechoslovakia in 1993, but it remains relatively high. According to Fidrmuc and Fidrmuc (1999), trade flows between the two countries in 1997 were estimated to be five times higher than normal, compared with 13 times higher than normal in 1991 and 7 1/2 times higher in 1994.[5]

The trade relations between the Czech Republic and the Slovak Republic, facilitated by their customs union, continue to be more intensive than those among selected former Soviet Union (FSU) countries and the Baltic States. In fact, the customs union is largely comparable to trade liberalization within the European Union. This trade intensity has been converging gradually to that prevailing among the EU countries.[6] Fidrmuc (1999b) concludes it could stabilize at this level with no further relaxation of economic relations. If, however, the Czech Republic joins the EU earlier than the Slovak Republic and they must abandon their customs union, Fidrmuc expects a further decline in trade intensity between the two countries. This issue is considered two sections below.

Trade Potential after Accession for Different Commodity Groups and Its Political Economy Implications

Analysis of trade flows between OECD countries indicates that free trade areas have positive effects on trade.[7] In particular, trade between two European Union countries is about 1 1/2 times higher than the normal trade level. Freer trade within the EU has the largest positive effect in the agricultural sector. Trade in agricultural products is nearly five times higher within the European Union than between two other countries not in the Union. Trade in raw materials and intermediate products is not significantly higher between countries within the EU than between countries outside of the EU.

Accordingly, agricultural firms are likely to benefit most from EU membership. Producers of intermediate products and raw materials will gain relatively less. Both of these industrial branches, however, are important for Slovak exports. Exports of intermediate products and raw materials contributed 39.4 percent and 5.1 percent, respectively, in 1994, and 34.4 percent and 4.4 percent, respectively, in 1997 to total exports.

Hence, nearly half of Slovak exports involve industries expected to gain little from membership in the EU, which may explain why the new owners of major privatized Slovak companies apparently did not support accession to the European Union. Accession will necessitate significant adjustment costs for these firms as they become bound by stricter EU environmental norms, face increased competition, and lose direct and indirect state subsidies. Indeed, some companies could benefit more from exploiting their low cost advantage if their country does not join the EU.

Trade Development under Different Scenarios of Eastern Enlargement of the EU

Following the opening of Eastern Europe, the importance of the EU countries as the Slovak Republic's trade partners has risen dramatically, driven by the normalization of trade relations between the Slovak Republic and the EU member countries. The European market (including the EU, EFTA, and all associated countries) is the largest export market for the Slovak Republic, compared with its importance for many other European countries (figure 9.2). In 1997, 85.7 percent of the Slovak Republic's exports went to the European market, and the figure is only slightly lower for the Czech Republic. The Slovak Republic is likely to have the highest share of exports to the Single Market in Europe after Hungary, Poland, and the Czech Republic join the European Union.

To assess the potential implications of different enlargement scenarios, Fidrmuc (1999b)[8] simulated the development of Slovak trade with six EU countries (Austria, France, Germany, Italy, the United Kingdom, and the Netherlands) and three Central European neighbors (Hungary, Poland, and the Czech Republic, CE3). These nine countries together accounted for 78 percent of total Slovak exports in 1996; the six EU countries (EU6) accounted for 91 percent of Slovak exports to the EU in the same year. The simulations considered three different scenarios:

- enlargement, in which the Slovak Republic joins the EU at the same time as the other CEECs;

- no enlargement: none of the CEECs joins the EU; and

- exclusion: the Slovak Republic does not participate in the enlargement.

Exports to the EU6 averaged a 25.8 percent annual growth in 1995 and 1996. Simulations of aggregate trade flows showed that export growth from the Slovak Republic to the EU6 is estimated to slow, which is not surprising because countries cannot sustain such high growth rates in exports in the long term. With no Eastern Enlargement, export growth is estimated to reach 9 percent per year between 1997 and 2010. In the enlargement scenario in which the Slovak Republic joins the EU at the same time as the other CEECs, export growth is estimated to reach 15 percent per year between 1997 and 2010. (For the rest of this section, discussion of estimated export growth refers to the annual export growth between 1997 and 2010).

Simulations of trade flows by commodity groups between the Slovak Republic and the EU6 show significant variation across commodity groups. The highest growth is estimated for exports of agricultural products and raw materials (35 percent per year under the enlargement scenario and 22 percent under the no-enlargement scenario). It is reasonable to expect, however, that actual growth for these products will be substantially lower, given the lack of a sound production basis for these categories. Exports of intermediate products, consumer products, and chemicals could grow by about 15 percent to 20 percent per year under the enlargement scenario, and about 10 percent per year without the enlargement. Growth of

FIGURE 9.2 EXPORT SHARES OF SELECTED EUROPEAN COUNTRIES, 1997

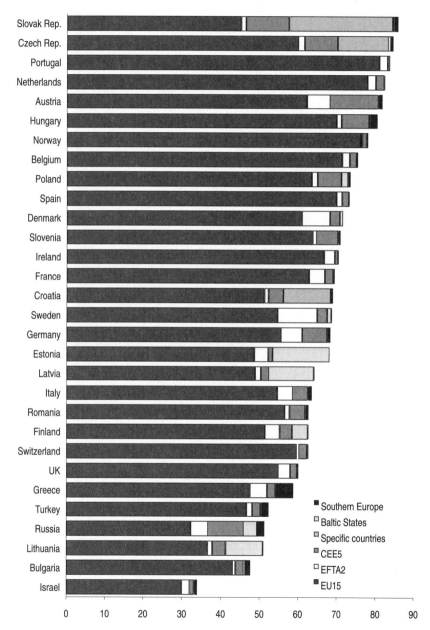

Note: The specific countries are: the Czech Republic for the Slovak Republic, the Slovak Republic for the Czech Republic, and Slovenia for Croatia.

machinery exports is estimated to be the lowest (10 percent per year under the enlargement scenario, and just below 1 percent under the no-enlargement scenario), though this group achieved the highest actual growth rate (56 percent) among all commodity groups in 1995–96.

The process of EU enlargement also can change the relationships significantly among Central and Eastern European countries. Slovak exports to Hungary are predicted to increase by about 3 percent annually without enlargement. If Hungary joins the EU before the Slovak Republic (the exclusion scenario), however, trade between the two countries will liberalize and Slovak exports to Hungary could increase by an additional 1 percentage point annually (and average annual growth by about 4 percent). Not surprisingly, growth gains are much higher if the Slovak Republic joins EU with Hungary. Then, Slovak exports to Hungary are to increase by about 6 percent per year (or 3.1 percentage points higher than with no enlargement).

The results are similar in the case of the Slovak Republic's exports to Poland. Estimates are that annual growth of the Slovak Republic's exports to Poland will be the highest under the enlargement scenario (10 percent), followed by the scenario in which Poland joins before the Slovak Republic (about 8 percent), and the lowest export growth expected with no enlargement (about 7 percent).

If the Slovak Republic joins the EU after the Czech Republic, analysis shows that there will a large drop in Slovak exports to the Czech Republic for all commodity groups. The most dramatic difference between joint enlargement and exclusion scenarios is predicted for agriculture: Slovak agriculture exports to the Czech Republic could fall by 7.3 percent annually under the exclusion scenario, instead of the significant growth of 11.0 percent per year under the joint enlargement scenario. This will be in the footsteps of the fall in Slovak agricultural exports to the Czech Republic of 10.7 percent on average in 1995 and 1996.

The simulation results for Slovak exports to the EU6 and the CE3 (see p. 196, above) show that if the Slovak Republic joins the EU after the other CEECs (the exclusion scenario), growth of its exports to all those countries will only be about 6 percent, compared with about 11 percent if it joins the EU at the same time as the others (the enlargement scenario). In fact, under the exclusion scenario, the Slovak Republic's export growth will be only marginally better (by half a percentage point) than under the no-enlargement scenario (in which its export growth would be about 5.5 percent).

Potential Effects of EU Accession on Slovak Labor Market

Background

As in many other transition countries, the Slovak Republic experienced a sharp increase of unemployment during the initial stages of transition. In 1990–91, unemployment rose sharply from virtually zero to about 12 percent.[9] From 1992 to 1997, the unemployment rate fluctuated between 12 percent and 15 percent. In 1998, the Slovak Republic reported the highest unemployment rate (15.6 percent) among the associated countries. In March 1999, the unemployment rate stood at a four-year high (16.7 percent). The developments in 1998–99 reversed the earlier trend (1995–96) when fast economic growth had a beneficial impact on unemployment. The unemployment rate had declined from a peak of 15.2 percent in January 1995 to 12.0 percent in October 1996.

Effects of EU Accession

The potential effects on employment arising from accession include the effects of improved economic performance and rising real wages, effects of labor market policies, effects of adopting EU labor market regulations, and the possibility of employment of Slovak workers in the current member states of the European Union. Each of these effects is considered, in turn, below.

ECONOMIC PERFORMANCE AND REAL WAGES

It is expected that accession will bring about considerable economic gains. One estimate indicates that the potential cumulative gain to the seven CEECs (Bulgaria, the Czech Republic, Hungary, Poland, Romania, the Slovak Republic, and Slovenia) of joining the EU can be between 1.5 percent (in the conservative scenario) and 18.8 percent of their GDP.[10]

The direct effects of the improved economic performance on employment, however, likely will be moderate. As in other countries (including developed and transition countries), labor demand is very inelastic in relation to GDP development. Haluska (1997) shows that GDP growth of 1 percentage point increases employment growth only by 0.28 percentage point in the Slovak Republic. This minimal change appears in the small employment effect of the recovery between 1995 and 1997. On the other hand, labor demand is negatively related to real wage growth. Haluska (1997) found that real wage growth of 1 percentage point lowers employment by 0.07 percentage point in the Slovak Republic.[11] Based on these elasticities, it could be postulated that accession will have only a slightly positive effect on employment.[12]

Active labor market policies could produce an indirect, positive effect on the labor market. Such policies could include retraining or subsidized employment of unemployed workers and public works, funded by the Slovak government from flows from EU budgets. Burda and Lubyova (1995) find that the elasticities of unemployment outflows (those who leave the pool of unemployed) with respect to expenditures on active labor market policy are positive (and higher than in the Czech Republic) and statistically significant. Similarly, Lubyova and van Ours (1999) find that the probability of transition from unemployment to employment is

150 percent higher for participants in active labor market policy programs than for nonparticipants.

EU LABOR MARKET REGULATIONS
Another consequence of accession is that the Slovak Republic will have to adopt the EU labor market regulations and institutions (such as those in the European Social Charter) that would make the labor market more rigid. This requirement could have a negative effect on employment.

Labor Mobility

Accession to the European Union sooner or later will introduce the possibility of seeking employment in the other member states of the European Union. The location of Bratislava right at the border with Austria and even a commuting distance from Vienna implies that the Slovak Republic could benefit from this possibility relatively more than the other acceding countries (perhaps except for the Czech Republic).

Walterskirchen (1999) estimates that up to 10,000 Slovaks (including commuters) could find new jobs in Austria annually if the accession occurs in 2005. The annual flows will decline over time as the income differentials diminish. Walterskirchen's estimate corresponds to about 0.4 percent of the 1997 Slovak labor force. Such an annual net outflow would have a non-negligible, although not a dramatic, effect on Slovak unemployment (because Austria is the only current EU country that shares a common border with the Slovak Republic, it most likely will receive the bulk of Slovak migrants). These estimates, however, appear unreasonably high. First, Walterskirchen uses results obtained for OECD countries to predict migration patterns for CEECs, which may not apply. Second, his income forecasts for the CEECs are rather low, which imply higher income differentials between the CEECs and EU countries, and hence higher levels of emigration.[13]

Fidrmuc et al. (1998) find that the Slovaks were relatively less mobile than both the Czechs and Western Europeans. In 1990, 0.69 percent of Czechs and 0.34 percent of Slovaks moved across the boundaries of administrative regions.[14] In comparison, internal migration amounted to 1.1 percent in the United Kingdom and Germany and 0.6 percent in Italy, according to Eichengreen (1998).

Despite growing regional disparities in unemployment rates and earnings, labor mobility actually declined during the economic transition. Slovak intercounty migration dipped from 0.94 percent of the population in 1990 to 0.81 percent in 1992, 0.78 percent in 1994, and 0.75 percent in 1996.

Migration across the Czech-Slovak border also declined. In 1990, 0.07 percent of Czechs and 0.19 percent of Slovaks migrated across the Czech-Slovak border. These figures declined to 0.01 percent and 0.06 percent, respectively, in 1996, despite the absence of significant barriers to movement of labor across the new border. About 59,000 Slovak citizens, however, including commuters, were employed in the Czech Republic in 1995 and about 72,000 in 1996. These figures corresponded to 2.3 percent and 2.8 percent, respectively, of the Slovak labor force and certainly helped to mitigate the Slovak unemployment problem, with the Slovak unemployment rate at 13.1 percent and 12.8 percent in the respective years.

An analysis to estimate the determinants of internal labor mobility in the Slovak Republic (appendix 3) suggests that high unemployment does not encourage labor mobility in the Slovak Republic, despite enormous regional differences (for example, the minimum and maximum unemployment rates for Slovak counties in December 1993 were 4.5 percent and 26.4 percent, respectively). The analysis also found that the higher the wages in a particular county, the higher the labor flows to that county (and vice versa), although the effect is not very strong.

A county with an average wage 10 percent above the national average will experience a net inflow of approximately 0.04 percent of its population annually. A county with double the national average wage will experience a net inflow of 0.4 percent per year. The magnitude of this effect indicates overall low intercounty migration. Although gross flows were not negligible,[15] the average net migration rate was only 0.01 percent annually during 1992–95.

While it is difficult to apply these results to international migration, they suggest the Slovaks are relatively not very mobile. Moreover, migration costs are much higher when crossing national boundaries because of linguistic and cultural differences, lack of social networks for migrants, and other factors. Therefore, the response of potential migrants to an earnings differential between the Slovak Republic and the current EU countries certainly will be much lower than estimated (see table 9.A7 in appendix 3).

The same analysis also seems to suggest that migratory patterns are quite different for different socioeconomic groups. In particular, the higher wage earners and the higher-skilled workers appear more mobile. The following results of the analysis support this point. First, as discussed above, the larger the difference between the wages in a particular county and the average wage in the country, the more the labor flows to and from that county. Second, the more entrepreneurs (excluding farmers) in a county, the more the labor flows to and from that county. This analysis implies that after the Slovak Republic's entry to the EU, the country may lose some highly skilled and most productive labor, although these outflows are not expected to be very high.

Finally, the same analysis shows that the Slovak labor market also could gain from the opening of labor markets in other Central European countries that also will join the European Union with the Slovak Republic. This development will affect mainly the Hungarian minority that lives along the border with Hungary. Fidrmuc (1995) shows that, in 1993, unemployment in the Slovak regions with a large ethnic Hungarian population was about 7 percentage points higher than average unemployment in the Slovak Republic and nearly 8 percentage points higher than unemployment in districts settled by the majority population. An increase in labor mobility between Hungary and the southern Slovak Republic could reduce regional unemployment, because this region is relatively closed to other regional labor markets in the Slovak Republic (including the relatively good labor markets in Bratislava and Kosice).

The Regional Effect of Accession

The aggregate picture of sectoral distribution within the Slovak Republic hides some of the diversity of regions in their "industrial mix." Fidrmuc et al. (1994) divide Slovak regions into industrial, agricultural, and structurally weak regions, depending on which sectors are relatively important within the region.

- The southern Slovak Republic is the bread basket of the nation, the center of agricultural production. Almost all of the country's agricultural produce comes from here.

- The northern regions are important for industry. About one-quarter of industrial output is produced here. The actual importance of these districts, however, is somewhat dwarfed by the two large industrial cities, Kosice and Bratislava, which are responsible for almost one-third of national industrial production. The north-central region of the Slovak Republic, in addition to its specializing in industry, is the nation's holiday resort. Almost one-third of the visitors to the Slovak Republic go to this region.

- Finally, the eastern region largely fails to fit into any of the above categories. Although the region has a high share of industrial and agricultural employment, it holds no significant share in the national production of either of these two sectors. That is, it represents a region specialized in, but not very productive in, either agriculture or industry.

Fidrmuc et al (1994) conclude that the regional specialization of the Slovak Republic occurs along a north-south axis, with the South more agricultural, and not between east and west. The east-west differential often cited in regional analyses of the Slovak economy refers more to productivity (and hence standard of living) differences among all sectors, which may well be caused by differences in infrastructural endowment.

The reorganization of Slovak regions in 1996 (see table 9.1) was based on the previous east-west classification. Therefore, the major regions are relatively similar but have many differences on more detailed levels. In particular, industrial regions, such as Trnava, Nitra, Banska Bystrica, and Kosice, were extended to include counties in the southern Slovak Republic that are dominated by agriculture (and the Hungarian minority).

TABLE 9.1 SELECTED INDICATORS BY SLOVAK REGIONS IN 1997

| | Share of sectoral employment (percent) | | | Unemployment rate | GDP per capita ratio to average |
Regions	Industry	Agriculture	Others	(percent)	(percent)
Bratislava	20.1	2.6	77.3	4.1	253.6
Trnava	37.4	13.9	48.6	10.6	93.8
Trencin	51.5	6.1	42.5	8.3	89.6
Nitra	33.4	14.4	52.2	14.3	74.5
Zilina	38.3	7.3	54.4	10.8	72.6
Banska Bystrica	36.7	10.7	52.5	14.9	85.9
Presov	31.1	11.6	57.2	17.8	55.8
Kosice	31.4	8.3	60.2	17.1	94.0

Source: Slovak Statistical Office.

The effects of accession to the European Union probably would distribute unevenly across regions in the Slovak Republic, but the developed industries in western Slovak Republic (including regions of Bratislava, Trencin, Trnava, and Nitra) stand to gain the most from the accession. This part of the country already has attracted a significant inflow of FDI. The other industrial parts of the Slovak Republic (Banska Bystrica, Zilina, and Kosice) that specialize in intermediate manufacturing products could face more significant adjustment costs.

Southern Slovak Republic may gain large agricultural subsidies. Agricultural regions also could benefit from the removal of trade barriers for agricultural products that still exist, despite the Association Agreements. In only this category did exports to the EU actually decline in 1995–96 (see table 9.A2 in appendix 2). This category also is expected to show the highest export growth in the enlargement scenario. Nearly all regions (except Bratislava, according to the present rules) will be eligible for subsidies from the structural funds. If the Slovak Republic joins the EU after the other CEECs, however, the agricultural sector will have the most to lose, concentrated in southern Slovak Republic.

Political Consequences of Accession

Besides important economic effects, the Slovak Republic's accession to the European Union also can have important political implications. Using regional data, Fidrmuc (1999a) analyzes the economic determinants of election results in the Slovak Republic in 1992 and 1994 and finds that differences in the patterns of electoral support of individual parties are significantly related to the underlying economic differences across regions. In particular, high unemployment is associated with high support for left-wing parties and low support for the parties advocating rapid economic reforms.

Similarly, the regions with high average wages tend to show more support for the pro-reform parties and less support for the left-wing parties. Regions with a larger share of industrial employment show low support for the pro-reform parties and high support for the left-wing parties. For example, HZDS (Movement for a Democratic Slovak Republic), the party of former prime minister Meciar, derives its support, according to Fidrmuc's analysis (1999a),[16] from regions with high unemployment, low wages, a high share of industrial employment, and a low share of agricultural employment.

Finally, among demographic determinants, the support for the HZDS relates positively to the share of pensioners and Roman Catholics and negatively to the share of Hungarian and Roma minorities in the population. The two junior partners in the previous government coalition, the far left ZRS (Workers' Association), the nationalist SNS (Slovak National Party), and the KSS (unreformed Communist Party, not represented in the parliament) share some common patterns of political support with HZDS: SNS and KSS benefit from high unemployment, and ZRS and SNS from high industrial employment.

Given such regional patterns of political support in the Slovak Republic, the economic effects of EU membership could help to stabilize Slovakian politics and especially increase the political support for the pro-reform parties (such as those that formed the current government). The assistance from the EU structural funds would go primarily to the depressed regions.

Stricken by high unemployment, low earnings, and outdated industry, these depressed regions are the major source of support for the HZDS, extreme left-wing, and nationalist parties. Improving the economic situation of these regions probably would reduce the support for extremist and authoritarian parties and increase the support for democratic parties.

Conclusions and Policy Implications

The Slovak Republic has a special position in the process of Eastern Enlargement of the European Union. On the one hand, the Slovak economy is firmly oriented toward the European Union and its Central European neighbors, already in accession negotiations. On the other hand, the policy of Slovak government from 1993 to 1998 resulted in a gradual deterioration of democracy and the rule of law and culminated in possible violations of the constitution, basic human rights, and the rights of minorities. This policy widened the gap between the Slovak Republic and the European Union, its neighboring countries, and the international organizations.

The potential gains and adjustment costs resulting from EU accession will spread rather unevenly in the Slovak Republic. Processing industries, including the iron and steel industry and intermediate manufacturing products, will face significant adjustment costs from stricter regulation, increased competition, and reduced government subsidies.

The industrial regions in western Slovak Republic could gain from increased liberalization of the trade and labor market with the European Union. The other industrial parts of the Slovak Republic that specialize in intermediate manufacturing products, however, could face more significant adjustment costs. Southern Slovak Republic could benefit from agricultural subsidies, while most of the country would be eligible for subsidies from the structural funds.

Empirical evidence suggests very low labor mobility internally in the Slovak Republic. The effect of wage differentials on internal migration is small, and the effect of unemployment differentials on internal migration is insignificant. EU membership is not expected to cause major emigration of Slovaks to current EU member countries. If some emigration occurs, the more highly skilled and educated workers will leave, because they face much lower migration costs and more potential gains from migrating.

Finally, EU membership can stabilize the political environment in the Slovak Republic and put the country firmly on a road to democracy and economic liberalization. While the European Commission has reversed its earlier decision and now has invited the Slovak Republic to start accession negotiations, the Slovak Republic still needs to address some internal political issues, including the still widespread corruption and cronyism. The treatment of the Hungarian minority is still unsatisfactory, despite the participation of an ethnic Hungarian party in the current government coalition. Finally, much can be improved for the Slovak Republic's Romanies.

The government also should focus on the industries and regions, particularly the intermediate manufacturing industries in the central and eastern Slovak Republic, likely to experience substantial adjustment costs following the Slovak Republic's entry into the EU. Effective restructuring of the formerly state-owned enterprises and inflow of FDI into these areas should be encouraged.

If the Slovak Republic joins the EU after its neighbors, it would be important for the Slovak Republic to maintain its customs union with the Czech Republic. The Czech Republic supports this policy, but the European Union seems poised to reject any irregular approaches in the cause of the Eastern Enlargement. This issue also will arise in the relations of Estonia with the other Baltic States and Slovene relations with Croatia.

If the negotiations for sustaining the customs union between the Slovak Republic and the Czech Republic succeed, the Slovak Republic can benefit from the EU accession of its neighbors, even if the enlargement excludes the Slovak Republic. Otherwise, its exclusion will result in significant aggregate welfare losses, which can further diminish the prospects for its future integration into the EU.

Appendixes

FIGURE 9.A1 GROWTH CONTRIBUTIONS BY COMPONENTS OF GDP, THE SLOVAK
REPUBLIC (%)

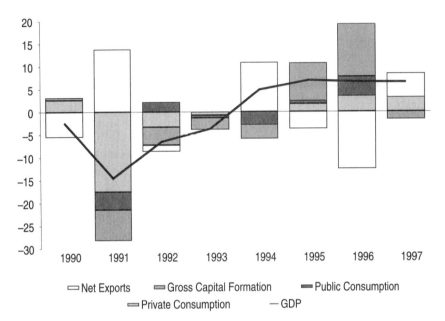

Source: Slovak Statistical Office and Institute of World and Slovak Economy of the Slovak
Academy of Sciences.

Appendix 1

Trade Potential after Accession by Commodity Groups

Fidrmuc (1998a) estimates gravity models for total trade and five major SITC one-digit groups[17] and the sum in 1989 of industrial products (SITC5-8) for 23 OECD countries (excluding Luxembourg and the newly admitted OECD countries, such as Mexico and Korea). The analysis chose that year because of the availability of trade flow data among all OECD countries. The estimates of trade aggregates closely approximate trade as shown in the high adjusted coefficient of determination (R^2) for total trade and for all commodity groups. Nevertheless, commodity groups—mainly products determined by factor endowments, such as raw materials and chemicals—rank slightly worse than high-processed industrial products, including machinery. The summarized results of the estimation are in table 9.A1.

TABLE 9.A1 ESTIMATIONS OF GRAVITY EQUATIONS FOR SELECTED COMMODITY GROUPS

	SITC 0-8 Total	SITC 5-8 Industrial products	SITC 0 Agriculture	SITC 2 Raw materials
Adjusted R^2	0.8937	0.8344	0.6533	0.5625
Constant	−4.981	−5.748	−6.157	−0.586
	(−6.131)	(−4.752)	(−2.762)	(−0.308)
GDP of importer	0.783	0.791	0.761	0.913
	(31.581)	(21.606)	(14.624)	(14.975)
GDP of exporter	0.762	0.926	0.493	0.477
	(34.979)	(29.023)	(8.093)	(8.239)
GDP per capita, importer	0.157	0.206	0.674	−0.243
	(2.781)	(2.342)	(3.445)	(−1.991)
GDP per capita, exporter	0.422	0.395	−0.083	0.272
	(7.796)	(5.873)	(−0.801)	(2.012)
Distance	−0.779	−1.025	−0.621	−0.820
	(−21.784)	(−17.678)	(−8.086)	(−9.113)
Dummy: EC12	0.410	0.358	1.566	0.076
	(5.652)	(3.684)	(10.003)	(0.573)
Dummy: EFTA	−0.089	0.071	−0.221	−0.340
	(−0.753)	(0.539)	(−1.057)	(−1.104)
Dummy: NAFTA	0.232	0.222	0.069	0.367
	(1.497)	(1.010)	(0.199)	(1.220)
Dummy: Neighboring countries	0.278	−0.017	0.580	0.480
	(3.022)	(−0.147)	(3.407)	(2.530)
Dummy: English	0.814	0.870	1.513	1.285
	(5.965)	(4.871)	(6.075)	(4.864)

(Continued on next page.)

TABLE 9.A1 CONTINUED

	SITC 5 Chemicals	SITC 6 Intermediate products	SITC 7 Machinery	SITC 8 Finished products
Adjusted R²	0.7601	0.7847	0.8105	0.7837
Constant	−11.185	−2.787	−15.345	−7.974
	(−6.228)	(−1.987)	(−9.541)	(−4.975)
GDP of importer	0.851	0.855	0.741	0.748
	(16.737)	(20.270)	(15.591)	(16.542)
GDP of exporter	0.850	0.785	1.086	0.995
	(18.437)	(19.529)	(27.190)	(25.783)
GDP per capita, importer	0.003	0.108	0.134	0.794
	(0.024)	(0.929)	(1.404)	(7.593)
GDP per capita, exporter	1.045	0.259	1.191	-0.164
	(9.160)	(3.465)	(10.246)	(−1.624)
Distance	−1.143	−1.166	−1.022	−1.079
	(−14.550)	(−16.456)	(−15.528)	(−16.545)
Dummy: EC12	0.573	0.186	0.642	0.506
	(4.096)	(1.679)	(4.735)	(3.824)
Dummy: EFTA	−0.219	0.275	0.085	0.153
	(−1.201)	(1.952)	(0.447)	(0.766)
Dummy: NAFTA	−0.799	0.270	0.372	−0.297
	(−2.782)	(0.988)	(1.035)	(−1.126)
Dummy: Neighboring countries	0.063	0.024	−0.088	−0.134
	(0.401)	(0.170)	(−0.541)	(−0.733)
Dummy: English	1.324	0.716	1.169	0.904
	(4.931)	(3.406)	(5.685)	(3.820)

Note: T-values within parentheses, 462 available observations for all commodity groups.
Source: Fidrmuc (1998a).

Appendix 2

Trade Development under Different Scenarios of Eastern Enlargement of the EU

Fidrmuc (1999b) uses a gravity model of trade to simulate the development of Slovak trade with six EU countries (Austria, France, Germany, Italy, the United Kingdom, and the Netherlands), and three Central European neighbors (Hungary, Poland, and the Czech Republic).

The model helps to estimate total trade flows for the main SITC one-digit groups. The simulations consider three alternative scenarios:

- enlargement, in which the Slovak Republic joins the EU at the same time as the other CEECs (Hungary, Poland and the Czech Republic);

- no enlargement, where none of the CEECs joins the EU; and

- exclusion, where the Slovak Republic joins the EU after the other CEECs.

The analysis assumes continued growth of GDP in the CEECs and in the EU during the period of simulations (1997 to 2010). All scenarios share the same assumptions on economic growth, although Baldwin, François, and Portes (1997) argue that the cumulative growth gain in Eastern European countries after their accession to the EU could range from 1.5 percent to 18.8 percent in the long run. They adopted this restrictive assumption to analyze only the direct effects of the enlargement on trade of the EU with CEECs (that is, the effects of trade liberalization) and to exclude the indirect effects through stronger growth in entrant countries.

TABLE 9.A2 PROJECTIONS OF SLOVAK EXPORTS TO EU6, AVERAGE ANNUAL
GROWTH RATES

SITC Groups	Description	Realized 1995–1996	No enlargement 1997–2010	Enlargement 1997–2010	Exclusion 1997–2010
SITC 0-8	Total exports	25.79	9.24	15.26	9.24
SITC 5-8	Industrial products	19.45	8.83	16.73	8.83
SITC 0	Agricultural products	–4.93	22.39	34.77	22.39
SITC 2	Raw materials	10.61	14.42	17.14	14.42
SITC 5	Chemicals	6.83	9.13	14.76	9.13
SITC 6	Intermediate products	3.28	10.91	18.93	10.91
SITC 7	Machinery	55.79	0.72	9.95	0.72
SITC 8	Consumer products	17.10	10.28	20.42	10.28

Note: See text for description of scenarios. EU6 includes Austria, France, Germany, Italy, the United Kingdom, and the Netherlands. The simulations produced the same results for the no-enlargement and the exclusion scenarios because the model does not take into account possible trade diversion effects of the other CEECs joining the EU before the Slovak Republic does.
Source: Fidrmuc (1999b).

TABLE 9.A3 PROJECTIONS OF SLOVAK EXPORTS TO HUNGARY, AVERAGE ANNUAL
GROWTH RATES

SITC Groups	Description	Realized 1995–1996	No enlargement 1997–2010	Enlargement 1997–2010	Exclusion 1997–2010
SITC 0-8	Total exports	5.01	2.97	6.10	3.97
SITC 5-8	Industrial products	1.56	6.59	7.16	6.36
SITC 0	Agricultural products	2.72	10.31	26.85	12.43
SITC 2	Raw materials	–4.56	–0.92	2.42	2.40
SITC 5	Chemicals	4.52	2.79	8.97	4.82
SITC 6	Intermediate products	–1.82	7.72	4.90	5.93
SITC 7	Machinery	10.57	3.66	6.37	3.29
SITC 8	Consumer products	–4.18	13.23	13.91	12.23

Note: See text for description of scenarios.
Source: Fidrmuc (1999b).

TABLE 9.A4 PROJECTIONS OF SLOVAK EXPORTS TO POLAND, AVERAGE ANNUAL GROWTH RATES

SITC Groups	Description	Realized 1995–1996	No enlargement 1997–2010	Enlargement 1997–2010	Exclusion 1997–2010
SITC 0-8	Total exports	50.17	6.94	10.18	7.98
SITC 5-8	Industrial products	34.27	7.54	8.11	7.30
SITC 0	Agricultural products	68.52	8.24	24.47	10.33
SITC 2	Raw materials	36.45	13.26	17.08	17.05
SITC 5	Chemicals	15.53	−1.34	4.59	0.61
SITC 6	Intermediate products	36.45	11.98	9.04	10.11
SITC 7	Machinery	62.84	3.49	6.21	3.12
SITC 8	Consumer products	41.29	7.21	7.86	6.27

Note: See text for description of scenarios.
Source: Fidrmuc (1999b).

TABLE 9.A5 PROJECTIONS OF SLOVAK EXPORTS TO THE CZECH REPUBLIC, AVERAGE ANNUAL GROWTH RATES

SITC Groups	Description	Realized 1995–1996	No enlargement 1997–2010	Enlargement 1997–2010	Exclusion 1997–2010
SITC 0-8	Total exports	4.61	−0.96	−0.96	−6.07
SITC 5-8	Industrial products	−3.98	−2.69	−2.69	−6.14
SITC 0	Agricultural products	−10.66	11.03	11.03	−7.27
SITC 2	Raw materials	−6.98	4.29	4.29	−1.64
SITC 5	Chemicals	1.42	−5.73	−5.73	−11.52
SITC 6	Intermediate products	−10.88	−2.08	−2.08	−5.14
SITC 7	Machinery	0.20	−6.64	−6.64	−8.81
SITC 8	Consumer products	2.67	−0.19	−0.19	−3.80

Note: See text for description of scenarios.
Source: Fidrmuc (1999b).

TABLE 9.A6 PROJECTIONS OF SLOVAK EXPORTS TO EU6 AND CEE, AVERAGE
ANNUAL GROWTH RATES

SITC Groups	Description	Realized 1995–1996	No enlargement 1997–2010	Enlargement 1997–2010	Exclusion 1997–2010
SITC 0-8	Total exports	15.60	5.98	10.88	5.48
SITC 5-8	Industrial products	8.70	5.93	12.39	5.55
SITC 0	Agricultural products	−5.84	15.42	24.83	12.33
SITC 2	Raw materials	1.89	10.30	12.73	10.20
SITC 5	Chemicals	4.69	3.28	8.14	2.91
SITC 6	Intermediate products	−2.14	7.78	13.95	7.23
SITC 7	Machinery	27.81	−0.71	6.97	−1.03
SITC 8	Consumer products	12.45	8.05	16.86	7.64

Note: See text for description of scenarios. The selected countries include Austria, France, Germany, Italy, the United Kingdom, the Netherlands, Hungary, Poland, and the Czech Republic.
Source: Fidrmuc (1999b).

Appendix 3

Determinants of Interregional Migration in the Slovak Republic

To assess the impact of unemployment and earnings differentials on labor mobility, Fidrmuc et al. (1999) regressed gross and net migration rates (that is, inflow, outflow, and net inflow divided by the county's population per end of the year) on the county unemployment rate, the average wage (divided by the national average wage), and additional economic and demographic characteristics, including:

- the number of small, private, unincorporated entrepreneurs, excluding farmers, as a percentage of the county's population;

- the employment in industry and agriculture, as a percentage of total employment;

- the share of the Hungarian minority;

- the proportion of county residents above retirement age;

- the proportion of county residents who have a university education; and

- the log of population density.

The results are in table 9.A7 below:

TABLE 9.A7: DETERMINANTS OF INTERREGIONAL MIGRATION IN THE SLOVAK REPUBLIC

	Inflow rate		Outflow rate		Net inflow rate	
Constant	−0.781 **	(−2.78)	0.067	(0.28)	−0.853 **	(−3.72)
Dummy 93	0.002	(0.06)	−0.097 **	(−3.83)	0.099 **	(3.24)
Dummy 94	−0.104 **	(−2.66)	−0.249 **	(−8.49)	0.145 **	(5.26)
Dummy 95	−0.192 **	(−4.63)	−0.303 **	(−9.84)	0.111 **	(4.26)
Unemployment rate (lagged)	−0.003	(−0.84)	−0.001	(−0.37)	−0.002	(−0.75)
Wage ratio (lagged)	0.942 **	(4.12)	0.567 **	(2.71)	0.381 *	(2.11)
Hungarian minority	−0.002 *	(−2.32)	−0.004 **	(−5.03)	0.001 *	(2.44)
Retirees	0.041 **	(6.96)	0.028 **	(5.98)	0.013 **	(2.97)
University educated	−0.002	(−0.21)	−0.026 **	(−3.03)	0.024 **	(3.44)
Population density [log]	−0.035	(−1.74)	0.011	(0.64)	−0.045 **	(−2.63)
Entrepreneurs	0.056 **	(2.92)	0.035 *	(2.38)	0.022 *	(2.39)
Industrial employment	−0.004 *	(−2.07)	−0.007 **	(−5.15)	0.003 *	(2.08)
Agricultural employment	0.006 **	(2.69)	−0.001	(−0.42)	0.007 **	(3.29)
Adj. R^2	0.556		0.656		0.365	

Notes: The data are pooled from 1992 to 1995. T-statistics (heteroscedasticity robust) are reported in parentheses. Significance levels: ** indicates variables significant at 1 percent level, * indicates variables significant at 5 percent level.

The dependent variables are the gross inflow and outflow rates and net inflow rate as a percentage of region's population, respectively. The wage ratio is the average wage divided by the national average wage of that year. The unemployment rate and the wage ratio are lagged one year. Hungarian minority is the percentage of a county's population, as of 1991.

Retirees are persons above the legally stipulated retirement age as a percentage of population, as of 1991. University educated are the county's residents with a university education as a percentage of the total population, as of 1991.

Population density is the log of persons per squared kilometer. Entrepreneurs are unincorporated entrepreneurs and self-employed persons, excluding farmers, expressed as a percentage of the county's population, as of 1992. Industrial and agricultural employment are expressed as a percentage of total employment, as of 1992.

Source: Fidrmuc et al. (1999).

Notes

* Prepared for the research project "Winners and Losers of EU Integration in Central and Eastern Europe," organized by the World Bank and the Bertelsmann Foundation. We are grateful to András Inotai and Helena Tang for many helpful comments and suggestions.

† Center for European Integration Studies (ZEI), University of Bonn, Walter-Flex-Strasse 3, 53113 Bonn, Germany, E-mail: Fidrmuc@united.econ.uni-bonn.de, Tel.: +49-228-73-1821, Fax: +49-228-73-1809.

†† Oesterreichische Nationalbank, Foreign Research Division (AUSA), Schwarzspanier-Str. 5, A-1090 Vienna, Austria. E-mail: Jarko.Fidrmuc@oenb.co.at; Tel.: +431 40420-5218, Fax: +431 40420-5299.

1. For an analysis of the causes of the break-up and some of its implications, see Fidrmuc, Horvath, and Fidrmuc (1999). Dedek et al. (1996) described the process of the break-up and the events preceding it.

2. See Appendix, Figure 9.A1.

3. The high growth rates the Slovak Republic reported probably also were achieved to some extent by creative statistics rather than economic growth. (According to the authors' estimates, creative statistics could account for up to a percentage point every year from 1995 through 1998).

4. These figures are based on statistics reporting deliveries of Slovak medium and large enterprises (enterprises with more than 25 employees) to and from the Czech Republic. Hence, these data are not directly comparable with customs statistics on trade flows available since 1993.

5. This analysis is based on a gravity model estimated by the authors. The estimated equation is $M = \beta1 + \beta2Ym + \beta3Yx + \beta4d + \sum i\beta iDi + \varepsilon$, where M denotes bilateral imports, Y is the GDP of the exporting and the importing countries (denoted by X and M, respectively), d is the distance between the capital cities of both countries, and ε is the disturbance term. All variables are in logs. Di denotes dummy variables for common border, common language, and preferential trade areas, such as the EU, EFTA, or the Czech-Slovak customs union. The normal level of trade flows is predicted by the gravity model, given the distance between the countries and their economic size, without the dummy.

6. Fidrmuc (1999b) explores this point in more detail.

7. Fidrmuc (1998a). Results are reported in Appendix 1.

8. Fidrmuc used a gravity model for the analysis. (See footnote 6 for an explanation of the model.) The simulations assume full convergence to trade potentials by 2010. Trade potential is the trade level predicted by the model.

9. The unemployment rates reported here are official unemployment rates, which probably overestimate the true extent of unemployment. In 1997, the internationally comparable International Labor Organization unemployment rate for the Slovak Republic was 11.6 percent, while the official rate was 12.5 percent.

10. The estimate is by Baldwin, et al. (1997). The gain stems from elimination of trade barriers for EU-CEEC trade, adoption of the more liberal EU external tariffs, and becoming part of the "Single Market." The latter figure based on the less conservative scenario also considers the effects of EU accession on reducing the risk premium on investments in the CEEC.

11. This result hinges, however, on the specific assumptions about long-term productivity growth. Haluska, for example, assumed exogenous productivity growth, captured by the trend variable.

12. This postulate is based on the assumption that accession will have a positive effect on GDP growth as well as real wage growth (which is likely), and that real wage growth will not exceed real GDP growth by more than four times (which is also likely).

13. The expectations of a large influx of foreign migrant workers following accession also are not corroborated by the experience of early 1990s. (Walterskirchen estimates that the total influx to Austria from the Czech Republic, Hungary, Poland, the Slovak Republic, and Slovenia will be 42,000 per year, if accession occurs in 2005.) According to Breuss and Schebeck (1995), during the first half of the 1990s, Austria received about 100,000 foreign migrants. Most of them, however, were from the traditional source countries, that is, former Yugoslavia and Turkey, not from the accession hopefuls.

14. The Czech Republic had 76 counties, and the Slovak Republic had 38. These counties further aggregated into eight regions in the Czech Republic and four regions in the Slovak Republic. The figures reported here are interregional migration, though the subsequent analysis focuses on intercounty migration.

15. The gross inflow and outflow rates were, respectively, 0.72 percent and 0.71 percent in the Slovak Republic.

16. The results presented here refer to the 1994 election. Unfortunately, Fidrmuc (1999a) does not analyze the 1998 election, which brought down Meciar's government.

17. The Standard International Trade Classification (SITC) is a commonly used classification in international trade. Beverages and tobacco (SITC1), fuels (SITC3), animal and vegetable oils (SITC4), and other commodities (SITC9) are excluded.

References

Baldwin, Richard E., Joseph F. François, and Richard Portes. 1997. "The Costs and Benefits of Eastern Enlargement: The Impact on the EU and Central Europe." *Economic Policy.* April.

Barro, Robert J., and Xavier Sala-i-Martin. 1995. *Economic Growth.* McGraw-Hill: New York.

Breuss, Fritz and Schebeck, Fritz. 1995. "Ostöffnung und Osterweiterung der EU," *WIFO Monatsberichte* 2, WIFO, Vienna, Austria.

Burda, Michael. 1998. "The Consequences of EU Enlargement for Central and Eastern European Labor Markets." European Investment Bank, *EIB Papers* 3 (1) 65–82.

Burda, Michael, and Martina Lubyova. 1995. "The Impact of Active Labor Market Policies: A Closer Look at the Czech and Slovak Republics." In David M. G. Newbery, *Tax and Benefit Reform in Central and Eastern Europe.* London: CEPR.

Dedek, Oldrich, et al., 1996. *The Break-up of Czechoslovakia: An In-Depth Economic Analysis.* Aldershot, England; Brookfield Vermont: Avebury.

Eichengreen, Barry. Autumn 1998. "European Monetary Unification: a *Tour d'Horizon.*" *Oxford Review of Economic Policy* 14 (3): 24–40.

Fidrmuc, Jan, Julius Horvath, and Jarko Fidrmuc. 1999. "Stability of Monetary Unions: Lessons from the Break Up of Czechoslovakia." *Journal of Comparative Studies*, forthcoming.

Fidrmuc, Jan. 1999a. "Political Support for Reforms: Economics of Voting in Transition Countries." Tilburg University. *European Economic Review*, forthcoming.

Fidrmuc, Jan, and Jarko Fidrmuc. 1997. "Slovakia." In Gacs, J. and R. Cooper, eds. *Impediments to Exports in Small Transition Economies.* London: Edward Elgar.

Fidrmuc, Jarko. 1995. "Ethnic Minorities and Regional Unemployment" In Scarpetta, Stefano and Andreas Wörgötter, eds. *The Regional Dimension of Unemployment in Transition Countries.* Paris: Organization for Economic Cooperation and Development.

Fidrmuc, Jarko. 1998a. "Application of Gravity Models to Commodity Groups and Trade Projections between the EU and the CEEC." Paper presented at European Meeting of Econometric Society, Berlin.

Fidrmuc, Jarko. 1998b. "Core and Periphery of World Economy, Outlier Analyses of Bilateral Trade Flows," Vienna: Institute for Advanced Studies, processed.

Fidrmuc, Jarko. 1999b. "Trade Diversion in 'Left-Outs' in Eastward Enlargement of European Union, The Case of Slovakia." *Europe-Asia Studies* 51 (4): 633–45.

Fidrmuc, Jarko; Wilfried Altzinger, and Gunther Maier. 1998. "Cross-Border Development in the Vienna-Bratislava Region: A Review," In U. Graute, ed. *Sustainable Development for Central and Eastern Europe, Spatial Development in the European Context.* Berlin: Springer Verlag.

Fidrmuc, Jarko, et al. 1994. *The Slovak Republic, After One Year of Independence.* Vienna: Bank Austria.

Fidrmuc, Jarko, and Andreas Wörgötter. 1999. "Structural Changes of East-West Trade." In Jarko Fidrmuc, et al. *East-West Trade: 10 Years After.* Vienna: Bank Austria.

Hajek M., et al. 1993. *Ceskoslovenska ekonomika v zaveru roku 1992.* Research Paper No. 3, Prague: Czech National Bank.

Haluska, Ján. 1997. "A Quarterly Econometric Model for the Slovak Economy SR-1Q." Eastern European Working Paper No. 47. Institute for Advanced Studies, Vienna.

Lubyova, Martina, and Jan C. van Ours. 1999. "Effects of Active Labor Market Programs on the Transition Rate from Unemployment into Regular Jobs in the Slovak Republic." Paper presented at CEPR Annual Transition Economics Summer Workshop for Young Academics, Budapest.

Walterskirchen, Ewald. 1999. "Pendler und Migranten im Zuge der EU-Osterweiterung." In *Österreichs Aussenwirtschaft: Das Jahrbuch 1998–99.* Ministry for Economic Affairs, Vienna, Austria.

CHAPTER 10

Slovenia

Peter Stanovnik
Boris Majcen
Vladimir Lavrač
Institute for Economic Research, Ljubljana

Introduction

It is a generally accepted opinion that the Eastern Enlargement of the European Union is a "positive-sum game," in which all partners concerned will gain more in the long run than they will lose. This expectation is true from the political and security perspectives and from the socioeconomic aspects. Because of institutional and structural changes within the EU and in the CEECs, however, the winners and losers will not spread evenly over time and space.

In Slovenia, the two continuing processes of transition and EU accession clearly overlap significantly. They complement and reinforce each other. With transition incomplete, the higher stages of integration into the European Single Market would be extremely difficult to reach. EU accession, however, gives a clear guideline for the direction of the transition process. Most of the market-oriented reforms conducted in Slovenia and in the other CEECs would need to be introduced, regardless of the European integration processes.

As a country in transition and in the process of integration with the EU, Slovenia should be concerned primarily with achieving economic stabilization and effecting the structural reforms needed for sustainable growth. This process implies that the economic system will achieve an adequate degree of compatibility with that of the EU; that the acceding country will develop an adequate level of competitiveness; and that a politically and socially acceptable adjustment process will give rise to conditions that permit sustainable growth within the newly open EU environment.

Although this paper deals with the political, social regional, and economic (trade, financial, and monetary) effects of Slovenia's EU integration, it focuses mainly on expected gains and losses from the standpoint of the Slovenian economy. Initial substantial preaccession costs (harmonization of legislature of acceding countries and practically full adoption of *acquis communautaire*) in the long term might turn into competitive advantages and benefits.

In financial and budgetary terms, the accession countries benefit from the structural and cohesion funds and being in the CAP. In a tendency among the EU incumbent countries, they generally concentrate more on the costs of enlargement rather than on its benefits, which in some cases may be less tangible than the costs.

With Slovenia integrating into the EU, an assessment of the long- and short-term costs and benefits is called for. Assessments of this kind constitute a basis for rational economic policy decisions and for decisions by individual enterprises. Officials still have room to maneuver on economic policy, even after making the political decision on accession. All of their decisions have a bearing on the negotiation process and are crucial for making the economic agents, the state, and citizens aware of the consequences they will face both during the transition period and upon entry into the EU.

Integration into the EU is basically a structural problem. The economy faces the consequences of structural change in individual sectors (agriculture, manufacturing, industry, transport, financial services, energy sector, environment, and others) and the effects of these changes on other sectors, in addition to the impact on macroeconomic aggregates. Partial sector analyses cannot evaluate the more complex effects at the aggregate level or at the level of individual sectors of the Slovene economy. Appropriate quantitative tools must be devised to permit analysis of various areas of economic policy.

Besides these problems, predicting the effects of Slovenia's entry into the EU is a difficult task. The present situation in both Slovenia and the EU most likely will be distinctly different from the situation five to six years from now, when actual entry may be expected. Consequently, an analysis and constant monitoring of the present situation in selected sectors in Slovenia is even more important if Slovenia is to prepare and adjust to EU requirements before its entry. An active policy of adjustment throughout the preaccession period could reduce the negative shock of entry.

Another problem relates to the different phases of accession to the EU. Two issues are important here. First, the gradual full-scale implementation of the Europe Agreement should be considered as part of the broader economic process of preparation for accession. Second, the effects of full accession closely depend on the level of economic, social, and political reform achieved prior to actual entry into the EU. It is therefore essential to distinguish between different (and significant) phases of the accession process and assess the full costs and benefits by adding estimates for individual phases.

Consequently, in estimating the effects of the adoption of the EU Common Customs Tariff, it is not enough to measure the consequences of changes in the tariffs adopted previously. In the preaccession period, the country must completely abolish all tariffs and other import duties (and nontariff barriers) on imports from the EU. These changes are certainly one of the steps to take while approaching the EU; they therefore should be considered.

Slovenia should meet the accession requirements the European Council spelled out in Copenhagen (June 1993) in the preaccession period. These requirements obviously will involve some costs and yield some benefits for the accessing countries. Research studies should aim at estimating total costs and benefits, in addition to estimating partial costs and benefits during specific phases of the accession process, in relation to a particular country's level of preparation for entry into the EU.

As mentioned above, it is somewhat difficult to distinguish between the effects induced by the essential economic and social policies aimed at completing the country's transition to a market economy and those caused by the need to approximate conditions in the EU. Hitherto, no such attempt has been made. Almost all studies on the costs and benefits of accession to the EU assess both effects together and fail to distinguish explicitly between the effects of the preaccession period (implementation of the Europe Agreement and its cumulative effects), actual accession, and the post-accession period of adaptation.

This paper is organized as follows: The second section deals with main political and social issues. The third section is focused on macroeconomic impact of Slovenia's accession to the EU. The fourth section discusses the evaluation of the continuing trade liberalization and restructuring processes.

After the short evaluation of the effects of the Slovenian inclusion into the EU and EMU at the aggregate level, the general equilibrium simulation results complement some partial equilibrium analyses of the trade reforms, further effects of the proposed new tariff schedule, lowering of tariff rates for imports from the EU, and the importance of FDIs in the restructuring process. It pays special attention to the agriculture and food-processing sector. In the last section, the paper briefly discusses financial, regional, and environmental aspects of winners and losers. Finally, it draws some conclusions and makes policy recommendations.

Political and Social Aspects of Winners and Losers

Political Aspects

Slovenia has regarded EU membership as a necessity to ensure it a better political, security, and economic position in the world. This membership is particularly important because, compared with other CEE candidate countries, Slovenia's political weight is much weaker than its economic weight.

Slovenia's historical and cultural tradition and background predetermines its joining the EU. Slovenians have not debated the political considerations of EU integration much, however, because all the important political parties and pressure groups have agreed with the official policy of the present coalition government, which emphasizes the necessity of EU accession. The exception is the opposition of some minor political parties and NGO organizations, such as the "Movement 23 December," which oppose EU accession on the grounds that Slovenia will lose its identity.

Even several EU supporters have expressed opinions that call attention to the possibly negative political effects of EU integration. Political losses relate to either losing or sharing of recently gained sovereignty with other people in policymaking, monetary sovereignty, national culture, ethnic identity, and language. For instance, these Slovenes have a high sensitivity about the ownership of land, partly historically rooted and partly from their awareness of the small size of Slovenia and the fear that foreigners might buy most of the Slovenian land (Svetlièiè and Stanovnik 1997). Such losses have not occurred, however, with previous EU enlargements. Moreover, in any case, the process of globalization would affect national sovereignty, regardless of Slovenia's EU accession.

The process of complying with EU structures will create many losers in domestic politics, such as from building new institutional structures (for instance, reorganizing public administration and regionalizing Slovenia). The losers will include those pressure groups within the main political parties that play on populist and local cards. "Changing the way the society and its particular sectors function requires an adjustment of the dominant political culture, as well. This, however, is a far longer and more complex process than the mere establishment of new institutions." (Hafner-Fink 1996)

Public opinion polls show that Slovenes, on the whole, support the full integration into the EU. Opinions about the influence of EU membership on different aspects of the Slovene society and economy also clearly indicate that the majority believes that joining the EU would have a positive effect on the development of Slovenia. Nevertheless, such support for EU membership has not always been so strong and unwavering.

Public opinion regarding the EU is highly influenced by the prevailing political and economic situation. Most of the population expects that Slovenia will gain from EU accession, but this opinion dropped to 47 percent in 1997 from 61 percent in 1996. The weakest support for accession was recorded after the elections, when some political groups and parties based their campaigns on nationalistic feelings linked with euroskepticism.

One factor behind the diminished enthusiasm for EU accession is a more realistic assessment of what it entails. During the EU negotiation process in the first half of 1999, it became clear that the taxpayers and private industry will bear the high costs of EU harmonization (the reform of agriculture and public administration and the costs of environmental adjustment and implementation).

Social Aspects

EU integration does not directly affect the social security of the population. For example, it does not change the level of social payments. It could have an effect, however, on the social security of the population through the "four freedoms," the core of the integration process (the free flow of goods, services, people, and capital). The country's adoption of these four freedoms, to a certain degree, will affect economic performance, the rate of employment, wage levels, and the migration of labor from and to Slovenia. All of these factors, in turn, will affect the standard of living and hence the social security of the Slovene population. For example, a strong economic performance will strengthen the social position of the population through higher employment and better funded social security funds.

A potentially negative effect of EU integration on the social security of the population would be the weaker competitiveness of Slovenian goods and services, in comparison with those from other EU states, which could reduce production and employment.

Assessing the Macroeconomic Effects of Accession to the EU for Slovenia

Several research studies estimate the costs and benefits of accession, mostly for specific sectors, while few studies analyze the effects of accession at a macroeconomic level.[1] One research study[2] found that Slovene firms, with integration into the EU, could reduce production costs by at least 5.3 percent. The same study also found that the overall cumulative effect on the GDP would be 8.8 percent,[3] about one-quarter of the predicted increase in Slovene GDP for 1996–2002.

One research study found that the effects of EU integration for Slovenia highly depend on the macroeconomic framework that the government sets and maintains with its short and long-term actions.[4] The study found that an economy that is already very open certainly has chances to survive the entire abolition of the remaining import duties without profound shock.

While further liberalization of foreign trade would lead to the substitution of imported products for domestic products, it also would increase GDP, employment, and exports. More specialized products could increase the variety and quality of the products offered to the domestic consumers. Budget revenues would fall as a result of lower import duties. The study also found, however, that appropriate steps toward more rational government consumption and lower energy consumption could result in even higher budget revenues.

Another research study[5] also found positive effects on the macroeconomic level. The study found that with EU integration, the real change of aggregate GDP (assuming full employment of labor and capital) would be small but positive (0.1 percent to 0.5 percent). Assuming that the quantity of labor will adapt (that is, implicitly assuming the existence of unemployment), the study found that further trade liberalization and the adoption of the EU Common Customs Tariff would increase employment (0.7 percent to 2 percent), aggregate GDP (0.8 percent to 1.9 percent), exports (5.8 percent to 10.6 percent), imports (5.9 percent to 10.6 percent), and decrease domestic prices (2.6 percent to 3.1 percent).

Research on the importance of the particular phases of further trade liberalization also found the heaviest influence (more than half of the total effects) derived from adopting the Europe Agreement. Adopting the new customs system, which incorporates Slovenia's obligations toward the WTO, amounts to 30 percent to 40 percent of the total effects, and the adoption of EU Common Customs Tariff includes 10 percent to 20 percent of the total effects.

These research studies all found positive macroeconomic effects of EU integration for Slovenia. They all analyze only one element, albeit an important one, of the accession process, however: in particular, further trade liberalization through the adoption of a new customs system, Europe Agreement, and the EU Common Customs Tariff. Recent research focused mainly on the preparation of partial studies as a basis for the preparation of the Slovenian negotiating positions in some of the 31 chapters. There has been no research to assess the effects of adopting the entire *acquis*. One important element also still missing in the implementation of the "EU Accession Strategy of the Republic of Slovenia" is the estimation of costs and benefits to the status quo of declared reforms for each particular policy and its possible effects.

Costs and Benefits of Joining the EMU for Slovenia

The main expected benefit of membership in the EMU, because of irrevocably fixed exchange rates and the use of the single currency, is that Slovenian trade with the EU would not be exposed to exchange rate fluctuations, uncertainties, risks and associated costs, and to conversion costs within the euro area. This benefit should lead to lower costs and to increased stability of trade, which in turn should result in larger trade and capital flows with the EU and in deeper integration with the EU internal market. This process would be of vital interest for the Slovenian economy.

Another benefit from the EMU is based on the expectation that the euro is likely to be a very stable currency. In this case, Slovenia can expect lower inflation and interest rates, with favorable effects on its monetary stability, investment, and economic growth. It also could participate in the seigniorage revenues from the creation and use of the euro and participate in the formulation and implementation of the European single monetary policy. It also could benefit from the economies of scale of pooling international monetary reserves and from using the euro as a potentially prestigious international currency, rivaling the dollar's leading role as an international currency.

On the costs side, Slovenia in principle will have to bear the same sacrifices from inclusion in the EMU as the EU members of the euro zone. First, the nation would lose its national currency, painful in itself, considering the symbolic and prestigious dimension of a currency. Slovenia, in this respect, is in no worse position than the EU members of the EMU.

For Slovenia, this sacrifice could be even less pronounced because its currency, the Slovenian tolar, has a short history and a poorer track record than the EU currencies. Second, the loss of autonomy in monetary policy and particularly the loss of the exchange rate as an instrument of adjustment could represent a problem, but not significant difficulty.

Monetary autonomy in itself remains a questionable concept to some extent, if a country is integrating in an area with a stable currency. In this case, monetary autonomy first means the possibility of less responsible monetary policy and of misusing monetary policy for some other (fiscal or redistributional) goals. In this sense, the loss of monetary autonomy need not necessarily be worth grieving. In academic circles, the prevailing view is that, for a small open economy without capital controls, monetary autonomy in fact is more or less just an illusion.

The loss of exchange rate autonomy may represent a more severe problem. To what extent the loss of the exchange rate instrument is really a cost of inclusion in the EMU depends mostly on two factors: First, the exposure to the so-called asymmetric shocks and, second, the functioning of alternative mechanisms of adjustment to these shocks, which substitute for the exchange rate when Slovenia gives up this instrument with its inclusion in the EMU.

Slovenia has the structural characteristics for benefiting from joining the EMU. According to the theory of the optimum currency area, the main structural characteristics that determine whether a country should join a monetary union are size, openness, diversification of production and exports, and geographical concentration of trade. After successfully completing transition and adopting the *acquis*, Slovenia will have the necessary structural characteristics for benefiting from joining the EMU.

For an economy with these structural characteristics, Slovenia can expect that benefits of the EMU would increase and costs decrease, so that net expected benefits from the EMU should increase, at least compared with other economies with different structural characteristics. Such an analysis for the moment, of course, is possible only in principle and generally. Concrete estimations and quantifications of costs and benefits of the EMU for Central European economies in general and for Slovenia in particular are a demanding task. It still needs to be done and was hardly accomplished even for the EU member countries.

As empirical research carried out in two PHARE ACE projects shows, Slovenia has a trade structure similar to EU member countries, which indicates that Slovenians can expect less asymmetric shocks than if they were dissimilar. The research also found that Slovenia's development is relatively well coordinated with cycles in the EU, especially those in Germany.[6]

Slovenia will need to make adjustments when joining the EMU, because of the possible or probable lower or, in time, declining competitiveness of its economy on the EU internal market (just like in the EU member countries in the EMU). An important adjustment will be greater flexibility of real wages and the labor market in general. For Slovenia, inclusion in the EMU will make sense only if the nation prepares itself beforehand to sustain the competitive pressures on the EU internal market. Not surprisingly, this is the main point and the main requirement in the negotiations for full membership in the EU.

In the opposite case, losing the exchange rate as an adjustment instrument when joining the EMU might really be too much of a sacrifice. If the exchange rate policy no longer is available while alternative mechanisms do not function (because they do not exist or are not flexible enough because of the built-in rigidities), a candidate country that faces problems with its international competitiveness on the EU markets might start to decline in economic growth and employment. It would become a depressed region in the EMU, the final high cost of an unsuccessful inclusion in the EMU.

Some Sector Effects of Slovenian Integration into the EU

Foreign Trade Liberalization

The issue of foreign trade liberalization hinges on certain processes and characteristics that are typical for Slovenia:

- First is the extent of foreign-trade protection originating from the former Yugoslavia and the process of trade liberalization that already has occurred in parallel with the process of political change and market reorientation.

- Second is the dissolution of the former markets for products, services, and production inputs.

- Third is the integration process throughout Europe, ultimately aimed at abolishing foreign trade barriers and simultaneously determining the framework of protection against states not members of the EU.

- Fourth is the adjustment process that will enable the Slovene economy to integrate successfully with the EU.

The effects of adopting the EU Common Customs Tariff after accession certainly will depend on the levels of foreign trade protection when Slovenia enters the EU. In the extreme situation of Slovenia's completely liberalizing trade, even for agricultural imports from the EU and adopting the Common Customs Tariff well before accession, the post-accession effects would be relatively low, but they would be high before accession.

The continuing trade liberalization of industrial products through implementing the Europe Agreement also is part of the preaccession process, aimed at arriving at an internal market. It is necessary, therefore, to analyze the complete process of foreign trade liberalization to determine its possible negative and positive effects on the Slovene economy.

Yugoslavia began to reduce import protection at the end of the 1980s, and this reduction continued into the early 1990s during the first years of Slovenia's independence. This policy appears in the reduction in the effective rates of protection from 1986 to 1993 (table 10.1). During that period, producers in the manufacturing, energy, and mining sectors already had experienced the main shock of foreign trade liberalization and reorientation from domestic to foreign markets.

The estimated rate of effective protection for manufacturing fell to only 4 percent in 1993 from 37 percent in 1986. From this level of protection, the liberalization process would proceed for EU integration. The future reduction in import protection would be considerably lower than that which already occurred during this first stage of foreign trade liberalization.

Tariffs on imports from the EU are being gradually phased out during the transition period (1997–2001) before accession. Implementation of the new tariff schedule and agreements signed with the EU will have major negative effects, pri-

TABLE 10.1 ESTIMATES OF THE EFFECTIVE RATES OF PROTECTION

Sector	1986 Total sales	1993 Total sales	1993 Home sales	1996 Total sales	1996 Home sales	1997 Total sales	1997 Home sales	2001 Total sales	2001 Home sales
1. Energy and mining	25.6	5.04	6.19	2.44	3.25	1.76	2.34	1.33	1.79
2. Manufacturing	36.7	4.18	11.93	3.93	10.51	2.72	6.64	0.85	2.26
– Capital goods	23.7	2.33	10.09	2.47	9.39	1.59	4.37	0.34	1.71
– Intermediate goods	45.4	4.40	8.99	3.86	7.57	2.80	5.19	0.81	1.66
– Consumer goods	32.7	4.67	16.41	4.60	14.71	3.08	8.98	1.09	3.25
3. Agriculture	8.7	18.2	17.3	25.9	25.1	26.3	25.8	26.7	26.4
– Basic materials	–5.7	9.79	8.02	8.95	6.68	9.60	7.61	10.1	8.35
– Processed goods	47.2	26.9	26.5	42.5	43.4	42.8	44.0	43.0	44.4
4. Total	30.9	7.03	12.11	7.89	12.34	7.09	9.86	5.85	7.07

Source: Majcen, B., and M. Lapornik (1989), Table, p. 6; Majcen, B. (1995), Table 4 in Appendix C; and authors' calculations.

marily on producers still serving the domestic market. At the end of the transition period, the Slovene economy will face negligible, nominal, and effective protection, except for agricultural products.

Given the expected low levels of nominal and effective rates of protection for the final year of the transition and preaccession period, Slovenians expect the adoption of the EU Common Customs Tariff to have a relatively low additional influence. The only exception would relate to the production of basic agriculture materials and particularly processed agricultural goods.

In the remaining short transition period, the need to redirect sales to foreign markets and simultaneously to open up the home market to foreign competition mean that the Slovene government cannot pursue the same protection policy as in the past. Classic price protection instruments will play an increasingly limited role. The protection of predominantly exported products has no significant effect, but export promotion activities are far more important and effective.

The government could use individual protective instruments but would be limited to those measures the WTO and European integration agreements permit. With state income decreasing rapidly because of continuing trade reforms and with expenses increasing after different measures taken to support production, the structure of the state budget, including the tax system, and the public sector in general will have to undergo a thorough transformation.

Structural Adjustments through Further Economic Integration of Slovenia—Effects on Industrial Structure

Market reforms and stabilization policies have forced enterprises to restructure. This reform reflects in the pattern of manufacturing output and trade over time. Industries with growing shares in output, exports, and imports include motor vehicles and furniture. Industries with shrinking shares in total output but with increased shares in exports include basic metals, metal products, and machinery.

Traditional industries with still negative trends and growing import shares include textiles, wearing apparel, and leather dressing. The food and beverages industry has a rather specific position. Increased protection has resulted in a lower import share and stable output share, but at the same time, the industry also has a shrinking export share. The trade balance for this industry has sharply deteriorated.[7]

Slovenia seems to have accomplished the first phase of transition relatively successfully and is in the process of economic recovery, but it still faces a number of serious challenges. Reform of the pension system and of the tax system are absolutely necessary. Further reducing inflation, curtailing the growth of wage and labor costs below productivity growth, and further liberalizing trade are necessary to increase export competitiveness.

The process of privatization is only in the first, formal phase when enterprises get new owners. The ownership structure is still far from desirable. During the privatization process, many enterprises have not undertaken the necessary restructuring to increase national competitive advantages. This restructuring is particularly important for a country so highly dependent on export markets. The rising deficit in the foreign trade balance suggests that enterprises, with some exceptions, have difficulties maintaining their export competitiveness, based on the present export pattern and structure of the manufacturing sector.

The next section attempts to assess the possible structural adjustment of the Slovenian industrial structure after further economic integration. Different factors affect the future industrial structure: a continuing transition and privatization process, further trade liberalization, the role of FDI, and the importance of comparative advantages and existing intra-industry specialization and their changes. The analysis has been restricted to the further trade liberalization process, with possible government policy actions and its complex impact on particular sectors and compared with the base year economic situation.[8]

Research Results

The results of the analysis show that the effects on Slovenia of full enforcement of the Europe Agreement depend on the government's macroeconomic policies (including exchange rate and public finance policies). According to this analysis, the effects on the Slovenian production sectors could divide into three groups.[9]

The first group includes the sectors with positive effects expected, irrespective of the exchange rate, public finance, or other economic policies adopted. These sectors are: fishery products, basic metals and metal products, machinery and equipment, electrical machinery, radio, TV and communications equipment, transport equipment, construction, trade, and financial and other market services.[10] The manufacturing and agriculture sectors within this group are export-oriented, with high shares of imports and a below-average rate of nominal protection (table 10.2). These sectors also have the highest shares of enterprises with FDI in their total output.[11]

The second group includes sectors where negative effects are expected, irrespective of the government policies adopted. These sectors are agricultural and forestry products, coal, crude oil and natural gas, food, beverages and tobacco, cellulose, paper and cardboard, coke and refined petroleum products, and basic chemicals and chemical products. On average, they are less open and more protected sectors.

The third group includes sectors where the effects depend largely on the exchange rate and public finance policies adopted. These sectors are ferrous, nonferrous ores and stones; textiles and wearing apparel; leather, footwear and leather products; wood and wood products; rubber and plastic products; nonmetallic mineral products; wooden furniture and miscellaneous goods; electricity, gas, steam and water; restaurants and hotels; transport, communications, travel agencies, housing, and nonmarket services. This group can further divide into those sectors

TABLE 10.2 SHARES OF BASIC MACROECONOMIC AGGREGATES IN PARTICULAR
GROUPS, ACCORDING TO THE SIMULATION RESULTS IN THE YEAR 1992

Group	Share in toal exports (%)	Share in total imports (%)	Share in total production (%)	Share in total GDP (%)	Exports/ GDP	Imports/ GDP	Average rate of nominal protection (%)
1 (+)	46.0	42.0	32.0	26.7	1.70	1.41	4.0
2 (-)	25.8	41.6	43.4	47.3	0.54	0.79	8.5
3 (+-)	28.2	16.4	24.6	26.0	1.07	0.56	6.3
TOTAL	100.0	100.0	100.0	100.0	0.99	0.90	6.4

Note: (+) indicates positive effects, regardless of government policies;
        (-) indicates negative effects, regardless of government policies;
        (+-) indicates effects dependent on the exchange rate and national policies adopted.
Source: Statistical Office of the Republic of Slovenia; calculations: Institute for Economic Research.

more sensitive to exchange rate policy and those more sensitive to public finance policy. They have an average share of exports and nominal rate of protection and a below-average share of imports in GDP.

The producers primarily oriented toward the domestic market thus particularly would feel the negative consequences of opening the domestic market still further. Whether they ultimately will adapt successfully to conditions prevailing on the world market depends on adjustments by individual producers to foreign competition and on the measures government bodies adopt. Further cuts in import duties, however, would positively affect export-oriented producers.

Despite the positive effects overall of further trade liberalization, sectoral results show that, if nothing changes from the base year situation, sectors that will experience possibly negative effects produce almost 50 percent of total GDP, while those sectors for which effects will depend on the policy measures adopted produce about 25 percent of GDP.

Additional simulations made on the adoption of the EU Common Customs Tariff yielded quite similar results, with the same directions but larger magnitudes of change.[12] Results of the simulations indicate the situation in two sectors—basic metals and metal products and machinery and equipment—deteriorated during 1992–95. Two other sectors experienced a positive change in the same period: refined petroleum products and nuclear fuels (a sector of only marginal importance in terms of size), and rubber and plastic products.

The most recent simulations[13] indicate negative effects in the energy, mining, and basic metals and metal products sectors. Agriculture and food, beverages, and tobacco also would have problems. Further foreign trade liberalization in manufacturing and agriculture will have a positive effect on growth in the service sectors, if government consumption decreased. If the sales tax on services increased as a compensation for the budget incomes reduced by the liberalization process, mainly trade, market services, and construction would be negatively affected.

It should be emphasized that the above results do not show the changes that will occur in real life. Rather, they indicate only the sensitivity of particular sectors to further foreign trade liberalization and assumed government actions, based on the actual situation in the particular sector in the base year of 1992. The consequences in real life will depend mainly on the level of awareness of individual producers of how necessary it is to adapt to foreign competition and on government policy actions.

Foreign Direct Investment and Their Role in the Restructuring and Integration Process

The stock of inward FDI in Slovenia in 1993–96 more than doubled, rising from US$954.3 million to US$1.9 billion. The present stock of inward FDI in Slovenia is somewhere between US$2.3 billion and US$2.4 billion (Rojec, 1998a).

At the end of 1996, most FDI in Slovenia came from Austria (34.3 percent), followed by Croatia (18.5 percent), Germany (14.1 percent), France (7.5 percent), Italy (7.4 percent), and United Kingdom (4.7 percent). The high shares in Croatia and France result from a particular situation and do not accurately reflect the overall picture. In Croatia, this result is the consequence of the co-ownership of the Nuclear Power Plant Krško, while in France, the high share derives mostly from Renault's investment in car manufacturing.

Among the major countries investing in Slovenia, Austria has become increasingly important. Austria's share in the total stock of inward FDI in Slovenia rose to 34.3 percent in 1996 from 19.0 percent in 1993. Shares of Croatia, Italy, and France in total inward FDI stock in Slovenia fell considerably in 1994–96. Only Austrian investors until now seem to have shown a genuine interest in investing in Slovenia.

Despite the relatively low importance of FDI in Slovenia (FDI stock or annual inflows as a share of GDP), compared with the developed countries and some other transition economies, enterprises that have FDI are becoming increasingly important in exports, imports, and profits.

FDI stock is distributed mainly between capital- (56 percent) and labor-intensive (37 percent) industrial groups (see table 10.3). The FDI stock in the R&D (research and development) and human capital-intensive group are of only minor importance. The high share of the FDI stock in capital-intensive industries, where Slovenia does not have revealed comparative advantages, implies that foreign investors must perceive these industries to be viable in the medium term. Over time, this FDI may lead to extensive changes in production and exports. Findings in the next sections certainly will confirm these expectations.

TABLE 10.3 FOREIGN DIRECT INVESTMENT STOCK IN INDUSTRIAL GROUPS IN 1995
(PERCENTAGES)

| | | Distribution between groups | | | Distribution within groups | |
| | | 10–50% foreign equity | 50% foreign equity | | 10–50% foreign equity | 50% foreign equity |
Industrial groups	Total	share	share	Total	share	share
1. Capital-intensive	55.5	19.7	61.7	100.0	5.2	94.8
2. R&D and human cap.-int.	6.1	13.3	4.8	100.0	32.2	67.8
3. Labor-intensive	36.6	66.3	31.1	100.0	26.9	73.1
4. Human capital-intensive	2.1	0.7	2.3	100.0	4.7	95.3
Total	100.0	100.0	100.0	100.0	14.7	85.3

Note: The data under "Distribution between groups" show the sectoral distribution (capital or labor-intensive, etc.) of enterprises with different shares of foreign equity participation. The group of data under "Distribution within groups" show for each sector, the distribution of enterprises with different shares of foreign equity participation.
Source: Bank of Slovenia, author's calculations.

In enterprises with 10 percent to 50 percent foreign equity share, two-thirds of total stock was invested in enterprises characterized as labor-intensive, but the capital intensity industrial group recorded 62 percent of FDI with more than 50 percent equity share. FDI with more than 50 percent foreign equity shares is very high for every industrial group, and particularly so for the capital and human capital-intensive industrial groups.

Table 10.4 shows the importance of enterprises with FDI in total value of output and exports. The overall share of output from enterprises with FDI in manufacturing output rose to almost 20 percent in 1996 from 15 percent in 1992. The highest share of production with FDI in total output appeared in the capital-intensive industrial group, rising to 40 percent in 1996 from 33 percent in 1992. The share of production with FDI in the R&D and human capital-intensive industrial group was relatively stable at about 14 percent. The lowest share of production with FDI in total output was in the labor-intensive industrial group, although this share was rising significantly over time.

The importance of enterprises with FDI in exports was even more significant. Their overall share rose from 20 percent to 26 percent from 1992 to 1996. The largest and fastest-growing share in total exports, in the capital-intensive industrial group, rose to 55 percent in 1996 from 45 percent in 1992. The share in the R&D and human capital-intensive industrial group depends on the production trend of enterprises with FDI in the sector "Manufacture of television and radio transmitters." Shares in the labor-intensive industrial group were below average but increasing rapidly.

Enterprises with FDI concentrated in the capital-intensive and R&D and human capital-intensive groups for the domestic market, but they concentrated in

TABLE 10.4 THE SHARES OF OUTPUT AND EXPORTS (ENTERPRISES WITH FDI) IN TOTAL OUTPUT AND EXPORTS*

Industrial groups	Share of output with FDI in total output (%)					Export share with FDI in total exports (%)				
	1992	*1993*	*1994*	*1995*	*1996*	*1992*	*1993*	*1994*	*1995*	*1996*
1. Capital-intensive	33.3	32.7	35.1	37.3	40.3	44.8	39.6	46.6	52.9	55.1
2. R&D and hum. cap.-int.	14.4	14.4	12.5	12.8	13.5	13.0	9.1	8.3	11.7	12.0
3. Labor-intensive	5.9	7.3	9.6	11.2	12.2	7.3	9.3	12.3	13.7	14.9
4. Human capital-intensive	8.4	9.5	6.2	3.6	3.7	3.5	4.8	8.4	3.6	5.2
Total	15.0	15.3	16.8	18.3	19.6	19.7	17.7	21.6	24.8	25.8

* Calculations prepared on data from enterprises' income statements sheets
Source: Bank of Slovenia, authors' calculations

the capital-intensive group for the export market. Domestic enterprises without FDI could be described mainly as producers of labor-intensive and human capital-intensive products and are becoming increasingly important in the exports of R&D and human capital-intensive products.

Considering the importance of sectors with increased output shares in the observed period of 1992–95, it can be concluded that, on average, they produced only one-third of total manufacturing production in 1992 and 46 percent in 1995. These changes undoubtedly reveal a rapid restructuring process in the Slovene manufacturing industry (table 10.5). From the different changes of shares within particular industrial groups, it can be concluded that DEs (enterprises without FDI) and FIEs (enterprises with FDI) behaved quite differently. On one hand, we have FIEs with a high share in the subgroup with increasing output shares (the "+" subgroup) and relatively low (and rapidly decreasing) shares in the subgroup with decreasing output shares (the "–"subgroup). On the other hand, DEs were mainly responsible for the overall results but also reveal rapidly increasing shares of the "+"subgroup.

Notable results regarding export orientation of enterprises, measured in export-output ratios, are presented in table 10.6. FIEs are characterized with higher average export orientation and higher export-output ratios in the two most important industrial groups (labor- and capital-intensive groups), compared with the DEs. They also had higher export-output ratios in the "+" subgroup and particularly low ratios in the "–" human capital-intensive subgroup. Low export-output ratios found in the "+" subgroup of capital-intensive DEs, together with decreased return-on-assets indicators (see below), certainly reveal still existing problems in competitiveness and unfinished restructuring process with still strong orientation of these enterprises on domestic market. Better results were found in the labor-intensive industrial group.

TABLE 10.5 THE OVERALL OUTPUT SHARES AND OUTPUT SHARES FOR
ENTERPRISES WITH FDI (FIEs) AND ENTERPRISES WITHOUT FDI (DEs) IN
PARTICULAR INDUSTRIAL GROUPS IN 1992–95
(in percentages)

Industrial groups	Total 1992	1995	Change 95/92	FIEs 1992	1995	Change 95/92	DEs 1992	1995	Change 95/92
1 CAPITAL-									
INTENSIVE	30.9	28.5	−7.6	68.4	58.8	−13.9	24.3	21.6	−11.0
+	12.2	15.6	28.1	82.9	86.8	4.6	19.9	27.2	37.1
−	87.8	84.4	−3.9	17.1	13.2	−22.4	80.1	72.8	−9.2
2 R&D AND HUM.									
CAP.-INTENSIVE	6.9	7.4	7.1	6.6	5.1	−23.4	6.9	7.9	14.0
+	70.8	76.9	8.6	19.2	25.8	34.1	79.5	84.4	6.2
−	29.2	23.1	−20.9	80.8	74.2	−8.1	20.5	15.6	−24.0
3 LABOR-									
INTENSIVE	58.2	58.2	0.0	22.8	35.0	53.1	64.5	63.5	−1.4
+	44.2	55.3	25.0	90.3	96.3	6.6	30.2	41.2	36.5
−	55.8	44.7	−19.8	9.7	3.7	−61.5	69.8	58.8	−15.7
4 HUMAN CAPITAL-									
INTENSIVE	3.9	5.9	50.3	2.2	1.1	−47.7	4.2	7.0	65.0
+	24.8	61.4	148.0	0.0	15.3	0.0	21.0	60.0	185.3
−	75.2	38.6	−48.7	100.0	84.7	−15.3	79.0	40.0	−49.4
TOTAL	100.0	100.0	0.0	100.0	100.0	0.0	100.0	100.0	0.0
+	35.3	45.9	29.9	78.6	86.2	9.6	30.7	42.9	39.8
−	64.6	54.1	−16.2	21.4	13.8	−35.4	69.2	57.1	−17.5

Source: Income statements, balance sheets, and authors' calculations.

To test the changes in the efficiency of the enterprises, the return-on-assets indicator was used (RAI; table 10.7). With their levels and changes in the observed period, we tried to find out if changes in the output shares accompanied appropriate changes in the efficiency indicator. As we analyzed average values, we found certainly particular sectors or enterprises within subgroups with different results, but our first aim was to compare these values between FIEs and DEs.

On the aggregate level, enterprises turned from the positive to negative RAI in the observed period 1994–96 due to the decreased positive RAI in the "+" subgroup and increased negative RAI in the "–" subgroup. Results, particularly for the "–" subgroup, once again only reveal the fact of still-unfinished restructuring process. We also could observe positive but rapidly decreasing RAI for the sectors in the capital-intensive and R&D and human capital-intensive "+" subgroups. Positive shifts in the "+" labor-intensive subgroup could be attributed mainly to positive developments in the FIEs.

FIEs have positive and increasing RAI on average, with the main contributor as enterprises in the labor-intensive industrial group. The situation in the capital-

TABLE 10.6 THE OVERALL EXPORT-OUTPUT SHARES AND EXPORT-OUTPUT
SHARES FOR FIEs AND DEs IN PARTICULAR INDUSTRIAL GROUPS, 1992–95

Industrial groups	Total		Change	FIEs		Change	DEs		Change
	1992	1995	(%)	1992	1995	(%)	1992	1995	(%)
1 CAPITAL-INTENSIVE	0.484	0.498	3.0	0.651	0.686	5.3	0.401	0.382	−4.8
+	0.523	0.589	12.6	0.733	0.753	2.8	0.251	0.254	1.2
−	0.479	0.482	0.7	0.254	0.241	−5.2	0.438	0.429	−1.9
2 R&D AND HUM. CAP.-INTENSIVE	0.604	0.642	6.3	0.545	0.588	8.0	0.614	0.650	5.9
+	0.644	0.671	4.1	0.477	0.364	−23.7	0.651	0.685	5.2
−	0.507	0.548	7.9	0.561	0.666	18.7	0.472	0.465	−1.5
3 LABOR-INTENSIVE	0.461	0.489	6.0	0.572	0.600	4.8	0.454	0.475	4.6
+	0.441	0.478	8.4	0.562	0.603	7.3	0.432	0.469	8.7
−	0.477	0.503	5.3	0.667	0.518	−22.4	0.464	0.480	3.3
4 HUMAN CAPITAL-INTENSIVE	0.219	0.171	-22.1	0.093	0.172	85.6	0.231	0.171	−26.0
+	0.119	0.041	-65.7	0.000	0.279	0.0	0.114	0.033	−71.0
−	0.252	0.378	49.7	0.093	0.153	64.6	0.262	0.378	44.1
TOTAL	0.469	0.484	3.3	0.614	0.645	5.0	0.443	0.448	1.0
+	0.469	0.479	2.0	0.684	0.688	0.6	0.433	0.431	−0.6
−	0.468	0.489	4.5	0.357	0.376	5.4	0.447	0.460	2.9

Source: Income statements, balance sheets, authors' calculations.

intensive group is different: The positive RAI in the "−" subgroup deteriorated and became negative, but the "+" subgroup revealed positive but decreasing RAI. The restructuring process for the capital-intensive FIEs apparently is not finished yet, and, because of high export-output ratios, they also are quite sensitive to the developments on the world market.

DEs had positive shifts in the shares of subgroups in the capital-intensive sector, but the relative growth of the output of the "+" subgroup was relatively low. A decreased positive RAI (because of increased loss of loss making enterprises) indicates some still problematic enterprises. Decreasing shares of the "−" subgroup with the highest negative RAI, which decreased further, point to the unfavorable developments in this part of capital-intensive DEs. Compared with the FIEs, they have very low export-output ratios in both subsectors and are thus more oriented to the domestic market. This is certainly another less favorable indicator for the future developments of capital-intensive DEs.

Labor-intensive DEs as a group experienced increases in the negative RAI. In both subgroups, they showed losses that decreased in the "+" subgroups (as a result of positive developments in the enterprises with profits and decreased loss in the

TABLE 10.7 RETURN ON ASSETS INDICATOR (%) FOR INDUSTRIAL GROUPS IN THE PERIOD 1994–96

Industrial groups	Total 1994	Total 1996	Difference 96-94	FIEs 1994	FIEs 1996	Difference 96-94	DEs 1994	DEs 1996	Difference 96-94
1 CAPITAL-									
INTENSIVE	−0.53	−0.13	0.39	2.02	1.24	−0.77	−1.23	−0.58	0.65
+	1.97	0.91	−1.05	3.54	2.65	−0.89	1.35	0.53	−0.82
−	−2.19	−1.08	1.12	0.88	−0.16	−1.05	−12.77	−21.36	−8.59
2 R&D AND HUM.									
CAP.–INTENSIVE	5.52	2.50	−3.03	−1.68	−2.88	−1.20	6.63	3.39	−3.24
+	7.97	4.04	−3.92	−1.68	−2.88	−1.20	6.96	3.45	−3.51
−	−7.11	−6.03	1.08	0.00	0.00	0.00	0.00	0.00	0.00
3 LABOR-									
INTENSIVE	−0.36	−0.45	−0.10	2.92	4.62	1.70	−0.63	−1.07	−0.44
+	−0.74	0.43	1.17	3.77	5.00	1.23	−0.27	−0.13	0.14
−	−0.13	−1.11	−0.98	−4.29	−3.26	1.03	−3.13	−9.93	−6.80
4 HUMAN CAPITAL-									
INTENSIVE	0.00	0.19	0.19	1.52	−7.34	−8.87	−0.13	0.55	0.68
+	−0.01	0.19	0.20	−4.65	−14.78	−10.14	−0.41	1.80	2.21
−	10.14	−8.60	−18.74	0.00	0.00	0.00	0.00	−0.01	−0.01
TOTAL	0.08	−0.06	−0.14	2.00	2.19	0.20	−0.20	−0.45	−0.25
+	1.37	1.04	−0.33	2.82	3.05	0.23	0.87	0.46	−0.41
−	−0.93	−1.58	−1.17	0.53	−0.27	−0.79	−5.90	−8.34	−2.44

Source: Income statements balance sheets, authors' calculations.

enterprises with loss), but increased in the "–" subgroups (as a result of negative developments in the enterprises with profits and increased loss in the enterprises with loss). Both subgroups of export orientation remained stable and far below the ratios of the FIEs. The labor-intensive group is the most important industrial group with high shares in almost all important variables: The actual and future success in the restructuring process of the DEs, therefore, is important for the overall performance of the Slovenian manufacturing sector.

In the remaining two industrial groups, DEs experienced increases in output shares. The R&D and human capital-intensive group, which was the most export-oriented group, decreased its high positive net profits. The human capital-intensive group, on the other hand, succeeded in turning from loss to net profit, despite the extremely low export orientation. In the future, problems thus may arise from the further liberalization of foreign trade and increased foreign competition.

We can conclude that, according to the return-on-assets indicator, both FIEs and DEs had, on average, positive RAI in the "+" subgroup, that is, decreasing for the DEs and increasing for the FIEs, as the result of positive developments in the labor-intensive group. We did not find positive shifts in the efficiency of the sectors in the "–" subgroup as negative RAI further decreased in the observed period, except for the FIEs in the labor-intensive group.

The restructuring process in the DEs is certainly not finished yet. Both most important industrial groups (capital- and labor-intensive) revealed rapidly increasing negative RAI in the "–" subgroups, with the only exemption in the labor-intensive "+" subgroup. FIEs revealed the best results in the labor-intensive group, with the fast-growing positive RAI in the "+" subgroup and positive development in the "–" subgroup.

FDI evidently played a positive role in the restructuring process so far, but it also increased competition for the DEs. It is thus quite questionable to conclude that sectors with increased output shares will lead industrial growth in the future. Positive shifts between the two observed periods, 1992–95 and 1994–96, certainly pointed out that the economy succeeded to some extent in the restructuring efforts (also with significant positive contribution of the FIEs), but it has still problems, especially within the DEs in the capital-intensive and labor-intensive groups.

We finally conclude that increasing output shares of sectors with high shares of FIEs can be regarded as sustainable, but for sectors where the shares of DEs are high, we should wait until the end of the continuing restructuring process. We should not be surprised if some now contracting sectors will lead to future industrial growth. Future developments certainly also will connect closely with Slovenia's approaching the EU. At the enterprise level, it seems that more DEs will be among the losers in the integration process, particularly those still oriented primarily to the domestic market.

Agriculture and Food Industry

Previous experience clearly had demonstrated that agriculture was often the key problem in accession negotiations, because of its special characteristics and features. The process of adjusting to the European Union will radically change the economic and political structure of Slovene agriculture. Agricultural adjustments will focus mainly on changes in policy measures related to the preaccession strategy. Economic analysis has shown that even small price variations and minor modifications in budgetary support may dramatically change the level of income earned by a particular farmer.

Erjavec, et al. (1997) estimated the possible effects of accession[14] and simulated the following scenarios:[15] Scenario A1 assumes the CAP in its present form, scenario B1 assumes modest reforms of the CAP oriented toward a liberalization of agricultural policy. Variations in these two simulated scenarios assumed that the new members would not receive compensatory payments (scenarios A2 and B2). The baseline simulation assumes full implementation of the Europe Agreement. Scenario W assumes the most far-reaching changes in agricultural policy, that is, complete liberalization.

The simulation results show that accession of Slovenia to the EU under the present form of the CAP (with higher support and foreign trade protection) would result in a higher GDP growth rate and a positive foreign trade balance in agriculture products (figure 10.1). The possibility that the new members would not be entitled to compensatory payments (scenario A2) reduces GDP growth and worsens the foreign trade balance. Further liberalization of CAP (scenarios B1 and B2) would cause further deterioration of both GDP and export growth, with a rise in import growth.

Results clearly indicate that both agriculture production and foreign trade are very sensitive to the level of budget support. Changes in the levels of foreign trade protection affect primarily the volume of imports. Considering that Slovenia will join the EU after 2003, the third scenario, B1 (or, worse, the fourth scenario, B2) is probably the most realistic. One could conclude that the effects of Slovene accession to the EU for agriculture and for the food industry will be negative, if Slovenia makes no structural adjustments in the transition period remaining.

Quite similar results were found using a partial equilibrium static net income model (Erjavec, Rednak, Volk, eds.). Results of the simulation estimations (figure 10.2) suggest that a better net income level in agriculture could be expected if Slovenia were to accept the present form of CAP, that is, scenario A1. Accession under the terms of scenario A1 would increase the prices of agricultural products (by 5 percent to 10 percent) and direct budget support in agriculture (from ECU 27 million to almost ECU 70 million). Costs also would increase, but less so than income, such that aggregate net incomes in agriculture would rise by 15 percent to 20 percent. Although Slovenia, as a new EU member, may not be entitled to compensatory payments (scenario A2), aggregate net income nevertheless would increase, in comparison with the current situation under this outcome. (Higher price increases may be expected in agricultural products than in farm input prices.)

FIGURE 10.1 REAL GROWTH RATES OF GDP, EXPORTS, AND IMPORTS, COMPARED WITH THE BASE SCENARIO RESULTS FOR MANUFACTURING INDUSTRY (=100)

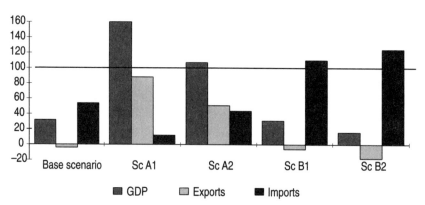

Source: Erjavec, Rednak, Volk, eds., 1997, figure 99, p. 341.

FIGURE 10.2 RELATIVE AGGREGATE NET INCOME CHANGES (NET VALUE ADDED)
BY VARIOUS ACCESSION SCENARIOS

(parity income = 100)

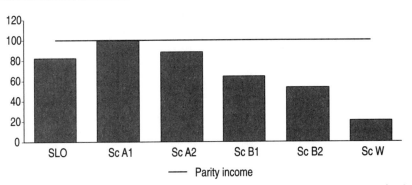

Notes: SLO stands for an estimate of the net income changes of Slovene agriculture for the
period 1992–95. Parity income refers to the average of the whole Slovene economy.
Source: Erjavec, Rednak, Volk, eds., 1997, figure 34, p. 191.

In the case of all scenarios demonstrating the effects of a partial or complete
liberalization in prices within CAP (a drop in the prices of agricultural products),
the aggregate net income in agriculture is expected to decline. EU agricultural price
reductions of approximately 20 percent (as the simulations within the scenarios B1
and B2 envisage) would lower net income in Slovenia by 20 percent (scenario B1)
and 35 percent (scenario B2), despite lower costs.

The results of scenario W (complete liberalization to the level of the world
prices) are mentioned only as an example of an extreme possibility and to present
a complete range of the various degrees of liberalization. The chances that the EU
will accept this scenario are slight, but such conditions might emerge in Slovenia
(a very pessimistic view) if (or as long as) it stays outside the EU (WTO, CEFTA
agricultural trade liberalization).

The effect of accession on Slovene agriculture is likely to vary substantially
between commodities (figure 10.3). Both positive and negative effects may occur
within the same scenario. As a rule, better net income levels can be expected for
those farm products with currently poor economic results, and vice versa. Based on
conditions expected in the EU, agricultural products can divide roughly into two
groups:

- Agricultural products with more protection under CAP (the highly regulated products, including cereals, oil seeds, fattened cattle, sheep, hops,
  milk, and sugar beets); and

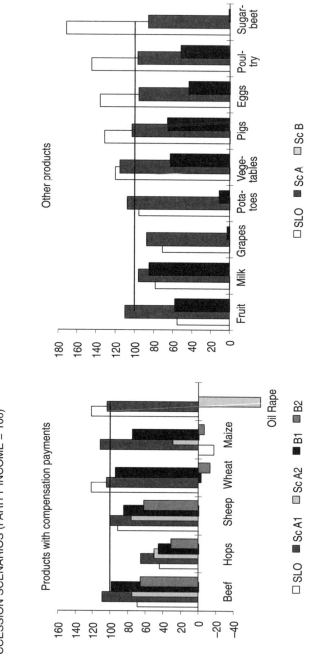

FIGURE 10.3 RELATIVE NET INCOME CHANGES FOR INDIVIDUAL PRODUCTS (NET VALUE ADDED) ACCORDING TO VARIOUS ACCESSION SCENARIOS (PARITY INCOME = 100)

Source: Erjavec, Rednak, Volk, ed., 1997, figure 35, p. 192

- Agricultural products with less protection under the CAP (products with insufficient regulative coverage, basically those not included in the first group, such as pork).

Concerning the products in the first group, the consequences of accession will depend mainly on the success of preaccession negotiations (quotas) and the status of the new EU members (compensatory payments). Should the negotiations conclude successfully, Slovenia may well expect better or at least very similar economic conditions for these products. Should the final outcome of the negotiations be unfavorable, conditions for those products could worsen markedly.

The EU market is noticeably less regulated for the second group of products. Price differences among countries are distinctively larger than in the first product group, and competition on world markets is stronger. Price levels in this group depend not so much on market policy interventions, but rather on the quality, market organization, marketing mix, tradition, and consumer attitudes toward domestic products.

The results vary according to the scenario. The effect would be positive (that is, net income increases) if products get into the medium or higher price range in the EU context (scenario A), but will be negative if products do not reach this price range (scenario B). There are a few exceptions and many uncertainties in both the first and second group, but we already can clearly foresee the expected changes overall for certain products. A very brief summary of the results of the simulation analyses is in table 10.8.

The various scenarios yield different simulation results that indicate the advantages and risks to expect for specific farm products after accession. It is highly unlikely, however, that exclusively good or bad forecasts will come true for all products. Development trends will move along the lines of some farm products

TABLE 10.8 CLASSIFICATION OF AGRICULTURAL PRODUCTS ACCORDING TO EXPECTED CHANGES IN INCOME LEVEL

| Probable improvement (low current income situation) | Uncertain predictions | | Probable deterioration |
	depends on compensatory payments	depends on actual price growth	(favorable current income situation)
beef	cereals	vegetables	sugar beet
hops	oil seeds	potatoes	eggs
fruit	sheep	grapes	
milk		pigs	
		poultry	

Source: Erjavec, Rednak, Volk, ed., 1997, table 35, p. 193.

coming close to the optimistic estimates, several agricultural products approaching the pessimistic scenarios, with the rest falling somewhere in between.

As discussed above, much will depend on the specific details of the final negotiations and the success with which Slovenia adapts to ever-changing market conditions. The real economic effects of accession will thus be found somewhere between the possibilities listed. The key factor will be the level of budgetary support to agriculture, and Slovenia might be relatively optimistic regarding forecasts on this issue.

Each increase in agricultural incomes primarily reflects a rise in expenditures on agriculture. What is good for an agricultural producer is certainly not beneficial for the consumer or taxpayer, and vice versa. Accession to the EU will directly affect the structure and volume of budget expenditures in Slovene agriculture. The transfer of competencies concerning market and price policies also means a transfer of CAP costs (compensatory payments, export refunds, intervention purchases). In this way, the appreciable pressures on national budgets will decrease. At the same time, however, harmonizing national policy to EU policy will call for higher expenditures in the Slovene budget. The EU budget only assists in cofinancing the structural changes that Slovenia would need to make at the national level.

Domestic food consumers will pay for most of the post-accession changes expected in agricultural income, and a considerable share also will come from taxpayers (table 10.9). The net increase in "income" is the difference between the changes in the agriculture income and the changes in expenditure by the Slovene taxpayers and consumers. As such, it represents the net effect of Slovene integration into the EU. The figure is positive only in those scenarios that assume that Slovenia will obtain compensatory payments from EU funds (scenarios A1 and B1); this assumption again underscores the vital importance of compensatory payments.

The effects of these possible changes on the processing industry and additional effects on food consumption (effects of price changes for foods not produced in Slovenia) are positive, as is the total net figure. Nevertheless, the figures are not so high as to have a critical bearing on the Slovene decision about accession.

Winners and Losers of Joining the Single European Financial Market for Slovenia

This section deals with the effects of financial integration, that is, the costs and benefits of EU accession, for the Slovenian financial services sector. The free flow of financial services relates to one of the four freedoms (goods, services, capital, people) that constitute the EU internal market. A candidate country such as Slovenia, after going through different phases of EU integration (Europe Agreement, pre-accession phase, negotiations for a full membership, EU accession), finally has to open its financial market completely to foreign competition. Its financial market has to become an integral part of the European Single Market for financial services,

TABLE 10.9 CHANGES IN AGRICULTURE REVENUE AND IN THE SOURCES OF
FINANCING BY DIFFERENT ACCESSION SCENARIOS
(ECU million)

	SLO	Sc A1	Sc A2	Sc B1	Sc B2	Sc W
The value of production (producer prices)	707	758	758	613	613	477
Direct and indirect budget support of agriculture	60	117	83	117	83	83
Total "revenues" in agriculture	766	874	841	730	697	560
Net budget expenditure of Slovenia in agriculture	38	76	76	76	76	76
(1) Change in "revenues" for agriculture		108	75	–36	–70	–206
(2) Change in the cost of the agriculture to						
Slovene taxpayers		38	38	38	38	38
(3) Change in consumer expenditure. for food						
produced in Slovenia		51	51	–93	–93	–230
Net effects of accession for agriculture (1–2–3)		19	–14	19	–14	–14
Net effects on food industry and additional effects						
on food consumption		17	17	34	33	48
Total net effects for agro-food sector		36	3	53	19	34

Source: Erjavec, Rednak, Volk, eds., 1997, table 37, p. 197.

based on the complete freedom to establish foreign financial institutions and to provide financial services from abroad to the domestic financial market.

Because of its effect on other sectors of the economy, we can consider the
financial service sector almost infrastructural for the economy as a whole.
Financial services accompany practically every transaction in goods and services,
so they play an important role in the intermediation of resources and in the transfer of capital flows, both within the country and in its external transactions.

From this perspective, it is essential for an economy that its financial sector functions well and efficiently, regardless of the ownership, foreign or domestic, of financial institutions. Having an efficient and competitive financial services sector is an
integral part of the Slovenian development agenda and a part of the structural adjustment required in the process of EU approximation. Therefore, at first sight, it would
seem that the EU integration can be only beneficial for the Slovenian financial services sector, because its opening, liberalization, and exposure to foreign competition
will contribute to a more efficient financial service sector in Slovenia. The issue is,
of course, more complex because there will be winners and losers in the process.

Slovenia's financial services sector, small in both absolute and relative terms,
has undergone significant restructuring in recent years, but it still is far from being
internationally competitive in terms of its soundness, efficiency (costs of financial
intermediation), and diversification (choice of financial institutions, financial instruments, and financial products or services). The main objective in the next few years

of the preaccession phase is to increase the international competitiveness of the financial sector so as to enable its successful integration in the EU internal market.

The Slovenian financial sector has been protected so far from serious foreign competition. At present, 25 banks, 6 savings banks, and 70 smaller savings cooperatives operate in the Slovenian banking sector. The insurance sector includes 10 insurance companies and 3 re-insurance institutions. Financial institutions dealing with securities in the capital market consist of 46 investment companies and 15 mutual funds, plus 42 stock exchange trading companies.

This chapter focuses on the banking sector, by far the most important segment of the financial market in Slovenia, not only in terms of size (its share in GDP and employment) but also in terms of its influence on other sectors and on the economy as a whole. Much of the analysis of the banking sector, however, *mutatis mutandis*, also can apply for the other two parts of the financial services sector in Slovenia.

The banking sector in Slovenia has been practically isolated from foreign competition until recently. Of the 25 banks in Slovenia, 11 banks are 100 percent domestically owned, 10 banks are in dominant domestic ownership, and 4 banks are in complete or dominant foreign ownership. Since the Europe Agreement and the new banking law took effect in early 1999, foreign banks can freely open branches in Slovenia, but up to now only one foreign bank has taken this opportunity. Except for the two largest banks, which went through the process of rehabilitation and were nationalized, all other banks are in dominant private ownership. The privatization of these two banks started recently after a considerable delay.

Even the largest banks (or the whole banking sector, for that matter) are small in size, compared with a potential competing bank from the EU. Until the early 1990s, the structure of the Slovenian banking sector was monopolistic, with one large bank dominating the banking system (its banking group, including some connected smaller banks, accounted for more than 80 percent of the total assets).

Later, the structure of the banking system became more dispersed, but the largest two banks still hold more than 50 percent of the market. Some peculiar regional monopolies also still exist in the Slovenian banking sector. At present and as a reaction to the forthcoming EU accession, there is a trend of intensive consolidation in the banking sector, with more or less friendly mergers and acquisitions. In a few years, this process is expected to result in a Slovenian banking sector better prepared to meet foreign competition.

Compared with EU banks, domestic banks are relatively inefficient and not yet ready for the challenges of opening to foreign competition. At midyear 1999 for the banking sector as a whole, the return on average assets was 1.1 percent, the return on average equity was 10.8 percent, and the ratio of labor costs to average assets was 1.7 percent.

The ratio of operating costs to average assets is slowly declining and is now 3.5 percent. Efficiency of the banking sector can best be assessed by net interest margin and interest spread. The former declined from 4.9 percent (at the end of

1997) to 4.5 percent (at the end of 1998) and to 4.1 percent at present. The interest spread also is declining and is now 5.6 percentage points.[16]

Assessment of the costs and benefits of financial integration as a consequence of Slovenian accession in the EU and the identification of winners and losers in the process would need to begin with exposure to foreign competition, that is, increased competition in the financial services sector and its consequences. For consumers, increased competition in the financial market can bring only benefits. Users of financial services will benefit from increased competition, by having a wider choice of financial institutions, instruments and services, lower costs of financial intermediation, and better quality of financial products.

Costs of financial integration arise only for financial institutions. They are to be exposed to challenges of intensive EU-wide competition. If they are not successful in the competition of the market, domestic financial institutions can lose their market share, with consequences on profits and employment. They have some starting advantages in this competitive fight, such as information capital (knowledge of Slovenian firms) and a retail distribution network, which a foreign financial institution cannot easily and quickly establish.

Most probably, foreign capital will be attracted into existing domestic financial institutions. This investment can have some benefits (additional capital, improvements in technology and information systems, knowledge and expertise, marketing skills, development of new products, and innovations). Dangers or costs of financial integration arise, however, from unfriendly mergers and acquisitions, which can lead to a loss of market share, level of activity and employment, loss of jobs for the management, or even to bankruptcies.

Truly, financial integration in principle is a mutual and symmetric process, but in Slovenia's small economy and less-developed financial market, this process may be quite asymmetrical. Domestic financial institutions may not easily recover their losses in the domestic market by their increased activity in the EU financial markets.

Regional Policy Issues

Official documents and some articles on regional development have one thing in common: they do not explicitly measure or estimate the costs and benefits of accession to the EU.[17] Some indirect estimates are in papers prepared for the White Paper on regional strategy in Slovenia. These estimates form an international comparison of regional differences in economic development and unemployment, a measurement of current economic policy actions, and an assessment of development possibilities of various regions in Slovenia.[18] Regional strategy should form the basis for the new Regional Development Promotion Act because it must precisely define the main goal of furthering sustainable regional development and establishing quantitative targets.

The analysis showed that Slovenia has an above-average rate of unemployment and a below-average level of economic development. Compared with the most highly developed EU regions, Slovenia certainly will lag behind for several decades to come. The question, however, is whether it is really necessary for Slovenia to try to catch up with the levels of development enjoyed by huge conurbations in the EU. Excluding 25 metropolitan regions, Slovenia (with ECU 10,216 in per capita income on a purchasing power parity basis) would be at around 73 percent of the EU-21 average, and we perhaps should measure the process of catching up in years, not decades.

In terms of central government interventions, Slovenia has almost no current regional policy. Apart from minimal funds provided for demographically endangered regions, the government pursues only horizontal and sectoral policies. The goal is to satisfy horizontal and sectoral interests; regional goals are not important.

In its preparations for joining the Union, Slovenia should observe the interests of the EU and reorganize its aid according to EU norms and regulations. A special EU committee that approves state aid authorizes the aid for different purposes in the common interest. This policy applies, in particular, to regional and horizontal aid (R&D, development of small and medium enterprises, training, and ecological aid).

The Slovenia government should change its implementation of regional policy, its interventions in state aid, in two ways. It should:

- Concentrate state aid regionally so that the primary goal of central government interventions becomes regional development (especially in less-developed regions) and the secondary goals become horizontal and sectoral goals; and

- Extensively modify its current mode of promoting horizontal and sectoral goals in connection with regional goals. This change would mean that, in the first case, it would determine sectoral policies with a large array of "regional instruments" and, in the second case, it would ensure regional development through both horizontal and sectoral policies (for example, including regional—rather than general—aspects in setting priorities for horizontal and sectoral policies, which would help direct aid toward less-developed regions).

A discussion of the effects of future EU enlargement should bear in mind that enlargement certainly will affect both current and future EU member states and their constituent regions. Enlargement will lead to increased competition, primarily between regions. One of the important factors in their future economic development will be the ability of enterprises to adapt rapidly to changes in demand and economic environment and the ability of regional administrations to attract new enterprises to their areas.

Accession to the EU, which will open up opportunities to trade with the EU, is just as important for regional development as the provision of structural and other funds, but the path previously taken by regional development is also important. The discussion should identify factors governing that path and estimate the development possibilities of existing regions (table 10.10).

TABLE 10.10 SYNTHESIS OF THE ESTIMATED DEVELOPMENT POTENTIAL OF THE SLOVENE REGIONS IN TERMS OF FACTORS CRUCIAL TO THE DEVELOPMENT OF INNOVATION AND ENTREPRENEURSHIP

Factors:	Central	Coastal	Gorenj.	Goriška	Savinj.	Dolenj.	Pomur.	Kras	Podrav.	Koroš.	Spod-posav.	Zasav.
1. General sociopolitical environs and region's image	+11	+3	+6	-3	-3	+1	-2	-2	-3	-2	-2	-5
2. Existing economic structure and infrastructure	+7	+10	+5	+4	-2	-3	-8	-2	-5	-3	-4	-5
3. Human capital	+13	+7	+11	+2	-1	+4	-13	-4	-3	+2	-11	-8
4. Quality of life in region	+8	+8	+8	+7	-3	+3	0	+4	+1	0	-2	-4
5. Access to information about market and technology	+4	+4	+3	+2	+2	-3	+3	-4	+4	+4	-1	+2
6. Investment financing possibilities	+4	+3	-1	-1	-1	+2	+2	-2	0	-3	-2	-3
7. Organization and management	+4	+2	+3	-2	-2	0	-2	-2	+2	0	-2	-2
Sum total	+51	+37	+35	+13	-10	+10	-20	-12	-4	-2	-24	-25
Rank	1	2	3	4	8	5	10	9	7	6	11	12

Note: The table shows aggregated results of '+' and '−' for seven categories of factors. Each category has more subfactors—the estimation of a single subfactor shows deviations from the Slovenian average. The region with better subfactor was marked as '+', the region where subfactor was worse than the Slovenian average was marked with '−'. Synthesis estimation in this table derived from summing up '+' and '−' for subfactors of each of seven broader categories of factors. Source: Kukar (1998)

It is not so surprising that ranking Slovene regions in terms of the crucially important factors, innovation and entrepreneurship, comes quite close to ranking regions (especially the most developed regions) in terms of their level of development, based on gross material product per capita. After accession to the EU, Slovenia should expect the toughest problems in the least developed regions with poor development possibilities.

With increased competition and rather low levels of development (in comparison with the EU) in even its most developed regions, Slovenia must launch an efficient economic reorganization of all regions and drastically change (or better, reconstruct) its recent, almost nonexistent regional policy.

Adjustment Costs to EU Environmental Legislation

In environmental protection, high costs will result from the adjustment to EU legislation, and Slovenia is not expected to adopt the whole environmental *acquis* before the accession (2002–2003). For this reason, the national environmental program will demand a negotiated transition period for the chapter ecology. The program translates the Environmental Protection Act into a series of objectives in four priority areas: water, wastes, biodiversity, and air. According to the National Environmental Action Plan, the general objectives of environmental protection are:

- promotion of sustainable development;

- holistic approach to environmental problems;

- harmonization of regulations with EU environmental *acquis* (transposition and implementation of framework legislation in priority areas); and

- active participation in international efforts addressing global pollution and degradation of the environment.

Since 1993, Slovenia has operated an environmental development fund that supports investments in state services on environmental protection, local environmental protection, public services, the purchase and development of equipment and technologies for ecology, the implementation of environmentally friendly technologies and products, and that supports polluters in their efforts to diminish pollution.

In 1998, the government projected that the environmental *acquis* and accompanying administrative procedures will be adopted by the end of 2000. Because the total investment costs amount to approximately DEM 5 billion[19] (or DEM 2,500 per capita), this projection is not realistic. Instead, it is expected that full compliance will be reached by 2007, with annual costs as high as DEM 750 million, which represent quite a large increase over the current investment of about DEM 240 million (0.7 percent of GDP). Institutional changes (expenditures for administration, monitoring, and enforcement) will require an additional DEM 50 million.

Investments in water quality are considered the most costly. The planned investment costs (DEM 2.3 billion) will focus on municipal waste water treatment and industrial waste water treatment plants, in compliance with EU directives. In waste management, national regulations are not yet compatible with the requirements of EU legislation. Investment in waste management will require substantial costs to comply with EU directives (approximately DEM 2.2 billion).

In biodiversity, the conservation strategy provides a policy framework for more sectoral activities. It contains general provisions in compliance with EU legislation providing for a very strict protection system. Implementation of the EU CITES regulation is foreseen. Air quality requires modest costs (DEM 480 million). Major polluters (the Šoštanj power plant on thermal energy and local heating plants) will be replaced by modern combined power plants.

The sum of these costs is sizable. The public sector (70 percent) and the private sector (30 percent) will share the costs. The taxpayers and the business sector will carry the burden of environmental adjustment.

Conclusions

No major political and social changes are expected after Slovenia's EU accession. Political parties and pressure groups within civil society with predominantly nationalistic or local political programs will be the main losers of the integration. We can expect that because of the transformation and integration process, about 15 percent of the population (the poorest part of unskilled workers and unemployed persons) will live below the poverty line. The winners of the integration and transformation will be private businessmen and people with high education and highly skilled employees in specific service sectors (banking, insurance, financial intermediaries, part of the public administration).

After accession to the EU, Slovenian economic and social policy will face severe problems in the least developed regions (Zasavje, Spodnje Posavje, and Pomurje) with poor development possibilities and high unemployment rates. Efficient regional public administration authorities, implementation of new regional policies, and cross-border cooperation with neighboring countries will be required to prevent more economic differentiation between developed and underdeveloped regions.

With Slovenia integrating into the EU, an assessment of the long- and short-term costs and benefits is required. This assessment will constitute a basis for rational economic decisions and for decisions by individual enterprises during the preaccession period and upon entry into the EU. Integrating countries face the consequences of structural changes in particular sectors. Evaluation of these effects is further complicated by the "moving target" problem and the continuing process of economic stabilization and structural reforms needed for sustainable growth.

Research studies on costs and benefits of Slovenian accession were mainly prepared for specific sectors, and only a few comprehensive studies analyze the effects of the accession on the macroeconomic aggregates. Simulation results of different models used to assess the possible overall or macroeconomic effects of Slovenia's approaching the EU (further trade liberalization and adoption of EU Common Customs Tariff) are positive, with differences in the character of the models and assumptions used. Unfortunately, there is no research on the effects of adopting the *acquis*, and one important element is still missing in the implementation of the "EU Accession Strategy of the Republic of Slovenia"—the estimation of costs and benefits of declared reforms for each particular policy and the possible effects of the status quo.

According to its structural characteristics, the Slovenian economy seems suitable for inclusion in the EMU. Slovenia can expect net benefits from joining the EMU, because it is not specifically exposed to asymmetric shocks. We can conclude that consumers will be winners in the financial and monetary integration, while some financial institutions (banks and insurance companies, for example) will be the losers.

Simulation results at the sector level indicate that the producers oriented primarily toward the domestic market would particularly feel negative consequences from further opening the domestic market. Whether they ultimately will adapt successfully to conditions prevailing on the world market depends on the ability of individual producers to adjust to foreign competition and on the measures that government bodies adopt. Further cuts in import duties and increased competition would positively affect export-oriented producers. Increased product specialization with an enhancement of variety and quality of the products and services offered also will have positive effects for domestic consumers.

Results for the agriculture and food-processing industry clearly indicate that both production and foreign trade are very sensitive to the level of budget support given. Changes in the levels of foreign trade protection affect primarily the volume of imports. Regarding the most probable CAP scenario at point of entry into the EU, the effects on these sectors probably will be negative if no structural adjustments are made in the preaccession period.

The net effect for agriculture (also considering changes in the expenditures of taxpayers and consumers) is positive only in those scenarios that assume that Slovenia will obtain compensatory payments from EU funds. The estimated total net effects for agriculture (also considering effects on the processing industry and on food consumption) are on the other hand positive regardless of the scenario assumed.

Analyses at the enterprise level show a growing importance of FDI, especially in capital and labor-intensive products. FDI evidently has played a positive role in the restructuring process so far, but these investments also have increased competition in the domestic market. Despite the observed positive developments in the restructuring efforts, the Slovenian economy still has problems, especially within domestic enterprises that have no FDI (DEs) in the capital-intensive and labor-intensive industrial groups. At the enterprise level, it seems that among the losers in the integration process will be more of these DEs, among them particularly those still oriented primarily toward the domestic market.

Integration of the Slovenian financial sector into the EU Single Market undoubtedly will bring benefits to consumers, while the balance between the costs and benefits of financial integration for domestic financial institutions will depend on their ability to cope with intensified foreign competition in the Slovenian financial market.

The adjustment costs to achieve harmonization with the EU environmental *acquis* amount to approximately 5 billion DEM. The bulk of investment will be devoted to meeting EU water quality standards, waste treatment, and air quality. For this reason, the Slovene government will negotiate either derogations or long transitional periods. In the next eight years, annual costs (investment and operating) would be about DEM 800 million. The public sector (70 percent) and the private sector (30 percent) will share these costs. The taxpayers and the business sector will carry the burden of environmental adjustment.

The current negotiations between the Slovene government and the EU commission show that numerous chapters of *acquis communautaire* remain open for negotiations: flows of goods, labor, services and capital; company and competition law, culture and audiovisual policy, customs union, foreign relations, security, and tax system. The issues already resolved because they will cause no problems after Slovenia's entry into the EU include: fishery, statistics, industrial policy, SMEs, science and technology, education and youth, telecommunications and information technology, health, and consumer protection.

The attempts to assess some short- and long-run effects show that accession into the EU will bring net benefits to the Slovenian economy, particularly in the long run. In the process of approaching the EU, there will be groups of winners and losers, but the expected positive effects will more than compensate for the expected negative effects.

Appendix A

The CGE model used is based on a consistent database, the social accounting matrix (SAM) for 1992, divided into 27 standard basic production sectors of NACE classification.[20] The model includes two production factors: labor and capital. The assumption was that they are mobile between sectors which means uniform production factor prices.

Three types of institutions were included in the model: enterprises, households, and government. Transfers of enterprises and households depend on the total income of the institutions and are established in relation to the income calculated from the base SAM data. All elements of government expenditure were determined exogenously in nominal terms.

Budget surplus or deficit was calculated as a residual of total government revenue after deducting fixed expenditure. The aggregate level of consumption depends on the total household income available. The amount of fixed capital formation as a whole depends on the funds collected for investment or, to put it in another way, the amount of savings determines the amount of investment (savings-driven model). The sectoral structure of investment goods, and of goods in stock, remains unchanged.

The model distinguishes between direct and indirect taxes (customs duties, sales taxes, state subsidies, and export subsidies). The largest block relates to activities and commodities. The functioning of the economy is described by means of a two-level CES function. At the first level, different production factors are aggregated into the value-added and at the second level value-added and intersector expenditures are aggregated (with zero elasticity of substitution) and form gross production.

Four forms of commodities are defined: domestic, imported, exported, and composite. The relations of domestic and imported commodities (from the EU and the rest of the world) are again modeled through the two-level CES function. Their interrelationship depends on the sector-relative prices and estimated values of elasticity of substitution.

On the supply side, the commodities produced are either consumed domestically or exported to the EU or the rest of the world. The division is modeled on the CET function. Domestic producers do not have any influence on world prices and all transfers with the rest of the world are determined exogenously.

The numeraire is the exchange rate. As regards the model closure, investment is determined endogenously, dependent on the funds available for investment. In the base variant, capital and labor are determined exogenously (neoclassical variant of the model closure) as their prices adjust.

The current account balance between the Slovene economy and both rest-of-the-world accounts is also determined exogenously. The model includes 3,760 equations and the same number of variables. One can conclude that it is an applicable variation of the CGE model with a sharp focus on an expanded analytical application. It was primarily developed to analyze the effects of Slovenia approaching the EU, although it can be used to analyze the consequences of numerous economic policy measures.

New versions of the CGE model were based on the new SAMs for 1993 and 1995 (Potoènik 1996, 1997) using the same equation specifications as the CGE model with the 1992 base solution.

Appendix B

TABLE 10.A1 THE EFFECTS OF TRADE LIBERALIZATION ON SECTORAL GDP CHANGES ON ACCOUNT OF THE EUROPE AGREEMENT, WITH REGARD TO DIFFERENT ECONOMIC POLICIES

		SIM 1	SIM 2	SIM 3	SIM 4	SIM 5	SIM 6	SIM 7	SIM 8
Agriculture	GDP	−	−	−	−	−	−−	−	+
	Labor	−	−	−	−	−	−−	+	+++
	Exports	−	−	−−	−−	−	−−	−	−
	Imports	−	−	++	++	+	+++	+++	+++
Manufacturing	GDP	+	+	+	+	+	++	++	+++
	Labor	+	+	+	+	+	++	+++	+++
	Exports	+	++	+	+	++	+	+++	+++
	Imports	+	++	+++	+++	++	+++	+++	+++
Services	GDP	+	−	+	−	+	+	+	+++
	Labor	−	−	−	−	+	+	+	+++
	Exports	−	+	−	+	−	+	++	++
	Imports	−	+	++	+	+	+++	+++	+++

Sector	Name	SIM 1	SIM 2	SIM 3	SIM 4	SIM 5	SIM 6	SIM 7	SIM 8
A	Agricultural and forestry products	−		−−	−	−	−−	−	+
B	Fishery products	+++	+++	++	++	+++	+	+++	+++
CA	Coal, crude oil, natural gas	−	−	−−−	−−−	−	−−	−−−	+
CB	Ferrous, nonferrous ores and stones				++		++	++	+
DA	Food, beverages, and tobacco	−	−	−	++	−	++	−	++
DB	Textiles and wearing apparel	−	+	−	−	+	−	+++	+++
DC	Leather, footwear, leather products	+	++	−	+	+	−	+++	+++
DD	Wood and wood products, excl. furniture	−−		−	+	−−	++	++	-
DE	Cellulose, paper, and cardboard	−		−		−	−	+	++
DF	Coke and refined petroleum					−−−	−−−	+	+

		SIM 1	SIM 2	SIM 3	SIM 4	SIM 5	SIM 6	SIM 7	SIM 8
DG	Basic chemicals and chemical products	+	–	– –	+	– – –	– –	– – –	+
DH	Rubber and plastic products	+	+	–	+	–	–	+	++
DI	Nonmetallic mineral products	– –	+	+	– –	+++	+++	+++	+++
DJ	Basic metals and metal products	+	++	+	+	++	++	+++	+++
DK	Machinery and equipment	++	++	++	+	+++	+++	+++	+++
DL	Electrical mach., radio, TV and commun. equip.	++	+	+	++	+	+	++	++
DM	Transport equipment	+	+	+	++	+	+	++	++
DN	Wooden furniture, miscellaneous goods n.e.c.	+++	+++	+++	+++	+++	+++	+++	+++
E	Electricity, gas, steam, and water	–	–	–	–	+	+	++	++
F	Construction	–	++	++	+	+++	+++	++	+++
G	Trade	+	+	+	+	+	++	+++	+++
H	Restaurants and hotels	–	–	+	–	+	+	++	++
I	Transport, storage, communication, travel agen.	+	+	+	–	+	+	++	+++
J	Financial intermediation, insurance	+	+	+	+	+	++	++	++
K	Dwelling services	+	–	–	+	–	+	++	+++
MS	Other market services	+	+	+	+	+	++	++	+++
NMS	Nonmarket services	– – –	–	– – –	–	– – –	– – –	– –	++

SIM 1 - SIM 4: aggregate GDP unchanged

SIM 5 - SIM 8: volume of the aggregate GDP may also change

SIM 1 and SIM 5: constant current account balance and government consumption (lower customs and other import duties offset by increased sales taxes - higher price of gasoline)

SIM 2: constant current account balance and lower import duties (offset by lower government consumption)

SIM 3 and SIM 6: current account balance adjusting and constant government consumption (lower customs and other import duties offset by increased sales taxes - higher price of gasoline)

SIM 4 and SIM 7: current account balance is adjusting and lower import duties (offset by lower government consumption)

SIM 8: constant current account balance and lower import duties (higher government consumption)

Source: The results of simulations using the Computable General Equilibrium Model of the Slovene economy, Potočnik and Majcen (1996).

In table 10.A1 the summary effects of the Europe Agreement at the aggregate and sectoral levels are presented. If as a result of simulation the variable in any one particular sector increased (decreased) by up to 5 percent, the change is marked "+(−)"; if it increased (decreased) by 5 percent to 10 percent, it is marked "++(− −)"; and if it increased (decreased) by more than 10 percent, it is marked "+++(———)". The first four simulations were based on the assumption that aggregate GDP would remain unchanged and the last three were based on the assumption that the volume of production factors would vary, or to put it differently, the volume of the aggregate GDP might also change. All simulations were based on the assumption of full implementation of the Europe Agreement (complete abolition of import duties with the exception of agricultural primary production and processed goods) and the adoption of different exchange and public finance policies.

Notes

1. An appropriate tool for this kind of analysis would be a macroeconometric model. But because of the lack of time series data of sufficient length, research activities in this area used partial or general equilibrium models based on social accounting matrices. The models developed focused primarily on estimating the effects of foreign trade liberalization due to the introduction of new customs tariffs, the full implementation of the Europe Agreement with the EU, the free-trade agreement with the EFTA countries, and the adoption of the Common Customs Tariff after accession to the EU (see Potoènik and Majcen 1996; Potoènik 1996 and 1997; Buehrer and Majcen, 1999, forthcoming).

2. Caf and Damijan, 1995.

3. The result showed here is one arising from oligopolistic competition, which seems more realistic in the case of Slovenia. If perfect and monopolistic competition were assumed, the cumulative increases in GDP would be 3.5 percent and 3.2 percent, respectively.

4. From CGE simulation results in Potoènik and Majcen (1996).

5. The research developed a computational general equilibrium model based on the 1993 Social Accounting Matrix (Buehrer and Majcen, 1999).

6. De Grauwe and Lavrač, 1999.

7. The pattern of manufacturing output, trade, and domestic demand and their changes in the 90s is more thoroughly presented in Majcen (1998, section 4, p. 20–37).

8. The analysis is based on simulations of a computable general equilibrium (CGE) model (Potoènik and Majcen 1996; Potoènik 1996, 1997; Buehrer and Majcen 1999). A brief explanation of the CGE model can be found in Appendix A.

The simulations were based on differing assumptions about the balance of payments and government consumption. The exogenously determined current account of the balance of payments implies some restrictions in external debts and is in the case of Slovenia a reasonable assumption. In line with the controlled floating exchange rate, the assumption is a permanent surplus in the current account balance.

The assumption of lower government consumption is in accordance with the policy Slovenia has adopted of reducing the burden on the economy. The assumption of increased sales tax on oil derivatives as a compensation for reduced import duties points to the need to cover this deficit and to adjust to Western economies.

9. Summary effects of the Europe Agreement at the aggregate and sectoral levels are presented in Table 10.A1 in Appendix B.

10. Effects on the service sectors are the result of government policies adopted and the liberalization process in the manufacturing sectors.

11. See Majcen (1998), p. 47–49.

12. Additional simulations were made with a new version of the CGE model based on Social Accounting Matrix (SAM) for 1993 and the most recent SAM for 1995 (Potoènik 1997).

13. Using the new CGE model developed by Buehrer and Majcen (1999).

14. A static deterministic net income model for Slovene agriculture coupled with a computable general equilibrium model (CGE model) of the Slovene economy was used. The scenarios were implemented through different foreign trade protection (tariffs and levies) and budget support. Further, it was assumed that at least one of the production factors, price, is exogenous. This meant that an equilibrium in the production factor market was achieved through the adjustment of quantities; this allows for the possibility of changing the aggregate GDP. Adjustment of the quantities of labor entailed an implicit assumption about unemployment; although quite a reasonable assumption, estimated growth rates of additional employment may in practice be difficult to realize as the labor force lacks adequate skills and mobility.

15. The authors were aware of the fact that integrating Slovene agriculture into the CAP constituted a moving target. The agricultural policy that Slovenia is likely to adopt on possible entry into the EU may well be very different from the current policy; it is thus extremely difficult to predict the exact nature of future changes. To depict the possible range of changes and their effects on Slovene animal husbandry and crop growing, simulation estimates were calculated on the assumption that basically the EU CAP offers a few possible developments —these are depicted in the scenarios. All the estimates in the scenarios were calculated for individual agricultural products and refer to producer prices,

direct budget supports, costs, and—as a new derived category—net incomes. The scenarios were compared with an estimate of the situation in Slovene agriculture for the period 1992–95.

16. The data are from the report on banking supervision in Slovenia in 1998 and the first half of 1999, Bank of Slovenia.

17. Several studies exist that assess (only) direct net outcome of Slovenia's transfers to the EU budget and EU transfers through different funds, taking into account the existing regulation and the changes announced by the European Commission. Strmšnik (1997) estimated the net budgetary effect for the year 2005—it ranges from ECU 570 m to ECU 870 m, accounting for approximately 2 percent of GDP that year. According to Breus (1996), the costs of the Slovenian accession should amount to ECU 1011 m or 5.24 percent of Slovenia's GDP, and Slovenia's transfers to the EU budget should amount to ECU 248 m or 1.28 percent of GDP, with the net positive effect at ECU 764 m or 3.95 percent of GDP. With an additional assumption of changed power of new members, Baldwin et al. (1997) estimated net budgetary effect for Slovenia in 2002 to amount to ECU 1.3–1.9 billion. Unfortunately there was no attempt to also estimate indirect implications of these potential transfers on the Slovenian economy and regional development as well as on the necessity to change the role of the existing industrial, agricultural and regional policies.

18. See Strmšnik (1997), Murn (1998), Kukar (1998) and Kukar et al. (1998)

19. World Bank estimates, 1999.

20. A detailed description of the model, together with model specification and all simulation results, can be found in Potoènik and Majcen (1996).

Literature

Baldwin, R. E., J. F. François, and R. Portes. 1997. "The Costs and Benefits of Eastern Enlargement: the Impact on the EU and Central Europe." Economic Policy, A European Forum. USA Blackwell Publishers.

Breus, F. 1996. "Austria's Approach Towards the EU." Paper presented at the Expert Meeting on the Economic Aspects of Slovenia's Integration into the European Union. Bled, Slovenia. April 12–13.

Buehrer, T. S., and B. Majcen. 1999. *Two-Regional CGE Model Slovenia–European Union.* Ljubljana: Institute for Economic Research, forthcoming.

Caf, D. and J. Damijan, 1995. "Welfare Effects of Trade Liberalization and Integration on Slovenian Economy: A General Equilibrium Analysis." Paper in the Proceedings of the East Central Roundtable Conference IV: "Dynamic Effects of Economic Integration" — RBMP '95. Ljubljana Center for Foreign Trade. Bled.

De Grauwe, P., and V. Lavrač. 1999. *Inclusion of Central European Countries in the EMU.* Boston: Kluwer Academic Publishers.

Erjavec, E., M. Rednak, T. Volk, eds. 1997. *Slovene Agriculture and European Union.* ÈZD Kmeèki glas, Ljubljana.

Hafner-Fink, D. 1996. *INTO Europe?* Ljubljana: Faculty of Social Sciences.

Institute for Macroeconomic Analysis and Development. 1997. *EU Accession Strategy of the Republic of Slovenia: Economic and Social Part.* Ljubljana.

Kovaèiè, A., and P. Stanovnik. 1999. *Ocena Stroškov Uveljavljanja Okoljske Zakonodaje.* Ljubljana: IER.

Kukar, S., et al., eds. 1998. *Thesis for the Strategy of Regional Development of Slovenia.* Ljubljana: Institute for Economic Research.

Kukar, S. 1998. "Utilisation of Regional Development Potentials and Estimation of Development Possibilities of Slovene Regions." Institute for Economic Research. Paper prepared for the Strategy of Regional Development of Slovenia. Ljubljana.

Kuzmin, F., et al. 1998. "HSL4: The HERMIN Macromodel of Slovenia." First draft. Institute for Economic Research, Ljubljana.

Majcen, B. 1995. "Zunanjetrgovinska Liberalizacija Industrijskih in Kmetijskih Proizvodov (Foreign Trade Liberalization of Industrial and Agriculture Products)." Institute for Economic Research, Ljubljana.

Majcen, B. 1998. "Industrial Growth and Structural Changes in the Associated Countries—The Case of Slovenia." Final report, prepared within the ACE Research Programme, 1996. "Trade Between the European Union and the Associated States: Prospects for the Future." Institute for Economic Research, Ljubljana.

Murn, A. 1998. "The Impact of Economic Policy on Regional Development and Directions of Changes and Completion of National and Sectional Economic

Policies for the Goal of Attaining More Congruent Regional Development."
Paper prepared for the Strategy of Regional Development of Slovenia. Institute
for Economic Research, Ljubljana.

Potoènik, J. 1996. "Analiza Posledic Vkljuèevanja v EU z Modelom Splošnega
RavnotežJa Slovenskega Gospoadrstva Temeljeèim Na Matriki DružBenih
Raèunov Za Leto," 1993. Institute for Economic Research, Ljubljana.

Potoènik, J. 1997. "Effects of Slovene Integration into the EU—CGE, 1995.
Institute for Macro-economic Analysis and Development, Ljubljana.

Potoènik, J., and B. Majcen. 1996. "Slovenija In EU: Analiza Posledic
PribližEvanja z Modelom Splošnega RavnotežJa." Possible Effects of Slovene
Integration into the EU—CGE Approach." Analize, Raziskave in Razvoj. Urad
Republike Slovenije za Makroekonomske Analize in Razvoj, Ljubljana.

Rojec, M., et al. 1998a. "Enterprise Restructuring as the Basic Process of
Slovenia's EU Accession." Prepared for the workshop, "Foreign Direct
Investment and Industrial Modernisation in Central Europe." PHARE-ACE
Project No. P95-2152-R.

Rojec, M. 1998b. "Restructuring and Efficiency Upgrading with Foreign Direct
Investment." Prepared for the project, "Impact of Foreign Direct Investment on
Efficiency and Growth in CEEC Manufacturing." PHARE-ACE Project No.
P96-6183R.

Stanovnik, Tine. 1997. "Dohodki in Socialni PoložAj Upokojencev v Sloveniji." *IB
Revija*, 5-6 (31) 23–39.

Stanovnik, Tine, and Nada Stropnik. 1998. "Impact of Social Transfers on Poverty
and Income Inequality in Slovenia: A Comparison between the Pre-Transition
and the Post-Transition Period." Institute for Economic Research, Ljubljana.

Strmšnik, I. 1997. *Expected Macroeconomic Effects of Integration into the
European Union, Analysis, Research and Development.* Ljubljana: Institute of
Macroeconomic Analysis and Development.

Strmšnik, I. 1998. "Regional Differences in Economic Development and
Unemployment—International Comparison." Paper prepared for the Strategy of
Regional Development of Slovenia. Institute for Economic Research, Ljubljana.

Svetlièiè, M., and P. Stanovnik. 1997. *Slovenia Integrating in the EU.* Ljubljana.

World Bank. 1999. Slovenia, Economic Transformation and EU Accession. Washington, D.C.

Žnidaršiè, Erika. 1996. "Analiza Revšèine Slovenskih Gospodinjstev Na Podlagi Podatkov iz Ankete o Porabi Gospodinjstev v Letu," 1993. Statistical Office of the Republic of Slovenia, Ljubljana.

PART III

EU Perspectives

Internal Problems of the European Union That Might Obstruct an Enlargement Toward the East

Martin Brusis
Bertelsmann Research Group on Policy Centre for Applied Policy Research

Introduction[1]

The following study explores internal problems of the European Union that might obstruct the project of enlargement toward the East. It does not conceive "internal" in a narrow geographic or legal-institutional sense. Rather, it tries to look beyond the problems of the current EU members and the current institutional and policy-related *acquis communautaire* to the problems of an enlarged EU.

"Obstruction" is also interpreted in a wider sense, denoting not only the block-ade of accession but also its postponement to an uncertain future. This approach implies that the study builds upon scenarios that try to anticipate possible problem constellations. The study's objective is to analyze their critical relevance for the enlargement process on the one hand, and the problem-solving capacities of the EU on the other.

The Eastern Enlargement will increase economic and social disparities in the EU more than any other enlargement in the history of the Union. To cope with their internal disparities, EU member states have developed a sophisticated cohesion and structural policy. The first section of the paper discusses the effectiveness of this policy tool in reducing the East-West gap. The second section of the paper dis-cusses the difficulties faced by regional economies in both Eastern and Western Europe as a result of transnational economic integration.

Eastern Enlargement entails an integration of the large agricultural sectors of the Central and East European countries. The third section of the paper discusses the effects of this sectoral integration. It will analyze the policy responses given by the EU agricultural ministers and the Berlin European Council with respect to the next WTO negotiations.

According to a perception shared by many EU citizens, the enlargement will affect the "space of freedom, security and law" created by the Treaty of Amsterdam. The fourth section of the paper discusses the political relevance of these fears. To ensure the functioning of an enlarged EU, the member states have agreed on the need to implement further reforms of EU institutions and procedures. The fifth section of the paper considers the interrelatedness and viability of crucial institutional reforms.

The war in the Federal Republic of Yugoslavia has affected the political and economic perspectives of South-East European countries in the enlargement process. The final section of the paper focuses on negative political and economic effects resulting from the war, the post-war EU policy towards the region and the role of enlargement.

Increasing Social and Economic Disparities

Enlargement toward the East will transform the European Union into an institution that is mainly concerned with overcoming gaps in socioeconomic development. Although the EU gains economic weight and increases its population by nearly a third, its average level of income will be reduced by much more than in all previous enlargements. In the Agenda 2000, the European Commission has stressed that an enlargement by 10 CEECs will reduce the EU average GDP per capita by 16 percentage points.[2]

This reduction is due to the relatively low level of economic development of the applicant countries, a feature that will persist for many years since the CEECs are only slowly catching up with the EU-15 (the current 15 members of the EU). According to Eurostat figures, in 1995 the applicant countries had an average GDP per capita of 38 percent of the EU average, measured in Eurostat purchasing power parities.

From 1995 to 1997 this indicator of economic development increased by only 2 percentage points to 40 percent of the EU average. In this period the gap between the two South-East European applicants, Bulgaria and Romania, and the EU average widened. Because of its severe economic crisis, Bulgaria even experienced an absolute decline of GDP per capita (see table 11.1). The persistence of large income disparities between the future member states of an enlarged EU implies that interests will diverge much more than in the EU-15 and, with joint decisions reflecting the lowest common denominator, steps of a "positive integration"[3] will be even more difficult to achieve.

The economic catch-up process has turned out to be much slower than initially expected. After nearly a decade of economic transformation, the GDPs of most

TABLE 11.1 GROSS DOMESTIC PRODUCT IN THE APPLICANT COUNTRIES
(according to Purchasing Power Parity)

	Amount		*Percentage of EU average*	
	1995	*1997*	*1995*	*1997*
Bulgaria	4,900	4,400	28	23
Czech Republic	10,800	12,000	62	63
Estonia	5,600	7,000	32	37
Hungary	7,800	8,900	45	47
Latvia	4,300	5,100	25	27
Lithuania	4,800	5,800	28	30
Poland	6,200	7,500	36	40
Romania	5,600	5,800	32	31
Slovak Republic	7,400	8,900	43	47
Slovenia	11,300	13,000	65	68
Average	6,600	7,500	38	40

Source: Eurostat.

of the CEECs have not yet recovered to their 1989 levels. According to data from the European Bank for Reconstruction and Development, in 1998 Slovenia and Poland were the only countries that had attained a GDP higher than their GDP level of 1989. The slow recovery can be explained partly by the insufficient inflow of FDI necessary to support a substantial modernization of the outdated capital stock in CEECs.

Although the region has increasingly attracted foreign investors, and Hungary attained particularly high FDI per capita, one has to take into account that, as a share of GDP, foreign direct investment in Central and Eastern Europe has reached only half of the level of investment South-East Asian countries attracted.[4] The allocation of foreign direct investment within the region shows a clear preference for the advanced transition countries, and the distance between Poland and Bulgaria or Romania in terms of cumulated FDI per capita has even increased.[5] The lagging behind of the southeast European countries is also reflected in the shares of investment in fixed assets that fell in Romania and Bulgaria but rose in Poland, Hungary, and the Czech Republic.[6]

The example of the German unification illustrates that, despite very high financial transfers, the economic catch-up process has taken a long time and has still not led to an alignment of West and East German levels. Gross public financial transfers of nearly 1000 billion DM effected an increase of East German GDP per capita from 31.3 percent to 54.0 percent of the West German level between 1991 and 1996.[7]

The low level of GDP per capita in the CEECs poses a challenge to the system of EU cohesion policy, which has not been designed to cope with such large income gaps. Upon its accession, the entire region would qualify as an Objective-1[8] area for the structural funds. (The eligibility criteria are less than 75 percent of EU average GDP per capita) and for the cohesion fund (the eligibility criteria being less than 90 percent of EU average GDP per capita).

The Commission has calculated that an enlargement by the 10 CEECs and Cyprus would increase the population living in Objective-1 areas from 94 million to 200 million. This increase means that the eligible population would rise from 25.3 percent to 41.9 percent of the total EU-26 population, which would be contrary to the principle of concentration of the cohesion policy.[9] Areas in the current member states will lose their eligibility for regional assistance because enlargement would reduce the average GDP per capita of the EU and the new regulations on the structural funds restrict the areas eligible for Objective-1 and Objective-2[10] support to 40 percent of the EU population.

The compromise found at the Berlin European Council has avoided and postponed a redistribution of cohesion policy resources beyond the end of the financial planning period. It did so because it has separated structural assistance for the new member states (envisaged from 2002 onward) from the structural operations for the EU-15, which will be only gradually reduced after 2001 (see table 11.2). As the eligible areas are determined for the entire period, the accession-induced reduction of the EU average GDP per capita will come into effect only after 2006. Structural assistance for the prospective new member states will not be granted according to the same criteria as for the current member states. Rather, the financial perspective envisages a gradual increase until the absorption capacity ceiling of 4 percent of GDP is reached in 2006.

The distribution of structural expenditures does not constitute an appropriate strategy to cushion the existing and increasing socioeconomic disparities in Europe for the following reasons:

- Expenditure on structural assistance is inversely related to the level of economic wealth. The higher a country's GDP per capita, the more resources are available to support economic growth.

TABLE 11.2 FINANCIAL RESOURCES ALLOCATED TO THE NEW EU MEMBER STATES
(as agreed by the European Council in Berlin, 24–25 March 1999)

Enlargement (appropriations for commitments) (million euros, 1999 prices)	2002	2003	2004	2005	2006
Heading 8 (Enlargement)	6,450	9,030	11,610	14,200	16,780
Agriculture	1,600	2,030	2,450	2,930	3,400
Structural operations	3,750	5,830	7,920	10,000	12,080
Internal policies	760	760	790	820	850
Administration	370	410	450	450	450

- Membership matters more than developmental needs. Although the poor member states of the current EU-15 (Greece and Portugal) receive structural assistance amounting to approximately 400 euros per capita annually, the 10 applicant countries are granted a preaccession assistance of approximately 30 euros per capita per year in 2000 and 2001.

- Incumbent member states remain privileged. Assuming that those applicant countries that have already started negotiations accede in 2002, they will receive an annual structural and agricultural assistance of 85 euros per capita (Cyprus excluded), rising to 247 euros in 2006, while structural assistance for the poor members of the EU-15 will not change significantly.

- Advanced transition countries receive more than laggards. Although the preaccession assistance will be divided among fewer countries after the first candidates have joined the EU and despite the establishment of a small catch-up fund, the distance between the new members and those that will join later will increase. If the countries that started accession negotiations in April 1998 join in 2002, those countries not belonging to this group will receive 73 euros per capita as preaccession assistance, which will only rise if further candidates join before 2006[11] (see table 11.3).

- If structural assistance is granted with respect to the ceiling of 4 percent of GDP, new member states with a higher GDP and higher growth rates will receive more assistance.[12]

Socioeconomic disparities between the EU and the CEECs are rooted in the different economic structures. With the exception of the Czech Republic, CEE economies still have a very high share of agricultural employment, ranging from 37.3 percent (Romania) to 6 percent (Slovak Republic) of total employment in 1997. In Poland, 26.7 percent of the labor force are still working in the agricultural sector whereas the EU average is only 5.1 percent.[13]

TABLE 11.3 FINANCIAL RESOURCES ENVISAGED FOR THE PREACCESSION ASSISTANCE TO THE APPLICANT COUNTRIES (AS AGREED BY THE EUROPEAN COUNCIL IN BERLIN, 24–25 MARCH 1999)

Preaccession instruments (million euros, 1999 prices)	2000	2001	2002	2003	2004	2005	2006
Preaccession instruments	3,120	3,120	3,120	3,120	3,120	3,120	3,120
PHARE	1,560	1,560	1,560	1,560	1,560	1,560	1,560
Agricultural	520	520	520	520	520	520	520
Structural	1,040	1,040	1,040	1,040	1,040	1,040	1,040

Modernization and structural adjustment of this sector will lead to large numbers of redundancies, a particular problem in the CEECs because of the comparatively low flexibility of the labor market. Unemployment in the CEECs can be characterized as a "stagnant pool,"[14] where only few unemployed manage to get employed again. High shares of long-term unemployed can be found primarily in rural areas lacking alternative job opportunities.

The current restructuring of industry will entail further labor shedding in the former state-owned enterprises and particularly in heavy industry, which is a typical example of state socialist industrialization. It is unclear to what extent the growth of the service sector and of private enterprises can absorb the unemployed from shrinking agricultural and declining industrial sectors.

As with structural expenditures, there is a certain mismatch between needs and problems on the one side, and policy programs on the other. While the economic integration with Western Europe accelerates structural changes in the CEECs, the preaccession assistance and the transfer of *acquis communautaire* regulations do not provide targeted support to cope with the consequences of the change.

Rapid structural adjustment is particularly hampered by bottlenecks in public infrastructure.[15] The transport, communication, energy, and environmental infrastructure built under the previous state socialist systems are inappropriate for the needs of modern economies. The new governments have not allocated much resources to infrastructure development because of declining revenues resulting from economic transition and budgetary constraints. Attempts to involve private sponsors in the financing of transport infrastructure have not yet been successful, for example, in the case of the Wien-Györ motorway.

The lack of appropriate infrastructure hampers growth in the region because it restricts the capacity of the CEECs to absorb a larger inflow of private investment and EU structural assistance. With respect to infrastructure, the enlargement strategy chosen by the EU appears particularly unsuitable because it expects the CEECs to establish a physical infrastructure for the implementation of the *acquis before* their accession while granting substantial support to build this infrastructure only *after* accession.

This suboptimal development policy results from the competing priorities the EU has to reconcile. The EMU and the Internal Market are the institutionalized results of bargaining between poorer and richer member states. The latter gained the economic benefits of further integration while the higher adjustment costs of the former were compensated by increased financial transfers.[16] The CAP apparently has become a kind of regulatory mechanism whose political logic is to ensure the participation of the agricultural sector (and mainly those countries with a traditionally structured agriculture) in the benefits generated by the integration of trade, services, and industrial production.[17] The institutions and cooperation procedures of the EU provide an arrangement to balance competing interests and priorities, which preserves the achievements of integration but restricts the options to respond with appropriate policies to new challenges.

Because of these constraints neither a quick and significant shifting of resources toward Eastern Europe (the frequently demanded "new Marshall plan") nor a partial membership for the CEECs became feasible options after 1989 (when the former socialist countries of Eastern Europe decided to introduce the western institutions of liberal democracy and market economy).[18] The constrained policy approach of the EU, as discussed in the preceding paragraphs, was successful for those CEECs that began their transition under auspicious conditions and could draw from their economic, social, and cultural resources of modernity. But EU integration and trade cooperation offer too few incentives and benefits to other countries in the region including Russia, Belarus, Albania, the Federal Republic of Yugoslavia, and Bosnia and Herzegovina. Its success appears still uncertain in the cases of Bulgaria, Romania, Croatia, and the former Yugoslav Republic of Macedonia (FYR Macedonia).

Consequences of Transnational Economic Integration

Despite the establishment of an Internal Market for goods, capital, services, and labor in Europe, economic differences between the regions of the EU have only slightly decreased. In a recent report on the impact of structural assistance, the Commission has stated that the gap in GDP per capita between Objective-1 areas and the rest of the Union has narrowed only slowly, with the level in the former having only risen from 64 percent to 68 percent of the EU average between 1988 and 1996.[19]

The difference in unemployment rates between the EU average and the Objective-1 areas has remained by and large the same. Among the cohesion countries, only Ireland has made significant progress toward the EU average while Greece could not improve its economic position relative to the EU average. According to the Commission's First Cohesion Report, disparities in GDP per capita between EU regions did not change significantly between 1983 and 1993, while disparities in unemployment rates increased.[20]

These results indicate that even the comparatively large resource inflows in the framework of the structural operations did not significantly affect the inherited interregional disparities within the EU, which are not as wide as disparities between Western and Eastern Europe.

With markets re-established, the economies of Central and Eastern Europe are undergoing a major structural change not only between agriculture, industry, and services, but also between and within subsectors, branches, and companies. A cause and consequence of this process is the fundamental re-orientation of foreign trade from the former Soviet Union and its successor states to the EU's Internal Market.

The emerging patterns of foreign trade and foreign direct investment in the CEECs exhibit specific spatial features. Foreign direct investment inflows tend to concentrate on regions that are easily accessible from Western Europe. Companies with a huge share of EU exports (usually these are companies with modernized production facilities and foreign ownership) tend to settle in regions close to western markets. The eastern regions of the CEECs are neglected, as reflected in the lower FDI per capita, lower per-capita incomes, a lower labor force productivity, and higher unemployment rates.[21]

Residents of the applicant countries perceive EU enlargement as a manifestation and a consequence of the global integration of factor markets, which will exacerbate regional differences within their countries. Three patterns of economic integration in the CEECs could be distinguished as affecting the prospects of regions within these countries. Some regions will become integrated into the world economy by foreign direct investments, others will be marginalized, and a third group of regions will be integrated by activation of their indigenous capacities.[22]

The development capacities of predominantly agrarian regions, monostructural industrial regions (regions dominated by a single industry), and prospering regions differ.[23] One example of a monostructural industrial area is the region of Katowice in Poland, dominated by metallurgical and mining industries suffering from the breakdown of the former CMEA trade relations and the excess supply of steel and coal products in the EU market.

The Accession Partnership has obliged the Polish Government to submit a restructuring plan for its steel and mining industry. In 1998 the government declared its intention to reduce the number of employees in the steel industry from 85,000 to 45,000 in 2003, and in coal mining from 244,500 to 139,500 in 2002. Labor shedding of any larger scale would hit the Katowice region in particular. The government has therefore decided to maintain the volume of steel production, although the EU Commission preferred a lower volume of production. Regions like Katowice have great difficulties in rebuilding their economic structure on the basis of their given endowments of economic, social, and human capital.

The predominantly agrarian regions of Central and Eastern Europe often lack the capacity to develop and implement a regional development concept tailored to their endowment of production factors and their specific development needs. Competitive programs for state grants or the programming-based regional policy approach of the structural funds may be biased toward regions with better initial conditions. Hungarian experiences with grant programs in regional policy have shown that very poor agrarian regions are not capable of competing with more developed regions for state funds.[24] Such regions may become locked in a development trap, lacking the means to mobilize resources that could enable them to overcome the barriers to further development.

Widening regional disparities pose a particular challenge to the CEECs. CEE governments lack the knowledge of regional policymaking under market conditions and have few opportunities to influence the restructuring process. Their domestic private sector provides neither sufficient resources to renew the outdated capital stock of the former state-socialist enterprises nor the required know-how of corporate governance.

As a consequence of these deficiencies, regional disparities may become an economic obstacle to further EU integration, undermining political support for the accession. CEE governments face a policy dilemma. On the one hand, they can support prosperous regions to facilitate a quicker catch-up with EU levels and wait until spillover effects induce economic growth in other regions, or until internal labor migration processes defuse the labor market crisis in declining regions. On the other hand, they can support a costly redistribution between regions and try to keep political and social tensions under control by cushioning and delaying the effects of structural change. Actors at the regional level usually have very limited resources to reverse a regressive development path triggered by transnational economic integration.

One may ask whether the EU's cohesion approach, which aims at enabling backward regions to catch up with advanced regions, is an appropriate strategy to facilitate the modernization of the CEECs, a process mainly driven by the growth dynamics of the advanced regions in the CEECs. This question has also been posed by the proponents of an efficiency-oriented regional policy approach in the CEECs. It can be argued that "priority should be given to the removal of bottlenecks in growth poles, which will promote faster convergence of the national income per capita towards the Union average but might increase regional disparities rather than giving assistance primarily to lagging regions, which might allow them to catch up to the national average to the possible detriment of national income growth."[25]

Through Eastern Enlargement, the EU may, on the one hand, be viewed as the source of economic decline and social crisis in lagging regions. Protest movements may mobilize the losers of economic transition against the enlargement project. National governments may shift responsibilities to the EU to avoid the blame on themselves. On the other hand, the EU institutions not only lack the financial means but they also lack the governance capacity to facilitate regional restructuring and a more equal interregional allocation of economic wealth.

This situation relates to a more general dilemma facing the EU. European integration has unleashed the unifying forces of the Internal Market and monetary union, both demanding more visible political control and political legitimation of decisions at the European level. Yet political developments in the European societies are eroding the "permissive consensus," which has buttressed integration until now. As a result, governments are stressing national interests and referring to the subsidiarity principle of the Maastricht and Amsterdam treaties, which provides for the protection of national sovereignty.

Blockades of Common Agricultural Policy Reform

With respect to the reform of the CAP, the Council of EU agricultural ministers and the Berlin European Council in March 1999 only partially adopted the proposals of the Commission's Agenda 2000. The intervention prices for milk, cereal, and beef were lower than envisaged by the Commission, and were later reduced even further. The member states did not agree to restrict direct income subsidies (compensatory payments) to small farms, as proposed in the Agenda 2000. Instead, degressive subsidy schemes (which focus financial support on smaller farms) may be applied by member states voluntarily. Contrary to the Commission's proposal, set-aside programs will be continued. The European Council agreed to limit the annual average expenditure on agricultural policy in the 2000–2006 period to 40.5 billion euros. The Council also set up fixed amounts of preaccession agricultural assistance and of agricultural assistance reserved for the new member states after their accession. These resources may not be spent for CAP purposes, nor may the CAP budget be used to support the accession and catch-up process of the applicant countries. The German government had proposed to introduce the principle of cofinancing CAP subsidies from national budgets, modeled according to the structural policy, but this was rejected mainly due to French resistance.

These reforms do not alter the CAP fundamentally. The compromise reached by the member states reflects the intention of the initial MacSharry reforms of 1992, that is, to liberalize the market for agricultural products by replacing price subsidies with direct income subsidies. With its reform approach, the EU separates the participation of CEEC in the CAP from the application of direct income subsidies and price subsidies. Eastward enlargement will bring about an integrated market for agricultural products but it does not comprise a transfer of direct income subsidies to CEEC farmers. According to the Commission's plan, CAP intervention prices will be introduced only gradually and after the end of the current financial perspective in 2006.

As a consequence, there will be different price levels for agricultural products in the enlarged EU. To prevent farmers of the prospective new member states entering the current Internal Market with products at a price lower than the subsidized price applied in the CAP, customs duties will have to be raised. This implies that border controls and tariffs have to be maintained after the accession date of the first applicant countries, a perspective that contradicts the core principles of the Internal Market.

If the bilateral agreements on price alignment with applicant countries differ, it also would be necessary to re-impose tariffs between the applicant countries.[26] Another implication is that the EU would have to accept that the CEECs continue to impose customs duties on agricultural imports from the EU. However, since it is of major importance for the CEECs to join the Union, they are in a weak position to bargain with the EU on the terms of accession.

Much depends on the uncertain development of price levels for agricultural products in Central and Eastern Europe. The quicker the prices of agricultural commodities in the CEECs converge to the EU level, the easier a full integration into the Internal Market of agricultural products. Currently, comparatively low labor, land, and production input costs in some CEE countries have allowed their farmers to sell their goods for a lower price than EU farmers. But the price difference for these countries is not transformed into a competitive advantage since agriculture in the CEECs is characterized by an enormous deficit in productivity compared with the EU-15.

Weakly developed food-processing industries, backward infrastructure, and inappropriate farm size restrict the farms' competitiveness. The CEE governments do not have the budgetary resources to support their farmers to the same extent as the EU.[27] This is reflected in a continuous deficit in the balance of agricultural trade with the EU (with the exception of Hungary). Restructuring will improve the CEEC's competitive position in agricultural trade, but it also will entail a convergence of product prices to the level of the EU.

The scope of price increases in the CEEC is limited, however, because consumers already spend a much larger share of their income on food than in the EU.[28] Market integration and the ensuing restructuring can be expected to trigger considerable resistance by the affected social groups, which are more reluctant to accept modern values than the rural population in most West European countries. In Poland, radical peasant organizations have already mobilized against subsidized agricultural imports from the EU, blocking border stations in January 1999.

The EU supports price convergence by reducing its guaranteed prices for EU agricultural products. This policy is mainly driven by the need to fulfill WTO commitments the EU has undertaken in the Uruguay round. The new WTO round entails further political pressure on the EU to adjust its CAP. The United States and other countries with export-oriented agriculture ("Cairns group") demand a further reduction of tariffs, export subsidies and, most problematic, of production-related direct income subsidies. Because most of the candidate countries of the first group have agreed on lower bounded tariffs than the EU, upon accession they will have to increase their levels of protection, which entails additional conflicts in the WTO negotiations.

Until now the EU has been able to achieve a political acceptance for a gradual liberalization of its agricultural market and a removal of trade barriers because it compensated farmers for their revenue losses with direct income subsidies. These subsidies are linked to the requirement that areas eligible for subsidies are de facto used for agricultural production.[29] The level of subsidies depends on the size and output of farms. Agricultural interest associations within the EU have a strong interest in maintaining this linkage between production and subsidies since it legitimizes their claim for continuous financial support.[30]

A de-linking of subsidies from production would reveal the CAP as a sectoral social policy and equalize CAP subsidies with other social policy expenditures. Defenders of CAP spending would then have to give accounts justifying the necessity of an expenditure while other spending objectives were being neglected.

Leaving subsidies linked to production, on the other hand, would not be tolerated by the Cairns group of agricultural exporters, which would cause a blockade in the WTO negotiations.

If only the market component of the CAP transfers in the Eastern Enlargement, EU farmers will receive income subsidies while farmers in the new member states of Central and Eastern Europe are excluded from this form of support. This exclusion not only would contradict basic principles of equality of member states in an enlarged EU, but it would also appear absurd and irrational in the face of large differences in economic wealth between the current and the future EU member states. Consequently, EU member states have to choose between accepting partial membership (in this context, the maintenance of border controls and tariffs for agricultural products) and further reforms of their CAP.

Threats to Internal Security and Their Perception by EU Citizens

Since the accession treaties have to be ratified by the national parliaments of the current EU member states, enlargement toward the East requires a favorable public opinion in the member states. Questions of internal security—illegal migration, refugee and asylum issues, transborder crime—are very delicate issues that can be used to mobilize public opinion against the integration of East European countries. This perceptual dimension appears to be even more important than the real threats to internal security originating from the CEECs.

Labor migration from the CEECs is expected to remain at an annual rate of far less than a million. According to an estimate of the German Institute of Economic Research, the integration of Poland, Hungary, the Czech and Slovak Republics, and Slovenia into the EU will entail a potential flow of 340,000–680,000 migrant workers per year from these countries.[31] This calculation assumes that an income difference of 10 percent between the average EU income and the average CEEC income triggers an annual net migration of 0.08 percent to 0.16 percent of the CEEC population.

According to a survey of citizens in Poland, the Czech and Slovak Republics, and Hungary conducted in 1996, approximately 700,000 persons have already applied for immigration and work permits while approximately 4 million citizens of these countries have gathered information on opportunities to work in the EU.[32] Germany and Austria are considered the most preferred destinations, with 37.0 percent and 24.4 percent of the overall potential migrants planning to stay in these countries, respectively. These comparatively low figures reflect the experience with other economic and institutional integration processes, and disincentives for migration from the CEECs arising from language, cultural, and bureaucratic barriers. In addition, one has to stress that increased migration would be an even more probable scenario if the applicant countries were not integrated and left to an uncertain economic future.

Fears about migrant workers from Eastern Europe who might enter the EU labor market, however, are widespread. In a *Eurobarometer* survey conducted in autumn 1997, 59 percent of the EU citizens surveyed felt that people from Eastern Europe wishing to work in the EU should be accepted only with restrictions while 23 percent did not want to accept East European migrant workers at all.[33] In Germany and Austria, countries with direct borders to Eastern Europe, the share of citizens rejecting any migrant workers amounted to more than 30 percent. A similarly high percentage of the EU population, 18 percent, would not (and 55 percent of the citizens would only with restrictions) accept people seeking political asylum in the EU.

Illegal migration and organized crime across borders are phenomena that have gained increasing importance in the accession preparation. For example, the number of illegal border-crossings at the East German border has risen sharply in recent years.[34] Because the EU member states perceived the liberalization process in Eastern Europe as facilitating immigration, they tried to involve the CEE governments into the EU cooperation on Justice and Home Affairs and to induce them to take preventive action against immigrants, refugees, asylum seekers, and criminals.[35] Having agreed upon the rule of the safe third country, EU member states signed readmission agreements with most CEECs.[36]

With some justification, the applicant countries that already have started negotiations consider themselves not the sources but transit countries of migrants and criminals arriving from the east or southeast. This implies that with the introduction of the Schengen border regime, these security threats can be controlled more effectively. Although the CEECs declared their willingness to adopt the Schengen provisions before their accession, technical and political problems persist. The technical improvement of border controls (qualification, staffing, and equipment) and their integration into the Europol network requires considerable financial assistance and time.

The political problem is that the adoption of Schengen provisions runs contrary to the CEECs' commitment of ensuring visa-free and open borders with their eastern neighbors. To prepare for the adoption of the *acquis* on Justice and Home Affairs, Poland had to introduce more restrictive immigration regulations for Russian, Belarussian, and Ukrainian citizens in 1998 and to conclude agreements with its Eastern neighbors on the re-admission of rejected asylum seekers. These steps blocked the flourishing petty trade in Poland's eastern border regions and were criticized by the governments of Belarus and Russia. The re-introduction of visa regulations also affects Hungarian interests in facilitating cross-border contacts with its ethnic Hungarian minorities in Ukraine and Romania.

The public in the EU-15, however, considers effective protection of borders and crime prevention in the applicant country as a high priority. According to the latest *Eurobarometer* of October and November 1998, 92 percent of the citizens of the EU-15 think that a country that wants to join the EU has to fight organized crime and drug trafficking.[37] This perception has to be taken into account by EU policymakers who want to convince the public to back enlargement. It also should be considered by the applicant countries trying to negotiate an early introduction of the freedom of movement. Applicant countries have to convince EU and national decisionmakers that they are capable of ensuring the same level of protection as the current EU member states. As the recent success of Austria's right-wing extremist FPÖ has demonstrated, resentments and prejudices against East Europeans may be incited by aspiring politicians, who could, once in power, abandon the enlargement consensus.

Failure to Implement Institutional Reforms of the EU System

The institutional reforms agreed in the Amsterdam Treaty have not sufficiently prepared the EU for enlargement.[38] It is unclear how an institutional arrangement initially designed for six member states can work efficiently in an EU with 21, 27, or even more members. In June 1999, the Cologne European Council decided to discuss three crucial institutional reforms at an Intergovernmental Conference. These issues are the size and composition of the Commission, the weighting of votes in the Council, and the extension of qualified majority voting in the Council.

Solving these problems is particularly difficult because all three issues are interrelated and determine the future profile of the EU. In the negotiations on the Amsterdam Treaty, the five largest member states made their willingness to give up their second Commissioner contingent upon a reweighting of votes. On the other hand, small member states will insist on their Commissioner if they are to accept a reweighting of votes. A shift to qualified majority voting (QMV) in the Council will raise the issue of how and according to which principles member states should defend their interests in the Council.

Large member states used to criticize that, if the current principles of vote distribution[39] persisted, the increasing number of member states would delegitimize majority decisions of the Council because the number of votes needed to attain a qualified majority would no longer reflect the majority of the population in the EU. In contrast, small states argue that the current system of weighting of votes in the Council could persist.

In their opinion, blocking coalitions of small states are very unlikely to occur because the states needed for such a coalition are characterized by huge disparities and do not share common interests that would induce them to vote against large member states. Their second argument is that in an EU with 26 members, a qualified majority of votes in the Council would still represent a majority of the EU citizens because the minimum population share needed for QMV would amount to 50.29 percent[40] (see table 11.4). A third argument is that the Council embodies the intergovernmental principle of legitimization whereas democratic legitimization is incorporated in the European Parliament (EP). Efforts to achieve a more "democratic" allocation of votes in the Council would therefore blur the genuinely inter-

TABLE 11.4 EFFECTS OF ENLARGEMENTS ON VOTING RIGHTS IN THE COUNCIL

Country	Population (millions)	Votes in the Council
Germany	81.5	10
United Kingdom	58.3	10
France	58.0	10
Italy	57.2	10
Spain	39.6	8
Netherlands	15.4	5
Greece	10.4	5
Belgium	10.1	5
Portugal	9.9	5
Sweden	8.8	4
Austria	8.0	4
Denmark	5.2	3
Finland	5.1	3
Ireland	3.6	3
Luxembourg	0.4	2
Subtotal	371.5	87
Minimum population and number of votes required for QMV	216.3 (58.30%)	62
Poland	38.4	8
Czech Republic	10.3	5
Hungary	10.1	5
Slovenia	2.0	3
Estonia	1.5	3
Cyprus	0.7	2
Romania	22.8	6
Bulgaria	8.8	4
Slovak Republic	5.4	3
Lithuania	3.7	3
Latvia	2.6	3
Subtotal	43.3	45
Grand Total	477.8	132
Minimum population and number of votes required for QMV	240.3 (50.29%)	94

Source: Giering, et al. 1999 and Stubb 1999. The votes in the Council and seats in the Parliament were calculated on the basis of a continuation of the current system. Compare the votes in the Council EU document CONF/3815/97 and similar calculations in Bieber and Bieber 1997.

governmental nature of this organ and restrict the relevance of parliamentary deci-sionmaking in the EU.

The compromises on procedures and institutions reached in Amsterdam suffer from a number of further shortcomings. Although the EU member states have agreed to limit the maximum number of EP deputies to 700, no decision has been made on how to redivide mandates among nations and to tailor electoral districts.

If the current deputy-citizen relations were applied to those applicant countries that have already applied for accession, the number of deputies would already exceed the upper limit of 700. The number and complexity of decision mechanisms could not be significantly reduced.

Moreover, there is no congruence between matters decided according to the codecision and the QMV procedure, although one might have expected such congruence since in principle the EP and the absence of member state veto rights should both help to strengthen the integrationist character of the EU.[41] The option of qualified majority voting in the Council prompts member states to build coalitions and compromises, and the codecision procedure provides Council decisions with parliamentary legitimation. The incongruence of decision procedures one can find in the treaties is an unintended outcome of intergovernmental bargaining, which reduces the transparency of EU decisionmaking.

In the Amsterdam Treaty, the member states have adopted a flexibility mechanism that allows groups of member states to establish a closer cooperation in certain policy areas. This flexibility mechanism, however, is not suitable for organizing enlargement because it is restricted to a differentiation *within* the Union. Flexibility requires a majority of member states and may not be applied to areas of exclusive community competence (for example, trade policy) or to the Union's second pillar, the Common Foreign and Security Policy. Irrespective of various and recurring proposals to apply a flexibility and differentiation mechanism with respect to accession candidates *outside* the EU, the EU has insisted on the entire *acquis communautaire* being adopted before an accession.

The main obstacle on the way to enlargement is that the process will stop short after a first group of countries have joined the Union. Irrespective of the recent Commission proposal to open accession negotiations with all applicant countries, this scenario appears realistic because of the political logic that has guided all the reforms of the EC and EU treaty since 1957. The competing interests of member states and the patterns of EU decisionmaking restrict the EU to a piecemeal approach institutional reform.

If negotiations on the reweighting of votes, QMV, and the composition of the Commission have moved into a deadlock, member states may be inclined to agree on incremental changes that permit an enlargement by a first group of "easy-to-handle" countries. This could be achieved if the current power relations and formulae were simply maintained and applied to the new member states. Each new member state could get its commissioner and its share of EP deputies while the current size of the Commission and the maximum size of the EP would not have to be changed. Qualified majorities in the Council would still represent a clear majority of the EU population and other organs and institutions like the European Court of Justice, the Court of Auditors, the Committee of Regions, or the Economic and Social Committee could be slightly enlarged while maintaining implicit and explicit national proportionality rules.

With a first group of Central European countries having joined the Union, the fragile balance between member states advocating enlargement and member states in favor of deeper integration could shift toward the latter. A German government concerned with domestic social and economic problems, less devoted to the ideas of European integration, and whose immediate neighbors have already become members would not continue to promote the early accession of problem-ridden countries of South-Eastern Europe or of the former Soviet Union.

In a declaration on the Amsterdam Treaty, more integrationist countries, such as Belgium, France, and Italy, had demanded substantial institutional reform to precede further enlargement. They would find more support for their agenda of EMU, political union, and stronger cohesion.

Faced with scarcer budgetary resources, smaller, old member states that had argued for an inclusive approach to enlargement, such as Sweden, Denmark, Greece, and the new CEE member states would be less committed to struggle for further enlargement.[42] Even if there were a committed coalition of member states, the required unanimity would be much more difficult to attain among 20 member states.

Negative Effects of the War in the Federal Republic of Yugoslavia

The war in the Federal Republic of Yugoslavia has affected the economic and political development prospects of the entire Balkan region. The IMF and the World Bank have estimated that Albania, FYR Macedonia, Bosnia and Herzegovina, Bulgaria, Croatia, and Romania require balance of payment support, budgetary support, and refugee-related support of US$1.9 billion to 3.0 billion because of the ramifications of the war.[43] The Kosovo crisis is expected to reduce economic growth in the six countries by 3 to 4 percentage points in 1999, with much larger declines in Bosnia and Herzegovina and FYR Macedonia since the trade of these countries heavily depends on transit routes through the Federal Republic of Yugoslavia. The Romanian Ministry of Foreign Affairs has estimated that losses incurred by Romanian enterprises and the state due to the sustained trade embargo and the blockade of the Danube amounted to US$840 million in 1999.[44]

It is true that the immense budgetary costs of the war do not affect the financial management of Eastern Enlargement since the European Council has agreed that the resources allocated for pre- and post-accession assistance cannot be used to cover the expenses of war and post-war reconstruction efforts in the Balkans. Yet the inclusiveness of the enlargement process appears threatened. As a consequence of the war, Bulgaria and Romania will face more difficulties in keeping pace with other applicant countries. The continuous political instability and economic chaos in Serbia and Bosnia and Herzegovina, the fragile political situation and severe economic crises in Albania and FYR Macedonia tend to have negative spillover effects for these countries, for example, by diverting foreign investments. The ambiguous status of Kosovo within the Federal Republic of Yugoslavia and the complete isolation of Yugoslavia from the international finance institutions impedes the effective implementation of reconstruction measures.

With its widely acknowledged proposal to open accession negotiations with those applicant countries that have not begun negotiations, the Commission has sent an important signal that the EU is aware of the risk that Bulgaria and Romania may lose pace and become drawn into the post-war economic and political calamities of their neighbors. Yet Bulgaria and Romania also have some reason to take an ambivalent position on the emerging EU policy approach toward South Eastern Europe. This is because, as a side effect of a region-oriented policy, they may be scaled back from the ranks of current candidate countries with an—albeit remote— accession perspective to the level of the Yugoslav successor states.

With the creation of its odd term of "Western Balkans," the EU has carefully tried to avoid this impression. However, the inclusion of Bulgaria and Romania into the Stability Pact for South-Eastern Europe, justified for expediency and neighborhood reasons, has put both countries at the same table as the countries of the Western Balkans. If the EU negotiates Association Agreements with FYR Macedonia and Albania or introduces a special category of "stabilization and association agreements" for the Western Balkan countries, it will be even more difficult to maintain the distinction between them and Bulgaria and Romania.[45]

Judged in economic terms only, Croatia is already now in a much better position than Bulgaria and Romania, although currently it does not even have a trade and cooperation agreement with the EU and is excluded from the PHARE program due to the situation of democracy and human rights in Croatia.

The current situation in post-war South-Eastern Europe suggests that the EU's association and enlargement approach is not a feasible strategy to address the complex and interdependent problems of the region. The enlargement perspective is too remote and the incentives provided too little, either to induce semi-authoritarian leaders to stop ethnic polarization, to democratize their state and transform their client-focused economies, or to sufficiently stabilize well-intended governments that have embarked upon economic reforms and face the critique of populist opposition forces.

Conclusions

This paper has analyzed internal problems of the EU that might hamper an enlargement toward the East. Six main obstacles have been identified. First, despite the recent reforms of the cohesion policy, it is doubtful as to whether the EU has appropriate policy tools to overcome large gaps in socioeconomic development between the East and West, which will persist after enlargement.

Second, enlargement and increased market competition in its wake may lead to even larger development gaps between prosperous and marginalized regions within the East or the West.

Third, the restriction of intervention prices to agricultural products in the current EU area would require the imposition of tariffs on agricultural products of the new member states and the maintenance of border controls within an enlarged EU. Intervention prices may be replaced by production-related income subsidies but these subsidies will run contrary to WTO principles, being rejected by agricultural exporting states. The de-linking of income subsidies from production would be a solution compatible with WTO principles but it would not be accepted by agricultural interest organizations opposing the transformation of the CAP into a social policy for a particular group of the rural population.

Fourth, enlargement has to be communicated to a Western public, strongly biased against immigrants and organized crime and susceptible to aspiring politicians who capitalize on these sentiments by linking threats to internal security to the enlargement project.

Fifth, experiences with previous reforms of EU institutions demonstrate that only incremental adaptations of the existing arrangement are viable. This may facilitate the accession of a first group of candidate countries, contributing to and resulting in a blockade situation, in which a wider and more fragmented EU lacks the commitment to continue the enlargement process.

Sixth, because of the effects of the war in the Federal Republic of Yugoslavia, Romania and Bulgaria will lag further behind the advanced transition countries, thus de facto losing their perspective of accession in the not too distant future.

In sum, socio economic disparities and deadlocks in agricultural policy may impede or postpone the entire enlargement project. Institutional problems and the effects of the Yugoslav war may not threaten enlargement as such but may lead to a uncoupling of Bulgaria, Romania, and other South-East European countries from enlargement. Thus, enlargement would cease to be an inclusive process, with EU membership no longer open toward all European countries "that so desire" (Copenhagen European Council).

Notes

1. The author expresses his gratitude to Claus Giering, Josef Janning, Wim van Meurs and the participants of the Bertelsmann-World Bank conference who provided valuable comments and insights on earlier versions of this article.

2. Europäische Kommission 1997, p. 119.

3. Scharpf 1997.

4. Weise et al. 1997.

5. According to UN-ECE calculations, the cumulated FDI per capita of Poland was US$276 in June 1998, US$152 and US$144 more than the respective FDI per capita of Bulgaria and Romania. In the previous year, the differences were US$115 and US$123 (UN-ECE: Economic Survey of Europe 1998 No. 1 and No. 3, quoted in: *Neue Zürcher Zeitung*, April 22, 1998, December 16, 1998.)

6. Welfens 1999, p. 36.

7. Jovanovic 1999.

8. Objective 1 (01) is the objective to promote the development and structural adjustment of regions whose development is lagging behind. Most of the regions designated as 01 are in the southern periphery of the Union, but 11 member states receive some allocation under 01.

9. Europäische Kommission 1997, p. 121; Ardy 1999, p. 110.

10. Object 2 (02) is the objective to promote development of regions seriously affected by industrial decline. Most of these 02 regions are traditional industrial areas in the northern member states, although the eligibility extends to other industrialized regions such as the Basque country in Spain.

11. Grabbe and Hughes 1997, p. 102.

12. Ardy 1999, p. 112–113.

13. Eurostat data.

14. Boeri 1997.

15. Ludlow and Hager 1998.

16. Axt 1999.

17. Rieger 1996.

18. Proposals to establish a member status for the CEECs in the second and third pillars of the EU (the second pillar is the Common Foreign and Security Policy and the third pillar is Justice and Home Affairs) did not gain the support of the majority of member states.

19. European Commission 1999.

20. Europäische Kommission 1996, p. 19, 25.

21. Dezséri, et al. 1999.

22. Gorzelak 1996; Krätke, et al. 1997.

23. European Commission. DG XVI 1996, p. 26–38.

24. Pálné Kovács 1997, p. 5.

25. Hallet 1997, p. 25.

26. Jovanovic 1999, p. 21.

27. In the Czech Republic, Hungary, and Poland, state subsidies for agriculture were 11 percent, 16 percent, and 22 percent of the production value, compared with an EU average of 42 percent. *Neue Zurcher Zeitung.* August 11, 1998.

28. Banse 1997, p. 8.

29. Banse 1997, p. 12.

30. Rieger 1999.

31. Weise 1997.

32. Fassmann and Hintermann 1997.

33. http://europa.eu.int/en/comm/dg10/infcom/epo/eb/eb48.html, p.69–70.

34. Rommelfanger 1998.

35. Lavenex 1998.

36. The policy of "safe third countries" is based upon the notion that asylum seekers coming to an EU member country from a third country (for example, the CEECs), where they are not subject to political prosecution, should not be entitled to claim asylum in the EU. To facilitate the readmission of these people, the EU member states have signed agreements with, and provided financial support for, the CEEC.

37. http://europa.eu.int/en/comm/dg10/infcom/epo/eb/eb49/eb50.html.

38. Weidenfeld 1998; Giering, et al. 1999.

39. The current system of vote distribution is biased in favor of small countries, which have more votes in proportion to their populations.

40. The minimum coalition necessary for QMV would consist of Italy, Poland, Romania, the Netherlands, Greece, the Czech Republic, Hungary, Belgium, Portugal, Sweden, Bulgaria, Austria, the Slovak Republic, Denmark, Finland, Lithuania, Ireland, Latvia, Estonia, Cyprus, and Luxembourg (see Stubb 1999; see also: Deubner and Janning 1996).

41. Weidenfeld and Giering 1998, p. 56. Seventy-two of 104 policy fields and issues decided by QMV are not subject to the codecision procedure, but 5 issues under codecision require unanimous voting in the Council.

42. See Kreile 1997 for a discussion of EU member states' strategic interests.

43. http://www.imf.org/external/pubs/ft/kosovo/052599.htm, p. 11–12.

44. *Neue Zürcher Zeitung*, October 5, 1999.

45. The Stability Pact for South-Eastern Europe, concluded on June 10, 1999, envisages "a new kind of contractual relationship" with the Western Balkan countries. The Commission has stressed that the agreements will not contain a formulation about a perspective of EU accession (see, for example, Agence Europe, July 9, 1999).

References

Ardy, Brian. 1999. "Agricultural, Structural Policy, the Budget and Eastern Enlargement of the European Union." In Karen Henderson, ed., *Back to Europe. Central and Eastern Europe and the European Union*. London and Philadelphia: UCL Press.

Axt, Hans-Jürgen 1999. Solidarität und Wettbewerb—zur Reform der EU-Strukturpolitik. Ein Gutachten mit zwei Reformvorschlägen, Gütersloh: Bertelsmann Stiftung (in publication).

Banse, Martin. 1997. Wird die Agrarpolitik zum Motor oder Hemmnis der Erweiterung der Europäischen Union? Vortrag auf dem 9. Leutherheider Forum, January 17, 1997 (unpublished manuscript).

Bieber, Roland and Florian Bieber. 1997. "Institutionelle Voraussetzungen der Osterweiterung der Europäischen Union." In Werner Weidenfeld, ed., *Europa öffnen. Anforderungen an die Erweiterung*. Gütersloh.

Boeri, Tito. 1997. "Transitional' Unemployment." In *Economics of Transition* 2: 1–25.

Deubner, Christian, and Josef Janning, 1996. "Zur Reform des Abstimmungsverfahrens im Rat der Europäischen Union: Überlegungen und Modellrechnungen." In *Integration* 19: 146–158.

Dezséri, Kálmán, et al. 1999. "The Winners and Losers of EU Integration in Hungary." Paper prepared for the Bertelsmann/World Bank Workshop, Budapest.

Europäische Kommission. 1996. Erster Bericht über den wirtschaftlichen und sozialen Zusammenhalt, Luxemburg: Amt für amtliche Veröff.

European Commission, DG XVI. 1996. "The Impact of the Development of the Countries of Central and Eastern Europe on the Community Territory." *Regional Development Studies* No. 16. Luxembourg.

European Commission. 1999. *6th Periodic Report on the Social and Economic Situation and the Development of the Regions in the European Union.* http://europa.eu.int/comm/dg16/document/doc1_en.htm.

Europäische Kommission. 1997. "Agenda 2000. Eine stärkere und erweiterte Union." In *Bulletin der EU Beilage*. May.

Fassmann, Heinz, and Christiane Hintermann. 1997. "Migrationspotential Ostmitteleuropa. Struktur und Motivation potentieller Migranten aus Polen." Der Slowakei, Tschechien und Ungarn. Wien: Verlag der Österreichischen Akademie der Wissenschaften.

Frohberg, Klaus. 1998. "Optionen für die Gemeinsame Agrarpolitik in einer erweiterten EU. In Wagener, Hans-Jürgen and Fritz, Heiko (Hg.). 1998. *Im Osten was Neues? Aspekte der EU-Osterweiterung*. Bonn: Dietz.

Giering, Claus, et al. 1999. *Demokratie und Interessenausgleich in der Europäischen Union*. Gütersloh: Bertelsmann Stiftung.

Gorzelak, Grzegorz. 1996. "The Regional Dimension of Transformation in Central Europe." *Regional Policy and Development Series*. Vol. 10. London: Jessica Kingsley Publishers and Regional Studies Association.

Grabbe, Heather, and Kirsty Hughes. 1997. "Enlarging the EU Eastwards." Royal Institute of International Affairs. Chatham House Papers.

Hallet, Martin. 1997. "National and Regional Development in Central and Eastern Europe: Implications for EU Structural Assistance." European Commission, Director General for Economic and Financial Affairs. *Economic Papers.* No. 120.

Henderson, Karen, ed. 1999. *Back to Europe. Central and Eastern Europe and the European Union.* London and Philadelphia: UCL Press.

Henriot, Alain and András Inotai. 1997. "Economic Interpenetration between the European Union and the Central and Eastern European Countries." In *EFA Review* 2: 167–196.

Jovanovic, Miroslav N. 1999. "Where are the limits to the enlargement of the European Union?" In *Journal of Economic Integration* (forthcoming).

Krätke, Stefan, Susanne Heeg and Rolf Stein. 1997. *Regionen im Umbruch. Probleme der Regionalentwicklung an den Grenzen zwischen "Ost" und "West."* Frankfurt u.a.: Campus Verlag.

Kreile, Michael. 1997. "Eine Erweiterungsstrategie für die Europäische Union." In Weidenfeld, Werner (Hg.). *Europa öffnen. Anforderungen an die Erweiterung.* Gütersloh: Bertelsmann, 203–274.

Lavenex, Sandra. 1998. "Asylum, Immigration, and Central-Eastern Europe: Challenges to EU Enlargement." In *EFA Review* 3: 275–294.

Ludlow, Peter and Wolfgang Hager. 1998. "The Fifth Enlargement: An Interim Progress Report." Paper presented to the Liechtenstein Conference, June 2–4. Vaduz, Liechtenstein.

Pálné Kovács, Ilona. 1997. "Merre halad a magyar vidék? A fejlesztési politika és a közigazgatás ellentmondásai a rendszerváltás után." In *Társadalmi Szemle* 52: February, 3–15.

Rieger, Elmar. 1996. In Wallace, Helen, and William Wallace. *Policy-Making in the European Union.* Oxford University Press.

Rieger, Elmar. 1999. *Agenda 2000. Reform der Gemeinsamen Agrarpolitik.* Gütersloh: Bertelsmann Stiftung.

Rommelfanger, Ulrich. 1998. "Wir brauchen die internationale Zusammenarbeit von Polizei und Justiz." In *Frankfurter Allgemeine Zeitung,* February 5, 11.

Scharpf, Fritz W. 1997. "Economic Integration, Democracy, and the Welfare State." In *Journal of European Public Policy* 4 (1) March 18–36.

Stubb, Alexander C.G. 1999. "Institutional Change and the Enlargement of the European Union: How and When to Compromise on the Reweighting of Votes, the Number of Commissioners and Qualified Majority Voting." In Wittschorek, Peter (Hg.) 1999. *Agenda 2000: Herausforderungen an die Europäische Union und an Deutschland.* Baden-Baden: Nomos Verlag.

Weidenfeld, Werner (Hg.) 1998. *Amsterdam in der Analyze: Strategien für Europa.* Gütersloh: Bertelsmann Stiftung.

Weidenfeld, Werner, and Claus Giering. 1998. "Die Europäische Union nach Amsterdam—Bilanz und Perspektive." In Weidenfeld, Werner (Hg.) 1998. *Amsterdam in der Analyze: Strategien für Europa.* Gütersloh: Bertelsmann Stiftung.

Weise, Christian, et al. 1997. "Osteuropa auf dem Weg in die EU—Transformation, Verflechtung, Reformbedarf." *Beiträge zur Strukturforschung des DIW,* 167.

Welfens, Paul. 1999. "Anpassungsprobleme in postsozialistischen Ländern Osteuropas im Vorfeld der EU-Osterweiterung," Jan. 15. In *ApuZ* 3–4, 1999, 29–42.

CHAPTER 12

Portugal's European Integration: Lessons for Future Enlargements[1]

Jorge Braga de Macedo
Faculty of Economics, Nova University at Lisbon

Introduction

European integration has combined deepening economic interdependence and mutual political responsiveness among EU members and widening membership. After the fall of the Berlin Wall significantly increased the potential for membership, however, fears surfaced that, if the EU simultaneously pursued deepening and widening, negative spillovers would more than offset the benefits from positive spillovers. The EU, therefore, adopted sequential approaches. Yet, if faster widening proves unacceptable to members and faster deepening hurts the expectations of candidate nations, chances are that both will continue to stall.

The requirements for accession are essentially a well-functioning, competitive economy and democratic institutions. In other words, they describe the aim of economic and political transition. The preparedness for subscribing to the legal framework of the EU, in turn, includes very detailed and demanding obligations. Some of them require the strengthening and adjustment of public institutions, for instance, regarding the regulation of product standards or of competition. Others will have strong implications, particularly for infrastructure, enterprises, and financial institutions.[2]

As shown below by the example of Portugal, where financial institutions were fully state-owned until accession, these institutions will be expected to perform to higher standards of financial strength and transparency than at present. They will have to demonstrate that the government regulates them well, as they show independence in their allocation of credits. Financial systems also are expected to play a larger role in funding small and medium-size enterprises than they do at present, because they are an important factor in stimulating innovation, competition, and growth.

The nature and requirements of membership have been shifting. The degrees of commitment to the union and to each of its main institutions have been changing in various issue areas, as a partial response to a more turbulent global and regional environment.

The euro was created in January 1999 among most of the 15 member states, but the resignation of the European Commission (EC) shortly thereafter delayed the accession calendar. The strains introduced in the balance of power between institutions were exacerbated after the parliamentary elections in the spring changed the majority from the European socialist to the popular party.

Another challenge had come from military actions in Kosovo, which brought the need for reconstruction and stability in the Balkans. Albeit conjunctural, these two developments may have changed the perception of Europe more than the euro, whose introduction had been planned for more than 10 years. We can only hope the new EC will be able to combine internal reform and external visibility. In any event, the interplay among political, economic, and social factors will continue to make the EU a shifting constraint for members and a shifting objective for candidates.

In that sobering context, it is helpful to remember that European integration comprises individual country responses to both external and internal pressures. Generally unknown success stories may provide lessons to the dozen accession countries likely to be involved in future enlargements.

Given a policy environment fraught with ambiguities, both deepening and widening are likely to be slow and differentiated processes and to make recent accessions of relatively poorer countries useful cases for comparison. Though Greece and Ireland seem to be polar cases in what pertains to the capacity to absorb structural funds, Portugal shares features with either one. The lessons may thus appear more relevant.[3]

Aside from the constraints imposed by membership are constraints imposed by past policies. Structural adjustments occur at different speeds, changing the attractiveness to investors and the degree of social cohesion in ways that lessen or exacerbate the ability to reach the moving target.

Past and present candidates for accession may have common features, but the relevant constraints largely reflect the specific country experience. This situation provides another reason to select one national case and understand it fully, rather than pick and chose between various allegedly polar cases of success or failure. Indeed, all accession processes will have successes and failures.

We rightly can consider the case of Portugal a success, but the government missed several opportunities, largely because of a defensive accession strategy and inappropriate domestic policies. The persistence of these policies reflects resistance from potential losers from integration. The defensive accession strategy is rather rooted in a lack of confidence about the ability of Portugal to "make the grade."

Such skepticism prevailed in business circles and civil society even during the phase when the authorities attempted to be "good students" of European integration. According to polls taken before the parliamentary elections of Spring 1999, the Portuguese continue to be among the nations who trust European institutions the most. The idea that success of integration could have been greater is therefore difficult to convey to public opinion. The groups whose ability to capture government transfers has diminished because of the Single Market perceive themselves to be losers but do not necessarily claim that integration was a failure.

The beginning of Portugal's European transition could trace back to membership in EFTA since its inception in 1960. The quarter-century in EFTA allowed Portugal to develop an export base in manufacturing, which proved decisive after the 1974 revolution—when policies were reversed. Paradoxically, by averting more serious balance of payments crises during the negotiations for EU membership from 1977 to 1985, the export base reinforced some of the interests vested in state intervention.

One reason for the paradox is that Portugal's transition to European integration did not balance mutual political responsiveness with economic interdependence. The *acquis communautaire* also is not equivalent to free trade, and in some sectors, such as agriculture, it actually goes the other way.

Indeed, the Portuguese experience suggests a trade-off between transition and integration. The imbalance between economic and political integration has social implications to the extent that it threatens the government's capacity to balance economic transformation and social cohesion so as to preserve political legitimacy. This capacity is needed even more for an implicit or explicit ranking of the progress of accession.

As Portuguese negotiations for membership continued during those of Spain, EU membership had the (almost unintended!) effect of bringing about free trade with Spain. Because of the geographical proximity, Portugal resisted Spanish imports and investment, especially in agriculture and banking. To pursue a defensive strategy with one partner and remain cooperative with others is easier with ambiguous responses to external liberalization. Coupled with gradualism, this ambiguity makes policy reversals likely.

The general lesson comes from Charles Kindleberger (1962), who argued that a country showing capacity to transform benefits more from international trade than a rigid economy. We do not always understand, however, that the result of a favorable external shock can be equivalent to that of natural rigidity.

When the state appropriates the surplus, perhaps as an instrument of powerful but uncoordinated social groups, it may damage growth prospects and leave society worse off than it was before the favorable shock. This enhanced rigidity of economies experiences a terms of trade or a productivity boom, redistributed to competing social groups, including state agencies and enterprises. Observed in several developing countries, it has been called the "voracity effect" by Aaron Tornell and Philip Lane (1999).

The Portuguese pre- and post-accession experience combined gradual adjustment and ambiguous responses to external pressure. This was based on the fear of economic integration with Spain, but the pattern also is consistent with domestic policies aiming at preserving state intervention, even if it reduces social welfare— because it makes vested interests voracious.

Constitutional constraints, both political and fiscal, best capture the defensive domestic policies followed when Portugal began on a transition from market to plan, inverse from that of the 10 CEECs to EU accession.

This attempt to disentangle the shifts in objectives and constraints—stemming from the Portuguese experience with successively tighter forms of European integration—is organized into four sections plus this introduction and a conclusion. In connection with the trade-off between integration and transition, the next section establishes the shifting balance between economic and political integration and shows its historical roots, in particular the political constitutional constraints on Portuguese integration. The subsequent section amplifies this discussion by describing the effect of these constraints on fiscal policy and how they delayed the implementation of a credible multi-annual fiscal adjustment strategy (MAFAS).

"Economic Management in an Open Economy" analyzes the changes in Portuguese economic policy as the economy became more open and integrated with Europe's. This section also reviews the type of international specialization followed since the application for membership was lodged and the resulting pattern of trade and investment, illustrating once again Portugal's ambiguous response to external liberalization. The final section analyzes the role of FDI in the integration process.

Imbalance between Political and Economic Integration and its Consequences

Portugal's integration with the rest of Europe has not always been balanced. Figure 12.1 illustrates the pattern of Portugal's transition by plotting economic and political integration into Europe along the horizontal and vertical axes, respectively. If this illustration is done so that the 45° line represents a balanced path, figure 12.1 shows how rising economic interdependence in the 1960s was followed by increased mutual political responsiveness in the 1970s.

The newly founded democratic parties (Socialist, Social Democratic, and Social Centrist), supported by external actors, such as the World Bank, the International Monetary Fund (IMF), and foreign nongovernmental organizations

FIGURE 12.1 PATTERN OF POLITICAL AND ECONOMIC INTEGRATION

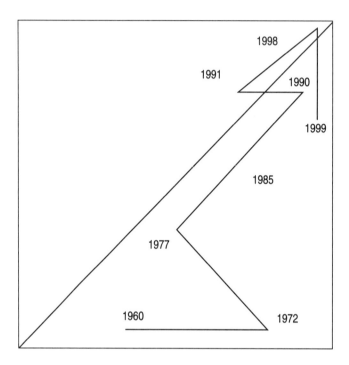

Note: Economic interdependence on horizontal axis, mutual political responsiveness on vertical axis, diagonal shows balanced path of economic and political integration.

(like the foundations linked to major German political parties), stimulated the process leading to European integration. Only the Communist Party opposed it, because membership threatened the transition of Portugal to a Soviet-style regime.

In the Portuguese system, two large parties have been competing for the median voter, but alliances with smaller parties on the right and the left have kept the structure of the party system fairly loose. Note that at the time of the application for membership, Portugal was economically less, not more, integrated with Europe than five years earlier, when the free-trade agreement was concluded.

Despite the balance between economic and political integration obtained during the EU Council presidency in the first half of 1992, perhaps the heyday of the "good student" phase, figure 12.1 shows two reversals. The leftward movement corresponds to a reduction in economic interdependence, because of exchange controls imposed in 1990–91. The downward movement reflects a drop in mutual political responsiveness following the veto of a cross-border bank merger in June 1999, just ahead—as it turns out—of a new EU Council presidency in the first half of 2000. The veto was lifted after the October elections, making the political reversal more short-lived than the economic change. The negative consequences in financial reputation and in the capacity to attract FDI, however, are likely to last beyond the presidency.

These reversals reflect fears of not being able to compete in a unified market and more specifically integration with Spain. To be sure, the escudo is part of the euro and the ratio to the EU average is expected to reach three-quarters in 2000 (allowing for the effect of German unification) from less than one-half 50 years earlier.

Nevertheless, fears of failure still prompt lobbying efforts aimed at delaying integration or at limiting its scope. Indeed, international cooperation in the business community did not start until the late 1990s. These doubts as to whether Portugal can maintain the catching-up already secured echo a fear of "geographic fundamentals," which would make Portugal follow Spain in bad times but not in good times.

For example, the economic sentiment indicator that the EC produced shows that the range between the peak in 1987–91 and the trough in 1991–95 is more than 7 percentage points in Portugal, more than twice as large as in Spain, though the unemployment rate in Spain was almost four times as high. The fear of "geographic fundamentals" is consistent with the prevailing expectation of an unfavorable unemployment performance in the future against the evidence of the past 10 years. "Geographical fundamentals" cloud national perceptions of the benefits of economic and political integration with Europe, insofar as the bilateral consequences are valued disproportionately.

These policy reversals also reflect that the constitutional system in Portugal has had difficulty creating stable parliamentary majorities, and economic policy has oscillated between earning credibility abroad and selling stability at home. Indeed, the division of powers between prime minister and president of the republic prevailed even within the strong single-party executive governments of 1985–95.

The reelection of a Socialist president in 1991 reintroduced the dilemma of the bipolar executive with a vengeance. The Social Democratic government did not resist the effects of the international recession and the slowdown of reforms it implied. The Socialists, led by Antonio Guterres, won the October 1995 general elections, again on a reformist platform. Cavaco Silva (the only prime minister who managed stable parliamentary majorities) had refused to run in February and was beaten in the presidential elections of January 1996 by the Socialist candidate. The recent electoral campaign suggests that ambiguities within the major parties will have a bearing on the future pattern of integration, comparable to that of the bipolar executive.

Until 1982, the parallel and sometimes competing legitimacies of the revolution and the results of general elections also exacerbated the negative consequences of the bipolar executive. This competition impaired the government's willingness and ability to stabilize and liberalize the economy. Liberalization was not accepted easily by any major political force until the mid-1990s, and, both in and out of power, the Social Democrats are more anxious than the Socialists to avoid branding as pro-business.

Their preference for some form of social pact was evident in efforts to accommodate the objectives of the noncommunist trade union—the General Workers' Union (UGT)—in the disinflation process initiated in 1985. The employers' confederations—especially the Confederation of Portuguese Industry (CIP)—also agreed to base wage increases on expected inflation in 1986, but the agreement broke down in 1988, when the inflation outturn was almost twice as high as the target.

Finally, these policy reversals also reflect the sometimes conflicting roles played by the minister of finance in a state-controlled developing economy. For decades, the absence of political parties and other democratic institutions made it easier for the government to coordinate between spending ministries and present and future taxpayers.

In the strong, single-party executive governments of 1985–95, finance ministers who sold stability at home by allowing increased deficits followed those who instead earned credibility abroad through structural reforms. The regime change toward currency convertibility and stability, brought about by the exchange rate mechanism, increased the independence of the central bank and withdrew the monetary constitution from the finance minister's responsibility. Nevertheless, its reversal in 1990–91 and difficulties in coordination between the Treasury and central bank in 1993–94 are consistent with the oscillating pattern described.[4]

The alternating pattern between international and domestic objectives in macroeconomic policymaking did not disappear when the escudo moved into the euro zone because the decision to veto a cross-border bank merger had a clear domestic objective. In any event, it is the failure to carry out structural reforms, not a specific decision—no matter how misguided—that threatens the benefits to people and to business of being endowed again with a stable and convertible currency.

If the awareness of the threat rises, the pattern may re-emerge, though one party has won both the presidency of the republic and the government, along with the major cities. This revived financial protectionism confirms that the run-up to the euro was not sufficient to eliminate the interests vested in public administration and some economic groups.

The Constraints on Fiscal Adjustment

All national economies face an external constraint. Foreign debt cannot become so large that international financial markets perceive that the government cannot service it. Export earnings must be sufficient to finance imports and debt service. Therefore, signs of internal imbalance, either excessive budget deficits or unacceptably high inflation, may be taken as indicators that a currently satisfactory external situation could become unsatisfactory in the future, as the internal imbalance spills over to the external sector.[5]

This spillover certainly existed in the Portuguese experience, but the pattern of export growth under limited financial development allowed intervention by the government and the central bank to remain high in the 1960s and 1970s, with very different ideological justifications but the same appeal to protectionism. In effect, a strong financial market implies not only less interference from the government but also a clearer notion of what the public sector is. Moreover, the increased factor mobility that the Single Market in financial services entailed eroded the major obstacle to a more transparent, revenue seeking fiscal policy.

Portugal has a bias toward a large public sector, as demonstrated by the continuous rise in the ratio of primary government expenditures to GDP from the early 1950s to the late 1990s. This bias leads to hidden taxation and disguised fiscal policy reminiscent of what CEECs were like before the transition began. In Portugal, the democratic regime suffered no public debt hangover: It agreed upon liberalization-cum-stabilization packages with the IMF, but this external pressure brought mounting public deficits.

The voracity effect remained, even when the government brought deficits under control. From 1991 to 1995, the effects of increased EU structural funds interacted with the electoral cycle and with the European recession, leading total expenditures to rise faster than GDP until a reduction in debt service offsets this increase. The pattern is the same from 1995 to 1999, to the extent that the adjustment process largely has spared government expenditure.

The absence of restrictions on public spending, central to the pattern of macroeconomic adjustment observed in Portugal since the revolution, implies larger increases in revenue and resorting to hidden forms of taxation. The pressure of the Single-Market deadline was not strong enough to affect the design of the 1988 Tax Act.

The introduction of comprehensive income taxation in 1989 did not increase the credibility of a future tax reform, in which concealed taxation would be reduced to a level consistent with external financial liberalization largely because of the priority given to selling stability at home ahead of the 1991 general elections.

On the contrary, the doubling of community structural funds secured in 1988 brought additional pressure on public investment expenditure, because of the requirement that recipient countries match these funds equally. It also increased rent-seeking within the private and public sector, along the lines of the voracity effect.

True, after the elections, the government tried to become a "good student" and, through a MAFAS, was able to commit itself to restoring control over public finances. This commitment did not prevent an increase in primary government expenditure, following the new duplication in EU structural funds decided in late 1992.

The government budget deficit was to be brought under control through the measures included in the convergence program presented after the 1991 elections. This program implied a credible MAFAS seeking to stabilize the accumulation of public debt through increases in revenue and decreases in expenditure, such that, excluding interest payments, there is a budget surplus. A variant of this benchmark, of course, is incorporated in the Stability and Growth Pact of 1996.

Before the MAFAS, the broader measure of public debt shows a ratio to GDP increasing at 4 percent a year for more than 10 years, despite high growth and negative real interest rates. Unreported lending operations by the Treasury and debt take-over operations by the government (to the benefit of autonomous funds and state-owned enterprises) make the decomposition of stock accumulation into well-defined flows difficult to interpret year to year.[6]

The continued pressure for a credible MAFAS notwithstanding, the previous pattern of slow adjustment on the tax and expenditure side continues. In particular, the improvement in tax administration has been in the government's program for more than 10 years. The reported government budget deficit was above the ceiling of 3 percent of GDP imposed by the EU Treaty until 1997, except for 1989 (when the introduction of comprehensive income taxation led to extraordinary revenue increases).

In 1991 (elections) and 1993–94 (recession), the downward trend of the deficit is reversed. The oscillations go a long way toward explaining how the public did not appreciate the change in regime until 1995. Unless public finances are reformed, a resumption of "stop-and-go" macroeconomic policies will be unavoidable, even within the euro zone.

The inability to reform the public sector reflects a propensity for state intervention and vested interests in the distribution of increased structural funds, which in turn reflect the imbalance between economic and political integration described in figure 12.1 (page 296, above) for the past 50 years. Hence, voracious vested interest, which may appear as the last hold-out from the constitutional ban on privatization, in fact is a reflection of the ancient inability to raise taxes in peacetime.

Economic Management in an Open Economy

EU membership implies accepting an economic regime based on nominal stability. The fulfillment of the convergence criteria for the euro is not part of the EU enlargement negotiations, but world financial markets already monitor the change in the economic regime of applicant countries toward nominal stability. The reason for this scrutiny is that the regime change requires that the national MAFAS be credible and that the macroeconomic framework be understood internationally.

Moreover, the euro deprives each participating nation's bank of the advantages of unique local market understanding and preferred access to institutional investors.

It also constrains the state's capacity to help the banks and the banks' reciprocal ability to help the state. In Portugal, engineering this change to an economic regime based on nominal stability has been a lengthy process that has included labor market adjustment, exchange rate policy, improvements in the financial sector, and a reduction in the fiscal deficit.

Labor Market Policies

Flexible labor markets have considerably facilitated the Portuguese transition to a open market economy. The ability to shift from inter- to intra-industry trade largely determines the capacity to transform and hence the pattern of specialization. Under the specialization based on the abundance of semiskilled labor, which happened under EFTA, the dislocation of labor and unemployment from agriculture and industry toward services faced more structural rigidities than if Portuguese firms had become competitive in differentiated products.

This dislocation of labor had a sectoral basis, such as from agriculture to industry or from one subsector of industry to another. The decline in agricultural employment has been compensated by increased employment in manufacturing and even more so in services, while employment in public administration also grew massively. These sectoral shifts have been associated with substantial migration from rural to urban areas. The activity rate in Portugal is slightly higher than in the EU, and so is the proportion of women in the civilian labor force.

Unemployment has not been a problem since the late 1950s, remaining low even by EU standards, so this factor has not led to lower public support for membership. The rate did jump in 1977 and kept rising to 8.7 percent of the labor force in 1985. It declined again until 1991, when it reached 4 percent, and rose to 6.8 percent in 1997 and dropped again to 5.1 percent in 1999.

Nevertheless, "underemployment" may be widespread because of the highly bureaucratic public (and private) administration and because of the high cost of adjusting manpower. If the organization of the economy changes, there will be a large potential to release workers to undertake new activities. These workers, however, are generally poorly trained and lack special qualifications.

Unions and other workers' organizations played an important role in this outcome. In the wake of the revolution, trade unions and other workers' organizations, which had been docile under the corporatist regime, engineered steep real wage increases. At the same time, because they had become accustomed to a stable exchange rate, workers were unaware of the erosion in real wages that currency depreciation caused between 1977 and 1985.

The "stop-and-go" policies of successive governments led to falling real wages during most of the post-revolutionary period. Despite the 1976 law, which confined layoffs to the most extreme cases, the labor market maintained a degree of flexibility, as employers hired employees on renewable short-term contracts (usually six months).[7]

In conclusion, workers tolerated brutal falls in real wages to keep their jobs and behaved as if they understood that when the relative price of their exports and imports decline, the real wage also has to decline. Whether the unions actually understood it or not is beside the point, which is that real wage adjustment worked much more efficiently in Portugal than in neighboring Spain, especially in the private, export-oriented firms.[8]

Financial Sector Policies

The crucial importance of building sound financial sectors and of catalyzing foreign direct investment became evident throughout the recent emerging markets crisis. Comparisons between the transition economies and the rapidly developing Asian "tigers" help demonstrate that the economies in transition need to renew efforts to keep their external balances under control, particularly through prudent fiscal management, and need to learn the lessons on exchange rate and debt management that the crises provide. Investing in structural reforms capable of improving the investment climate, of promoting the effective functioning of markets, and of strengthening institutions and standards of corporate governance becomes an essential requirement for a sustainable transition.

The process of income convergence requires deep economic restructuring, including in the financial sector. The banking sector, through privatization or other means, had to absorb the overhang of inefficiency. As with trade and industry, the pressure for financial readjustment came mostly from outside.

No excessive regulation in Portugal is likely to last without severe damage to financial development, because business will cross the border to Spain. Against the slow evolution of Portuguese nationalized banks, financial restructuring in Spain began several years earlier and continues, in the form of mergers among large banks, often encouraged by the monetary authorities.

International capital mobility and free trade in financial services, by significantly increasing the competition among banks, was bound to make Portuguese banks unwilling and unable to finance the deficits of the public sector at rates substantially below comparable borrowers. Given the fiscal constitution, this competition increased the cost of collecting the implicit intermediation tax from depositors, borrowers, and shareholders. The new behavior began in 1985 with the new banks and became stronger as banks began to be privatized in 1989. At the same time, the liberalization of capital movements across Europe was delayed until after capital controls were ineffective.[9]

Hence, in view of the opening up of domestic capital markets required by the Single Market objective, the public finance situation in Portugal threatened the sustainability of external liberalization. This threat led to suggestions that countries with high inflation and high public debt, such as Greece and Italy, might together pursue financial repression in a "soft-currency club," which would crawl relative to the ERM, so as to stabilize relative prices throughout the union. The case for such a halfway house was not convincing in the early 1990s, and it is not attractive today, either.[10]

Monetary and Exchange Rate Policies

Even when the aversion to open markets was most vocal, Portugal always kept an export sector in private hands. This export sector, which had boomed in the 1960s thanks to EFTA, always had behaved as a kind of enclave. It did not receive much attention from the authorities but also did not appear to contribute much more than the ironic reference to a "pajama republic."[11]

At this time, foreign exchange was abundant and industrial policy was targeted at national integration with Portugal's larger African territories, Angola and Mozambique. The threat of a balance of payments crisis appeared soon after the revolution and the independence of the colonies, but the government ignored it with the argument that the Portuguese economy was set to become centrally planned and the private export sector would dwindle.

Though Portugal achieved external balance by devaluation and a credit squeeze, monitored by the IMF, the fact is that government expenditure and transfers to state-owned enterprises did not adjust. This is the lesson mentioned above, to which the voracity effect was added.

The conflicting needs to undertake sizable public investments for meeting EU standards, especially in physical infrastructure, and to reduce the fiscal deficit were not reconciled through public sector reform coupled with improvements in competitiveness, including lessening labor and capital market rigidities. Instead, fast growth and a slower disinflation than desirable facilitated the adjustment.

The 1983–85 structural adjustment spared the public sector, however, so that rising nominal wages and interest rates exacerbated the appreciation of the real exchange rate and may have pushed beyond the sustainability level in the early 1990s as controls on capital inflows also were imposed. These controls resulted in a further misalignment and threatened the sustained output and employment expansion.

Credit ceilings, a feature of closed capital markets, proved quite effective in Portugal during periods of stabilization. Interest rates were kept low to alleviate the burden of public debt, showing again how the political element creeps into financial discipline. The only credible measure to end the direct financing of the Treasury by the banks would have been an agreement among the central bank, the finance ministry, and the spending ministries on a plan of deficit reduction involving both expenditure and revenue, and including tax reform.

This policy is the essence of what the Convergence Program attempted in November 1991, but the domestic coordination did not match the commitment at the EU level.

In early 1992, the sequencing changed with the introduction of a MAFAS, with nominal ceilings on primary expenditure (rather than in the ratio to GDP) and entry into the ERM, which involved an initially misunderstood Pre-Pegging Exchange Rate Regime (PPERR).

In spite of the fear of sudden reversals of capital inflows during the ERM crises, the authorities were able to realign the exchange rate without losing credibility because they followed the peseta. In this case, the "geographic fundamentals" actually helped to avoid an exchange rate misalignment, which could have threatened moving the escudo into the euro. The lesson for CEECs is that a rule-based exchange rate regime provides a credibility bonus compared to various forms of domestic discretion, even if these forms belong to an independent central bank.[12]

As discussed above, political and social variables explain some of the oscillations in the path to integration. Macroeconomic indicators, such as productivity and relative prices of goods and factors tell the same story. Figure 12.2 illustrates the cyclical pattern of labor productivity relative to the EU average. Accession is associated with a jump in the relative growth of productivity, which seems inversely related to disinflation policy as it rose in 1989–90.

The pattern shown in figure 12.2 also suggests a "double-dip" recession, in 1991 and 1994, when productivity growth in Portugal was 2 percent below the EU average. In 1991, this dip was due mostly to the creation of high employment, but in 1994, it was a consequence of a delayed recovery from the 1993 trough. The recession hit harder in 1993 than in 1992, and the productivity boom resumed in 1995. Note that both output and employment data have been subject

FIGURE 12.2 RELATIVE PRODUCTIVITY CYCLES

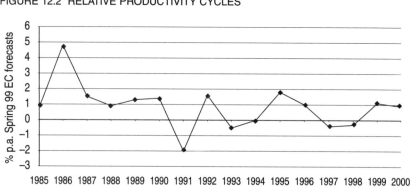

to substantial revisions, so that the more recent swings may well disappear in future revisions.

Nominal relative factor rewards reflected the ups and downs of relative productivities and the succession of exchange-rate arrangements. Thus, wage increases and long-term interest rates converged and diverged before they converged again to the European average. The pattern of relative nominal wage increases and long-term interest rates (what the government called financial moderation, shown in figure 12.3) was erratic until the mid-1990s. Wage and financial immoderation certainly contributed to obscure the significance of the PPERR for firms, trade unions, and the public.

In any event, the real and nominal effective exchange rates against 23 industrial countries, produced by the EC and shown in figure 12.4, stabilized only after the ERM bands widened in August 1993.[13] As mentioned above, the rules of the ERM allowed the escudo to realign following the peseta without loss of financial reputation or with a smaller loss than otherwise would have been the case.

The PPERR avoids the "inconsistent trio" of fixed exchange rate, free capital movements, and independent monetary policy by freeing monetary policy to be targeted on external balance, represented by a suitable reserve position. The MAFAS then sets fiscal policy to maintain internal balance, as represented by a low inflation rate.

Membership in the euro zone seems to suggest that Portugal's experience was an unqualified success, relative to Greece. Yet, inflation may not have been fully eradicated in Portugal, where it is now higher than in Greece. Put in another way, the credibility of Portugal's MAFAS/PPERR must be supported by additional mea-

FIGURE 12.3 WAGE AND FINANCIAL MODERATION

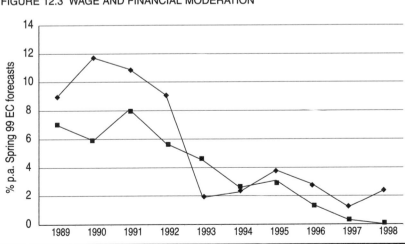

FIGURE 12.4 NOMINAL AND REAL EXCHANGE RATES

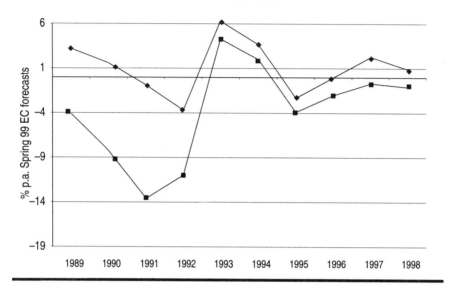

sures of a microeconomic and structural nature, designed to enhance the competitiveness of production and therefore sustain the catching-up process.

We must acknowledge, then, that the credibility of the MAFAS cannot be considered definitive, especially if public sector reform does not support it, as is the case in Portugal. This lingering internal imbalance and the failure to carry out public sector reform makes for an unfavorable business environment, which has led to a recent acceleration of outward direct investment. The absence of reforms has included the rejection of a regionalization proposal in 1998, which would surely have led to greater bureaucracy.

Indeed, if the current drive to make business international is not accompanied by reform of tax administration and justice, social security and public health, and decentralization toward municipalities, it may erode the legitimacy of integration. I will call this threat the "euro holdup," following the conjecture of Buiter and Sibert (1997).

Structural Adjustment and Foreign Investment

Available indicators still show more openness in the current account than the capital account: exports and imports rose from two-thirds to three-fourths of GDP from 1993 to 1997, while nonmonetary transactions remain around 10 percent.

Patrick Honohan (1995) presents the stock of foreign assets and liabilities as roughly equal to GDP in 1993 and shows that, in that year, cross-border bank assets in escudos jumped more than 10-fold, especially at the short end. This increase shows that, in spite of the better access to information and the widespread financial globalization in Europe, Portugal needed almost a decade to spread financial freedom to its citizens.

The common external tariff brings the possibility of trade diversion, which in Portugal was sizable in the agricultural sector, and integration exacerbated the decline that began in the 1960s. The contribution of agriculture to growth declined to 4 percent in the 1960s from about 25 percent in the 1940s.

The situation deteriorated further in the 1970s. The chaotic "agrarian reform" conducted by the Communist Party in the southern provinces of Alentejo in the summer of 1975 had a decisive negative effect on output and productivity. At the same time, wage increases in the urban sector swelled the demand for food, so that agricultural imports rose by 25 percent in 1976 and 50 percent in 1977. It also prevented an attack on the problem of small, low-output farms in the north.

With accession, a specific program to support agriculture brought new investment, but modernization did not proceed fast enough. By 1992, the government decided to move ahead with full liberalization, and this policy reversed the effects on investment.

In spite of the failure to transform traditional agriculture, the trend toward intra-industry trade is undisputed. The Single Market review the EC produced in 1997 for the four cohesion countries, summarized by Abel Mateus (1998) shows that Portugal benefited by far the most. The static effects on production and consumption associated with inter-industry trade are embedded in a macroeconometric model, which is also capable of tracking dynamic effects.

These firm relocations result from foreign direct investment, more openness (which in turn increases the multiplier effect of foreign growth), and stronger economies of scale. They further foster intra-industry trade in the manner Paul Krugman pioneered (1981). The estimate for Portugal is an additional GDP growth of 0.7 percent per annum between 1995 and 2010, with 0.5 percent for Ireland and Spain and no visible effect in Greece.

The pattern of foreign investment reinforces the trade effect. Hans-Peter Lankes and Anthony Venables (1997) have analyzed the determinants of a country's attractiveness to foreign direct investment projects, with a focus on CEECs. They conclude that—in spite of the heterogeneity of the projects in size, function, technology, location, and control mode—the progress in transition matters more than the association to the EU, or lack of it. This analysis is equally relevant to the Portuguese situation before accession and is worth summarizing.

With respect to any particular project of foreign direct investment, its function may be a predominantly market access motive (as close to consumers) or a predominantly cost motive (as a low-cost production). Projects in distribution or local supply are more concerned with access- than export-oriented projects, which, in turn, tend to be more closely integrated in the activities of the firm, and somewhat more upstream.

Aside from the function, the control mode is also relevant: licensing or joint venture projects differ from establishing a fully owned subsidiary. The choice depends on the need to gain access to local contacts and information about markets, as compared with the need to safeguard technology and product quality. Wholly owned projects tend to be both more export-oriented and have more of their output transferred within the firm.

Countries with perceived political stability and low perceived risk levels are not only more likely to receive larger flows of foreign direct investment but also less likely to have projects postponed or abandoned. The tighter security of supply makes these countries more likely to have projects that are relatively export-oriented and integrated in the sales orientation of the firm. This is the nature of projects located in Portugal during the "good student" phase, especially Auto Europa, a joint venture by Ford and Volkswagen established in 1991 and now responsible for sizable exports of differentiated products.

This example shows how such projects bring with them the benefits of technology transfer, quality control ,and the development of marketing channels. They certainly seem to be more in line with the comparative advantage of the host economy. The example suggests that, in determining the flow of foreign direct investment and the type of this investment to Portugal, policy credibility was more important than the proximity to EU markets. The converse could be gathered from some recent examples of disinvestment, to the extent that they may be exacerbated by the drop in policy credibility observed in 1999 and pictured in figure 12.1, above.

Conclusion

Portugal is rightly considered a success of EU accession, but the accession strategy was mostly defensive, because business circles and civil society doubted they could "make the grade." Inappropriate domestic policies persisted because of resistance of potential losers from integration.

The lack of confidence in the country's capacity to transform and an exaggerated fear of negative influence from Spain prevailed even during the phase when the authorities attempted to be "good students" of European integration. At the time, though, several ERM realignments initiated by Spain and partly followed by Portugal actually dampened the escudo's real appreciation ahead of entry into the euro.

Portugal until now has lost the opportunity for sustained structural change afforded by the euro and the associated improvement in fiscal discipline, thus Portugal became a potential victim of the "euro holdup." Public administration has remained incapable of reforming itself in such issues as justice, home affairs, social welfare, education, and others.

The absence of structural reforms is especially grave in what pertains to the enlarged public sector and the discretionary regulation of private enterprise. For this reason, the MAFAS/PPERR was such a decisive signal of the change in economic regime. As it turned out, the 1993 recession and the (general and local) election cycles have hindered the implementation of public sector reform.

The competitive forces the euro unleashed will not suffice to bring about the public sector reform that has been urged for more than three decades. To be sure, joining the euro multiplied the effects on firms and consumers of the Single Market in financial services established in 1993.

Nevertheless, the positive response of Portuguese firms to globalization, based on the current virtuous cycle, cannot be divorced from a stronger social anxiety than during the vicious cycles before accession. This threat, of course, is more serious for such catch-up countries as Portugal.

Moreover, a better balance between the European and Lusophone allegiances of the Portuguese population, which is currently observed, did not erase the rise in inequality and the suspicion of widespread corruption, suggesting that the propensity for excessive state intervention and perverse redistribution remains. Both have become social concerns, echoed in the news media.

That a society without expecting to alleviate poverty may suddenly fracture, of course, is familiar from Europe and elsewhere. The accession experience of Portugal is useful politically, economically, and socially. Political integration encompasses not only the executive system and voting patterns, but also public administration institutions and procedures, including governance and the fight against corruption.

Economic transformation toward making firms competitive in the European Single Market requires sound macroeconomic management, coupled with well-functioning capital and labor markets. Political and financial stability deliver growth, which, given preferences about inequality, sustains social cohesion during the accession process and beyond.

With the benefit of hindsight, the lessons Portugal's experience could offer for reducing the costs of adjustment for its accession negotiations may relate to the long adjustment period implied by the negotiations. Though gradual adjustment is desirable in principle, when it combines with an ambiguous response to external liberalization, it may lead to defensive policies and increase rather than decrease the costs of adjustment.

In Portugal's case, this effect was not as severe as one might have expected because unemployment benefits were not large enough to create a strong disincentive to work. There were other domestic policies (such as worker retraining), but they do not seem to have dealt with the social costs of adjustments resulting from accession.

The social dimension is both the most fundamental long-term objective and an immediate constraint on public policy, ensuring that the EU will remain a shifting objective for accession countries. The lessons from Portugal, nonetheless, will remain essential.

Notes

1. This research was conducted as part of the joint program of the Bertelsmann Foundation and the World Bank, *Toward European Integration,* and the results were presented at a conference in Guetersloh, Germany, on November 3, 1999. Comments from participants are gratefully acknowledged. A longer version is available as Nova Economics Working Paper No. 369, December 1999, with the subtitle, "The Limits of External Pressure."

2. In infrastructure, there will be emphasis on integrating transport and communication systems to ensure the smooth functioning of the Single Market. For enterprises, EU rules for health and safety of processes in the workplace and environmental standards will be of particular significance, with major implications for restructuring and investment. Accession will imply that enterprises must conform with the stringent standards of the EU on the safety of products. Investment requirements for municipal services (such as the treatment of waste and water), for power generation, and for heavy industries (emission standards) would appear to be especially large. This discussion follows EBRD (1998).

3. The advantages of differentiated integration for enlargement are in Bertelsmann (1999). The general argument is in CEPR (1995). The Portuguese parliament promoted a similar view in connection with the revision of the EU Treaty, see Magone (1997).

4. In emerging markets, and especially in CEECs, the special role of the minister of finance and of the central bank governor may lead to the same oscillation.

5. Policies for internal and external balance in CEECs are discussed in joint work with William Branson and Jurgen von Hagen (1998).

6. Before the revolution, the reported surplus was hiding a deficit, except in 1972, when the reported deficit was hiding a surplus. Between 1977 and 1985, leaving out 1980 because of a debt write-off operation, the implied deficit was, on average, double the reported deficit, though there were substantial year-to-year variations. This is the same as saying that, on top of the reported deficit, there was a hidden deficit of equal size. In 1986–88, however, while the reported primary budget deficit was about zero, there was a hidden deficit of 6 percent. See Braga de Macedo (1990).

7. But the share of short-term labor contracts dropped from a peak of 20 percent in 1989 to about 12 percent, according to Mateus (1998).

8. This information was first noted in work with Paul Krugman (1981).

9. Exchange controls kept interest rates in Portugal artificially low, indicating that barriers to capital outflows operated very stringently. The average covered interest differential against the dollar between 1984 and 1988 was 0.6 percent in Spain and about -3.0 percent in Portugal. See Braga de Macedo (1990) and note 12 below.

10. Comparing the rate of crawl and the change in an effective exchange rate with the same weights suggests that the crawling peg of the escudo, introduced in 1977 upon advice from the IMF, no longer altered relative prices in 1986–88. The change in cost competitiveness was mostly due to the discrete devaluations of the 1978–79 and 1983–85 periods. See Braga de Macedo (1990) and (1998).

11. The chemical industry, plastics in particular, was perhaps more important than textiles in establishing the roots of intra-industry trade specialization, which nowadays features exports of auto parts and other technology intensive goods. As discussed in section 5, however, EFTA favored inter-industry trade.

12. This point is discussed in Braga de Macedo, Luís Catela Nunes, and Francisco Covas (1999). See also note (13) below.

13. The weekly pattern of exchange rate volatility against the DME shows that the PPERR followed alternative imposition and relaxation of capital controls and retreat from, then return to, international borrowing. See the reference in note 12 and EC (1997).

References

Bertelsmann Foundation. 1999. *Central and Eastern Europe on the Way into the European Union*. Strategy Paper for the International Bertelsmann Forum. Warsaw, June 25–26.

Branson, William, Jorge Braga de Macedo, and Jurgen von Hagen. 1998. "Macroeconomic Policy and Institutions in the Transition to European Union Membership." NBER Working Paper No. 6555, May.

Buiter, Willem, and Anne Sibert. 1999. *Transition Issues for the European Monetary Union*. CEPR Discussion Paper No. 1728, November.

Center for Economic Policy Research. 1995. "Flexible Integration: Toward a More Effective and Democratic Europe." *Monitoring European Integration* 6. London.

de Macedo, Jorge Braga. 1990. "External Liberalization under Ambiguous Public Response: The Experience of Portugal." In Bliss, Christopher, and Jorge Braga de Macedo, eds. *Unity Diversity in the European Economy. The Community's Southern Frontier.* Cambridge: Cambridge University Press, p. 310–354.

de Macedo, Jorge Braga. 1998. Portugal. In Fukasaku, Kiichiro, and Ricardo Hausmann, eds. *Democracy, Decentralisation and Deficits in Latin America.* OECD Development Centre, Paris.

de Macedo, Jorge Braga. 1999. "Portugal's European Integration: the Limits of External Pressure." Nova Economics. Working Paper No. 369. December.

de Macedo, Jorge Braga, Luís Catela Nunes and Francisco Covas. 1999. "Moving the Escudo into the Euro." CEPR Discussion Paper No. 2248. October.

European Bank for Reconstruction and Development. 1998. *Transition Report 1997.* London.

European Commission. 1997. "The Economic and Financial Situation in Portugal in the Transition to EMU." *European Economy* special reports.

Honohan, Patrick. 1995. *Measuring European Financial Integration: Flows and Intermediation in Greece, Ireland and Portugal*, ESRI Working Paper 60, Dublin, June.

Kindleberger, Charles. 1962. *Foreign Trade and the National Economy.* New Haven: Yale University Press.

Krugman, Paul. 1981. "Intraindustry Specialization and the Gains from Trade." *Journal of Political Economy*, 89 (5) October.

Krugman, Paul, and Jorge Braga de Macedo. 1981. "The Economic Consequences of the April 25th Revolution." Braga de Macedo, Jorge, and Simon Serfaty, eds. *Portugal Since the Revolution: Economic and Political Perspectives.* Boulder, Colo.: Westview Press.

Lankes, Hans-Peter, and A. J. Venables. 1996. "Foreign Direct Investment in Economic Transition: The Changing Pattern of Investments." In *Economics of Transition*, 4(2) 331–347.

Magone, José. 1997. *European Portugal: The Difficult Road to Sustainable Democracy.* London: Macmillan.

Mateus, Abel. 1998. *Economia Portuguesa desde 1910.* Lisbon: Verbo.

Tornell, Aaron, and Philip Lane. 1999. "The Voracity Effect." In *American Economic Review.* March.

.

Index